# MODERNISM AND COLONIALISM

# Modernism and Colonialism

*British and Irish Literature, 1899–1939*

*edited by*

RICHARD BEGAM

*&*

MICHAEL VALDEZ MOSES

DUKE UNIVERSITY PRESS
DURHAM & LONDON 2007

Printed in the United States of America on acid-free paper ∞

Designed by Jennifer Hill
Typeset in Bembo by Keystone Typesetting, Inc.

Library of Congress Cataloging-in-Publication Data
appear on the last printed page of this book.

*For our parents*

HELEN GERTRUDE BEGAM
& ROBERT GEORGE BEGAM

*and*

JUDITH GLORIA MOSES
& THOMAS DONALD MOSES

# CONTENTS

Acknowledgments ix

*Richard Begam and Michael Valdez Moses* ⋮ Introduction 1

PART ONE ⋮ Victorian Backgrounds

1 *Nicholas Daly* ⋮ Colonialism and Popular Literature at the Fin de Siècle 19

PART TWO ⋮ Modern British Literature

2 *Michael Valdez Moses* ⋮ Disorientalism: Conrad and the Imperial Origins of Modernist Aesthetics 43

3 *Jed Esty* ⋮ Virginia Woolf's Colony and the Adolescence of Modernist Fiction 70

4 *Andrzej Gąsiorek* ⋮ War, "Primitivism," and the Future of "the West": Reflections on D. H. Lawrence and Wyndham Lewis 91

5 *Vincent Sherry* ⋮ T. S. Eliot, Late Empire, and Decadence 111

6 *Brian May* ⋮ Romancing the Stump: Modernism and Colonialism in Forster's *A Passage to India* 136

7 *Rita Barnard* ⋮ "A tangle of modernism and barbarity": Evelyn Waugh's *Black Mischief* 162

PART THREE ⋮ Ireland and Scotland

8 *Richard Begam* ⋮ Joyce's Trojan Horse: *Ulysses* and the Aesthetics of Decolonization 185

9 *Nicholas Allen* ⋮ Yeats, Spengler, and *A Vision* after Empire 209

10 *Maria DiBattista* ⋮ Elizabeth Bowen's Troubled Modernism 226

11 *Ian Duncan* ⋮ "Upon the thistle they're impaled": Hugh MacDiarmid's Modernist Nationalism 246

PART FOUR ⋮ Toward the Postcolonial

12 *Declan Kiberd* ⋮ Postcolonial Modernism? 269

13 *Jahan Ramazani* ⋮ Modernist Bricolage, Postcolonial Hybridity 288

Contributors 315

Index 319

# ACKNOWLEDGMENTS

First, we would like to thank the contributors to this volume, who have shown remarkable patience and forbearance through too many proposals, drafts, submissions, revisions, and deadlines. Again and again, they have reminded us of how fortunate we are in having such generous and understanding colleagues. We also gratefully acknowledge the detailed and attentive reports submitted by our outside readers. They brought just the right mix of sympathetic engagement and critical distance to comments that were both instructive and constructive. We also deeply appreciate the expert counsel and consummate professionalism of the staff at Duke University Press, most especially Reynolds Smith (senior editor), Pam Morrison (assistant managing editor), and Sharon Torian (senior editorial assistant). Finally, our work on this collection has been made immeasurably easier, and the manuscript itself substantially improved, by the splendid efforts of three research assistants: Jack Dudley, Mark Estante, and Jesse Wolfe.

*Richard Begam and Michael Valdez Moses*

⋮

# INTRODUCTION

It has now been nearly twenty years since Fredric Jameson published "Modernism and Imperialism." What was perhaps most striking about the essay when it first appeared in 1988 was its title: with a modest but provocative copula, Jameson willed into syntactic unity two concepts that had previously seemed alien, even antithetical.[1] What, after all, could modernism—reputedly that most aestheticized and rarefied of literary movements—have in common with the brute realities of conquest and empire? Where might one discover affiliations between the formal audacities of avant-gardism and the historical atrocities of colonialism? In short, how might one connect the culture of the cosmopolitan center with the politics of the imperial periphery? If we do not always agree with the answers Jameson supplied to these questions—indeed we often disagree with him—we nevertheless recognize that he was among the first to think searchingly about the ways in which modernist literary practice might be related, both formally and thematically, to the experience of empire.

Today the idea of joining the terms "modernism" and "colonialism" in a title provokes neither alarm nor surprise. Over the last two decades, numerous articles and books have examined how individual authors responded to empire (Conrad, Forster, Joyce), and a host of well-known critics have produced influential works on the subject (Bhabha, Eagleton, Gikandi, Parry, Said, and Suleri).[2] Yet, despite this scholarly activity, few studies have provided a sustained and comprehensive account of the relation of modernism to colonialism. The comparative absence of such scholarship is puzzling, given the political and historical imperatives of the modernist period. For while it is something of a commonplace to identify the nineteenth century as the age of empire and the twentieth century with the end of empire, matters are a good deal more complicated than such a formulation would suggest.[3] It should be remembered, for instance, that the British empire reached the height of its geographic expansion not in 1877, when Victoria was proclaimed Empress of India, nor in the 1880s and 1890s when England made substantial territorial gains in Africa, but during the boom years of modernism: the early twentieth century, especially the period between the two World Wars. In fact Britain's imperial influence expanded after the First World War on virtually all fronts, with new acquisitions in the Middle East (Palestine, Trans-Jordan, and Iraq), Africa (Tanganyika and South West Africa), and Melanesia (Samoa, Nauru, and the Bismark Archipelago).[4]

It was also in the early twentieth century that communications technology finally made it possible to consolidate the British empire into a single network of overland telegraphs and submarine cables. Of special importance was the laying in 1902 of the first trans-Pacific line, which joined Western Canada to Queensland and New Zealand. As William Roger Louis observes, the establishment of this link had "almost metaphysical significance," radically transforming the experience of time and space, while, on a more practical level, placing merchants throughout the empire "in direct touch with sources of supply."[5] By the 1920s, in a striking anticipation of globalization, Great Britain's imperial cables and wireless beams had unified its colonial holdings into a vast communications system, extending from New Zealand, Australia, and India, through East and West Africa, to the Falkland Islands, British Guiana, and the Dominion of Canada. Between the two world wars, Britannia ruled not only the waves but also the airwaves, and this meant that if the sun never set on the English empire, the language of Shakespeare and Milton never fell silent in any of its domains. The military and political extension of empire had, in other words, cultural consequences, consequences that were felt in London, just as surely as they were in Dublin, Cape Town, Sydney, or Bombay.

Admittedly, the opening of the twentieth century, marked by Victoria's death in 1901 and the public reversals England suffered in the Boer War between 1899 and 1902, has often been seen as foreshadowing the decline of the British empire. Such a view appears all the more credible if we construe history retrospectively, reading backward from the vantage of 1947–60 when most of England's colonies gained their independence. But if we examine history from the perspective of the moderns, attempting to imagine how it might have appeared to them, then the British empire looms large and indomitable, the kind of weighty edifice that inspired the famously pessimistic conclusion to *A Passage to India* (1924). Certainly a transformation did occur around 1900, but it was not the empire that changed so much as the attitude of a rising generation toward it. Many of the writers we associate with modernism were part of a new spirit of opposition, which challenged the social, economic, and political status quo in fundamental ways. Obviously central to this challenge was the question of England's imperial mission; as one contemporary observed: "The present generation is the first of a new order, and looks forward upon a prospect in which the idea of conquest and expansion find no place."[6] Even those who had a more ambivalent reaction to colonialism nevertheless recognized it as a topic of enormous importance, one that was intimately bound up with the defining issues of the day. If to be a modern meant thinking these issues anew, then to be a modern meant thinking empire anew.

Of course, how one thinks about empire largely depends on the terminology one employs, and it will therefore be helpful to say a few words about the distinction we draw in the present volume between "imperialism" and "colonialism." While these terms are often used interchangeably, especially in the United States, they carry different connotations and evoke different associations.[7] It is not surprising, for example, that Jameson prefers the term "imperialism," since Marxist criticism has historically tended to view colonialism as a discrete phase within the broader history of imperialism. As it happens, the terms "colonialism" and "imperialism" did not enter into English until the nineteenth century, and Marx himself never employed the word "imperialism."[8] In the twentieth century, however, Marxist theorists have made wide use of the term—Lenin most notable among them—treating imperialism as the geographic extension of the acquisitive and expansionist practices of capitalism.[9]

In the present volume, we employ both these terms but with different emphases. For us "imperialism" refers to both the policy and practice whereby a nation establishes rule over another country or group of countries through the application of military force or conquest, while "colonialism" designates the institution and administration of an imperial power's foreign holdings and dependencies. Obviously imperialism and colonialism represent related aspects of the larger project of empire, but we have chosen to focus our discussion principally (though not exclusively) on colonialism

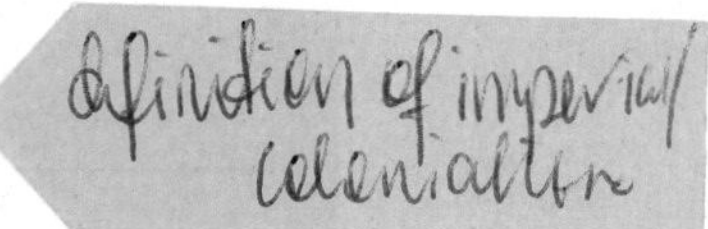

for a number of reasons. First, according to the *OED*, "colonialism" indicates not only the "colonial system or principle" (def. 2) but also "the practice or manner of things colonial" (def. 1a) and the "practice or idiom peculiar to or characteristic of a colony" (def. 1b).[10] In contemporary usage, the word is probably more often associated with the second definition, but we wish to emphasize the first as well, since many of the essays in this collection deal directly with the colonial scene, as viewed at the local level. Considered from this vantage, "colonial" underscores the hybridity of a culture born out of conflict and compromise and shaped by what is native and alien, what is negotiated and imposed.

Second, the term "imperialism" derives from a Latin verb, *impero, imperare*, which literally means "to order, govern, command."[11] Yet insofar as the word conveys a sense of complete or absolute domination, it misses a revealing aspect of British colonialism. For the latter often followed, for better or worse, what Michel Foucault has called the "gentle way" in exercising administrative authority, aiming at conversion as much as coercion.[12] Hence, the preferred English model of "indirect rule" often permitted greater local autonomy of colonial elites than did its French, German, and Belgian counterparts. Even where England relied upon a direct form of colonial rule, it employed a relatively spare and economical method of governance that allowed for lower administrative costs and smaller deployments of imperial military forces than would otherwise have been necessary.[13] Of course, it must be remembered that Foucault himself treats "soft" power not as more "humane" than "hard" power but as more effective in achieving social control, and there is no doubt that such a system was ultimately designed to serve the interests of the Colonial Office.[14] Nevertheless, the preferred English method of governance tended to produce a distinctive approach to the management of empire, one that—whatever its motivation—was often less imperious than that pursued by the other European powers.[15]

Third, precisely because British colonialism was committed to a strategy of cultural co-optation and absorption, education acquired special importance as a vehicle for disseminating the English language and English values. It is no accident that when Obi Okonkwo, the hero of Achebe's *No Longer at Ease* and an exemplary instance of the colonized subject, applies for a position in the colonial government of Nigeria, the job interview turns into an examination on his knowledge of English literature. He impresses his prospective employer, securing the job in the process, by demonstrating that his familiarity with English culture is not confined to the writers he has read in colonial schools but also extends to such contemporary figures as Graham Greene and W. H. Auden.[16] Obi has learned—as did Achebe, the title of whose novel is drawn from a T. S. Eliot poem—that cultural capital commands respect and enables advancement within the British colonial system.

Finally, as a concept colonialism admits of temporal delimitation—one can speak meaningfully of precolonial, colonial, and postcolonial periods—and such temporal delimitations enable historical discriminations. Of course, the chronological parameters we have set for the present volume are artificial, but they are not arbitrary. The year 1899 marks the publication of Conrad's *Heart of Darkness* on the eve of the new century, and 1939 marks the death of William Butler Yeats on the eve of the Second World War. With the exception of the Victorian romances discussed in the first chapter and the postcolonial poetry discussed in the last chapter, all the major works treated in this volume fall within the forty-year period that runs from 1899 to 1939. Obviously the Second World War represents a turning point in Great Britain's colonial venture. In the immediate aftermath of the war, the United States emerged as the dominant military power in the world, while Great Britain was left with its economy in shambles and, to a large degree, dependent on its American ally. The dissolution of the British empire, which followed hard upon the end of the Second World War, was mostly completed by 1960.

Each of the essays in *Modernism and Colonialism* examines the modernist rethinking of empire by focusing on an author, a formal problem or a literary theme. One of the key issues linking these essays is the question of how aesthetic innovation and formal experimentation, so often associated with modernism, is related to British colonialism. While we do not propose a simple or single answer to this question—so complex a phenomenon as modernism does not admit of such a response—we nevertheless believe that it is essential to investigate how modernist literary practice was variously shaped by the contemporary geopolitical scene, and how the modernist revolution can be understood as a critical and artistic engagement with the British and, more broadly, European quest for empire. We therefore devote considerable attention in these essays to placing the work of leading modernist writers within its historical context and to exploring the related developments of literary and political forms during the period.

Given such an approach, it is inevitable that this collection should engage

—sometimes explicitly, sometimes implicitly—with a number of current debates concerning the scholarly and institutional definition of modernism, or as it is sometimes called, the "new modernisms." It is our hope that the present volume will serve to complicate and contest two of the dominant accounts of modernism, one older and the other more recent. The older account, inspired by formalist and humanist criticism, often ignored the connections that exist between modernism and politics, connections that we feel are of vital importance. For these critics, modernism bore little or no relation to colonialism.[17] The more recent account, drawing on postcolonial and cultural studies, has sometimes pushed modernism too far in the opposite direction, treating it as indistinguishable from colonialism, a structure of ideological oppression that aided and abetted empire. The problem with both these accounts is that they tend to overlook the historical and cultural reality of modernism, which more often than not challenged the prevailing values of English culture, including its most powerful institution, the British empire.[18]

Having said this, we recognize that different modern writers responded to empire in different ways. We have attempted to register the diversity of their responses through individual chapters, many of which are devoted to examining in detail a single writer and his or her major work. At the same time, the organization of the volume underscores our conviction that modernism is not a unified or monolithic phenomenon so much as a series of intersections and overlappings, linked according to a principle of Wittgensteinian family resemblances. Hence, we approach Anglo-modernism as occupying a number of discrete cultural and geographic locales—not only in England, Ireland, and Scotland, but also in Africa, Asia and the Americas—which opens up the possibility of positing a series of "vernacular modernisms." We also wish to consider the continuities that connect modernism to earlier and later forms of cultural expression, and we therefore begin our collection with Nicholas Daly's essay, which looks back to Victorian themes, and end with Jahan Ramazani's essay, which looks forward to postcolonial forms.

While the essays in this volume present a largely revisionary account of the relation of British and Irish modernism to English colonialism, one that challenges the occasionally reductive dichotomies of some postcolonial criticism, we do not want to be understood as in any sense attempting to justify or mitigate the horrors (we deliberately use this Conradian word) that empire has inflicted on its victims, most particularly its native subjects. The contributors are unanimous in their unqualified condemnation of colonialism and imperialism, so much so that we have taken it as the unspoken—and therefore unwritten—starting point for our essays. In our view, the matter at issue is not whether one should defend the politically and morally discredited system of empire but how literary scholarship might unfold the enormously complicated relationship that exists between modernism and colonialism. It is this question that shapes and animates the chapters that follow.

Here we believe it is also important to address the scope and focus of the present volume. Obviously a collection of essays that includes among its topics Conrad, Forster, Woolf, Eliot, Lawrence, Yeats, and Joyce is weighted toward "canonical" modernist literature. Two principles have guided our selections. First, it is the traditional modernists who have most often been censured for being receptive to, or complicitous with, the project of empire. Insofar as this is a point of view we wish to interrogate, and in some instances to contest, we have found that our choices were often already made for us. In other words, the writers we examine in this volume have been selected as much by their critics as by us. Second, we fully appreciate that a strikingly different collection could be produced that would view modernism from outside our own largely metropolitan perspective. Such a work might not only explore how non-European writers like Coetzee, Desani, Emecheta, Naipaul, Ngugi, Rhys, Rushdie, Roy, Walcott, and others adapted and transformed modernism but could also engage more extensively with postcolonial theory and criticism than we do. A volume conceived along these lines might stand as a valuable companion piece to our own, but it would have its own logical and historical integrity—one that we have not presumed to reproduce in our study.

To date one other collection of essays has been published on the subject before us: *Modernism and Empire*, edited by Howard J. Booth and Nigel Rigby (2000). A welcome entry into the field, the Booth-Rigby volume brings together a series of penetrating and provocative essays. The approach that Booth and Rigby take is, however, different from our own. Their volume assembles essays on a variety of topics and authors, each interesting and valuable in itself, but it does not attempt to cover comprehensively those writers that several generations of modernist critics regarded as central to British and Irish literature. Hence, there are no individual chapters on

Conrad, Forster, Woolf, Eliot, Lewis, and Pound, while less prominent figures such as Elizabeth Bowen, Hugh MacDiarmid, and Evelyn Waugh are never mentioned. In our view, a fully articulated account of British and Irish modernism on the one hand, and English colonialism on the other, should include those authors and works that historically have been most influential in shaping the literature of the period and the body of criticism that has accumulated in relation to it. Such an approach enables one to see the extent to which the moderns often focused on a set of shared issues and problems, while producing distinctive, even idiosyncratic, responses to them.

We have presented these issues and problems in a structure that is organized into historic and geographic sections. Part I, "Victorian Backgrounds," features an essay by Nicholas Daly that deals with the relation of colonialism to popular culture at the end of the nineteenth century. It is generally accepted that the so-called imperial romance, which inspired later writers like Conrad and Forster, had its origins in popular adventure novels. Focusing on two examples of this kind of literature, Robert Louis Stevenson's *Treasure Island* (1883) and H. Rider Haggard's *King Solomon's Mines* (1885), Daly proposes that these treasure-hunt novels connect the imperial project of competing for plunder abroad with the mass-market project of competing for profit at home. For Daly the marketplace—often viewed as antithetical to the interests of modernism—is key to understanding how we move from the Victorian romanticization of colonialism to modernism's more negative attitude toward it. Yet if Stevenson's and Haggard's narratives seem to glamorize colonialism, they also betray a deep ambivalence, even anxiety, over their own efforts at pandering to the marketplace, suggesting that even for writers of the imperial romance, notions of morality and materialism could be as complicated as they were for the modernists.

Part II, "Modern British Literature," brings together six essays that trace a series of varied but largely critical responses to colonialism. Chapters 2 through 4 examine how British imperialism inspired Conrad, Woolf, and Eliot to seek new aesthetic forms appropriate to the sense of dislocation and decadence which they associated with empire. In chapter 2, Michael Valdez Moses reads two seminal works by Conrad, *Heart of Darkness* (1899/1902) and *Lord Jim* (1900), arguing that the experience of a European consciousness confronting an alien culture, an experience regularly enacted at the peripheries of empire, played a crucial role in generating formal modernism. Contesting the view that modernist innovations implicitly serve (or explicitly promote) the larger projects of colonialism and Orientalism, Moses maintains that Conrad's use of avant-garde literary devices—delayed decoding, anachrony, perspectivism, *mise-en-abyme*—transformed and subverted the Victorian imperial romance. More specifically, Conrad's narrative experimentalism functions to disorient the reader, thereby undermining his or her confidence in the morality and legitimacy of British imperialism and European colonialism. In chapter 3, Jed Esty also addresses the question of how modernist innovations remade and unmade Victorian literary forms. Taking Virginia Woolf's *The Voyage Out* (1915) as his principal example, Esty considers how the developmental logic of the bildungsroman is drastically revised in the modern period, as national economies expanded and fractured into colonial and global systems, and the allegorical pair of nationhood/adulthood was destabilized. What resulted was a nonteleological bildungsroman in which the hero lingers in adolescence, forever deferring the closure that adulthood implies. The political consequence of such anti-*Bildung* is a hero who, failing to assume the duties and responsibilities implied by the Victorian imperial romance, does not become a servant of empire. In chapter 4, Vincent Sherry turns to the issue of imperial decadence in Eliot's *Poems* (1920), showing how it inspired both the form and content of the ironically detached "quatrain" poems. While Eliot's own views on empire were ambivalent—Sherry discusses both the figures of Bolo and Sweeney—the poet's interest in literary decadence, especially as it developed out of Swinburne and Rossetti, indicates that he took a decidedly elegiac perspective toward empire. One can read this attitude as lamenting a fading ideal or as acknowledging a failed ideology, but in either case Eliot was not among those who, in the aftermath of the First World War, still regarded the empire as an integral part of Great Britain's mission.

Chapters 5 through 7 deal less with an imperial imaginary and more with a colonial reality. In chapter 5, Brian May challenges the claim that *A Passage to India* (1924) reenacts a colonialist appropriation of India through overly symbolic landscape descriptions that serve to de-realize what they are supposed to represent. On the contrary, May contends that the novel acknowledges India's material otherness, even as it resists reducing it to colonialist stereotypes of the natural or primordial. Indeed, it is only by means of a modernist epistemology of skepticism that Forster is able to strike a balance between an object world that is bereft of meaning and one so symbolically freighted that it ceases to be real. In chapter 6, Andrzej Gąsiorek considers the topic of primitivism—of obvious importance to colonialism—in the fiction of D. H. Lawrence and Wyndham Lewis. While both authors were critical of nationalism and imperialism, their divergent views on the "primitive" indicate two highly distinct approaches to it within modernism. Lawrence believed that the cultural renewal of the West could only be achieved by turning to the animism and atavism he identified with non-Western cultures, such as the "Indians" of New Mexico. Lewis, on the other hand, equated atavism with the destruction of the war and opposed to it a Hellenic aesthetic that stressed clarity and order. Completing part II of the collection, Rita Barnard analyzes Evelyn Waugh's notorious *Black Mischief* (1932) in chapter 7. Concentrating on colonial mimicry, she demonstrates that the novel reverses the typical logic of European original/African imitation, suggesting that Waugh's view of imperialism was far less sympathetic than critics have alleged. She goes on to connect the novel's treatment of geographical dislocation to the modernist technique of collage, revealing how Waugh's handling of experimental form—ironic juxtapositions, rapid shifts in point of view, and so on—mirrors the geographical and epistemological dislocations that characterize the colonial experience.

Part III, "Ireland and Scotland," brings together five essays, but here colonialism is viewed from the perspective not of the colonizer but the colonized. Matters are further complicated by the fact that the colonized themselves represent an array of perspectives, from Irish to Anglo-Irish to Scottish, from Catholic to Protestant, from nationalist to cosmopolitan. The first three essays in this section plot Irish reactions to colonialism by probing the stresses and strains that occur as aesthetic imperatives confront political and historical reality. In chapter 8, Richard Begam investigates how *Ulysses* (1922) also employed modernist techniques for anticolonial purposes. Focusing on a number of metafictional moments, Begam maintains that the novel strategically situates its modernism in relation to two of the dominant trends of the Irish 1890s: Oscar Wilde's aestheticism (which dared not speak its Irishness) and Douglas Hyde's nationalism (which spoke nothing but its Irishness). Seeking an alternative to both these traditions, Joyce constructs what is in effect a literary Trojan horse, designed at once to advance the claims of an international modernism and to smuggle within itself a distinctly Irish modernism. Begam then proceeds to show that two of modernism's most frequently cited techniques, stream-of-consciousness and the "mythical method," are deliberately used by Joyce not so much to establish the novel's universalism as to insist on its decolonizing particularism.

Chapter 9, by Nicholas Allen, turns to a markedly different use of myth, W. B. Yeats's spiritualist experiment, *A Vision* (1926). Often dismissed as occult escapism, the book occupied Yeats for almost ten years and was written during a historically tumultuous period, which included the First World War, the Russian Revolution, and the Irish Civil War. Reading *A Vision* alongside Oswald Spengler's *Decline of the West*—books Yeats himself regarded as companion pieces—Allen reveals that both works function as narratives in search of authority in the aftermath of empire. The effect of Allen's reading is to cast *A Vision* in a new light, seeing it as a work whose multiple voices and modernist collage connect literary form to the disorienting experience of empire. In chapter 10, Maria DiBattista also considers the question of how one writes history under the pressures of a dissolving empire, only in the case of Elizabeth Bowen's *The Last September* (1929) that history is envisioned not as universal but as personal and is viewed prospectively as well as retrospectively. Of special interest to DiBattista is the way Bowen's self-consciously Proustian novel uses formal innovation as a vehicle for working through her divided loyalties during the Troubles (Bowen was Anglo-Irish). Here that innovation involves what DiBattista calls "retrospective intimation," a narrative device that intimates an event carries great significance for the story, while acknowledging that its significance can only be understood after the fact. Such a device makes time move both forward and backward, integrating a lyrical present with a historical past through the manipulation of voice and point of view.

Chapter 11 shifts the scene from Ireland to Scotland, as Ian Duncan focuses on Hugh MacDiarmid's modernist masterpiece, *A Drunk Man Looks at the Thistle* (1926). Duncan uses the MacDiarmid poem to analyze, as a number of other essays have, the problematic relation between nationalist aspirations and modernist commitments, especially insofar as they are linguistically expressed as an opposition between "provincial" Scots and "global" English. It is Duncan's larger claim that Scotland's position in the 1920s, as a culturally distinct but politically subordinate part of the United Kingdom, proved a vexing obstacle for a nationalist and modernist like MacDiarmid. The result is a conflicted and self-canceling modernist work, whose very success depends, paradoxically, on the announcement of its own failure, its inability to discover a suitable form for the expression of a modern and modernist Scottish identity.

Part IV, "Toward the Postcolonial,"concludes the volume with essays by Declan Kiberd and Jahan Ramazani. In chapter 12, Kiberd examines how, in the immediate aftermath of World War Two, literary critics such as Hugh Kenner and Richard Ellmann institutionalized modernism as an internationalist and universalist phenomenon. While Kiberd, unlike other contributors to this volume, views T. S. Eliot as an unambiguous apologist for the universalism of empire, he regards Wilde, Yeats, and Joyce as firmly rooted in and committed to the Irish scene. Taking *Ulysses* as his test case, Kiberd argues that in Ireland colonization meant that the country never progressed from an aristocratic phase (associated with the epic) to a bourgeois phase (associated with the novel). Ireland's historical underdevelopment had, in Kiberd's view, aesthetic consequences, opening up the possibility for radical experimentation, which led in the case of *Ulysses* to the novel's famously mixed form—part epic and part novel. Finally, in chapter 13, Jahan Ramazani takes up the relation between modernist and postcolonial poetry. While modernism is generally assumed to stand in opposition to postcolonialism, Ramazani points out that writers such as Yeats, Pound, and Eliot provided their postcolonial followers with a set of poetic models that were both formally radical and politically liberating. More particularly, a range of techniques that Ramazani identifies with modernist bricolage provided non-Western poets with precisely the aesthetic tools they needed for exploring their own hybrid cultures and postcolonial experiences. As for such modernist poets as Yeats, Pound, and Eliot, while they all exemplify some degree of Orientalist appropriation, their handling and quotation of the East signal a far more critical attitude toward the West than has generally been recognized. If Kiberd's chapter asks in its title whether Irish modernism wasn't always already postcolonial, Ramazani's essay suggests that we might extend that question to modernism per se, not to ignore the differences between Anglo-modernism and postcolonialism, but to understand that these categories are fluid and the writers who inhabit them given to change.

The arguments mounted in these final two chapters recapitulate and reaffirm the polemical thrust of the volume as a whole. Again, while we do not wish to reduce modernism to a single or unitary phenomenon, or to airbrush away its more objectionable attitudes, we believe that the moderns were significantly more varied in their views of colonialism and substantially more critical of empire than their critics have allowed. If, for example, the racial views or ethnocentric perspectives of Conrad, Waugh, or Eliot were often deplorable, it is nevertheless worth considering that such attitudes paradoxically and unexpectedly helped to generate a skeptical modernist interrogation of empire and of its deleterious effects upon English and European culture. Although Anglo-modernism was Eurocentric—how could it not be?—it was nevertheless deeply committed to thinking beyond its cultural moment. The conclusion to *A Passage to India* tellingly evokes the situation we are describing. Fielding asks Aziz, "Why can't we be friends now? It's what I want. It's what you want." But the friendship is impossible, because in 1924 the forces of history seemed as implacable as the forces of nature. As the two friends attempt to embrace they are separated by the earth itself, which, along with the sky, answers their plea for brotherhood with a cosmic "No, not yet," "No, not there."[19] It is as though time and space, the categories of knowledge itself, have rendered impossible the desired communication between Fielding and Aziz, between the cosmopolitan center and the colonial periphery. But what is perhaps most interesting about the novel's conclusion is Forster's own paratextual addendum, the postscript: "Weybridge, 1924." Here Forster acknowledges with quiet eloquence the limitations of his own position. Yet the matter is more complicated still. For Forster has situated himself, through an act of triangulation, outside the defining binary of empire—the cosmopolitan center and the colonial periphery. His own point of view may be partial and restricted, but by dislocating it from the center, by relocating it along a divergent axis of perception, he raises the possibility of producing a kind of cultural anamorphosis. Modernism proposed to do much the same. Like Forster, it could not see beyond its field of vision—could not achieve a universalist high ground—but it could and did imagine alternatives to its own perspective. Among those alternatives was a radically different conception of England, one in which the shadow of empire would fall less darkly and less comprehensively around the globe.

## Notes

1 Jameson's essay was first published as a pamphlet by Field Day Theatre Company; it was later collected in Eagleton, Jameson, and Said, *Nationalism, Colonialism and Literature*, 43–66.

2 Bhabha, *The Location of Culture*; Eagleton, "Nationalism, Irony and Commitment," in *Nationalism, Colonialism and Literature*, 23–39; Gikandi, *Maps of Englishness*, and *Writing in Limbo*; Parry, *Delusions and Discoveries*; Said, *Culture and Imperialism*, and "Yeats and Decolonization," in *Nationalism, Colonialism and Literature*, 69–95; Suleri, *The Rhetoric of English India.*

3 Historians often date the high-point of empire as the last third of the nineteenth century and the early years of the twentieth century, running up to the beginning of World War I; see, for instance, Hobsbawm, *The Age of Empire*, and Shannon, *The Crisis of Imperialism.*

4 See map 1.1 in *The Oxford History of the British Empire*, ed. Brown and Louis, 4.

5 Ibid., 5.

6 Quoted in *Oxford History of the British Empire*, 3.

7 Williams and Chrisman discuss this distinction in the opening of *Colonial Discourse and Postcolonial Theory*, where they cite Hobson's *Imperialism*, as well as Lichtheim's *Imperialism*; for another view, see Koebner and Schmidt, *Imperialism.*

8 On Marx and the word "imperialism," see Williams and Chrisman, *Colonial Discourse and Post-Colonial Theory*, 2. According to the *OED*, "imperialism" was first used in 1858 (*COED*, vol. 1, 1385) and "colonialism" in 1864 (*COED*, vol. 1, 469).

9 See Lenin, *Imperialism*; Bukharin and Luxemburg are among the other notable Marxist thinkers from the early century to offer a sustained consideration of imperialism in their works.

10 *COED*, vol. 1, 469.

11 This sense is expressed by definition 1 in the *OED:* "An imperial system of government; the rule of an emperor, esp. when despotic or arbitrary" (*COED*, vol. 1, 1385).

12 In part 2 of *Discipline and Punish*, see chapter 2, "The Gentle Way in Punishment," 104–31. Although *Discipline and Punish* deals with penal institutions and the "carceral" network, many of its claims can be extended to colonialism, something Foucault occasionally does himself.

13 To be sure, if the British looked askance at the genocidal methods of the Germans in their African colonies, the use of virtual slave labor in the Belgian Congo, and the dreaded *corvée* in French colonies, they were willing to maintain control of their colonies by means of violent military interventions and unequivocally brutal methods when it suited them: witness the wholesale slaughter of the Mahdist "rebels" at Omdurman in 1898, the razing of 30,000 farms and herding of Boer women and children into pestilential concentration camps from 1900 until 1902, the massacre of hundreds of un-

armed Indian civilians at the Jallianwalla Bagh in Amritsar in 1919, and the violent outrages of the Auxiliaries and Black and Tans in Ireland in 1920, to name only a few of the more notorious instances of Britain's use of "hard" as opposed to "soft" power.

14 In the opening pages of *Discipline and Punish*, Foucault observes that the "disappearance of torture as a public spectacle . . . has been attributed too readily and too emphatically to a process of 'humanization' " (7). He later remarks that the result of penal reform was "not to punish less, but to punish better; to punish with attenuated severity perhaps, but in order to punish with more universality and necessity" (88).

15 Of course, government authorities, pro-imperial statesmen, and jingoists in the press certainly recognized the advantages to be gained by stressing that English colonial policies were more "progressive" or "enlightened" (to employ the parlance of the day) than those pursued by the other (mainly) European empires against which Britain struggled in the global contest known as "great power politics."

16 For Obi's exchange with the colonial office, see the beginning of chapter 5, *No Longer at Ease*, 42–44. That Achebe is also providing an anticolonial gloss on how to read the ending of *Things Fall Apart* enhances the irony of the scene.

17 The two major anthologies on modernism from this period are *The Modern Tradition*, ed. Ellmann and Fiedelson, and *Modernism*, ed. Bradbury and McFarlane; neither offers any discussion of modernism's relation to colonialism or addresses the issue of empire. Even a recent collection on modernism, the excellent *Cambridge Companion to Modernism*, ed. Levenson, omits any discussion of how the experience of empire influenced modernist writing.

18 Representative of this school of thought is the discussion of modernism in *The Empire Writes Back*, ed. Ashcroft, Griffiths, and Tiffin, esp. 156–60.

19 Forster, *A Passage to India*, 362 (pages citations are to the 1952 reprint edition).

## Works Cited

Achebe, Chinua. *No Longer at Ease*. New York: Ballantine Books, 1960.

Ashcroft, Bill, Gareth Griffiths, and Helen Tiffin, eds. *The Empire Writes Back: Theory and Practice in Post-Colonial Literatures*. London: Routledge, 1989.

Bhabha, Homi K. *The Location of Culture*. London: Routledge, 1994.

Booth, Howard J., and Nigel Rigby, eds. *Modernism and Empire*. Manchester: Manchester University Press, 2000.

Bradbury, Malcolm, and James McFarlane, eds. *Modernism: A Guide to European Literature, 1890–1930*. London: Penguin Books, 1976.

Brown, Judith M., and William Roger Louis, eds. *The Oxford History of the British Empire: The Twentieth Century*. Oxford: Oxford University Press, 1999.

*The Compact Edition of the Oxford English Dictionary*, Vol. 1 AO. Oxford: Oxford University Press, 1989.

Eagleton, Terry, Fredric Jameson, and Edward Said. *Nationalism, Colonialism and Literature*. Minneapolis: University of Minnesota Press, 1990.

Ellmann, Richard, and Charles Fiedelson, eds. *The Modern Tradition*. Oxford: Oxford University Press, 1965.

Forster, E. M. *A Passage to India*. New York: Harcourt Brace and Jovanovich, 1924. Reprint, 1952.

Foucault, Michel. *Discipline and Punish: The Birth of the Prison*. Translated by Alan Sheridan. New York: Vintage Books, 1979.

Gikandi, Simon. *Maps of Englishness: Writing Identity in the Culture of Colonialism*. New York: Columbia University Press, 1996.

——. *Writing in Limbo: Modernism and Caribbean Literature*. Ithaca, N.Y.: Cornell University Press, 1992.

Hobsbawm, Eric. *The Age of Empire, 1875–1914*. New York: Vintage Books, 1989.

Hobson, J. A. *Imperialism*. London: Nisbet, 1902.

Koebner, Richard, and Helmut Dan Schmidt. *Imperialism: The Story and Significance of a Political Word, 1840–1960*. Cambridge: Cambridge University Press, 1964.

Lenin, Vladimir Ilyich. *Imperialism, The Highest Stage of Capitalism*. New York: International Publishers, 1939.

Levenson, Michael, ed. *The Cambridge Companion to Modernism*. Cambridge: Cambridge University Press, 1999.

Lichtheim, George. *Imperialism*. London: Allen Lane, 1971.

Parry, Benita. *Delusions and Discoveries: Studies on the British Imagination, 1880–1930*. London: Allen Lane, 1972.

Said, Edward W. *Culture and Imperialism*. New York: Vintage Books, 1994.

Shannon, Richard. *The Crisis of Imperialism, 1865–1915*. London: Paladin Books, 1976.

Suleri, Sara. *The Rhetoric of English India*. Chicago: University of Chicago Press, 1992.

Williams, Patrick, and Laura Chrisman, eds. *Colonial Discourse and Post-Colonial Theory: A Reader*. New York: Columbia University Press, 1994.

# VICTORIAN BACKGROUNDS

*Nicholas Daly*

⋮

ONE

# Colonialism and Popular Literature at the Fin de Siècle

Stark walls and crumbling crucible,
Straight gates, and graves, and ruined well,
Abide, dumb monuments of old.
We know but that men fought and fell
Like us—like us—for love of gold.

ANDREW LANG, "Zimbabwe"

Once upon a time there was a thing called modernism that disdained the mass market, and made its way in the world by appealing to a small but discerning clientele; poor but honest, it eventually triumphed over the shoddy cultural goods that surrounded it, saved from commodification by its formal difficulty. Or so the story went. It was a moving story, with even a certain amount of suspense and melodrama, almost as if the very narrative qualities that modernism was supposed to have rejected in its practice had returned with a vengeance in its literary history. These days, of course, we have grown somewhat skeptical of such tales. The work of Lawrence Rainey, among others, has alerted us to the extent to which modernism ambivalently courted the market; if it appeared bashful about commercial success, this sometimes worked all the better to attract it.[1] A once monolithically conceived Modernism has been replaced by a more modest lowercase modernism, or by a variety of modernisms. But if we have begun to rethink modernism, we have also begun to consider the extent to which those shoddy cultural goods that once seemed just the opposite of the gleaming artifacts of modernism may in fact not have been so very different after all. It has become a good deal easier to argue that far from being polar opposites, modernism and mass culture enjoyed a variety of more complex relations. At a very basic level it has become clearer that, forged in the same historical moment, modernism and the popular are often concerned with the same things: for example, new conceptions of gender, new technologies, ideas of professionalism and expert culture, the coming of the mass market, and an increasingly globalized world.

Here I want to look at a small slice of British literary history, not the "high modern" 1920s, but the late nineteenth century, when modernism and modern mass culture were growing up together. The contemporaneous growth of the popular and modernist novel in these years can in part be ascribed to developments in the publishing industry. The demise of the three-volume novel was one such development. In 1828 the *Athenaeum* declared that "no Englishman in the middle class of life buys a book," and this remained true for most of the century, at least as far as new fiction was concerned. Artificially high prices, sustained by a comfortable arrangement among authors, publishers, and the circulating libraries, meant that novels, priced at a standard 31s 6d, were more often rented from Mudie's, or one of the other circulating libraries, or were read in part-published form (a mode popularized by the success of Dickens's *Pickwick Papers* in 1836–37), or as serials in periodicals ranging from the *Cornhill* to the *Graphic*. When the circulating libraries forsook the three-volume novel toward the century's end, their immense power over the market weakened, and the homogenizing power that for much of the century they had exercised on the public's reading habits weakened too. Reading patterns became increasingly "niched" as people began to buy the books they wanted to read rather than those that the libraries wanted to rent them. As bookrenting yielded to bookbuying, what developed was not, then, an opposition of a homogeneous mass market and a more rarefied market for elite cultural goods, but rather an increasingly fragmented market in which modernism would come to be another niche, albeit a more prestigious one.[2]

In terms of British modernism, these were the years of such protomodernists as Joseph Conrad, Henry James, and the young W. B. Yeats (though none of these was actually British); in terms of popular literature—or more accurately middle-brow literature—people were reading a wide variety of subgenres: historical novels, regional novels, "New Woman" novels, "slum novels," and novels of religious doubt, to name a few.[3] But they were also reading a new type of adventure fiction that was the fruit of the "revival of romance" launched by Robert Louis Stevenson's *Treasure Island* (1883). While one can detect the pressure of empire in early and mid-Victorian fiction, it has become a critical commonplace that these late-nineteenth-century adventure novels, the so-called imperial romance, constituted a more or less explicit part of the propaganda of empire, leading a whole generation of schoolboys—but also soldiers, sailors, adventurers, and businessmen—to believe that Britain's colonies promised exciting adventures and limitless wealth for those who were bold enough.[4] Even the very titles of such novels as *Treasure Island* and *King Solomon's Mines* seem to equate exotic territory and fabulous wealth before the narratives themselves do. Of course this equation was one that was being made far more forcefully in other places: in these same years the European powers were—not always amicably—carving up Africa among themselves, though the treaties of the Berlin Conference (1884–85) were to put a more diplomatic gloss on their rapacious scramble for the spoils. It is tempting then to see the adventure romances as providing a series of celebratory myths of empire for a mass audience, in counterpoint to the more complex, ironic, and demystifying protomodernism of, say, Conrad, aimed at a smaller and more discerning audience suspicious of the enthusiasms of empire and jingoism. Such a polar model does not, however, adequately describe the terrain of late Victorian literary production. For one thing, Conrad was very much part of the mainstream literary culture of the time, and his work appeared in serial form in such journals as *Blackwood's Magazine* and *T. P.'s Weekly*, not in "little magazines" of the kind that would later facilitate the circulation of the work of Joyce, Pound, and others. Moreover, as Peter D. MacDonald has shown, Conrad was extremely anxious to secure the approval of W. E. Henley, that formidable late Victorian editor, reviewer, poet, and literary promoter, who had helped to establish the reputations of Stevenson, Rudyard Kipling, and H. Rider Haggard, among others.[5] Here, though, I want to focus not on the complexities of Conrad's position but on those popular writers whose work has largely been placed outside the history of modernism (Stevenson is a partial exception in this respect).[6] While assessing their creation of a popular adventure literature consonant with Britain's imperial phase, I want to complicate our view of their work by considering the extent to which their the creation of Kimberley in 1871, and the excavation of the Big Hole, the world's largest man-made hole.[8] Haggard, though, is circumspect in his own way about the sources of colonial wealth: the diamonds that are recovered have not been mined by the present inhabitants of Kukuanaland; they are part of the fabulous treasury of a biblical king, and thus the men are happily restoring to Europe wealth that is perceived to be part of its Judeo-Christian heritage. But of course excavation is not confined to the search for mineral wealth. Both Stevenson and Haggard are also mounting a different kind of dig, one into the literary-historical past. If Stevenson seeks to revitalize the novel by mining the work of Sir Walter Scott, Haggard is prepared to dig deeper still. As his supporter, promoter, and sometime collaborator Andrew Lang explained in his essay "Realism and Romance" in 1887, Haggard was also trying to reach some very deep-lying seams in the reader—nothing less than "the natural man within . . . the survival of some blue-painted Briton."[9] The romance, then, was to put the modern reader back in touch with the inner savage by reviving the very roots of narrative in epic storytelling. Kukuanaland has been so isolated from history that in it heroic society still flourishes. As the choice of Africa as setting would allow that later primitivist, Ernest Hemingway, to write a certain kind of pared-down modernist sentence, here it underpins Haggard's attempts to write a more basic—and violent—kind of narrative, and to present as his heroes such bloodthirsty modern savages as that man's man, Sir Henry Curtis, described variously in the novel as an "ancient Dane" or "white Zulu."[10]

But for whose benefit was this work of literary and narratological excavation being effected? Why did Lang and others think that the English novel needed to be reinvigorated anyway? Was the three-volume domestic novel to be eschewed because it was inappropriate reading matter for empire boys? Up to a point, perhaps, but there is another reason why these short and involving yarns of lucrative adventure should appear when they do. It was not just the empire that was facing a phase of expansion in the 1880s: so was the publishing industry. There had for some time, of course, been a more or less indifferent awareness of that "unknown public," a readership "beyond the pale of literary civilization" to whom Wilkie Collins referred in 1858, but by the 1880s authors began to reimagine this unknown public as a veritable virgin continent of readers, an enormous untapped resource.[11] While many other factors contributed, the Education Act of 1870 and its sequels played a particular role in fostering this vision of a mass of literate but not literary readers who were at once a new territory to be profitably conquered, and a hostile mob whose low appetites threatened to overwhelm literature.[12]

That unknown public was itself fragmented, and one of the exemplary instances of the literate but not literary reader was the child. Stevenson conceived of *Treasure Island* as a "story for boys," at a time when he was also working on a number of what he hoped would be lucrative ghost stories. In August 1881, he writes to W. E. Henley, editor of the *National Observer*, and his sometime collaborator:

> See here—nobody, not you, nor Lang, nor the devil will hurry me with our crawlers. They are coming. Four of them are as good as done, and the rest will come when ripe; but I am now on another lay for the moment, purely owing to Lloyd, this one; but I believe there's more coin in it than any amount of crawlers: now, see here,
> "The Sea Cook,
> or Treasure Island:
> A Story for Boys."[13]

He signs the letter "R. L. S.—Author of Boys' Stories." Thanks to the intervention of Stevenson's acquaintance Dr. Alexander H. Japp, "The Sea Cook" was serialized in *Young Folks*, one of the less prestigious magazines then targeting the younger reader.[14] It appeared there from October 1881 to January 1882, now rechristened *Treasure Island; or the Mutiny of the Hispaniola*, by Captain George North. The pseudonym suggests that Stevenson felt that no critical benefit would accrue to him by his association with *Young Folks*. He was at some pains, however, to convince Henley that what might appear to be a whimsical venture into children's literature was a sound commercial venture for "coin." A subsequent letter to Henley reasserts the commercial point: "I'll make this boy's business pay; but I have to make a beginning. When I'm done with *Young Folks* I'll try Routledge or some one. I feel pretty sure the *Sea Cook* will do to reprint, and bring something decent at that."[15] This tale of buccaneers, then, was to be treated as a commercial property, to be rendered as profitable as possible by publication in different formats. Although he was paid less than he had hoped by *Young Folks* (£37. 7s .6d), he was able to hold onto his copyright, and the novel was published by Cassell and Co. (not Routledge) on November 14, 1883, in an edition of two thousand copies priced at five shillings. In the same letter Stevenson confesses his ambition to be the "Harrison Ainsworth of the future,"[16] a reference to the incredibly prolific author of *Rookwood* (1834), *Jack Sheppard* (1839), and other swashbuckling tales in the early and mid-nineteenth century, and he boasts that *Treasure Island* will be a better tale than Captain Marryat's *Pirate* (1836). He adds that this sort of work is a "D-sight gayer than Mudie-ing, you bet."[17] Not only, then, was *Treasure Island* to generate profits, and provide a break from writing for the genteel audience of the circulating libraries, but it was also to achieve the rather less commercial task of placing him among the great children's authors of his own youth: "coining it" is to take place in conjunction with a more complicated act that is half nostalgia, half Oedipal displacement, Stevenson's own effort to make it new.

Stevenson's genuine ambitions as a children's writer should not blind us to the fact that at least some of his defensiveness about his new generic direction stems from an awareness that it is not just the children's market he is courting but a more general mass readership. Such an awareness informs the poem which acts as a sort of preface to the book version. This poem addresses the "studious youth," who, "his ancient appetites forgot," may no longer hanker after the rip-roaring yarns of "Kingston, or Ballantyne the Brave" (W. H. G. Kingston and R. M. Ballantyne, authors of such adventure novels as *Peter the Whaler* and *The Coral Island*); but the poem's title, "To the Hesitating Purchaser," acknowledges that his book is a commodity competing for attention in an emergent mass market. He is targeting the adult as much as the juvenile reader, and, crucially, the *buyer* rather than the reader. That Stevenson had a deep personal as well as financial need to succeed in the market is attested to by his later account of his self-doubts during the novel's composition: "I was thirty-one; I was the head of a family; I had lost my health; I had never yet paid my way, never yet made £200 a year; my father had quite recently bought back and cancelled a book that was judged a failure: was this to be another and last fiasco?"[18] But it was not to be a failure, of course, and Stevenson received £100 from Cassell's, as well as a royalty of £20 for every thousand copies sold after the first four thousand.[19] His letter of May 1883 to Henley, who had negotiated with Cassell's on his behalf, reveals his mingled delight and relief at the deal that had been struck, and anxiety lest it should slip away. His high spirits carry the letter into comic verse, though the encomium to Henley has a tinge of hysterical hostility:

> Dear Child, O golden voice, enchanting warbler of the evening glade, sun of the ardent tropic, angel friend:
> One Hundred Pounds
> (and to a beggar)
> TAKE, O TAKE IT!
> LET IT WAVE
> . . .
> Take, O Take it
> Or your head
> I'll break, O break it
> And kill you dead
> . . .
> O I am happy, O my fortune's made.[20]

A letter to his parents written on the same day suggests that Stevenson was more focused on the immediate prospect of £100 than on any possible royalties (it is indeed possible that he did not know there were to be any): "My dearest people, I have had a great piece of news. There has been offered for *Treasure Island*—how much do you suppose? . . . A hundred pounds, all alive, oh! A hundred jingling, tingling, golden, minted quid. Is not this wonderful." He signs himself their "loving and ecstatic son, Treesure Eilan," and declares that "It has been, for me, a Treasure Island verily."[21] A letter to Henley of May 7, 1883, indicates that he felt he had done better out of the deal than Cassell's: "Really £100 is a Bloody Sight more than *Treasure Island* is worth."[22]

It is scarcely surprising, then, that a story developed as part of a plan to exploit a hitherto untapped, or at least undertapped, source of readers, and written at a time when Stevenson was in dire need of a commercial success, should be so concerned with digging for treasure. The early reviewers often highlight two (related, I would argue) aspects of the text: the importance of its hidden hoard, and its potential crossover appeal. As the *Academy* noted, Stevenson had appealed to "the old boy as well as the young" by recreating the fictions of Tobias Smollett, Dr. Moore, and Captain Marryat, but he had also stripped the exoticism from his tale "to depict an island the sole attraction of which lies in its hidden treasure."[23] The review in the *Athenaeum* also picked out the importance of treasure, noting the link to Poe's "Gold Beetle" [*sic*].[24] Stevenson's friend and negotiator Henley, in an unsigned review in the *Saturday Review*, assured his readers that "buried treasure is one of the very foundations of romance." "This is the theory on which Mr Stevenson has written *Treasure Island*," he expanded. And although it is a "book for boys," it is one "which will be delightful to all grown men who have the sentiment of treasure-hunting."[25]

Treasure, then, comes to function as a sign of the novel's semi-allegorical treatment of the new relations of author and the mass market. Nor is it the only sign: Jim Hawkins finds himself on board a ship, the *Hispaniola*, that seems to provide a microcosm of the class structure of Victorian Britain, "the whole ship creaking and groaning like a manufactory" (68). (We are reminded that Stevenson himself had spent a voyage to the United States in 1879 as a "second cabin" passenger, one step up from steerage.)[26] But this is a novel of class warfare rather than of peaceful stratification by deck level. The gentlemen (Squire Trelawney, Dr. Livesey, Captain Smollett—though not Jim) have unknowingly shipped with a crew that is largely comprised of pirates: a rough and lawless bunch of individuals who do not respect their betters, and who do not speak "correct" English. The partial exception here, of course, is the Sea Cook himself, Long John Silver, who, whatever his attitude to his social superiors, is better educated than his fellow pirates, and who seems to be the figure most likely to seduce Jim from his class allegiances. " 'He's no common man, Barbecue [ Silver's nickname],' said the coxswain to me. 'He had a good schooling in his young days, and can speak like a book when so minded' " (54). I am not suggesting, though, that Silver represents the post–Forster Education Act half-literate reader. Stevenson admitted to Henley that he had based his most memorable pirate on him, which suggests that if the social chameleon, Jim, is one figure for the late Victorian writer, the piratical Silver may be another.[27]

The treasure, the "coin" that this crew—and, I am arguing, Stevenson himself—are after, is problematic at a number of levels. At the level of plot, and in terms of the novel's class divisions, since it is the treasure of another pirate, Captain Flint, it might be thought that (a) the pirates have as much a claim to it as the gentlemen, or (b) that neither of them has any claim to it, and that the gentlemen wish to acquire what are in effect stolen goods, ill-gotten gains. At the level of the novel's allegory of writing, Stevenson's ambivalence about the mass market as a source of wealth leaves its mark in a number of ways. Before Jim Hawkins tells us of the treasure, he recalls the song that Billy Bones sings as he drunkenly bullies the customers of the Hawkins's inn, "Fifteen men on the dead man's chest." The way to buried treasure, that is, lies through a pile of buried men. As it happens, the six men (rather than fifteen) that Flint kills on the island when he is burying his treasure are not buried with it, though one of them has become a skeletal compass point showing the way to the spot of its interment. When Jim finally sees the treasure in Ben Gunn's cave, he is moved to think of its blood-soaked past: "That was Flint's treasure that we had come so far to seek, and that had already cost the lives of seventeen men from the Hispaniola. How many it had cost in the amassing, what blood and sorrow, what good ships scuttled on the deep, what brave men walking the plank blindfold, what shot of cannon, what shame and lies and cruelty, perhaps no man alive could tell" (185). Most curiously, in his prefatory poem, Stevenson seems to imagine himself interred with Kingston, Ballantyne, and their creations, and his own pirates, if his tale fails to find an audience: "And may I / And all my pirates share the grave / Where these and their creations lie" (xxx). Are we to imagine Stevenson himself consigned to the ash-heap of literary history, or transformed into a form of buried treasure, or to equate the wages of literary sin with death? But then this is a novel where the chief villain, Silver, is lost at the end, just like the bullion that shares his name ("The bar silver and the arms still lie, for all that I know, where Flint buried them; and certainly they shall lie there for me" [191]). One thinks of another letter to Henley regarding the American publication of *Treasure Island*, where he stressed that he "wish[ed] to imbrue himself in gold for it."[28]

But even before we come to the treasure of Treasure Island, the curious landscape that is half-Caribbean, half-Californian island is itself marked out as unhealthy. Here again it is tempting to see Jim's forebodings about the island as in some way reflecting doubts about the late Victorian imperial project, but they also seem to suggest some ambivalence about the sources of literary wealth:

> Grey-coloured woods covered a large part of the surface. This even tint was indeed broken up by streaks of yellow sandbreak in the lower lands, and by many tall trees of the pine family, out-topping the others—some singly, some in clumps; but the general colouring was uniform and sad. . . . The Hispaniola was

> rolling scuppers under the ocean swell . . . and the whole ship creaking and groaning like a manufactory. . . . Perhaps it was [seasickness]—perhaps it was the look of the island, with its grey, melancholy woods, and wild stone spires, and the surf that we could both see and hear foaming and thundering on the steep beach—at least, although the sun shone bright and hot, and the shore birds were fishing and crying all around us, and you would have thought that anyone would have been glad to get to land after being so long at sea, my heart sank, as the saying is, into my boots; and from that first look onward, I hated the very thought of Treasure Island. (68–69)

No island paradise this; I have already commented on the use of the term "manufactory" to describe the *Hispaniola*, but the description of the island as a gloomy and melancholy place is no less striking. Ashore the foliage has a "poisonous brightness" (69), and Dr. Livesey sniffs disapprovingly at the stench of decaying vegetation: " 'I don't know about treasure,' he said, 'but I'll stake my wig there's fever here' " (70). The island subsequently appears in a less sickly light, the deployment of the maroon, Ben Gunn, seeming to push Stevenson toward the more Edenic islands of the Robinsonade tradition, and nutmeg trees displace gloomy pines in the text. But the last lines of the novel see an older Jim still haunted by the island's real nature: "Oxen and wain-ropes would not bring me back again to that accursed island; and the worst dreams that I ever have are when I hear the surf booming about its coasts, or start upright in bed, with the sharp voice of Captain Flint still ringing in my ears: 'Pieces of eight! Pieces of eight' " (191). Again, although it is possible to read this dread of the treasure's origins as an oblique critique of Britain's increasingly imperial turn, it also marks Stevenson's uneasiness at his own financial expedition into uncharted waters.

This uneasiness would grow. If the dark continent of the book-buying public could still be thought of as populated by children of all ages in the early 1880s, by 1885 Stevenson's attitude had hardened, as we see from a letter to Edmund Gosse in connection with the hostile critical reception accorded his novel of 1885, *Prince Otto:*

> Let us tell each other sad stories of the bestiality of the beast whom we feed. What he likes is the newspaper; and to me the press is the mouth of a sewer, where lying is professed as from an university chair, and everything prurient, and ignoble, and essentially dull, finds its abode and pulpit. . . . As for respecting the race, and above all, that fatuous rabble of burgesses called "the public," God save

> me from such irreligion!—that way lies disgrace and dishonour. There must be something wrong in me, or I would not be popular. . . . We [ writers] were full of the pride of life, and chose, like prostitutes, to live by pleasure. We should be paid if we give the pleasure we pretend to give; but why should we be honoured?[29]

This was written at a time when Stevenson was making his most determined play for the heart, or stomach, of the same "beast": *The Strange Case of Dr Jekyll and Mr Hyde* (1886). If he had used the children's story as a way out of the triple-decker format in *Treasure Island*, with *Jekyll and Hyde* he appeared to his contemporaries to be writing an actual "shilling shocker." As James Ashcroft Noble pointed out in the *Academy*, it is "not an orthodox three-volume novel; it is not even a one-volume novel of the ordinary type; it is simply a paper-covered shilling story, belonging, so far as external appearance goes, to a class of literature familiarity with which has bred in the minds of most readers a certain measure of contempt."[30] (He goes on to argue that despite "the paper cover and the popular price" of one shilling, it is a literary triumph.) Stevenson himself writes nervously about having such a shilling shocker in hand. However, as he explained in a letter to F. W. H. Myers, "the wheels of Byles the Butcher drive exceeding swiftly," and he had to write for money.[31]

As critics have noted, a number of phrases seem to link Hyde to a sort of imperial recoil, as if England has been invaded by the dark forces that were supposedly opposed to the civilizing mission.[32] Much, for example, has been made of the scene in which Hyde clubs to death the elderly Member of Parliament, Sir Danvers Carew: "The old gentleman took a step back, with the air of one very much surprised and a trifle hurt; and at that Mr Hyde broke out of all bounds and clubbed him to the earth. And next moment, with ape-like fury, he was trampling his victim under foot, and hailing down a storm of blows, under which the bones were audibly shattered and the body jumped upon the roadway."[33] This extraordinary scene lends itself to interpretation as a species of symbolic rape, as a post-Darwinian account of degeneration, or of the violence of the mob. As Patrick Brantlinger and Richard Boyle have argued, it might more specifically have reminded contemporary readers of the Victorian cartoon portraits of the Irish Fenians that veered between Frankenstein monsters and shillelagh-wielding ape-men primitives, but also of the 1882 Phoenix Park murders in Dublin, in which the "Invincibles" had stabbed to death the chief secretary of Ireland, Lord

Frederick Cavendish, and his under-secretary Thomas Henry Burke.[34] Colonial violence is perceived by the colonizer to emanate from the colonized, to derive from their primitive, bestial nature—to be the opposite, that is, of the modernity of the colonial power. *Jekyll and Hyde* might seem, then, to bring one of the most infamous episodes of the Land War onto the streets of London itself.

But as with *Treasure Island*, the colonial theme here too seems to be linked to Stevenson's own self-perception as a writer. With *Jekyll and Hyde*, though, the allegory of the market goes one stage further. In the earlier novel, Stevenson's quest for gold seems to lead to a splitting of narrative energy between the upwardly mobile Jim Hawkins and the piratical Long John Silver; here our narrator has actually been torn in two—he shape-shifts between professional gentlemen and undersized street-thug with vicious appetites. At the end of *Jekyll and Hyde*, what remain are Hyde's body and Jekyll's confession ("Here then, as I lay down the pen and proceed to seal up my confession, I bring the life of that unhappy Henry Jekyll to an end" [62]). This may be a prescient example of the "death of the author," but it is one that appears at a particular moment in British literary culture, and in Stevenson's career, which suggests that Jekyll's divided self (and the novel's patchwork structure) mimics Stevenson's sense of his own fragmentation within a fissive literary market. The end of the tale seems to suggest that the belletristic author's only option is to disappear, to leave the field to the beast. The "wild man within" that Lang liked to evoke as the proper audience for the romance has been literalized and seen to be less a noble savage to be nurtured than a monster, a misshapen monster who grows stronger as his appetites are fed. Stevenson, though, implicitly acknowledges that like Jekyll he is both beast and beast-feeder.

⋮ ⋮ ⋮

Between *Treasure Island* and *Dr Jekyll and Mr Hyde* there appeared a novel that has also been taken as an exemplary instance of the "revival of romance," and that also seems to deal with the perils and treasures of colonial space: H. Rider Haggard's *King Solomon's Mines* (1885). Unlike Stevenson, Haggard was someone who had a good deal of personal knowledge of Britain's colonial possessions, having been dispatched to South Africa at the tender age of nineteen to work on the staff of Sir Henry Bulwer, Governor of Natal. He had played a part in the annexation of the Transvaal in 1877, and in the same year he was made Master of the High Court in the new colony. In a letter home he expressed to his father his hopes of eventually rising to the position of a Colonial Governor, though he later quit the colonial service to try his luck as an ostrich farmer.[35] While the Zulu War of 1879 seems to have done nothing to dampen his enthusiasm for the colonies, he returned to Britain early in 1881 during the uprising of the Transvaal Boers, which led to the retrocession of the Transvaal in August of that year.

Back home he studied for the bar examinations (his experience as a colonial judge seemed to cut little ice with the British Bar), while also writing an account of the political state of South Africa, *Cetywayo and His White Neighbours, or Remarks on Recent Events in Zululand, Natal and Transvaal* (1882), and two unsuccessful novels. It was while he was working as a fledgling barrister that he wrote *King Solomon's Mines*, which was rescued from the obscurity of his previous publications when first Henley and then Andrew Lang took an interest in it.[36] Cassell's appears to have realized its potential to follow the success of *Treasure Island*, and it was issued in a similar binding, and at the same five-shilling price. Posters were placed all over London to advertise "The Most Amazing Book Ever Written." The advertising campaign paid dividends, as it sold even more briskly than *Treasure Island*, some 31,000 copies in the first year in England, a phenomenal number at the time, and further proof that the one-volume, six-shilling format could be far more lucrative than the 31s 6d triple-decker.

Haggard had written his novel after reading Stevenson's treasure tale, convinced he could do better. Unsurprisingly, then, the treasure map is central to the narrative (and appeared as a fold-out inclusion in the first edition), but Haggard replaces Stevenson's young first-person narrator with the figure of Allan Quatermain, a fifty-five-year-old white hunter and sometime trader and miner who first came to South Africa in his teens, like Haggard himself. Though describing himself as "not a literary man" (7), he recounts his most recent adventure, the search for King Solomon's Mines and the discovery of the lost kingdom of Kukuanaland.[37] Two other Englishmen recruit him for the testing trek across deserts and frozen peaks: Sir Henry Curtis and his friend, a former naval officer, Captain John Good. Sir Henry Curtis has come to trace his brother, George, who disappeared in the South African interior while hunting for the diamonds of Solomon's Mines, though it is Quatermain himself who possesses an old map that purports to show the location of the mines. To complicate matters, their expedition is joined by one Umbopa—a formidable Zulu warrior whom Quatermain employs along with a Hottentot tracker, Ventvögel, and another Zulu, Khiva—who, when they finally reach Kukuanaland, claims to be the rightful heir to the throne. They side with him in the civil war that ensues against the corrupt reign of Twala and his adviser and witch-hunter, the ancient sorceress Gagool. After some epic battles, the Englishmen's chosen side prevails, and Umbopa—whose real name is Ignosi—is installed as the rightful king of Kukuanaland, and the men set off in search of Solomon's Mines again. Here, the ignominiously named Big Hole of Kimberley appears to be transformed into something ancient and mysterious. They are guided by Gagool, who leads them to the vast mines, the entrance to which is guarded by three large statues of forbidding appearance, and inside which they find the bodies of the kings of Kukuanaland, transformed into so many stalactites. Inside the mines Gagool opens a secret entrance to the treasure chamber itself, where they find huge stores of ivory, twenty boxes of "gold pieces, of a shape that none of us could have seen before, and with what looked like Hebrew characters stamped upon them," and at last the diamonds themselves:

> "Look!" he repeated, hoarsely holding the lamp over the open chest. We looked, and for a moment could make nothing out, on account of a silvery sheen that dazzled us. When our eyes got used to it, we saw that the chest was three-parts full of uncut diamonds, most of them of considerable size. Stooping, I picked some up. Yes there was no mistake about it, there was the unmistakable soapy feel about them. I fairly gasped as I dropped them.
>
> "We are the richest men in the whole world," I said. "Monte Cristo is a fool to us."
>
> "We shall flood the market with diamonds," said Good.
>
> "Got to get them there first," suggested Sir Henry. (216)

And this turns out to be their problem, as Gagool releases the lever that holds the chamber's enormous stone door in place, and traps them inside with their wealth. Foulata, the native woman who has fallen for Good, tries to stop her and is stabbed for her pains, though Gagool herself is caught by the slowly closing door and crushed to death. After some grim moments they find a passage that leads them to a small egress: "A squeeze, a struggle, and Sir Henry was out, and so was Good, and so was I: and there above us were the blessed stars, and in our nostrils was the sweet air; then suddenly something gave, and we were all rolling over and over, through grass and bushes, and soft, wet soil" (229).

This timely escape recalls a very different rite of passage by ordeal that they earlier undergo: after being baked in the desert and frozen in the mountains, they escape death just in time by eating the raw heart and liver of an antelope, which restores to them their "life and [their] vigour" (105), making men of them again. As Nancy Armstrong has argued, this aspect of the narrative reflects the extent to which their African adventure seems to be a course in remasculinization: just as Andrew Lang saw the red meat of the revival of romance as saving the novel from the feminizing effects of too much drawing-room self-consciousness, the characters themselves are given a healthy dose of masculine vigor through quite literally eating Africa raw.[38]

But their ordeal in the mines points to a more anxious aspect of the novel's self-reflexivity. Here, as with Stevenson, exotic treasure can be seen to figure the profitability of the domestic literary market. Quatermain's map, as a number of critics have noted, shows the landscape as a recumbent female body: the mouth of the treasure cave lies in a pubic triangle of mountains; the entrance into Kukuanaland itself lies through two peaks, Sheba's Breasts. Anne McClintock has argued that the men's trajectory is to impose their masculine will on the feminized body of Africa and ultimately, in effect, to rebirth themselves from the orifice of the mines.[39] I would argue, though, that the men's burial alive in the mines is rather more anxious, and that the very specific kind of claustrophobia it represents—being trapped in a woman's body—can again be read in terms of the author's place in the literary marketplace. That Haggard's novel equates making colonial money (diamonds) with being immured in a female body is difficult to interpret in light of the masculine myths of colonialism, but it does resonate with the contemporary equation of the lucrative market for popular books with women readers. The "beast" that Stevenson feared to feed was for many of his contemporaries not a dwarfish street-thug like Mr. Hyde but an omnivorous female consumer. Nor was this a fear exclusive to "hearties" like Haggard and Lang: one of the principal problems with what he styled the "tyranny of the novel" for a more aesthetically oriented critic like Edmund Gosse was that women, and particularly young married women, were "the main audience of the novelist."[40] One might expect Haggard, the former colonial administrator and ostrich-farmer, to have written a novel celebrating the (profitable) adventure of the colonies, a settler's myth in which Africa would appear as a peach ripe for plucking, but *King Solomon's Mines* is something rather different: it celebrates Africa as a place where the nonmodern should be allowed to survive, providing a healthy antidote to European modernity.[41] However, its fantasies about Africa's mineral wealth are also overshadowed by Haggard's sense that writing for the market was a feminizing task, that he might find himself with diamonds in his pockets but trapped forever in the mines. The adventure novel promised to transport the reader from the claustrophobic domesticity of the triple-decker novel of love and marriage, but for the author it seems to risk immurement in an even more feminized space.

⋮ ⋮ ⋮

I have dwelt at some length on one aspect of the revival of romance, those outward-bound narratives of adventure, the better to make a point about the colonial imaginary and the mass market. But of course there are also many novels and stories of the period that represent not expeditions but incursions into Britain by various alien forces. I mean, of course, the many invasion narratives of this period, which range from tales of actual military conquest in the 1870s (George Chesney's *The Battle of Dorking* [1871]) to later scientific romances (Wells's *The War of the Worlds* [1898]), and to narratives of supernatural invasion (Conan Doyle's "Lot No. 249" [1892], Stoker's *Dracula* [1897], Richard Marsh's *The Beetle* [1897]). A number of critics have diagnosed these too as being part of a colonial imaginary, and Stephen Arata's essay on *Dracula* as a supernaturally encoded tale of colonial recoil has been particularly influential in recasting these invasion stories as the nightmares of an aggressive and overextended Britain, one that projects its own imperial ambitions and colonial violence onto a variety of others.[42] But as with the treasure-expedition narratives, it is difficult not to see these too as at once part of the colonial imaginary and part of an extended coming to terms with the mass market for literature. As a transition narrative between the tale of treasure and the tale of invasion, we might consider Arthur Conan Doyle's *The Sign of Four* (1890), in which plundered colonial treasure has the effect not only of "Orientalizing" its possessor but also of drawing into Britain dangerous foreign entities, notably the diminutive assassin from the Andaman Islands who murders Bartholomew Sholto. Doyle, no less than Stevenson and Haggard, was someone who wanted to court the serious reader, and who was driven by financial exigencies to write for the kind of publications he would rather have avoided. He sent the draft of the first Holmes novel, *A Study in Scarlet*, to Smith, Elder and Co., to Arrowsmith, and to Frederick Warne and Company before, stung by their rejections, sending it to the rather less prestigious Ward, Lock and Company, where it was first published in their *Beeton's Christmas Annual* of 1887, before appearing the following year in their "shilling dreadful" series. He received £25 for the outright sale of the copyright rather than the royalty agreement he had hoped for. While *The Sign of Four* was published under much more auspicious circumstances by Lippincott and Spencer Blackett in 1890, it is tempting to read this tale of the blighting effects of treasure as again figuring the price that the author pays for going to market. Whatever forces are invading Britain in the 1880s might be seen to be as much the recoil from the Education Act of 1870 and its sequels as from Britain's overseas adventures.

In the novels of the 1890s there is less emphasis on the perils and pleasures of possessing treasure and rather more on being oneself possessed. The villains of George du Maurier's *Trilby* (1894), *Dracula*, and *The Beetle* are able to achieve ascendancy over their victims by a species of mind control: mesmerism, or sheer supernatural force in the case of *Dracula* and *The Beetle*, allows foreign villains to get their hands on British women—Trilby O'Ferrall, Lucy Westenra and Mina Harker, and Marjorie Lindon. But access to the nation's women seems also to guarantee dominion over its men. Svengali's use of Trilby is the clearest instance of this: his control over Trilby turns her from artist's model and laundress into a singer of consummate ability, which allows Svengali indirectly to spellbind huge audiences. While it is possible to see Svengali as du Maurier's nightmare version of Oscar Wilde, as Daniel Pick and Pamela Thurschwell have argued, or of James McNeill Whistler, as I have argued myself, it is also possible to see the novel focusing less specific fears about the mass market audience for literature, and their susceptibility. While Stevenson and Haggard were more concerned about their own implication in the mass market, here the unscrupulous Jewish manipulator is a figure projected outside the self and nation.

In conclusion, the novels of the revival of romance take part in the shaping of Britain's colonial imaginary, but their vision of Britain's place in a new global order always appears to be refracted through their authors' efforts to map cognitively their place in another emerging order, the mass market. In this respect they were not so very different from the contemporary social reformers who presented their perception of social problems "at home" in the language of the colonial space, in such titles as William Booth's *In Darkest England and the Way Out* (1890), with its evocation of H. M. Stanley's best-selling travelogues of 1879, *Through the Dark Continent*, and 1890, *In Darkest Africa*.

In the face of the mass market, the writers of the 1880s and 1890s tended to huddle together in all-male bands: the hearties of the (W. E.) "Henley Regatta," the aesthetes from the Rhymer's Club or Savoy, or the members of the *Idler* coterie (Jerome K. Jerome, James Barrie, Israel Zangwill, and Robert Barr). They saw safety in numbers and comradeship in the face of a mass market that sometimes wore a woman's face, sometimes that of a swarthy and dwarfish male. Small wonder that they could enjoy the all-male expeditions described so vividly by Stevenson and Haggard into dangerous exotic spaces, and perilous confrontations with dark others, and femmes fatales like Haggard's Ayesha. In this too, of course, they resembled the culture at large, where these same years saw a burgeoning of male professional societies and associations, and the privileging of hermetic vocational languages that, as Thomas Strychacz has suggested, also have their equivalents in high modernism. But despite the prevalence of such fantasies of impenetrability, that at least some of the writers of the romance revival could also, like Stevenson, see themselves as prostitutes serving the market suggests that writing, money making, and selfhood were far from simple issues for them any more than they were for the twentieth-century modernists.

## Notes

1 See, for example, Rainey, *Institutions of Modernism*, and "The Cultural Economy of Modernism."

2 On this "niche" aspect of modernism, see Strychacz, *Modernism, Mass Culture, and Professionalism*.

3 For a broad and even survey of literary production in these years, see Keating, *The Haunted Study*.

4 See, for example, Green, *Dreams of Adventure*. For accounts of the presence of empire in Victorian literature more generally, see, for example, Brantlinger, *Rule of Darkness*, and Said, *Culture and Imperialism*.

5 MacDonald, *British Literary Culture*, 22–67.

6 See, for example, Sandison, *Robert Louis Stevenson and the Appearance of Modernism*.

7 This is not to say that Stevenson invented his novel from whole cloth. See, for example, Watson, *Coasts of Treasure Island*.

8 In his autobiography Haggard claims that his story is partly based on rumors he

had heard during his time in Africa in the 1870s of the mineral wealth of what would later be Rhodesia (now Zimbabwe). See *Days of My Life*, 1: 242. On the Big Hole, see Pakenham, *The Scramble for Africa*, 46.

9 Lang, "Realism and Romance," 685.

10 Haggard, *King Solomon's Mines* (1885; reprint, Oxford: Oxford University Press, 1998), 11, 226. Further references to this edition are given in the text in parentheses.

11 Collins, "The Unknown Public," 2: 251, 263.

12 See, for example, MacDonald, *British Literary Culture*, 7–9.

13 Booth and Mehew, eds., *The Letters of Robert Stevenson*, 3: 224.

14 *Young Folks* was aimed at a broader audience than such public schoolboy–oriented publications as *The Boy's Own Paper*. See Letley, Introduction, xi.

15 *Letters*, 3: 229.

16 Ibid., 3: 230.

17 Ibid.

18 "My First Book," first published in *The Idler*, August 1894, reprinted in Letley, ed., *Treasure Island*, 192–200 (197).

19 *Letters*, 4: 119 n.

20 Ibid., 4: 117–18.

21 Ibid., 4: 119–20.

22 Ibid., 4: 120.

23 Unsigned review, *The Academy*, December 1, 1883, 362. Reprinted in *Critical Heritage*, ed. Maixner, 128.

24 Arthur John Butler, unsigned review, *Athenaeum*, December 1, 1883, 700. Reprinted in *Critical Heritage*, 130.

25 Henley, unsigned review, *Saturday Review*, December 8, 1883, lvi. Reprinted in *Critical Heritage*, 737–38.

26 McLynn, *Robert Louis Stevenson*, 149.

27 *Letters*, 4: 128–29.

28 Ibid., 4: 99–100.

29 Ibid., 5: 171.

30 Review in *Academy*, January 23, 1886, 55. Reprinted in *Critical Heritage*, 203.

31 *Letters*, 5: 216.

32 See, for example, Brantlinger, *Rule of Darkness*, 232–33.

33 *The Strange Case of Dr. Jekyll and Mr. Hyde*, ed. Linehan, 22. Further page references to this edition are given in the text in parentheses.

34 Brantlinger and Boyle, "The Education of Edward Hyde."

35 On Haggard's colonial ambitions, see the letter to his father of June 1, 1877, reproduced in *Days of My Life* 1: 101–3.

36 See *Days of My Life* 1: 226–28.

37 *King Solomon's Mines* (1885; Oxford: Oxford University Press, 1998), 7. Further references cited in parentheses in the text.

38 Armstrong, "The Occidental Alice."

39 McClintock, "Maidens, Maps, and Mines."

40 Cited in MacDonald, *British Literary Culture*, 6.

41 Laura Chrisman suggests that it is a mistake to conflate the young Haggard, colonial administrator and settler farmer, with the author of the novel, who sees Africa as a valuable heterotopia to European modernity. See her "Gendering Imperial Culture."

42 Arata, "The Occidental Tourist."

## Works Cited

Arata, Stephen. "The Occidental Tourist: *Dracula* and the Anxiety of Reverse Colonization." *Victorian Studies* 33 (1990): 621–45.

Armstrong, Nancy. "The Occidental Alice." *Differences: A Journal of Feminist Cultural Studies* 2.2 (1990): 2–39.

Booth, Bradford A., and Ernest Mehew, eds. *The Letters of Robert Stevenson*, 8 vols. New Haven, Conn.: Yale University Press, 1994.

Brantlinger, Patrick. *Rule of Darkness: British Literature and Imperialism, 1830–1914*. Ithaca, N.Y.: Cornell University Press, 1988.

Brantlinger, Patrick, and Richard Boyle. "The Education of Edward Hyde: Stevenson's 'Gothic Gnome' and the Mass Readership of Late-Victorian England." In *Dr Jekyll and Mr Hyde after One Hundred Years*, ed. William Veeder and Gordon Hirsch, 265–82. Chicago: University of Chicago Press, 1988.

Chrisman, Laura. "Gendering Imperial Culture: *King Solomon's Mines* and Feminist Criticism." In *Edward Said and the Gravity of History*, ed. Keith Ansell-Pearson, Benita Parry, and Judith Squires, 290–304. London: Lawrence and Wishart, 1997.

Collins, Wilkie. "The Unknown Public." *My Miscellanies*. Vol. 2. London: Chatto and Windus, 1875.

Green, Martin. *Dreams of Adventure, Deeds of Empire*. New York: Basic Books, 1979.

Haggard, H. Rider. *The Days of My Life*. 2 vols. London: Longmans, 1926.

——. *King Solomon's Mines*. 1885. Reprint, Oxford: Oxford University Press, 1989.

Keating, Peter. *The Haunted Study: A Social History of the English Novel, 1875–1914*. London: Secker and Warburg, 1989.

Lang, Andrew. "Realism and Romance." *Contemporary Review* 52 (1887): 683-93.

Letley, Emma. "Introduction." In Robert Louis Stevenson, *Treasure Island* (1883), ed. Emma Letley. Oxford: Oxford University Press, 1998.

MacDonald, Peter D. *British Literary Culture and Publishing Practice, 1880–1914*. Cambridge: Cambridge University Press, 1997.

Maixner, Paul, ed. *Robert Louis Stevenson: The Critical Heritage*. London: Routledge, 1981.

McClintock, Anne. "Maidens, Maps, and Mines: *King Solomon's Mines* and the Reinvention of Patriarchy in South Africa." In *Women and Gender in Southern Africa*, ed. Cheryl Walker, 97–124. Cape Town: David Philip and James Currey, 1990.

McLynn, Frank. *Robert Louis Stevenson: A Biography*. London: Hutchinson, 1993.

Pakenham, Thomas. *The Scramble for Africa, 1876–1912*. London: Abacus, 1971.

Rainey, Lawrence. "The Cultural Economy of Modernism." In *The Cambridge Companion to Modernism*, ed. Michael Levenson, 33–69. Cambridge: Cambridge University Press, 1999.

——. *Institutions of Modernism: Literary Elites and Public Culture*. New Haven, Conn.: Yale University Press, 1991.

Said, Edward. *Culture and Imperialism*. New York: Knopf, 1993.

Sandison, Alan. *Robert Louis Stevenson and the Appearance of Modernism: A Future Feeling*. Basingstoke: Macmillan/St. Martin's, 1996.

Stevenson, Robert Louis. *The Strange Case of Dr. Jekyll and Mr. Hyde* (1886). Edited by Katherine Linehan. Reprint, New York: Norton, 2003.

——. *Treasure Island* (1883). Edited by Emma Letley. Reprint, Oxford: Oxford University Press, 1998.

Strychacz, Thomas. *Modernism, Mass Culture, and Professionalism*. Cambridge: Cambridge University Press, 1993.

Watson, Harold F. *Coasts of Treasure Island: A Study of the Backgrounds and Sources for Robert Louis Stevenson's Romance of the Sea*. San Antonio, Texas: Naylor, 1969.

MODERN
BRITISH
LITERATURE

*Michael Valdez Moses*

⋮

TWO

# Disorientalism: Conrad and the Imperial Origins of Modernist Aesthetics

At the heart of *Heart of Darkness*, aboard a steamboat he captains on the upper reaches of an African river, Marlow experiences a moment of extreme vertigo, of radical disorientation. Somewhere downstream from Kurtz's station, Marlow and his passengers find themselves befogged as day breaks. The mist lifts momentarily to reveal the dense jungle canopy, and then a "white shutter" abruptly drops:

> What we could see was just the steamer we were on, her outlines blurred as though she had been on the point of dissolving, and a misty strip of water, perhaps two feet broad around her—and that was all. The rest of the world was nowhere, as far as our eyes and our ears were concerned. Just nowhere. Gone, disappeared; swept off without leaving a whisper or a shadow behind. (68)[1]

When the station manager suggests he should pilot the boat upriver through the fog, Marlow does not bother to reply:

> I knew and he knew, that it was impossible. Were we to let go our hold of the bottom, we would be absolutely in the air—in space. We wouldn't be able to tell where we were going to—whether up or down stream, or across—till we fetched against one bank or the other—and then we wouldn't know at first which it was. Of course I made no move. I had no mind for a smash-up. You couldn't imagine a more deadly place for a shipwreck. (72)

This pivotal scene proves paradigmatic not only for Marlow but also for Conrad's later fiction and indeed for modernist literature in general. Jim adrift at night in an open boat on the Indian Ocean shortly after he abandons the *Patna*, Razamov blinded by a snowstorm on the streets of Saint Petersburg, Nostromo and Decoud lost in the intense darkness of a nighttime crossing by boat from Sulaco to the Isabels, all find themselves disoriented, isolated, alienated, and imperiled. The Conradian scene of existential vertigo is replayed with subtle variations in many subsequent canonical modernist texts: by the traumatized Mrs. Moore and Adela Quested at the Marabar Caves in Forster's *A Passage to India*, by the mentally handicapped Benjy on the edge of the golf course in the opening chapter of Faulkner's *The Sound and the Fury*, by the psychologically ravaged World War I veteran Septimus Warren Smith at Hyde Park in *Mrs Dalloway*, by Stephen and Bloom at Bella Cohen's brothel in the "Circe" episode of *Ulysses*, by Anna Morgan coming out of anesthesia following her abortion in *Voyage in the Dark*.

If the experience of darkness, of radical alienation, of psychological vertigo and emotional disorientation becomes a topos of modernist narrative, it behooves us to ask if it matters that Conrad sets the Ur-text of what will become a generic, even obligatory modernist scene not in a cosmopolitan center or *unreal city* of modern Europe but in the apparently "uncivilized," peripheral, and decidedly non-European region of imperial Africa. In the first place, Conrad's colonial setting invites us to consider whether there is something deeply problematic about the common theoretical assumptions that underlie many contemporary postcolonial characterizations of modernist literature. In fact, Marlow's disorientation suggests that the imperial encounter of the representatives of Western imperial power with non-European colonial "realities," (be it the subaltern condition of the native or the alterity of a non-Western culture) does not easily conform to the interpretive model popularized by Edward Said and other founders of postcolonial theory. In *Orientalism* and *Culture and Imperialism*, Said argues that Western imperialism imposed a specifically modern occidental *episteme* upon recalcitrant, but historically subordinate "oriental" cultures. A la Foucault, Said maintains that "the Orient" is a construct of Western colonialism made possible by a modern European power-knowledge continuum that energizes, directs, and legitimates the imperial project. Subjugated cultures under the dominion of Western imperial authority are the products of specifically Western epistemological, (social) scientific, rational, and linguistic categories that make possible the "investigation" and control of non-Western peoples and places. But as we will see, if Said's theory provides an interpretative schema within which to read some of the better-known British imperial romances, such as those of Rider Haggard, it singularly fails to offer a satisfactory critical model for understanding Conrad's seminal modernist work. As I will argue, the paradigmatic Conradian scene of the imperial encounter is one of *disorientation*, one in which the Western mind, far from subjugating the pliable native environment to the scientific and epistemological categories of its omnipotent and omniscient European intelligence, finds itself at a loss, overthrown, confused, panicked, frustrated, and turned back upon itself. This Conradian scene typically culminates not in an act of Western epistemological mastery and political domination but one of uncertainty and alienation, radical skepticism, and intense critical self-examination. The very categories of Western knowledge and power are thereby unsettled and cast into doubt.[2]

Second, the imperial setting for Conrad's scene of disorientation draws into question prevailing critical assumptions concerning the urban origins of European modernist aesthetics. Malcolm Bradbury offers a concise articulation of what has become the common critical understanding of the cosmopolitan origin and nature of European modernism:

> In many respects the literature of experimental Modernism which emerged in the last years of the nineteenth century and developed into the present one was an art of cities, especially of the polyglot cities, the cities which, for various historical reasons, had acquired high activity and great reputation as centres of intellectual and cultural exchange. In these culture-capitals, sometimes, but not always the national political capitals, right across Europe, a fervent atmosphere of new thought and new arts developed. . . . When we think of Modernism, we cannot avoid thinking of these urban climates. . . . Such cities were more than accidental meeting places and crossing points. They were generative environments of the new arts. . . . But they were also often novel environments, carrying within themselves the complexity and tension of modern metropolitan life, which so deeply underlies modern consciousness and modern writing. . . . And if Modernism is a particularly urban art, that is partly because the modern artist, like his fellow-men, has been caught up in the spirit of the modern city, which is itself the spirit of a modern technological society.[3]

The urban environment as the matrix of European modernism and the individual's experience of the modern city as generative of modernist style have been brilliantly analyzed by several distinguished critics, notably Marshall Berman in *All That Is Solid Melts Into Air* and Franco Moretti in *Modern Epic*.[4] Moretti, for example, has argued that stream-of-consciousness evolves as the means by which Joyce successfully represents the hyperstimulation of a stereotypical urban *flâneur*, Leopold Bloom, who is subject to a massive bombardment of sense data (including that of modern advertisement) intrinsic to the daily experience of the modern city, even a provincial capital such as Dublin. But however persuasive these accounts (and I for one am largely persuaded), they necessarily leave out the crucial generative experience of the modern European individual at the edges of empire. Focusing on two of Conrad's early works, *Heart of Darkness* and *Lord Jim*, I will argue that the prevailing theory of the geographic origins of European modernism needs to be amended. Given the relatively early publication dates of Conrad's seminal works (both narratives were serialized beginning in 1899; *Lord Jim* was revised and republished in book form in 1900, *Heart of Darkness* in 1902) and their widely acknowledged influence on later practitioners of English literary modernism (including Woolf and Eliot), our theory of the origins of the aesthetic form of modernist literature must take account of the decisive contribution made by the peculiarly disorienting experiences of the modern European consciousness at the imperial periphery.

Third and finally, our investigation of the link between the experiences of the modern European individual at the edge of empire and the birth of modernist literary aesthetics will challenge an increasingly influential theory of modernist style as an artistic and ideological feint, a highly elaborated form of superstructural occlusion and compensation that effectively *hides* and *sublates* the grim realities of imperialism in the late stages of industrial capitalism. In Fredric Jameson's widely circulated account, Conrad's impressionism, like Forster's literary modernism, is understood as the aesthetic means by which the exploitative nature of imperial capitalism is first briefly revealed to the reader of Conrad (and Forster) and then just as quickly hidden from view. In a highly sophisticated updating of Lukács's critique of modernism as a literary form that distorts and disguises the real nexus of social relations, Jameson maintains that the depredations of European imperialism are ultimately occluded by a modernist literary style that offers in place of the contradictions of imperial capital the commodified and consumable literary objet d'art.[5] Contra Jameson, I will argue that Conrad's literary modernism, at any rate, not only provides a sustained and unflinching exposé of European colonialism and imperialism at its worst (including its economic depredations) but also attempts to generate in the reader a cognitive and emotional dissonance that is the experiential "aesthetic" correlative of the shock felt by Conrad's characters when confronted with the unsavory realities of Western imperialism.

⋮ ⋮ ⋮

Before embarking on a detailed critique of several of Conrad's most influential formal and stylistic innovations and of the cultural and political significance of his contributions to modernist literary practice, it will be helpful to consider an instructive example of the "conventional" late Victorian imperial romance against which he intended his revolutionary literary achievements to be measured, the sort of work with which both *Heart of Darkness* and *Lord Jim* were intended to compete in the literary marketplace. While relatively neglected by critics in recent decades, H. Rider Haggard's *Allan Quatermain* (1887) offers us a particularly useful standard of comparison. Rider Haggard's first sequel to *King Solomon's Mines* (1885), *Allan Quatermain* was an immediate bestseller after its serialization in *Longman's Magazine;* even before it was published in book form, Charles Longman had received a record-setting ten thousand subscriptions for Rider Haggard's forthcoming novel in London alone.[6] In chapter 3, "The Mission Station," Rider Haggard's plucky group of imperial adventurers, Allan Quatermain, Sir Henry Curtis, Captain John Good, the Zulu warrior Umslopogaas, and their native crew make their way by canoe up a great river in the interior of darkest Africa. At a "sudden bend in the river," Quatermain and his fellows come upon a "substantial-looking European house" encompassed by a verandah, the home of Mr. Mackenzie, a Scottish gentleman and missionary, his wife, and daughter, Flossie, all conspicuously attired in "ordinary English-looking clothes":

> [The house was] splendidly situated upon a hill, and surrounded by a high stone wall with a ditch on the outer side. Right against and overshadowing the house was an enormous pine, the top of which we had seen through a glass from the last two days, but of course without knowing that it marked the site of the mission station. I was the first to see the house, and could not restrain myself from giving a hearty cheer, in which the others, including the natives, joined lustily. (40)

Quatermain waxes enthusiastic over "the outbuildings and grounds of the station," which he considers "the most successful as well as the most beautiful place of the sort I have seen in Africa" (47). He is particularly struck by MacKenzie's massive single-storied stone house, his fenced-in orchard planted with "rows upon rows of standard European fruit-trees," and Mrs. MacKenzie's elaborate flower garden featuring a "beautiful fountain" amid roses, gardenias, and camellias grown from seeds and cuttings "sent from England" (42). The whole mission is secured by a "stone wall eight feet high," prompting the Reverend MacKenzie to boast that behind this defensive perimeter he "can defy all the savages in Africa" (42). From the top of the pine that towers above the station, Quatermain admires the panoramic view of the African interior: "It is a glorious country, and only wants the hand of civilized man to make it a most productive one" (57).

Quatermain's detailed description of the MacKenzie mission station—a veritable oasis of European civilization in the interior of Africa, the delights of which include the culinary offerings of Alphonse, the station's resident French chef—provides an illustrative example of Said's thesis, manifesting at least three separate Orientalist rhetorical tropes that correspond to what David Spurr, who has applied Said's conceptual insights to colonial discourse, terms "appropriation," "affirmation," and "idealization."[7] Rider Haggard here employs his narrative skills and rhetorical talents to represent, via his eponymous narrator's seemingly unornamented and straightforward late Victorian realist prose, how the rational, technological, and cultural tools of European civilization successfully appropriate and transform the African landscape and people. Only let a single Scottish missionary and his small family, sustained by nothing more than a faith in Christianity, commerce, and (Western) civilization, loose in the interior of the dark continent and immediately they assume the white man's burden, turning the savagery and unproductive violence of warring African tribesmen into a paradisiacal garden redolent of the virtues of modern European (or more precisely, Victorian British) society. Rider Haggard's set piece would hardly merit critical comment, so strenuous is its chest-thumping ideological posturing, were it not that it likely provides a literary source for one of the most famous scenes in Conrad's *Heart of Darkness.*

Approaching Kurtz's inner station by river for the first time, Marlow describes what he sees:

> Through my glasses I saw the slope of a hill interspersed with rare trees and perfectly free from undergrowth. A long decaying building on the summit was

> half buried in the high grass: the large holes in the peaked roof gaped black from afar; the jungle and the woods made a background. There was no enclosure or fence of any kind; but there had been one apparently, for near the house half-a-dozen slim posts remained in a row, roughly trimmed, and with their upper ends ornamented with round carved balls. The rails, or whatever there had been between, had disappeared. (86)

The historical (as opposed to the literary) source for Kurtz's compound was Stanley Falls Station, located at the last great bend in the navigable reaches of the Congo River, which Józef Teodor Konrad Korzeniowki visited in September of 1890.[8] Oddly, Marlow's description bears little or no resemblance to what Conrad saw of this inner station at "the bend in the river."[9] Marlow's account does, however, appear to be a thoroughgoing revision and literary deflation of Quatermain's description of the MacKenzie mission station in Rider Haggard's novel. Both Quatermain and Marlow first view the respective stations literally through the optics of Western science and technology; the former relies upon a "glass" (telescope or field glasses), the latter on his "glasses" (binoculars). But whereas Quatermain unexpectedly finds a well-ordered compound of massive stone house, cultivated orchards, luxurious garden, church, and outbuildings, all surrounded by a protective wall, Marlow sees only a decayed house "half buried in grass," surrounded by the bare remnants of a protective perimeter fence (or so it would seem). Kurtz's compound seems the very opposite of MacKenzie's testament to the civilizing mission of the white colonialist in Africa. It marks a conspicuous failure on the part of Conrad's "emissary of light" to tame the wilderness and set down the rudiments of European civilization in darkest Africa.

But of course, in one of the most striking uses of what Ian Watt has termed "delayed decoding," Conrad radically revises Marlow's initial description of the compound a few pages later.[10] During his first conversation with the vagabond Russian sailor who is Kurtz's admirer, Marlow once more turns his attention to the compound. As a quintessential instance of Conrad's innovative modernist narrative technique, the passage is worth quoting at length:

> I had taken up my binoculars while we talked, and was looking at the shore, sweeping the limit of the forest at each side and at the back of the house. . . . I directed my glass to the house. . . . And then I made a brusque movement, and one of the remaining posts of that vanished fence leaped up in the field of my

> glass. You remember I told you I had been struck at the distance by certain attempts at ornamentation, rather remarkable in the ruinous aspect of the place. Now I had suddenly a nearer view, and its first result was to make me throw my head back as if before a blow. Then I went carefully from post to post with my glass, and I saw my mistake. These round knobs were not ornamental but symbolic; they were expressive and puzzling, striking and disturbing—food for thought and also for the vultures if there had been any looking down from the sky; but at all events for such ants as were industrious enough to ascend the pole. They would have been even more impressive, those heads on the stakes, if their faces had not been turned to the house. Only one, the first I had made out, was facing my way. I was not so shocked as you may think. The start back I had given was really nothing but a movement of surprise. I had expected to see a knob of wood there, you know. I returned deliberately to the first I had seen—and there it was, black, dried, sunken, with closed eyelids,—a head that seemed to sleep at the top of that pole, and, with the shrunken dry lips showing a narrow white line of teeth, was smiling too, smiling continuously at some endless and jocose dream of that eternal slumber. (94)

As it turns out, the modern Western optic, the narrator's binoculars, quintessential talisman of the Western colonialist and adventurer, has not enabled Marlow's immediate mastery of his field of vision, nor has it, at least initially, provided him with a capacity for an accelerated processing of sense data that would enhance his knowledge of or power over the imperial scene he confronts. The instruments of Western science (or at any rate, the European gestalt that Marlow brings to his observation of the scene) serve merely to deceive him. Conrad's use of delayed decoding, particularly if it is viewed against the background of Rider Haggard's realistic set piece in *Allan Quatermain*, upsets an entire complex of cultural, political, and ethical assumptions that Conrad expects his English audience to bring to their reading of *Heart of Darkness*, assumptions concerning the relative superiority of modern European civilization and its capacity to uplift and improve non-Western peoples as part of its sacred imperial mission. This subversion of European cultural superiority and imperial confidence is registered literally as *shock*. That Marlow insists that he was not as shocked as we might have supposed only underscores his momentary disorientation: after all, his final decoding of the scene makes him throw his head back "as if before a blow." Most suggestively, Conrad does not merely allow his narrator to *tell us* that he is shocked but stylistically delivers the blow to the reader (and at the level of *story* that blow is also felt by Marlow's auditors aboard the *Nellie*, including the frame narrator) by withholding, for many paragraphs, a crucial fact—those wooden ornamental knobs are shrunken heads upon stakes. Indeed, *even* after Marlow tells us that he sees his "mistake," he continues to withhold this crucial detail from his auditors for several more independent clauses, thus replicating for the reader the extended period of phenomenological confusion, psychological anxiety, and cultural disorientation that he himself undergoes.

The "blow" delivered to both Marlow and Conrad's readers thus prepares the way for Marlow's irony, another characteristic of Conrad's anticonventional modernist style (though it is by no means the exclusive literary property of the high modernists). Bound by contract with the trading company for whom he captains the steamboat not to reveal "trade secrets," Marlow concludes:

> I am not disclosing any trade secrets. In fact the manager said afterwards that Mr Kurtz's methods had ruined the district. I have no opinion on that point, but I want you clearly to understand that there was nothing exactly profitable in these heads being there. They only showed that Mr Kurtz lacked restraint in the gratification of his various lusts, that there was something wanting in him . . . he was hollow at the core. (94–95)

Conrad, via his narrator, thus savagely ironizes the pecuniary motives of the company that employs both Marlow and Kurtz. And while Marlow has already exposed for his auditors the exploitative nature of the company's treatment of African laborers—"brought from all the recesses of the coast in all the legality of time contracts, lost in uncongenial surroundings, fed on unfamiliar food, they sickened, became inefficient, and were then allowed to crawl away" to languish and die (35)—he now suggests that the depravity of Kurtz is something more, and less, than the effects of mere greed or the effects of protectionist trade monopolized by a European company with the connivance of Western governments. "Hollow at the core": the phrase is later seized upon and memorialized by Eliot in "The Hollow Men." "Hollow at the core": the phrase conveys to Conrad's reader the political bankruptcy, the cultural nihilism, the ethical groundlessness that is at the heart of the Western imperial project, all conspicuously manifest in its most talented, high-minded, and exemplary representative, Mr. Kurtz, the emissary of light and the leader of the new gang of virtue, who so utterly loses his way. The specifically modernist narrative technique—delayed decoding—thus serves directly to undermine the ideology of Western imperialism and to reveal, with all the forceful shock that any merely literary technique can render, the full horror of that political and economic enterprise.

⋮ ⋮ ⋮

I have thus far dwelt on a single feature of Conrad's modernist style—delayed decoding—with only a brief mention of Conrad's additional penchant for literary irony. It is undoubtedly true that delayed decoding, like other techniques I discuss below, can be (and has been) adapted to other geographic venues (Conrad himself, for example, later employed delayed decoding in both *The Secret Agent* and *Under Western Eyes*, set respectively in London, Saint Petersburg, and Geneva). Moreover, it is by no means the case that the imperial setting of Conrad's fiction *necessarily* generates a modernist aesthetic—witness Rider Haggard's imperial romances, or for that matter Conrad's first two published novels, *Almayer's Folly* and *An Outcast of the Islands*, neither of which evidences the modernist style of Conrad's mature fiction. And it is certainly the case that a few of Conrad's innovative modernist narrative devices might be found in earlier works of fiction (such as those of Henry James or Lawrence Sterne) that owe little or nothing to an imperial setting. Nonetheless, it is highly suggestive that these techniques tend to proliferate in Conrad's mature fiction, and that these constellations of modernist innovations come fully into view for the first time within an imperial setting. I would argue that one very plausible reason for their sudden and decisive emergence within a colonial environment is that they answer to Conrad's formative experience as a participant in European imperialism: like his many characters, the former officer in the British merchant service feels the sudden immersion in the colonial and non-Western world as a shock to his system. What he vividly captures in his major fiction is a sense of near total estrangement from a cultural and geographic reality radically different from that of urbanized Western (or Central) Europe. Interestingly, Conrad's imperial world (unlike that of Kipling or Forster) is never, or almost never, that of the settled formal and bureaucratized colony (India makes only an oblique appearance in *Lord Jim*). His characters almost always operate at the edge of empire, where they repeatedly experience the shock of cultural disorientation, of a sudden and unnerving dislocation of their moral, epistemological, political, and (more rarely) religious convictions.

⋮ ⋮ ⋮

In the remainder of this essay, I propose to examine in abbreviated fashion a few of Conrad's other conspicuous formal and stylistic innovations, those that give *Heart of Darkness* and *Lord Jim* a distinctively *modernist* aspect, in order to suggest how these techniques respond to the peculiar features of life on the periphery of European empire. In addition to delayed decoding, Ian Watt has identified several of Conrad's most innovative narrative techniques, including *anachrony* (a term, along with *prolepsis*, *analepsis*, and *syllepsis* that Watt borrows from Gérard Genette), manipulation of point of view (perspectivism or the abandonment of omniscient narration), and *progression d'effet*.[11] I would add to Watt's list of characteristic Conradian techniques, shifting levels of interpolated and mediated narrative, fragmentary and elliptical dialogue, generic hybridization and modulation, the proliferation of abstract or impressionistic language—particularly in scenic description, and the work of involuntary memory (a special employment of anachrony). A comprehensive account of the imperial origins of Conrad's modernist style ought to consider all these techniques in their various manifestations, but here I must be selective in my treatment.

While the structuring devices of his stories are among Conrad's most distinctive contribution to modernist literary form, his innovations in prose style, perceivable at the level of the paragraph or sentence, are no less striking. What I call Conrad's impressionistic use of language may be illustrated by a representative passage from *Heart of Darkness:*

> Going up river was like traveling back to the earliest beginnings of the world, when vegetation rioted on the earth and the big trees were kings. An empty stream, a great silence, an impenetrable forest. The air was warm, thick, heavy, sluggish. There was no joy in the brilliance of sunshine. The long stretches of the waterway ran on, deserted, into the gloom of overshadowed distances. On silvery sandbanks hippos and alligators sunned themselves side by side. The broadening waters flowed through a mob of wooded islands; you lost your way on that river as you would in a desert, and butted all day long against shoals, trying to find the channel, till you thought yourself bewitched and cut off for ever from everything you had known once—somewhere—far away—in another existence

> perhaps. There were moments when one's past came back to one, as it will sometimes when you have not a moment to spare to yourself; but it came in the shape of an unrestful and noisy dream, remembered with wonder amongst the overwhelming realities of this strange world of plants, and water, and silence. And this stillness of life did not in the least resemble a peace. It was the stillness of an implacable force brooding over an inscrutable intention. (59–60)

The passage exhibits several of Conrad's most striking stylistic mannerisms: an increasing dependence on abstract as opposed to concrete nouns ("an implacable force brooding over an inscrutable intention"); a reliance on an ever proliferating set of adjectives and a corresponding suppression of "grammatically necessary" parts of speech in favor of paratactic constructions ("An empty steam, a great silence, an impenetrable forest"); the increasing dilation of meandering sentences freed of conventional grammatical and syntactical constraints ("The broadening waters flowed," etc.). Here Conrad anticipates, as it were, the formal effects of later high modernist prose stylists—the dilated paratactic sentences of Woolf's *Mrs Dalloway*, the increasingly abstract lexical register of Lawrence's *The Rainbow*, the Proteus episode of Joyce's *Ulysses* ("ineluctable modality of the visible"), and the fragmented, grammatically "loose" constructions of Rhys's *A Voyage in the Dark*, Faulkner's *As I Lay Dying*, and Lowry's *Under the Volcano*.

But if Conrad's style proves highly adaptable to other times and places, in *Heart of Darkness* it emerges out of a crisis of language that is integral to the disorienting experience of the Western colonialist at the fringes of empire. For the *alien* environment of the (Congo) river places Marlow's linguistic capacities under an immense, near fatal pressure. It is as if the exotic landscape Marlow encounters places an insupportable strain on the linguistic conventions of gentlemanly English discourse. No set of terms or linguistic constructions seems fully adequate to represent accurately either the objective details or the subjective experiences of his imperial encounter with colonial Africa. Conrad has been accused of rendering the Congo and its peoples as more primitive than they were at the end of the nineteenth century.[12] But surely part of Conrad's "failure" in this regard derives from the fact that Marlow lacks the vocabulary and linguistic resources and precise vocabulary to describe what he sees—the plants, trees, animals, topography, peoples, and cultural institutions and practices he encounters for the first time. Hearing the "roll of drums" along the river, Marlow cannot tell "whether it meant war, peace, or prayer" (62). A linguistic exile, suddenly cut off from the European languages with which he is familiar, Marlow, like the Russian sailor who does not understand the "dialect of [Kurtz's] tribe," finds crucial conversations within his hearing utterly lacking in meaning: "They [the tribesmen] shouted periodically together strings of amazing words that resembled no sounds of human language" (100). That Marlow insists on his common humanity with the African natives only underscores his radical linguistic estrangement from his immediate cultural environment (63). If Marlow is overwhelmed by his linguistic impotence, he is nevertheless astute enough to link the systematic imperial violence and exploitation going on around him with the linguistic and representational crisis he shares with his fellow European imperialists. When informed by Kurtz that those infamous heads on stakes belong to "rebels," Marlow mocks the epistemological slippage and linguistic absurdity of Kurtz's words: "Rebels! What would be the next definition I was to hear? There had been enemies, criminals, workers—and these were rebels. Those rebellious heads looked very subdued to me on their sticks" (96).

The cumulative strain placed upon Marlow's lexical reserves by his imperial encounter with a radically alien place often leads to linguistic paradox and to a representational aporia: "the earth seemed unearthly" (62). As J. M. Coetzee has suggested with respect to European poets and painters in South Africa, the imperial artist (whether he works in a visual or literary medium) has from his first arrival in sub-Saharan Africa been faced with the inadequacy of the particular set of representational tools that are the legacy of his "foreign" cultural heritage. Linguistic or painterly modes and techniques well adapted to a European landscape prove unable to capture faithfully the distinctive topographic features and atmospheric conditions that pertain in a non-European environment. The temptation is for the ill-equipped artist to render the African landscape *as if* it were just another version of its European counterpart; thus the European concept of the "picturesque" or "sublime" is inappropriately imposed upon a subject ill-suited to its application.[13] (Rider Haggard's *Allan Quatermain* might be taken to illustrate an instance of formal maladaptation of representational technique to the African environment). Marlow's confrontation with a *new* physical (and cultural) reality, however, prompts the invention of a novel set of techniques and formal devices by which it can be more accurately represented (a phenomenon that Coetzee suggests is characteristic of a *late* phase of European colonial cultural adaptation to the new African environment). Thus it is that Conrad, via his narrator Marlow, improvises an experimental set of representational devices meant to capture both the subjective experience and objective lineaments of a non-European, nonurban, and premodern reality, and in so doing, he helps generate a new *style* that we come to recognize retrospectively as *modernist*, a style subsequently employed and readapted by himself and other literary artists to the "new" (and consequently) alienating conditions of the modern European imperial city.

As if to excuse his inadequate, even bizarre linguistic performance, Marlow tells his auditors that "it seems to me I'm trying to tell you a dream" (50). As Marlow learns to his horror, even the most ordinary conversations between Europeans speaking a common tongue are distorted by the weird gravitational force of this alien world. Of his talk with Kurtz, for example, Marlow reports: "I've been telling you what we said—repeating the phrases we pronounced,—but what's the good? They were common everyday words,—the familiar, vague sounds exchanged on every waking day of life. But what of that? They had behind them, to my mind, the terrific suggestiveness of words heard in dreams, of phrases spoken in nightmares" (107). No doubt the linguistic and representational difficulties that Marlow encounters are considerably aggravated by his succumbing to a nearly fatal case of tropical fever, another distinctively colonial experience common enough among maladapted Europeans engaged in their "fantastic invasion." In the most literal sense, the colonial environment begins to infect and alter the linguistic and narrative functioning of Conrad's principal narrator. The conventional logos of late Victorian imperial narration gives way to the associative "logic" of *fever*, of *dreamwork*. What ultimately emerges out of the politico-physio-linguistic crisis of imperial adventure is a new kind of hallucinogenic dreamscape that can be represented, it seems, only by a new, distinctively modernist form of narrative. Marlow's feverish and oneiric prose, his efforts to render his experiences on the Congo River *as if* they were a dream anticipate later experiments in literary surrealism (and expressionism), such as those of Joyce, Woolf, Lowry, Rhys, and Beckett.

When Marlow returns to the sepulchral city (presumably Brussels) and once more regains his health, his (that is to say, Conrad's) narrative prose momentarily loses its peculiarly modernist texture (114–17). But in proto-Proustian fashion, an involuntary memory of Kurtz returns to haunt Marlow, "a shadow insatiable of splendid appearances, of frightful realities; a shadow darker than the shadow of the night, and draped nobly in the folds of a gorgeous eloquence" (117), and with it, the narrative voice once more assumes the distinctive aspects of Conrad's modernist style that I have catalogued. Partly the effect of tropical fever, the hallucinogenic and oneiric style has been transported like a contagion back to the European imperial metropolis, where it breaks out unpredictably and with renewed virulence at the heart of conventional bourgeois life, the drawing room of Kurtz's Intended:

> She went on, and the sound of her low voice seemed to have the accompaniment of all the other sounds, full of mystery, desolation, and sorrow, I had ever heard—the ripple of the river, the soughing of the trees swayed by the wind, the murmurs of wild crowds, the faint ring of incomprehensible words cried from afar, the whisper of a voice speaking from beyond the threshold of an eternal darkness. (121)

Like a rare foreign bacillus, Conrad's emergent modernist style is transported back to the heart of urban European modernity by a contagious agent of empire. Marlow's consciousness, still reeling from its disorienting encounter with an alien and hostile colonial world, finds itself unexpectedly out of place even after its return to its European homeland. Marlow thus anticipates a whole range of characters from modernist fiction whose disoriented, deranged, disaffected, or diseased modern consciousnesses are rendered by stylistic effects that bear comparison with, if they are not directly derived from, those that Conrad pioneers in his seminal imperial narrative: Septimus Warren Smith, Benjy Compson, Stephen Daedalus, Anna Morgan, Bertha Mason, Geoffrey Firmin, and Watt to name only a few of the better known progeny.

⋮ ⋮ ⋮

Turning from *Heart of Darkness*, I conclude my examination of Conrad's "imperial" contributions to modernist aesthetics by considering three narrative devices—interpolated or mediated narration, perspectivism (manipulation of point of view), and anachrony—devices present in Conrad's famous African tale, but even more insistently and conspicuously employed in *Lord Jim*. These three techniques are formally discrete and ideally should receive separate detailed analyses. However, here I examine them as an interdependent set of narrative devices that enable Conrad to represent a few crucial features of imperial existence at the peripheries of European colonial power. In *Lord Jim*, as in *Heart of Darkness*, Marlow's narrative is embedded within a frame tale told by an anonymous narrator who is also one of Marlow's auditors. At crucial junctures in his oral narration, Marlow directs a comment to one of these auditors or is interrupted momentarily by him. Occasionally, Marlow's narration is interrupted not by a *verbal* comment of the frame narrator or one of his other auditors but rather by the narrator's (written) remarks to his (Conrad's) reader. The interpolated structure of *Lord Jim* is further complicated by the fact that the final part of Jim's story is not communicated orally by Marlow to an assembled group of listeners but rather by way of Marlow's written correspondence to a "privileged man" (one of the original auditors of Marlow's oral narrative), who in turn remains embedded within the frame tale related by the anonymous narrator. Marlow's written communication to the "privileged man" in fact consists of four separate items: an unfinished letter written by Jim shortly before his death in Patusan; a letter written by Jim's father to Jim before he joins the crew of the *Patna;* a narrative account of Jim's last days in Patusan written by Marlow; and a cover letter to the privileged man also composed by Marlow. Not all these materials are presented directly or in their entirety; the letter from Jim's father is abridged and its content summarized by Marlow in his cover letter, while Jim's letter receives Marlow's editorial commentary in the same piece of correspondence.

Moreover, it is not entirely certain that Marlow's oral narration is delivered to the same set of auditors, gathered in a single location on a single evening. Although Conrad's "Author's Note" to the 1917 (second) English edition of *Lord Jim*, reprinted in all subsequent editions, lends credence to this supposition, Conrad's frame narrator suggests otherwise: "And later on, many times, in distant parts of the world, Marlow showed himself willing to remember Jim, to remember him at length, in detail and audibly. Perhaps it would be after dinner, on a verandah draped in motionless foliage and crowned with flowers, in the deep dusk speckled by fiery cigar ends" (24). The implication here is that Marlow's narration is related on many different occasions, in widely varied geographical settings, to a varying group of listeners, and inevitably, with slight variations from one telling to the next. The frame narrator's use of the conditional hints at his apparent attempt to provide a sort of idealized redaction of Marlow's oral performance, though it is important to remember that when(ever) Marlow relates the *oral* portion of his narrative, he does not *yet* know how Jim will end his life in Patusan; Marlow's "audible" narration ends with his taking leave of Jim at the conclusion of his visit to Patusan, that is, before the frame narrator or Conrad's reader has heard of Gentleman Brown and of the tragic events in Patusan that culminate in the deaths of Dain Waris and Jim and the subsequent flight of Jewel and Tamb' Itam to Stein's home (199).

Conrad's complexly interpolated and highly mediated narrative (and it should be noted, contrary to what most critics have suggested, that the structural complexity of the novel is not limited only to the first half of the tale concerned with events aboard the *Patna*) is further complicated by Marlow's extensive use of a great many different informants or "reflectors" (to use the Jamesian term). Conrad's perspectivism is manifest in the editorial function that Marlow doggedly fulfills as principal chronicler of Jim's story: he assembles the crucial events of Jim's life from interviews with a formidable number of different sources, whose credibility, knowledge, and reliability vary widely: the shipping master Archie Ruthvel, the first (anonymous) engineer of the *Patna* who suffers from the DTs, the elderly French lieutenant of the gunboat that tows the *Patna* to port, Captain Brierly and his first mate Mr. Jones, the rapacious entrepreneur and adventurer Chester, the rice mill owner Mr. Denver, the trader and ship supplier Egström, Stein, Jewel, Cornelius, Gentleman Brown, Doramin and his wife, an unnamed Dutch government official, and Tamb' Itam (even this list is not exhaustive). While Marlow synthesizes the mass of testimony with considerable finesse, the fact that he conspicuously foregrounds his informants suggests that our "final" view of Jim is nevertheless a speculative synthesis, a narrative construction assembled out of multiple, sometimes unreliable, often prejudicial or partial, and frequently contradictory views of the novel's eponymous character. For all his narrative skill, Marlow insists upon the incomplete, distorted, and opaque character of his synthetic portrait of Jim: "I am fated never to see him clearly" (146); "It is impossible to see him clearly—especially as it is through the eyes of others that we take our last look at him" (201).

Accounts of the origin and function of perspectivism and interpolated narrative within modernist aesthetics have tended to emphasize the importance of new understandings of the processes of human psychology and sensory perception made possible by emergent disciplines such as psychoanalysis and (depth) psychology (e.g., Freud, W. James, Köhler) and of comparable theoretical breakthroughs in epistemology, phenomenology, and the philosophical critique of time (e.g., Nietzsche, Husserl, Bergson). Still other accounts in the field of modernist studies, noted above, credit the new modes of European urban existence as the immediate inspiration for the new representational techniques and narrative forms of modernism. By contrast, I would like to suggest that it is the peculiar characteristics of the systems of communications and of social and professional organization that temporarily obtain at the turn of the century for those Europeans (particularly the British) operating at the peripheries of empire to which several of Conrad's innovative representational techniques are a response.

The European community at the edges of empire is not an organized citizenry in regular, predictable, routinized, and intimate contact with one another. It hardly forms a cohesive community at all. In fact, Marlow, his auditors, and his informants are a highly *dispersed* community of individuals scattered about an imperial archipelago that stretches for thousands of miles across the Pacific, the South Seas, Australia, and Asia (to say nothing of the Middle East and Europe!). They are never in the same place at the same time, meeting only infrequently (or not at all), often unexpectedly and by chance, and resorting to extraordinary efforts to maintain even minimal contact with one another. Their difficulties in communication are augmented by the fact that so many members of this "community" are highly *mobile* (e.g., Marlow, the privileged man, Brierly, Chester, the first engineer, the French lieutenant, Stein, Cornelius, Brown, Jim). Their movements are often quite unpredictable, even erratic, and thus they can find it difficult or even impossible to locate or contact one another at any given moment. Even if we consider just those *Europeans* occupying (however temporarily) official positions within the formal and informal sphere of the British empire, we find that they are a heterogeneous group of individuals—multiethnic, multilingual, multinational—whose interests, goals, and enterprises are by no means coordinated, centrally planned, or even compatible. One might say that in some crucial respects, the *dispersed, disorganized, heterogeneous,* and *nomadic* character of this peripheral imperial community of Europeans presages, in an outsized and exaggerated manner, that of the European cosmopolis. The allegedly defining features of modern urban life—the random meeting of strangers on the city streets, the polyglot character of urban discourse, the fluid and overlapping associations of modern urbanites, the constant exposure to the serendipitous nature of commerce and trade—are already present at the fringes of empire, are, in fact, the daily and even "ordinary" experiences of Conrad's narrators and characters. The European imperial "community" is, if anything, even farther removed from an idealized form of the premodern *Gemeinschaft* than are its counterparts living in the modern metropolitan centers of Europe.

A decisive feature of life in the European "community" at the periphery of the British empire, one on which Conrad's plots turn and that is generative of his modernist aesthetic, one that distinguishes it from its metropolitan counterpart in Europe, is its peculiarly "anachronistic" system of communication, one that suffers from what we might call "uneven development." As James Morris points out, a crucial concern of the British empire was its modes of communication; its "life-lines" were secured at the turn of the century by an extensive and technologically sophisticated network of global shipping routes (on which traveled the most modern steam ships), refueling and supply stations, naval ports, and submarine cables, all collectively secured by the world's largest and most imposing navy and merchant service.[14] But even if, as Morris tells us, the Victorians believed that steam had "annihilated distance," communication throughout the empire was hardly instantaneous and the flow of information not by any means uniform even in 1897. Mail service from London to Sydney took "only" thirty-eight days, London to India seventeen, and London to Ottawa eight.[15] The submarine cable system was nearly complete by the time of the Queen's Diamond Jubilee in 1897, but even then a number of inhabited British territories—Fiji, British Honduras, Tobago, the Falkland Islands, Turks Island, and New Guinea—lacked cable service altogether. Moreover, the lines were subject to deterioration, interference, and unpredictable "black outs," and required constant maintenance, which rendered them less than entirely dependable.[16] In practice, the empire, and most particularly that part of it that Conrad represents in his early modernist novels, depended on a wide variety of overlapping and varied modes of transportation and communication to carry on with its business: submarine cables and telegraph, steamship, sailing vessel, pack animal, carrier pigeon, and human carrier (to name just a few of the immense variety of means employed). The critical modes of communication thus comprised a hodgepodge of overlapping systems: electronic, written, and oral.

The upshot of this brief aside into the history of British imperial communication and transportation is to draw attention to an obvious if nevertheless neglected fact about Conrad's imperial world: the gathering, synthesizing, and distribution of news and information within the imperial periphery was an arduous, imperfect, slow, and technically difficult task. The facts of a "story" were often difficult or even impossible to attain with any degree of certainty. Moreover, *when* and *by what means* a particularly crucial "fact" might be gathered, analyzed, collated, and relayed was a serendipitous affair. To put the matter plainly, the peculiarly dispersed, mobile, heterogeneous, decentralized, and unorganized European community on the fringes of empire was unusually dependent on and particularly challenged (even disadvantaged) by the unevenly developed and distributed system of communication that prevailed. There is thus more than a structural homology between the organization of Conrad's European imperial "community" and its system of communication; they comprise parallel and linked systems of communal organization and communication that pose particularly recalcitrant and deeply embedded problems when it comes to the *representation* of any "story" or event that occurs within their mutual spheres of experience.

I am now in a position to state what, I hope, will have suddenly *become* obvious: Conrad's representational techniques, such as shifting and highly mediated narration, constantly shifting point of view, and his otherwise inexplicable alternation between oral and epistolary forms of storytelling, are *the concrete manifestations of the systems of social organization and communication that prevail at the peripheries of empire.* Conrad's narrators and informants, most particularly (but not exclusively) Marlow, collect, collate, and distribute the facts of Jim's story by the only (if highly varied) means available to them. Marlow crisscrosses the Australasian quarter of the empire over *several years*—and in the course of his travels visits Sydney, Bombay, Singapore, Hong Kong, Penang, Samarang, Ban(g)kok, and Patusan, to say nothing of an almost infinite variety of locations on the open sea—in his efforts to piece together Jim's "whole" story. In the course of his excursions, he talks to a large and varied group of eyewitnesses and informants—some reliable, some not—most of whom can offer Marlow only a few relevant (if uncoordinated) facts that are, by necessity, related in no particular (chronological) order, and which, often consisting only of hearsay, have been mediated and filtered several times over even before they reach Marlow's immediate sources. (The frame narrator is similarly mobile—he too has visited Stein, for example, and has spent much of his life at sea, though Conrad does not reveal to us the precise coordinates of his movements.) Marlow's task is made all the more difficult by virtue of Jim's own notorious and obsessive nomadism; in the course of his brief career, Jim travels to Aden, Bombay, Singapore, Rangoon, Penang, Ban(g)kok, Samarang and Patusan. Given the relative brevity of his stay in any one place, his eagerness to conceal as much of his personal history as possible, and his reluctance to form intimate and lasting social bonds, Jim makes for an unusually difficult subject for Marlow or the frame narrator to represent accurately and comprehensively. As Marlow puts it to the privileged man: "I put it down here for you *as though* I had been an eyewitness. My information was fragmentary, but I've fitted the pieces together, and there is enough of them to make an intelligible picture" (203, emphasis mine). Although Conrad's readers are understandably struck by the "difficulty" of his narrative presentation, by the complexity and multitude of the narrative devices he deploys in *Lord Jim*, the final version of Jim's life offered by the frame narrator is considerably *less* elliptical, disorganized, and anachronous, *more* cohesive, linear, and comprehensible than those fragmentary materials, testimonials, eyewitness accounts, rumors, and outright lies both written or spoken and compiled over many years out of which Marlow composes his narrative. One might say that the "reality" of Jim's story, as subjectively experienced by Marlow prior to his own delayed decoding of the relevant facts, would have had an even more strikingly and disorienting *modernist* feel than the one the frame narrator relates or the story published in *Blackwood's Magazine* in 1899.

In fact, Jim's story repeatedly turns upon the anomalous, unreliable, nonuniform, and most importantly, *anachronous* flow of information on the imperial periphery. When the *Patna* runs over a derelict vessel and appears to be sinking, Jim finds himself in one of the "blank places" on the map of the imperial communications system. It is possible neither to send a distress signal nor to receive vital information on the stricken vessel. But the *Patna* has not quite fallen off the edge of the earth; the crew and later its passengers are soon picked up at sea precisely because they are drifting "right in the track of all the [Suez] Canal traffic" (77), that is, in one of the principal shipping lanes of the empire. It takes Jim and the surviving officers of the *Patna* ten days to reach port (a conflation of Bombay and Singapore), where Conrad's hero will face a disciplinary hearing. But while the deserters reach port assuming that the *Patna* has sunk, the fact of its having been towed into

Aden by a French naval vessel has already been communicated to the British authorities in Bombay (or Singapore) by "that mysterious cable message from Aden" (25).[17] It is the uneven distribution of information, its anachronous flow, which reaches different places of the imperial community at different and unpredictable times, that makes Jim's already seriously compromised position even more humiliating and disgraceful. His story has been told and circulated in port *before* he arrives to tell it himself. Critics of the novel will do well to recall the particular surprise, shock, (and literary pleasure) of their first encounter with *Lord Jim*, and in particular of Conrad's narrative coup of concealing the fate of the *Patna* from his readers until well into the story (a crucial clue is dropped by Marlow in chapter 7, but definitive confirmation of the *Patna*'s survival does not come until chapter 12). This famous example of modernist anachrony, which may be taken as representative instance of Conrad's intricate and subtle manipulation of prolepsis, analepsis, and syllepsis throughout his novel, provides for the reader the literary equivalent or experiential complement of the anachronous flow of information that was the subjective reality of life as it was lived on the British imperial periphery at the turn of the century.

In any case, the anachronous flow of information on the periphery of empire proves critical for the whole of Jim's career. Following his hearing and loss of his officer's license in the Merchant Service, Jim attempts to take advantage of the unevenly developed system of communication that helped to reveal his own gross failings as a representative member of the imperial service class. He seeks to hide himself in those places where the story of the *Patna* is not known, or not current, or at least where his role in the affair may not circulate. Jim can't go home to England, because his father "has seen it all [the story of the *Patna*] in the home papers by this time" (51). In less than a month, a distant imperial event is a current news item in the Home Counties. Nor can Jim idle away his days in the port city where his trial has taken place. His lengthy confessional dinner with Marlow at the Marabar House reveals that the city is a nodal point in the imperial communications system: their conversation takes place amid the company of effusive and vocal British *tourists* traveling to the picturesque spots of the empire! So for nearly three years Jim tries to stay ahead of the news of his disgrace, traveling over an immense imperial territory, always seeking the place where *récit* has yet to catch up with *histoire*, where narration lags behind the event. One might say that Jim's ambition at this stage of his life, such as it is, is only conceivable or realizable, however temporarily, on the imperial periphery. Where communications and the flow of information are nearly instantaneous, or at least synchronous for all members of society (e.g., London), such a hope couldn't be contemplated. It's only because there are still backwaters, eddies in the temporal flow of information in the imperial periphery, that Jim can attempt to escape the news that hounds even someone so unimportant in the imperial system as himself. But as Marlow, once more with characteristic modernist irony observes, "this was the funniest part: he did after a time become perfectly known, and even notorious, within the circle of his wanderings (which had a diameter of, say, three thousand miles) in the same way as an eccentric character is known to a whole countryside" (119). The story of the *Patna* eventually circulates everywhere on the imperial periphery. As Marlow puts it to his auditors, "the affair . . . seemed to live, with a sort of uncanny vitality, in the minds of men, on the tips of their tongues. I've had the questionable pleasure of meeting it often, years afterwards, thousands of miles away, emerging from the remotest possible talk, coming to the surface of the most distant allusions. Has it not turned up to-night between us?" (84).

It is thus no coincidence that the only place left to Jim, the one blank space on the imperial map in which he can attempt to remake himself according to the heroic self-image that haunts his youth, is Patusan. It is suggestive that Marlow's auditors (experienced men well acquainted with obscure corners of the imperial periphery), like Conrad's readers, hear of Patusan for the *first time* from Marlow, who asks rhetorically, "I don't suppose any of you have heard of Patusan?" Patusan is the geographic and cultural anachrony par excellence. It is, as Marlow points out, "*far from the beaten tracks of the sea and from the ends of submarine cables*" (212, emphasis mine). It is the one location to which Jim can go that lies beyond the periphery of the imperial system of communication and information, if only temporarily. This "primitive" locale where Jim can for a time escape the notice of the modern world is also the place where many of Conrad's modernist representational techniques that characterize the *Patna* episode suddenly fall into relative abeyance. Beginning with the first mention of Patusan, Conrad instead employs a series of generic modulations, such that the traditional literary forms of epic, romance, and tragedy are once more revitalized and become the appropriate vehicles for communicating Jim's story.[18] To be sure, Conrad's hybridization of literary form, his extensive use of heterogeneous generic forms within a single narrative, will itself become a distinctive characteristic of the emergent modernist novel (consider Joyce's *Ulysses*, Dos Passos's *U.S.A.* trilogy, and Woolf's *Between the Acts*), and thus his apparent *reversion* to seemingly antiquated literary forms can be understood to have been contained by and expressive of a distinctively modernist aesthetic. In any event, Jim's enclosure within the distinctive chronotope that is Patusan cannot and does not last. First Jim, then Marlow, and finally Gentleman Brown break the hermetic temporal seal of this premodern idyll, and in the final section of *Lord Jim*, thanks to the flight of Jewel and Tamb' Itam from Patusan back to the imperial periphery and to Marlow's dogged investigative efforts, the hero's story begins once more to circulate via the emergent system of communication that characterizes the imperial archipelago.[19] It is thus a central irony of Conrad's novel that Jim's heroic and tragic career in Patusan comes to be known and brooded about by those modern representatives of the empire whose notice he had sought so assiduously to escape; he remains, in Marlow's equivocal sense, "one of us," a memorable and representative protagonist of high modernist fiction not despite, but by virtue of, his dubious entanglements with European imperialism.

⋮ ⋮ ⋮

If we are now in a position more fully to appreciate the distinctive and generative role played by European imperialism in the modernist literary revolution, our new vantage point also makes possible a reassessment of the complex relationship between modernist and postcolonial literature. Partly because postcolonial literary studies (at least in the United States) came into its own at roughly the same time that literary theorists began to distinguish sharply between postmodernism and modernism, a prevailing critical assumption has taken hold: even if postcolonial literature and postmodern literature are not (always) one and the same, these two interrelated literary movements nonetheless *both* mark a sharp break with the literary modernism that preceded them. Just as the emergence of postmodern literature signaled a rupture with the formal principles and underlying teleological and epistemological premises of modernism, so too did the advent of postcolonial literature mark a repudiation of the "retrograde" political affiliations and social values of high modernism. The rise of postcolonial literature, it was claimed, presaged the end of literary and cultural dominance by the European metropole and ushered in a new emancipatory era in which the subjugated voices at the periphery of Western colonial influence could "write back" to those at the center of the old empire. But if our revised conception of the multiple and varied origins of modernist literary aesthetics is correct, we might also consider the possibility that the reemergence or adaptation of (Conradian) high modernist formal innovations in the works of postcolonial authors was made more likely by continuities between the colonial and postcolonial conditions of literary cultural production. My analysis of the imperial sources of Conrad's modernism thus opens the way to a reconsideration of many of the most eminent postcolonial novelists—Coetzee, Rushdie, Naipaul, Ngugi, Rhys, Carpentier, García Márquez, Vargas Llosa, Fuentes, Donoso, Cabrera Infante, Roa Bastos, Khatibi, and Ben Jelloun—as practitioners of *late modernism*. Obviously, such a claim cannot be substantiated, only suggested here. But if, as I have argued, literary high modernism has a source in the European experience of empire, then it would stand to reason that the very same formal techniques and stylistic devices invented to represent the peculiar features of the imperial periphery might be effectively and brilliantly redeployed by a later generation of "postcolonial" writers who, like Conrad, underwent their formative experiences far from the metropolitan capitals of the old European empires. Nor should we be surprised to find that a revivified postcolonial modernism could effectively serve the political objectives of writers opposed to the apocalyptic failures of European imperialism, for it answered just such a need in Conrad's case, to say nothing of other earlier modernists such as Rhys, Joyce, and Forster, who also knew something about the ill winds of colonialism. If, as Conrad's anonymous narrator would have it, the "tranquil waterway" in which the *Nellie* is moored leads to "the uttermost ends of the earth . . . into an immense heart of darkness," and the Thames and the Congo form one continuous stream, then the cultural cargo that the great river bears back to the European capital includes not only the tarnished booty of imperial conquest but also the disorienting effects of the colonial encounter. The same flowing body of water that bears the products of empire and paradoxically nourishes the growth of European literary modernism, "by a comodius vicus of recirculation," flows outward again, carrying the literary freight that will come to rest in locales far distant from London's imperial metropole, in those very sites destined to become competing centers of culture in the emerging global network that will sustain literary modernism.

## Notes

1 Conrad, *Heart of Darkness* (London: Penguin, 1995); all page references are to this edition and are given in parentheses in the text.

2 Chinua Achebe's very different but no less influential postcolonial critique of *Heart of Darkness* rests on the charge that Conrad demeans African peoples and ignores the complexity of their cultures by presenting them as mere background in a Eurocentric narrative focusing on the crisis of a single Western consciousness. While I acknowledge the force of Achebe's characterization of the epistemological limits of Conrad's narrative vision, I will argue that Marlow's failure to comprehend African cultural realities and assimilate them to a more familiar set of European social norms is nonetheless essential to and even generative of Conrad's critique of Western imperialism. If Conrad's limited European perspective is illustrative of racism, paradoxically it is thereby all the more productive of his subversive representation of Western colonialism. For Achebe's critique of Conrad, see Achebe, "An Image of Africa: Racism in Conrad's *Heart of Darkness*," in Joseph Conrad, *Heart of Darkness* (New York: W. W. Norton, 1987), 251–61. Further citations to this edition in the notes will be to *Heart of Darkness* (Norton Critical Edition).

3 Bradbury, "The Cities of Modernism," 96–97.

4 Berman, *All That Is Solid Melts Into Air*, and Moretti, *Modern Epic*, 123–67.

5 Jameson, *The Political Unconscious*, 206–80, and "Modernism and Imperialism."

6 Denis Butts, Introduction, *Allan Quatermain*, by H. Rider Haggard (Oxford: Oxford University Press, 1995), vi. All page references to Rider Haggard's novel are to this edition and are given parenthetically in the text.

7 Spurr, *The Rhetoric of Empire*, 13–27, 109–40.

8 Korzeniowski had his name legally changed to "Joseph Conrad" in 1886 (when he became a British subject), but he continued to use his given Polish name in personal correspondence with friends and relatives in 1890 while he traveled up the Congo River.

9 For Conrad's description of and reaction to his first sight of Stanley Falls Station, see "Backgrounds and Sources" in *Heart of Darkness* (Norton Critical Edition), 186–87.

10 Watt, *Conrad in the Nineteenth Century*, 175–79, 270–71, 357. Watt defines delayed decoding as a "narrative device" that "combines the forward temporal progression of the mind, as it receives messages from the outside world, with the much slower reflexive process of making out their meaning" (175).

11 Ibid., 55, 201–17, 286–310; also see Genette, *Narrative Discourse*, 35–85.

12 See, for example, Achebe, "An Image of Africa."

13 J. M. Coetzee, "The Picturesque, the Sublime, and the South African Landscape" and "Reading the South African Landscape," in *White Writing*, 36–62 and 163–78.

14 Morris, *Pax Britannica*, 23–35.

15 Ibid., 26, 30.
16 Ibid., 31–34.
17 The London—Gibraltar—Malta—Alexandria—Suez—Aden—Bombay submarine cable was opened in 1870, some thirteen years before the fictional events aboard the *Patna* take place; see Morris, *Pax Britannica*, 32–33.
18 See Moses, *The Novel and the Globalization of Culture*, 74–76, 95–96.
19 Ibid., 98–104.

## Works Cited


Berman, Marshall. *All That Is Solid Melts Into Air: The Experience of Modernity*. New York: Penguin, 1988.

Bradbury, Malcolm. "The Cities of Modernism." In *Modernism*, ed. Malcolm Bradbury and James McFarlane, 96–104. Harmondsworth: Penguin, 1976.

Coetzee, J. M. *White Writing: On the Culture of Letters in South Africa*. New Haven, Conn.: Yale University Press, 1988.

Conrad, Joseph. *Heart of Darkness*. London: Penguin, 1995.

——. *Heart of Darkness*. Norton Critical Edition. Edited by Robert Kimbrough. New York: W. W. Norton, 1987.

Genette, Gérard. *Narrative Discourse: An Essay in Method*. Translated by Jane E. Lewin. Ithaca, N.Y.: Cornell University Press, 1980.

Haggard, H. Rider. *Allan Quatermain*. Oxford: Oxford University Press, 1995.

Jameson, Fredric. "Modernism and Imperialism." In Terry Eagleton, Fredric Jameson, and Edward Said, *Nationalism, Colonialism, Literature*. Minneapolis: University of Minnesota Press, 1990.

——. *The Political Unconscious: Narrative as a Socially Symbolic Act*. Ithaca, N.Y.: Cornell University Press, 1981.

Moretti, Franco. *Modern Epic*. London: Verso, 1996.

Morris, James. *Pax Britannica*. London: Folio Society, 1992.

Moses, Michael Valdez. *The Novel and the Globalization of Culture*. New York: Oxford University Press, 1995.

Spurr, David. *The Rhetoric of Empire: Colonial Discourse in Journalism, Travel Writing, and Imperial Administration*. Durham, N.C.: Duke University Press, 1994.

Watt, Ian. *Conrad in the Nineteenth Century*. Berkeley: University of California Press, 1981.

*Jed Esty*

⋮

# THREE
# Virginia Woolf's Colony and the Adolescence of Modernist Fiction

Edward Said's insistence on the "cultural integrity of empire" still offers a vital challenge to the humanities today, and particularly to literary scholars of the period 1880–1940, for whom Said's concept makes it at once more difficult and more necessary to reconceive the relationship between modernism and colonialism.[1] The dominant model established by Said identifies a flexible, often aesthetically complex, yet ideologically purposeful discourse of colonialism that projected Western superiority, secular rationality, economic progress, and bourgeois triumphalism to the far corners of the earth. Yet the dominant models of aesthetic modernism describe the latter movement as a critical voice whose dissonant strains within European culture are unified by a deep suspicion of precisely those same projected narratives of Western superiority, rationalism, and progress. These alternative propositions raise a key question for the politics of modernism: do modernist works critique imperialism and its associated values or do they, by contrast, renovate Western art by exploiting the cultural and epistemological privileges that Raymond Williams has memorably described as "metropolitan perception"?[2] Of course, the answers to this question are as various as modernism's disparate expressions in art, literature, music, and philosophy—and by now most scholars attempt to chart a middle course, eschewing both implausible claims of an ideological chasm between modernism and imperialism and equally implausible claims of direct ideological correspondence. Still, this way of framing the cultural politics of modernism, with its unfortunate Manichaean and moralistic overtones, continues to define much of the commentary on modernism and colonialism. As a result, many scholars restrict themselves to considering texts with obvious imperial content and, more to the point, end by charging or crediting particular modernists with pro- or anti-imperial views—even if the ratios of political intention are mixed, nuanced, and ever-shifting.

While Conrad stands as an obvious instance of a modernist writer whose relationship to colonialism has often been framed in largely intentionalist terms, the same problem has come to define postcolonial or colonial-discourse readings of Virginia Woolf. In the last fifteen years, such readings have consolidated the notion of Woolf's intertwined and impassioned suspicion of imperialism and patriarchy.[3] Jane Marcus's groundbreaking reading of *The Waves* established this interpretive position, arguing that that novel contains a veiled but unmistakable and cogent attack on the power/knowledge structures of British imperialism.[4] In a subtle rejoinder to Marcus, Patrick McGee insists that *The Waves* offers an "implicit and partial critique," rather than an explicit denunciation, of imperialism, drawing attention away from Woolf's own political attitudes and toward her form's symbolic mediations of the colonial context. McGee objects, in other words, to viewing Woolf as outside the ideology of imperialism that she anatomizes (and reproduces) in her fiction.[5] If we take Woolf's fiction as a key example of how modernist writing frames—both in terms of authorial intentions *and* formal effects—its historical relationship to colonialism, it is worth considering in more detail the literary devices that mediate between those two layers of textual meaning.

Toward that end, I want in this essay to examine Woolf's most obviously colonial novel, *The Voyage Out* (1915), focusing on its temporal structures in relation to its setting in a South American coastal enclave. I will not emphasize the postcolonial thematics of alterity (in the form, for example, of Rachel's oblique identification with colonized peoples) nor even the direct presentation of anti-imperial politics (in the form, for example, of Woolf's acerbic satire of the Dalloways and their fatuous jingoism), in part because the novel itself takes pains to establish the limited effectiveness of both cross-cultural identification and bourgeois dissent as types of counterdiscursive action. Instead, the reading will concentrate on the novel's assimilation of a certain uneven—and markedly colonial—temporality into its narrative and characterological language, which is to say, on the formal problem of how *The Voyage Out* undoes the generic protocols of the bildungsroman. How [illegible] n hypermodernization in the metropolitan core [illegible] he colonial periphery—a defining feature of the [illegible] elf felt in the very fabric of novelistic time?[6] This [illegible] ether Woolf's characteristically modernist aver[illegible] r idiosyncratic representation of an ersatz Amazonian landscape in order to propose a deep-structural link between the fiction of adolescence and the politics of colonialism—between, that is, modernist aesthetics and modern colonialism.

⁝ ⁝ ⁝

My essay begins, then, with one guiding question: is there a significant symbolic relationship between uneven development in colonial modernity (in the post–Berlin Conference era, 1885–1940) and antidevelopmental plots in canonical fiction of the same period? Before pursuing the question with regard to *The Voyage Out* in particular, I want to explore some generic and literary-historical backgrounds that help set Woolf's text into a broader context of European novels that cast colonial underdevelopment in terms of frozen or stunted youth. It is commonly observed that the bildungsroman had its heyday in the nineteenth century and that modernism tended to avoid its generic dictates or to revise them out of recognition. Consider the landmark fictions of European modernism: Kafka's "Metamorphosis," which short-circuits and hideously travesties the development of its late-adolescent protagonist; Proust's *Remembrance of Things Past*, which not only displaces the plot of development with the plot of recollection but distends its temporal frame over hundreds of pages; Mann's *The Magic Mountain*, which describes Hans Castorp wasting away, literally *un*becoming himself in an Alpine sanatorium; Wilde's *The Picture of Dorian Gray*, which inverts the aging process, yielding a protagonist whose endless youth anticipates another fin de siècle Orientalist tale, Kipling's *Kim*. Metamorphosis, dilation, truncation, consumption, inversion: these forms spectacularly thwart the realist proportions of biographical time that had, from its inception, defined the bildungsroman.

And this is not even to mention the stylized pattern of temporal compression and expansion in the work of Anglophone modernists such as Conrad, Woolf, and Joyce. In their fictions, characterization does not unfold in smooth biographical time but in proleptic fits and retroactive starts, in epiphanic bursts and encyclopedic mental inventories, in sudden lyric death and in languid semi-conscious delay. In *Lord Jim, The Voyage Out*, and *A Portrait of the Artist as a Young Man*, Conrad, Woolf, and Joyce rework narrative time via youthful protagonists who conspicuously *do not grow up*. Moreover, these texts establish the deferred or blocked attainment of a mature social role through plots of colonial migration. All three novels are antidevelopmental fictions set in underdeveloped zones. From Conrad's Asian straits to Woolf's South American riverway to Joyce's Irish backwater, colonialism disrupts the bildungsroman and its humanist ideals, producing jagged effects on both the politics and poetics of subject formation. Although many factors might be adduced to account for the anti-teleological shape of various modernist bildungsromane, the novels of Conrad, Woolf, and Joyce exemplify a specific and surprisingly underexplored connection between modernist aesthetics and modern colonialism. Moreover, the argument can extend to include, for example, Olive Schreiner, Oscar Wilde, Elizabeth Bowen, and Jean Rhys—all colonial emigrés whose fictions cast doubt on the ideology of progress and who make those doubts visible through the figure of stunted youth.

At one level, it is not surprising that a group of imperial fictions should feature endless youth; such a trope would seem to conform nicely to the wish-fulfilling aspects of imperial romance, indeed of imperial adventurism *tout court*. But the novels mentioned above are not simple romances. Their anti-bildungsroman temporality, combined with colonial content, suggests a more complicated history, with implications for the emergence of modernism's antinarrative techniques. To pursue these connections, we might turn to Franco Moretti's provocative argument that the European bildungsroman's historical vocation was to manage the effects of modernization by representing it within a safe narrative scheme. During the golden age of European realism (from Goethe and Austen to Flaubert and George Eliot), youth was the master trope of modernity itself, signifying the constant transformation of industrial society and the growing interiority and mobility of middle-class subjects. However, "to become a 'form,'" Moretti writes:

> Youth must be endowed with a very different, almost opposite feature to those already mentioned: the very simple and slightly philistine notion that youth "does not last forever." Youth is brief, or at any rate circumscribed, and this enables or rather *forces* the *a priori* establishment of a formal constraint on the portrayal of modernity. Only by curbing its intrinsically boundless dynamism,

> only by agreeing to betray to a certain extent its very essence, only thus, it seems, can modernity be *represented*.[7]

The young protagonist's open development is ultimately and rather artificially contained by the imposition of a static state of adulthood. In Moretti's model, the classic bildungsroman of Goethe and Austen turns on its ability to reconcile narrativity and closure, youth and adulthood, free self-making and social determination. It both reflects and produces social consent, modeling for its middle-class readers a fragile compromise between inner and outer directives in subject formation.

If this standard novel of socialization figures modernity's endless revolution in the master trope of youth, then what is the social referent for the countertrope of adulthood? If capitalism never rests, what symbolic equivalence can explain the capacity of adulthood to put the brakes on developmental time, preventing the bildungsroman from becoming a never-ending story? Here we arrive at a possibility that remains somewhat buried in Moretti—that the discourse of the nation supplies the realist bildungsroman with an emergent language of historical continuity or social identity amid the rapid and sweeping changes of industrialization. What Moretti leaves unexplored is the crucial symbolic function of nationhood, which gives a "finished" form to modern societies in the same way that adulthood gives a finished form to the modern subject.[8]

At a socially symbolic level, then, the dynamic tension between youth and adulthood in the nineteenth-century bildungsroman plays out as a struggle between the open-ended temporality of capitalism and the bounded, countertemporality of the nation. The discourse of romantic nationalism in the late eighteenth century was of course crucial to the philosophical milieu of the early bildungsroman in Germany. Indeed, the classic genealogy of *Bildung* begins with Goethe, Schiller, Lessing, and Herder. This lineage establishes the genre's roots in a burgeoning nationalism based on an ideal of organic culture whose temporality and harmony could be reflected in the developing personality at the core of the bildungsroman. This historically specific notion of becoming defines an ideal process of acculturation: the aesthetic education of the subject (Schiller) and the emergence of the folk into the historically meaningful form of the nation (Herder).

M. M. Bakhtin codified the literary-critical application of the concept when he claimed that a true (and thus truly modern) bildungsroman presents "an image of *man growing* in *national-historical time*."[9] For Bakhtin, the possibility of a narrative that fuses individual experience and social development requires an explicitly national (and tacitly masculine) form of emergence. These are the premises woven into Bakhtin's taxonomic and teleological account of the bildungsroman's pride of place in the history of realism:

> Along with this predominant, mass type [the novel with the "ready-made" hero], there is another incomparably rarer type of novel that provides an image of man in the process of becoming. . . . Changes in the hero himself acquire *plot* significance. . . . Time is introduced into man, enters into his very image, changing in a fundamental way the significance of all aspects of his destiny and life. This type of novel can be designated in the most general sense as the novel of human *emergence*. . . . Everything depends upon the degree of assimilation of real historical time.[10]

"National-historical time" allows the Goethean bildungsroman to reconcile the open-ended time of an expansive modernity and the cyclical time of local tradition.[11]

We can now begin to see the defining tension between the "realism" of the bildungsroman (bounded by "national time") and the potentially unbounded forms of temporality associated with supranational forces that emerged in the wake of the French and Industrial revolutions. Those expansionist forces—whether identified as political rationality or economic hegemony, as capitalism or imperialism—threatened the concept of culture itself insofar as they threatened to spill outside the borders of the nation. In the British sphere, Burke and Coleridge consolidated this central opposition between a national culture (in which proportionate social and personal growth can occur) and a multinational civilization (in which unrestrained growth has no organic checks or balances). What this suggests—and what the centrality of Goethe to Marxist theories of the bildungsroman would seem to confirm—is that the contradictory relationship between capitalism and culture, between alienated labor and aesthetic education, can only be harmonized by realist fiction during a brief heroic phase of bourgeois hegemony and European industrialization. By the late Victorian period in Britain, for example, a symbolic split had opened up between the insular nation (a culture proper to the bildungsroman's allegory of development) and the imperial state (a culture-diluting unit whose spatiotemporal coordinates did not conform to realist or *national-historical* time).

In other words, the bildungsroman's generic capacity to stabilize the rollicking tempo of dynamic modernization became attenuated as an increasingly global model of imperialism challenged the pretense of an organic relationship between culture and the state. Colonial modernity unsettles the discourse of national culture by breaking up its cherished continuities linking a people to its language, its territory, and its political history. It is not just the accelerating pace of economic and technological change that has this effect, nor even the values conflict between, for example, Britain's liberal heritage and the New Imperialism, but also—and more directly to the narratological point—it is that imperialism brings the bildungsroman and its humanist ideals into the zone of uneven development, breaking the Goethean bond between biographical and "national-historical time." A structural and historical analysis of the bildungsroman at this turning point in literary history is, in this sense, also a commentary on the fate of developmental thinking more broadly during the eclipse of nineteenth-century positivist historicism and the massive but strained expansion of European political hegemony.

In colonial fictions like Conrad's *Lord Jim* or Kipling's *Kim* (or, to cite a less-known example, Olive Schreiner's *The Story of an African Farm*), the temporality of deferral and dilation structures the entire novel in question; it is not just ascribed to individual characters or social dynamics on one side or the other of the colonial divide. As many commentators have noted, imperialism generally casts its subject people, the colonized, not as radically different but as an underdeveloped or youthful version of their rulers, not quite ready for self-government. But imperialism also casts its own agency as youthful and rejuvenating; its beneficiaries are rendered young outside the finite markets and social constraints of the Old World. In a sense, symbolic maturity is recurrently deferred for both colonizer and colonized in a fantasy of perpetual emergence without closure. And yet such exorbitant youthfulness, though it seems to represent a revitalizing frontier fantasy, also has a more troubling story to tell us about imperial time.

Following Sara Suleri's approach to Kipling, for example, we might read Kim's resplendent youth as a condition precipitated by a master plot of uneven development. In Suleri's view, the novel's structural emphasis on youth testifies to the futility of the imperial project, which must confront "the necessary perpetuation of its adolescence in relation to its history":

> Here "imperial time" demands to be interpreted less as a recognizable chronology of historic events than as a contiguous chain of surprise effects: even as empire seeks to occupy a monolithic historic space, its temporality is more accurately characterized as a disruptive sequence of a present tense perpetually surprised, allowing for neither the precedent of the past nor the anticipation of a future. . . . Kipling's narrative internalization of the superficiality of imperial time engenders both the adolescent energy of his tales and—in a text like *Kim*—the immanence of tragic loss, of an obsessively impelled discourse that lacks any direction in which to go.[12]

Kipling's anti-bildungsroman literalizes the problem of colonial development, giving an aesthetic form to what Dipesh Chakrabarty has called the endless Not-Yet of imperial history.[13] When we consider how central this same temporal-tropic device is for Conrad, Joyce, and Woolf, it becomes possible to read a colonial thematics of backwardness, anachronism, and uneven development as the basis for the anti-teleological model of subject formation that became a hallmark of modernist style. With this sketch of the intertwined problematic of colonial and narrative development in place, we can now turn to *The Voyage Out*, a book that seems to blend a species of imperial romance with the plotline of a female bildungsroman, only to invert the temporal logic of both forms by combining them.

⋮ ⋮ ⋮

Readings of *The Voyage Out* have long turned on two broad interpretive questions that organize feminist and postcolonial approaches respectively.[14] First, why does the novel initiate a trajectory of apparent self-determination, spiritual enlargement, or at least social adjustment for its protagonist Rachel Vinrace, only to close down those possibilities in a long spiral of illness, driving the plot into an antipatriarchal ground zero of death and renunciation? Second, why does Woolf stage this process in an obscure South American tourist colony? What narrative, symbolic, or stylistic purposes does the colonial setting serve? To put the two questions together: since in the end the colonial distance from England only highlights the durability and portability of the social conventions that domesticate Rachel, why voyage out there in the first place?

My answer to this last question turns on the novel's capacity to shift the trope of development freely between psychic and political registers. *The*

*Voyage Out* breaks from the narrative dictates of the bildungsroman, avoiding the baleful teleology of late Victorian womanhood with a protagonist who remains somehow, at age twenty-four, relentlessly, even insipidly, young. Woolf describes the impression Rachel makes: "Her face was weak rather than decided . . . denied beauty, now that she was sheltered indoors, by the lack of colour and definite outline"; she seems "more than normally incompetent for her years."[15] Rachel's development in the novel is not so much absent as staccato: thrust in and out of her amorphous youthfulness by turns, she is now frustratingly pillowed in innocence, now suddenly alert to adult possibilities. More to the point, Woolf sets this story of fits and starts, of beckoned and deferred maturity, in an unevenly developed coastal enclave, Santa Marina, a somewhat misbegotten tourist colony that seems to have deferred its own modernity only to have it arrive belatedly.

Woolf invents a syncopated, suspended, then accelerated history of settlement for Santa Marina; first dimly Spanish, then briefly English, then Spanish again for three hundred years of apparent social stasis, then English again, made over into a holiday spot for the shabby-genteel. Like Rachel, Santa Marina develops arrhythmically, first languishing, than suddenly catapulting forward, reeling with anachronism. Having failed to form itself into something firmly British and thus modern the first time around, Santa Marina appears as a cultural backwater. We learn that "in arts and industries the place is still much where it was in Elizabethan days" (80). And here, a few chapters earlier, is a description of Rachel Vinrace: "Her mind was in the state of an intelligent man's in the beginning of the reign of Queen Elizabeth" (26). Woolf persistently links these subjects of arrested development together through an Elizabethan (and Conradian) motif of the "virgin land behind a veil" (79).

The echo of Conrad is quite apt since Rachel is, like Lord Jim, a kind of supervirgin in a bubble of blushing egoism, a virgin not just to sex but to intersubjectivity, an innocent forced to face disillusionment yet stubbornly refusing it, a willfully adolescent adult whose unwillingness to age leads to death in an obscure colonial outpost. Like Jim (and for that matter, Kipling's Kim), Rachel is a classic symbolic orphan, a many-parented figure who, as the object of other characters' projections and desires, stands as a kind of "semantic void," the null function that can carry the symbolic weight of *Bildung* as both a biographical and social process.[16] Toward this end, Woolf often casts Rachel's consciousness and the South American landscape as figures for each other, each prone to a certain epistemological incontinence. Here is Rachel on the cliff's edge with her suitor, the plump and hapless Terence Hewet:

> Looking the other way, the vast expanse of land gave them a sensation which is given by no view, however extended, in England; the villages and the hills there having names, and the farthest horizon of hills as often as not dipping and showing a line of mist which is the sea; here the view was one of infinite sun-dried earth, earth pointed in pinnacles, heaped in vast barriers, earth widening and spreading away and away like the immense floor of the sea, earth chequered by day and by night, and partitioned into different lands, where famous cities were founded and the races of men changed from dark savages to white civilized men and back to dark savages again. Perhaps their English blood made this prospect uncomfortably impersonal and hostile to them, for having once turned their faces that way they next turned them to the sea, and for the rest of the time sat looking at the sea. (194)

The protagonists' discomfort stems not just from the infinite space (which would invoke a familiar mode of the colonial sublime) but from the almost-glimpsed cities that are ruled by an unaccountable, nonlinear history, a round of racial leapfrog with no clear progress toward civilized, stable self-possession. A lack of self-possession, in fact, stands as the most persistent motif linking Rachel to Santa Marina, "the sunny land outside the window being no less capable of analysing its own colour and heat than she was of analysing hers" (210). Cutting from psyche to setting, Woolf establishes a consistent figural scheme in which protagonist and colony share a generalized unboundedness and a resistance to purposeful or smoothly clocked development.[17]

The uncivilized South American landscape (however inauthentically rendered) serves as both figure and context for Rachel's ego-dissolution; as in the long passage above, the regress of the horizon disorients Rachel while signaling its actual—and her potential—alienation from English norms. Rachel's identification with uncouth nature becomes, for Woolf, a technique for indicating resistance to a mature identity, to the traps and trappings of bourgeois womanhood.[18] In this sense, Woolf's experiment in suspending Rachel's identity-formation depends on the colonial setting as both a figurative index and a causal agent in the mix. But what is in some ways most striking about the novel is the rapid, almost skittish permutation of figures established for Rachel: she is not just a lost colony or virgin land, she's also a ship, a river, a butterfly, a piano string, a breeze. The intermittency and inconsistency of these metaphors is not, as is sometimes thought, a flaw but the point of a novel seeking to disrupt the momentum of *Bildung*. *The Voyage Out* displaces all the potential plots of development (Victorian social mobility, naturalist tragedy, bohemian compromise) by creating a narrative stasis or long threshold wherein Rachel does not so much develop an ego as accumulate metaphors. She remains a bundle of crisscrossing libidinal vectors, a human nebula, poised between becoming and unbecoming herself, until she falls ill and dies.

The novel thus produces a systematic and astringent inversion of the Goethean ideal of male destiny, documenting Rachel's inability to cultivate her own selfhood through a set of linked images, through a set of averted narrative outcomes, and sometimes (as in the following passage) through explicit narratorial commentary:

> For the methods by which she had reached her present position, seemed to her very strange, and the strangest thing about them was that she had not known where they were leading her. That was the strange thing, that one did not know where one was going, or what one wanted, and followed blindly, suffering so much in secret, always unprepared and amazed and knowing nothing; but one thing led to another and by degrees something had formed itself out of nothing, and so one reached at last this calm, this quiet, this certainty, and it was this process that people called living. (297)

In this passage, the repetitive cadences evoke Gertrude Stein's characteristic method for forestalling narrative momentum, condensing into syntax the larger antidevelopmental logic of the text. Rachel's lack of self-knowledge at the level of plot also works at the level of language or style by generating an extreme mobility of perspective that slowly transforms itself from psychological quirk into narrative device. If a juvenile and estranged perspective on adult realities is a relatively common conceit (from Dickens's Pip to Faulkner's Vardaman), Woolf actually dramatizes the migration of that youthfully coded viewpoint from its explicit source in a discrete character into a diffusely adolescent principle of narration. In other words, Rachel's character yields (to) a narrative trope of undevelopment, an erratic, semi-omniscient, semi-embodied third-person perspective from which Woolf's key writerly innovations begin to emerge. Rachel cannot interpret or describe the effects of her own self-dissolution, but Woolf absorbs the subject/object dissolve into an experimental fictional language. In a sense, style transforms and even displaces plot; that is to say, style *has* a plot, while the novel itself, dilating and distending arrhythmically for long stretches, often does not.

This reading provides a new, more precise, and more specifically colonial explanatory framework for what is a fairly common observation about *The Voyage Out*, which is that the failed bildungsroman of Rachel Vinrace is a pretext or precondition for the ultimately successful artistic development of Virginia Woolf.[19] To elaborate my initial hypothesis about the connection between Rachel's ego dissolution in the colonial setting and the development of Woolf's modernist style, we might return to a comparison between *The Voyage Out* and Conrad's Marlow fictions. When Marlow encounters a socially or epistemologically unassimilable human figure (Mr. Kurtz or Lord Jim), he carries back some bounty of existential insight. But this two-man drama is feminized and internalized in *The Voyage Out,* where Rachel acts both parts, the peering protagonist and the blurry human figure. She cannot interpret or describe the effects of her own self-dissolution. Moreover, Rachel's stubborn innocence is repeatedly thematized as blocked knowledge about the imperial system itself, an incapacity to read the deep links between imperial capitalism and domestic humanism. As Rachel's merchant father summarizes this entire structuring motif, so crucial to the novel's shape and to its author's social experience: " 'If it weren't for the goats [commerce] there'd be no music [culture], my dear; music depends upon goats' " (16).

Rachel's uncultivated selfhood is not just, in other words, figured in the colony; it is in some sense routed through colonialism itself as a system of exchange and production. If we take Woolf's cue here, we can zero in on the mechanism that allows the trope of underdevelopment to shuttle between the novel's stylistic and generic registers on the one hand and its colonial context on the other. For the novel addresses itself quite explicitly to the problem of women's incomplete access to knowledge about imperial economics and politics, while more slyly assimilating this foreclosed knowledge into its own revision of the bildungsroman's temporal imperatives. In other words, some of the novel's most distinctive features can be traced to a specifically imperial kind of political unconscious, of the kind that Fredric Jameson has identified in his essay on the encrypted signs of empire in the language of Forster's *Howards End*.[20] Jameson's argument—that colonialism's dispersed and unknowable forms of economic activity filter into modernist works at the level of style—has seemed highly speculative to some critics. But *The Voyage Out* invites us to consider its departure from generic conventions precisely in terms of the unknowable geography of production in the imperial metropolis. In the opening scene, Rachel's aunt, Helen Ambrose, muses on the West End of London: "It appeared to her a very small bit of work for such an enormous factory to have made. For some reason it appeared to her as a small golden tassel on the edge of a vast black cloak" (6). Woolf foregrounds uncertain appearances ("It appeared to her. . . . for some reason it appeared to her") and vast cloaked realities, gesturing toward the lost intelligibility that Jameson sees as part of life in modernism's "unreal cities," where key parts of the society's basic daily life take place out of sight. Helen's bohemian and feminized image of the city's visible golden tassel marks this as a gendered instance of the broad screens and epistemological decoys that are symptomatic of capitalist and colonial modernity. Those screens and their gendered dimensions are further highlighted as we shift focus from Helen to Rachel, the underdeveloped heroine who continually strains to trace the lines of power and production connecting her inner life to the great world-spanning activities of men like her father and Richard Dalloway.

Moreover, Woolf's keynote theme of nonsynthesis between aesthetic culture (your music) and mercantile capitalism (my goats) represents another quite direct revision of the bildungsroman, which in its classic form aims to reconcile these forces via its narration of a harmony between desire and social convention, between self-production and production per se. Of course, there is a long dissenting tradition in the female bildungsroman where this symbolic reconciliation is not only not performed but is exposed and critiqued. *The Voyage Out* embeds that feminist critique into the problematic of colonial development. Among the many reasons that Rachel cannot reconcile the rules of art and commerce is that she, like Conrad's cloistered women in *Heart of Darkness*, represents the gendering of the imperial unconscious, the split between civilizing and chivalric ideals on the one hand and the grubby deeds of empire men on the other.[21]

From several important perspectives, the gendered dimensions of Woolf's project in *The Voyage Out* distinguish its plot of underdevelopment rather sharply from those of *Kim* and *Lord Jim;* however, all three novels share a certain kind of binary logic that structures the relation between acculturation and accumulation in the colonies. In each of these novels, the Goethe-Schiller model of aesthetic education displaces the real work of production. In *Lord Jim*, Jim's failure to *accumulate* experience or to amass a personality is registered reciprocally by Conrad's colonial economy—in which, as in *Kim* and *Voyage Out*, the main preoccupation seems to be the production of character, not wealth. Indeed Jim does not develop, which is precisely why he charms and horrifies Marlow (and the reader) in equal proportion. He is not so much a psychologically dynamic character as a walking principle of imperial time, a cipher or figure, a colonial Dorian Gray to Marlow's picture, since Marlow takes on all the sad, sagging weight of ethical complexity and temporal experience that Jim manages to repel. In the colonial fantasyland of Patusan, Jim's sense of an authentic and special destiny for himself aligns with the necessity of his removal to an obscure, unwanted outpost. But this alignment of inner and outer destinies, of the pedagogical project of soul-making with the practical work of colonial administration, can only be temporary. In Patusan as in Woolf's Santa Marina, the temporality of underdevelopment, shaping both adolescent heroes and colonial hinterlands, doesn't just prolong youth, it also snaps back into sudden death.

Like Jim, Rachel dies from a fateful encounter with a kind of native infection—an Amazonian virus in her case. Her death, like Jim's, is a Pyrrhic victory that symbolically affirms the marginalized values of the willfully innocent protagonist. A colonial romance lies buried in *The Voyage Out,* but it is an encapsulated romance (as in *Lord Jim*) whose logic is inverted and exposed by the closural process. In this sense, both novels reveal the ideological romance of permanent adolescence by insisting, with clear-eyed political realism, that neither human aging nor socialization nor modernization can be forestalled. Woolf and Conrad seem at first to reenchant the bildungsroman—to hold out hope for a reconciliation between the soul's private longings and its social obligations—but finally come to disenchant it with a vengeance. For Rachel, the voyage out to Santa Marina initially seems to promise some kind of enlarged possibility for semi-autonomy within patriarchal social relations; her courtship with the fatuous Hewet seems, under the spell of the Amazon, to break from some of the rigid sexual conventions that threaten Rachel's happiness. However, when—at the heart of the novel's Amazonian darkness—Rachel looks into the eyes of the native women who are staring back at her, she recognizes that a vast and impersonal system, in which sex, gender, labor, and power are socially organized, will always impinge on her subjective and autonomous sense of self: "So it would go on for ever and ever, she said" (270).[22] Rachel's sense of entrapment in patriarchy, her lost myth of Goethean subjectivity and freedom, unspools in the language of horrifying stasis, the permanent absence of a special developmental destiny, as the gears of patriarchy grind on.

⋮ ⋮ ⋮

As these remarks suggest, once cut free from its embedded teleologies, the trope of adolescence reveals a most cruel lesson: that endless youth is merely the obverse of sudden death. This temporal split helps explain the oddly bifurcated plot of *Lord Jim* as well as the imposed death spiral in the second half of *The Voyage Out*. Without age—or to be more precise, without aging—youth mutates from the very figure of vitality into the sudden, static ping of lifelessness. What is structured in these texts as an existential conflict between the forward momentum of duty and the playful stasis of desire can also be understood as the political contradiction between the imperial ethos of development and the facts of colonial underdevelopment. To frame the central political and generic contradiction of *Lord Jim* in this way is to name a specific crisis of under/development as a driving force in what Fredric Jameson presents as the broad modernist dialectic of "romance and reification."[23] Like *Lord Jim, The Voyage Out* divides into the romance time of youthful adventure and the naturalist time of late Victorian tragedy, falling to either side, as it were, of the temporal mean of linear, realistic (in Bakhtin's restrictive sense) growth. This particular plotting of imperial time's endless present uses tragic closure to reassert a kind of historical reality principle, reopening the gap between work and aesthetic education rather than magically suturing it a là Moretti's Goethe. In other words, the original contest between culture and capitalism that was so effectively knitted together by the symbolic mechanisms of the bildungsroman (with its implicitly national *telos*) is exacerbated, revealed, or given form as a contradiction by modernist fiction in the high imperial age.

If the conclusions I have drawn so far seem to indicate an improbably deterministic relationship between colonial conditions and modernist literature, I hasten to emphasize that my claim is neither that modernist writers were constrained by geopolitical factors to revise the traditional bildungsroman nor that modernism's manifold experiments in the interruption of narrative flow need be understood exclusively according to the problematic of "imperial time." Nor, certainly, were modernist novelists the first to vex the developmental plot with delays, inversions, and other assorted forms of silence, cunning, and exile (one need only mention *Tristram Shandy* as an earlier example). Yet there is, I think, a highly suggestive and prominent relationship between colonialism and adolescence in *The Voyage Out* and in a related cluster of important British novels, a relationship that demands literary-historical explanation. The more strongly materialist version of my argument might claim that these texts register a new phase in colonial capitalism, but even if we remain skeptical about that claim, even if the intertwined trope of frozen youth and colonial underdevelopment reflects not so much an implacable geopolitical base as a handy symbolic affinity, the trope seems to play a crucial role in the emergence of experimental modernist fiction. Separating adolescence from the dictates of *Bildung*, modernist writing created an autonomous value for youth and cleared space for its own resistance to progressive, linear plots while registering the temporal and political contradictions of colonialism as a discourse of progress. In short, whether we account for the currency of antidevelopmental logic according to changes in the material predicates or the symbolic proclivities of the bildungsroman, the texts in question—of which *The Voyage Out* is but one good example—highlight the genre's founding tensions between youth and adulthood, between modernization processes that never sleep and national discourses that posit origins and ends.

Viewed from this perspective, Woolf and Joyce find an unexpected prehistory in Conrad and Kipling, a constellation of writers that challenges Edward Said's influential notion of a split between imperial romance and domestic novels of disillusionment. One consequence of my argument, then, is to see colonial fiction as part of the history of the art novel rather than as a middlebrow detour. I propose this constellation not to construct a direct line of influence or even a web of intertextuality but to try to isolate a common formal feature that seems to shed light on the specific historical relationship between modernism and colonialism without granting too much force to the imagined political intentions of this or that modernist. In this argument, modernism acts neither as a counterdiscourse to the imperial metanarrative of modernity (the West civilizes the rest), nor as its apologetic discursive partner, but exposes modernity's temporal contradictions, particularly in zones of colonial encounter. The modernist texts in question represent the myth of universal progress, revealing its immanent contradictions rather than laying claim to a position of ideological transcendence. By the same token, we should not imagine that Western culture already had all its autocritical and anti-imperial resources in place before the anticolonial movements (and later postcolonial studies) came along to challenge the hegemony of European power and knowledge. If this essay has viewed colonial modernity from a metropolitan perspective, it is worth remembering that at the core of the formal problem I have discussed lies the historical challenge raised by colonial underdevelopment and by the resistance of colonized peoples.[24] Those unseasonable youths, Conrad's Jim, Kipling's Kim, Woolf's Rachel Vinrace, and Joyce's Stephen Dedalus, all register and embody the powerful unsettling effects of the colonial encounter on humanist ideals of national culture and aesthetic education that had, from the time of Goethe and Schiller, determined the inner logic of the bildungsroman.

Of course, that inner logic has always been more stable in theory than in practice. It will be immediately apparent to literary scholars that the generic definition of the bildungsroman can be loosened to include almost any novel or tightened to the point where no novel fits. Here as we look in vain for a *true* bildungsroman, we tumble quickly from Woolf and Joyce to Hardy to Eliot to Dickens to Brontë to Austen to Scott to Fielding and finally even to Goethe, whose *Wilhelm Meister*, most Germanists now agree, appears to violate most of the generic rules invoked in its honor. This problem has been laid out in a superb book by Marc Redfield, who argues that the bildungsroman is itself a "phantom formation."[25] Redfield's poststructuralist liquification of the genre makes sense, but the fact remains that the concept of *Bildung* has shaped not just literary criticism but also literary practice for generations—a fact that is not altered by its nonfulfillment in any given text. Indeed genres are almost always empty sets that shape literary history by their negation, deviation, variation, and mutation—and such deviations can be tracked, grouped, interpreted, even historicized. To put it another way, even if the bildungsroman's unmaking is always coeval with its making (in literary history writ large as well as in individual texts), it remains worthwhile to try to see patterns in the process of its unmaking and even—at a metacritical level—to explain why a phantom genre is such a recurrent object of theoretical desire.

It is with this in mind that I have adduced a positivist notion of the genre derived from Marxist narrative theory while also breaking with that tradition in seeing novels like *The Voyage Out* as something more than the disjecta membra of a postrealist age in which the bourgeois novel, folded in on its own subjectivity, could no longer synthesize the inner and outer world, no longer project the true shape of history. These dilatory, adolescent novels managed to encode anti-developmental time into the very language of human interiority and to objectify the deep-structural allegory binding the development of souls and nations. They stand as the narrative art of an era in which the time of modernization seemed increasingly *hyper* and *retro*, futurist and barbaric—all at once. Such works give form, I think, to the central contradiction of modernity, a contradiction especially vivid in the arena of colonialism, which is that modernity must always refer at once to a process of becoming and an ontology of being. If, as Adorno put it, modernity is the state of permanent transition, then its most trenchant literary incarnation is the figure of endless youth. Where the classical novel of education was shaped by the eschatology of nineteenth-century industrialization and nationbuilding, the modernist version assimilates the temporality of a global and imperial era when nations spilled beyond their borders and when the accelerating yet uneven pace of development seemed to have thrown the time of modernity out of joint. In this sense, the form of the modernist anti-bildungsroman manages, in fact, and against all odds, to fulfill the original function assigned to it by Bakhtin: the assimilation of "real historical time."

## Notes

1 Said, *Culture and Imperialism*, 97.

2 Williams, *The Politics of Modernism*, 44.

3 In *Virginia Woolf against Empire*, Phillips offers the most thorough presentation of this general view. Her broad thesis is certainly persuasive, though as the title suggests, Phillips tends to see the case mostly in terms of Woolf's criticism of, rather than implication in, colonialist modes of thought and forms of appropriation.

4 Marcus, "Britannia Rules *The Waves*."

5 McGee, "The Politics of Modernist Form, 631–32. McGee's political formalism produces similar conclusions to Raymond Williams's biographical essay on Woolf and the Bloomsbury group, in which Williams suggests that these liberal intellectuals were both beneficiaries and critics of British imperial power ("The Bloomsbury Fraction"). At a formal level, McGee argues against shunting the "negative aspects" of imperial politics onto Woolf's characters (such as

Bernard in *The Waves*) in order to argue for the author's own detached perspective on the corruption of imperial patriarchy (635). Mark Wollaeger offers a similar reading of *The Voyage Out*, suggesting that the novel's anti-imperial elements must be weighed against its representation of native women as mere object-symbols of global patriarchy ("Woolf, Postcards, and the Elision of Race," 44).

6 I use the terms "underdevelopment" and "underdeveloped" in this essay to describe what, from a Western perspective, appears as the uneven economic and technological development of the colonial periphery. Seeking to analyze rather than to replicate the progressivist and Eurocentric logic of imperialism, I do not attach any cultural valuation to the terms "developed" and "underdeveloped."

7 Moretti, *The Way of the World*, 6.

8 Moretti suggests at one point that "[c]apital . . . must grow and change form, and never stop: as Adam Smith observed in *The Wealth of Nations*, the merchant is a citizen of no country in particular. Quite true, and this is precisely the point: the merchant's journey can never come to a conclusion in those ideal places [of Goethe and Austen]" (26). Moretti does not explore the symbolic opposition between the merchant and the citizen, but the implicit logic is that the latter's achievement of cultured happiness and proportionate growth requires a relationship of belonging and of reciprocal allegorization with the nation. Within this allegorical scheme, the subject and nation do not just possess analogous forms of existential stability but generate a mutually reinforcing narrative that confers on the nation the organic coherence of a soul and confers on the individual the apparent temporal destiny of a nation.

9 Bakhtin, "The *Bildungsroman* and Its Significance in the History of Realism," 25.

10 Ibid., 21.

11 Hence Bakhtin's emphasis on the "concrete perception of the locality" that undergirds Goethe's deep historical vision (34). Bakhtin specifically excludes from Goethe's concrete and "realistic" historical imagination the far-away realms of the exotic, the sublime, and the wild, i.e., the world beyond those emergent and shapely intra-European national distinctions on display in works like *Italian Journey*.

12 Suleri, *The Rhetoric of English India*, 111, 113.

13 The temporal obverse of empire's "illusion of permanence" is the perpetually deferred future of the colony as an autonomous and fully modern society; for Chakrabarty, this ruse of imperial thinking is written into the protocols of historicism itself. See *Provincializing Europe*, 8.

14 For examples of feminist interpretation, see Froula, "Out of the Chrysalis," and Friedman, "Spatialization, Narrative Theory, and Virginia Woolf's *The Voyage Out*." For recent interpretations that emphasize travel and colonialism while integrating feminist insights, see Lawrence, "Woolf's Voyages Out," and Wollaeger, "Woolf, Postcards, and the Elision of Race."

15 Woolf, *The Voyage Out* (London: Penguin, 1992), 13; hereafter cited parenthetically in the text by page numbers.

16 For more on the *Bildungsheld* as semantic void, see Moretti, *The Way of the World*, 11.

17 Where Bakhtin's Goethe can see progressive time inscribed virtually everywhere —in sedimented landscapes, in wrinkled faces, in arboreal rings—Woolf's characters almost always seem to be apprehending the signs of atavistic and regressive time. For a thorough reading of Woolf's generalized skepticism about "developmental narratives," see Gillian Beer, *Virginia Woolf*, 13 ff.

18 As DeKoven (among others) points out, Rachel seems averse to a certain rigid set of social expectations and institutional arrangements associated with marriage, but she is not especially averse to heterosexual experience itself. See DeKoven, *Rich and Strange*, 127.

19 On this point, see Froula, "Out of the Chrysalis," 63; and Friedman, "Spatialization," 131.

20 Jameson, "Modernism and Imperialism."

21 In *The Voyage Out*, Richard Dalloway crystallizes the gender ideology that is anatomized by the novel and intensified in a colonial setting, where the gendered spheres of action and contemplation are even more rigorously separated. Dalloway expatiates on this principle to Rachel: "I never allow my wife to talk politics. For this reason. It is impossible for human beings, constituted as they are, both to fight and to have ideals" (56).

22 Wollaeger rightly notes that this episode is the scene "on which the entire narrative hinges," where the uncanny stares of the native women "bring home to [Rachel] the pressures of domestication and normalization" ("The Woolfs in the Jungle," 52 and 62).

23 Jameson, *The Political Unconscious*, 206–7.

24 The representation of uneven development as both a political and characterological trope in British modernism is, to borrow a formulation from Cooper and Stoler, a phenomenon "*viewed from* but not *determined at* the center" ("Tensions of Empire," 617; emphasis mine).

25 Redfield, *Phantom Formations*.

## Works Cited

Bakhtin, Mikhail M. "The *Bildungsroman* and Its Significance in the History of Realism: Toward a Historical Typology of the Novel." *Speech Genres and Other Late Essays*. Translated by Vern W. McGee. Austin: University of Texas Press, 1986.

Beer, Gillian. *Virginia Woolf: The Common Ground*. Edinburgh: Edinburgh University Press, 1996.

Chakrabarty, Dipesh. *Provincializing Europe: Postcolonial Thought and Historical Difference*. Princeton, N.J.: Princeton University Press, 2000.

Cooper, Frederick, and Ann Stoler. "Tensions of Empire: Colonial Control and Visions of Rule." *American Ethnologist* 16.4 (November 1989): 609–21.

DeKoven, Marianne. *Rich and Strange: Gender, History, Modernism.* Princeton, N.J.: Princeton University Press, 1991.

Friedman, Susan Stanford. "Spatialization, Narrative Theory, and Virginia Woolf's *The Voyage Out.*" In *Ambiguous Discourse: Feminist Narratology and British Women Writers*, ed. Kathy Mezei, 109–35. Chapel Hill: University of North Carolina Press, 1996.

Froula, Christine. "Out of the Chrysalis: Female Initiation and Female Authority in Virginia Woolf's *The Voyage Out.*" *Tulsa Studies in Women's Literature* 5.1 (Spring 1986): 63–90.

Jameson, Fredric. "Modernism and Imperialism." In Terry Eagleton, Fredric Jameson, and Edward Said, *Nationalism, Colonialism and Literature.* Minneapolis: University of Minnesota Press, 1990.

——. *The Political Unconscious.* Ithaca, N.Y.: Cornell University Press, 1981.

Lawrence, Karen. "Woolf's Voyages Out." *Penelope Voyages: Women and Travel in the British Literary Tradition.* Ithaca, N.Y.: Cornell University Press, 1994.

Marcus, Jane. "Britannia Rules *The Waves.*" In *Decolonizing Tradition: New Views of Twentieth-Century "British" Literary Canons*, ed. Karen Lawrence, 136–62. Urbana: University of Illinois Press, 1992.

McGee, Patrick. "The Politics of Modernist Form; or, Who Rules *The Waves*?" *Modern Fiction Studies* 38.3 (Autumn 1992): 631–52.

Phillips, Kathy J. *Virginia Woolf against Empire.* Knoxville: University of Tennessee Press, 1994.

Moretti, Franco. *The Way of the World.* London: Verso, 1987.

Redfield, Marc. *Phantom Formations: Aesthetic Ideology and the Bildungsroman.* Ithaca, N.Y.: Cornell University Press, 1996.

Said, Edward. *Culture and Imperialism.* New York: Vintage, 1994.

Suleri, Sara. *The Rhetoric of English India.* Chicago: University of Chicago Press, 1992.

Williams, Raymond. "The Bloomsbury Fraction." *Problems in Materialism and Culture.* London: New Left Books, 1980.

——. *The Politics of Modernism.* London: Verso, 1989.

Wollaeger, Mark. "The Woolfs in the Jungle: Intertextuality, Sexuality, and the Emergence of Female Modernism in *The Voyage Out, The Village in the Jungle,* and *Heart of Darkness.*" *MLQ* 64.1 (March 2003): 33–69.

——. "Woolf, Postcards, and the Elision of Race: Colonizing Women in *The Voyage Out.*" *Modernism / Modernity* 8.1 (January 2001): 43–75.

Woolf, Virginia. *The Voyage Out.* London: Penguin, 1992.

*Andrzej Gąsiorek*

⋮

FOUR

# War, "Primitivism," and the Future of "the West": Reflections on D. H. Lawrence and Wyndham Lewis

The impact of the First World War on literary modernism in England has long been the subject of critical discussion, but comparatively little work has been done on how this impact was influenced by writers' concerns about the legacies of colonialism and imperialism. While histories of colonialism and imperialism abound and debates about strategies for reading texts inflected by these histories proceed apace, the complex overlappings of modernist and colonialist discourses have received scant attention. This is puzzling, since the First World War provides an obvious point of departure for consideration of the modernism/colonialism nexus: its fratricidal carnage called the idea of European civilization into question, prompting reflection on its alleged superiority over the non-European nations in opposition to which it was defined. If an influential view among historians is that the First World War briefly safeguarded the British empire and that political decolonization should be dated from after the Second World War, it is nonetheless apparent that there was instability in the Empire throughout the 1920s, especially in Ireland and India.

The terms "colonialism" and "imperialism" need always to be treated carefully. The word "colonialism" was associated with British expansionism up to around 1870, after which the term "imperialism" gained ground, especially in relation to the Scramble for Africa in which rivalry between established colonial powers was at its most intense.[1] It was not until the 1870s that talk of imperialism started to dominate political debate, a shift associated with Disraeli's foreign policy, given currency by the publication of John Robert Seeley's *The Expansion of England* (1883), and developed by Joseph Chamberlain and supporters of "social imperialism" at the turn of the century. Conflicting views over the moral validity and economic viability of the empire lay at the heart of political debate in this period. Whereas Seeley's was a pragmatic view, other apologists for imperialism defended it on grounds of racial and moral superiority, identifying the work of Providence in the growth of the British empire. Hierarchical conceptions of race informed the idea of imperial trusteeship, which depended for its rationale on the belief that the British were superior to the peoples they had colonized in terms of national character and mode of government.[2] Although the Boer War called British foreign policy into question, the connection between imperialism and hierarchical views of race remained strong.[3]

Imperialist discourses that rely on racial distinctions depict the colonial other as inherently inferior, thereby validating the conquering nation's imposition of alternative cultural values and political modes of governance. Christine Bolt has argued that in the Victorian period "the attributes of the British race and British civilization were invariably confused," and this blurring of two discourses—ethnological and sociopolitical—is still evident in debates after the First World War when racial and cultural assumptions came under pressure.[4] Racially inflected anxieties about the future of society are discernible in works such as Sinclair Kennedy's *The Pan-Angles: A Consideration of the Federation of the Seven English-Speaking Nations* (1914), Madison Grant's *The Passing of the Great Race* (1916), Lothrop Stoddard's *The Rising Tide of Color against White World Supremacy* (1920), Oswald Spengler's *Decline of the West* (1918–22), and Henri Massis's *Defence of the West* (1926). Explicitly racist, and in some cases eugenicist, these works deployed racial categories and abstract concepts (East-West, Occident-Orient) to distinguish among civilizations. At a time when Europe had all but destroyed itself, the threat to its integrity and future was projected onto "alien" peoples and societies. Massis and Spengler, for example, deployed a crude East/West binary, combining topos with *Geist* in a move that mapped culture onto space. Rhetorically producing "the whole of Asia" as a single entity, Massis asserted that it "is the soul of the West that the East wishes to attack," while Spengler, insisting on the ineradicable difference between Russia and Europe, concluded that " 'East' and 'West' are notions that contain real history, whereas 'Europe' is an empty sound."[5]

Christopher GoGwilt rightly argues that these moves do not denote "a crisis of Western culture" but rather "a crisis that produces, in reaction, the idea of Western culture."[6] In Edward Said's terms, the discourse deployed by figures like Spengler and Massis approaches "a heterogeneous dynamic, and complex human reality from an uncritically essentialist standpoint"; framing difference according to a hierarchical conception of race, it is "a discourse of power originating in an era of colonialism."[7] But once terms such as "West" and "East" come into play it is difficult to avoid using them as markers of unitary entities, and it has been objected of Said's work that he too essentializes "the West," making an ontological distinction between Europeans and non-Europeans, which denies that the former can produce knowledge about the latter.[8]

Issues of ontology, knowledge, and otherness are central to any discussion of D. H. Lawrence's and Wyndham Lewis's attempts to rethink colonialist assumptions in their elaborations of two modernist trajectories. Both writers were equally preoccupied with the fate of Europe as a political and cultural entity, and although they were critical of each other's aesthetic commitments, both questioned the alleged preeminence of "European" or "Western" artistic traditions, social structures, and political arrangements. It would, however, be misleading to suggest that in their work the concept of "the West" somehow subsumed that of "Europe," as they tended to use the two concepts interchangeably. Lawrence during the war was obsessed with the imminent self-destruction of Europe, arguing that an entirely new way of life was required. Lewis was equally hostile to such self-destructiveness, writing after the war that "the white races seem almost incurably brutal, and always ready, after the regulation press provocation, to slaughter themselves."[9] Both writers criticized nationalism, imperialism, and materialism; questioned the benefits of democracy; favored natural aristocracies; and urged the transformation of Western civilization. But there the resemblances between them end. Lawrence turned for his vision of cultural rebirth to what he saw as the intuitive, animist view of life expressed in other cultures—principally the "Indians" of New Mexico and the ancient Etruscans—which he counterposed to the sterile, mechanical view of life that supposedly characterized white civilization; colonialism was associated primarily with a conflict between opposed (and racially conceived) modes of consciousness, a position that utilized "primitivism" by locating a lost authenticity in the "being" of nonwhite peoples.[10] Lewis, in contrast, defended the intellectual legacy of what he saw as a still developing "Western" tradition of thought; he viewed the postwar turn to intuitionism as a disintegrative atavism. Colonialism was the expression of European arrogance and its predilection for violence; Lewis thus rejected its racist rhetorics, arguing in favor of a modernism that drew on non-European, antinaturalistic artistic modes.

The disagreements between Lawrence and Lewis turned on opposed conceptions of the self, the aesthetic, and society itself. Lewis held to a fixed notion of species being in which the possibility of human self-overcoming was viewed as a fantasy. Because he insisted on the role of the intelligence in the process of subject-formation, he resisted conceptions of identity that construed it in terms of a self-liberation that would permit some authentic nonrational kernel of being to burst through. This meant that he defended an external aesthetic that stressed clarity and structure, which he opposed to Hellenic naturalism and subjectivist modernism alike. Inasmuch as Lawrence and Lewis invoked "primitivist" discourses, they conceived them completely differently: one defended an intuitionism that informed his mythopoeic art; the other valued antinaturalist canons that supported his insistence on the separation of "art" and "life." These aesthetic disagreements point to significant differences between their readings of Europe's postwar plight. Lewis's invocations of "primitivism" reveal that the artifacts that most influenced him were those he saw as nonorganic. Lawrence, in contrast, sought to transform self and society in quasi-spiritual terms that amounted to a kind of *Aufhebung*, a sublation of outworn categories that would create a new synthesis—the shattering of the old world of conceptual knowledge and materialism would enable a suppressed realm of knowledge and being to emerge. This led him to see in the animism of the "Indians" of New Mexico a corrective to the destructive form of life he identified with Europe.[11] Whereas Lawrence's belief in a transformed and regenerative consciousness was *mystical*, Lewis's attempted reformation of European culture was *practical* in that it sought to develop and to radicalize existing traditions of thought.

⋮ ⋮ ⋮

In the years immediately after the war, Lewis was still hopeful that modernism could play a significant role in forging a new society, whereas Lawrence was already turning away from England and Europe. In early postwar essays, Lewis reasserted his Vorticist credentials, urged the continuation of aesthetic experimentation, and insisted that art should be in the vanguard of social change. For Lewis, the avant-garde art of the prewar years, which had developed in dialogue with non-European traditions, represented the best hope for cultural renewal. Lawrence, in contrast, embarked on the travels that would take him to Italy, Ceylon, Australia, and New Mexico. His letters from this period reveal not only the depth of his anger at what he perceived as the decay of his homeland but also his uncertainty as to the remedy for its sickness. Despite the oft-repeated dreams of creating Rananim—that fantasy of a utopian community somewhere far away—his letters are full of doubts and prevarications: detestation of England, hostility to Europe, and contempt for Western civilization vie with his confusion about viable alternatives to a seemingly universal decline.

From *The Rainbow* (1915) onward, Lawrence was groping toward a form of life in which his version of the dissociation of sensibility might be overcome through a fusion of felt experience with conscious thought. In later works, especially *Fantasia of the Unconscious* (1923), *St Mawr* (1925), and *Mornings in Mexico* (1927), this division is articulated in predominantly racial and historical terms: the development of "white" civilization, in Europe and in America, is associated with Christian-Platonic idealism and the sterility of scientific-industrial "progress," whereas the aboriginal peoples whose ways of life have been overthrown by colonial expansion are seen as the custodians of a visceral knowledge that has barely survived into the modern world. Various essays and letters, as well as elements of *St Mawr*, *The Plumed Serpent* (1926), and *Fantasia of the Unconscious* suggest that Lawrence believed this older mode of consciousness had originally belonged to a variety of "races" and/or civilizations (such as the Celts, Iberians, Aztecs, Druids, Chaldeans, Etruscans, Amerindians, and Chinese), but that its erosion over time had left it in the hands of a few isolated peoples.[12] With its reification of the rhetorics of progress, democracy, and social amelioration, Western modernity had blocked the cycle of destruction-creation in which Lawrence believed and had lost contact with the natural world's "inward vision and its cleaner energy" as it fell into an "Augean stables of metallic filth."[13]

This turn away from the natural creation was a "white" phenomenon, the consequence of industrial-technical advance. Thus in *Women in Love*, Gerald Crich's "plausible ethics of productivity" is denounced by Birkin, for whom modern life "is a blotch of labour, like insects scurrying in filth."[14] Hostility to the nation is a marked feature of *The Rainbow* and *Women in Love*, associated as it is with commercial imperatives, racial rivalries, and proprietary instincts. For Lawrence, "internationalism of the cultured spirit" was no match for such instincts: "Nationalism, as we have it, is established upon *interest:* material interest, commercial interest. . . . Mentally, we are all cosmopolitan nowadays. But passionally, we are all jealous and greedy and rabidly national."[15] Birkin defends an individualism in which truth to the inviolable self takes precedence over social ties, a dream of human autonomy that communicates Lawrence's political skepticism. But inasmuch as Lawrence's critique of national life focuses on social conditions at home, looking to transcend them, it also recognizes the links between these conditions and the country's involvements overseas. Nationalism is rejected not just because it upholds crass materialism and provokes vicious rivalries but because it belongs to a system of thought in which myths of racial superiority express the desire for self-aggrandizement. In *The Rainbow*, Ursula's disavowal of the present-day world follows her rejection of Skrebensky, who is consigned to a dead past associated with the ambiguities of colonial rule. Whereas her initial response to Skrebensky's function as a colonial administrator in India accepts the hierarchical conception upon which imperial rule is based, she later criticizes him as a power-hungry individual who represents corrupt values.[16]

Lawrence refused to consider the modern English nation as a source of value because he believed it was undergoing an inexorable process of decline. Ursula's rejection of Skrebensky's choice of life is motivated by her belief that colonialism is the outward expression of an empty, mechanical society: it exports the nation's degeneracy and corruption abroad. Colonialism is here conceived as a *product* of the metropolitan order itself, and this order is associated with a generalized will to power. But Lawrence does not see any necessary connection between this *Machtkult* and the English character. Whereas Gerald Crich embodies the drive for dominion in its most brutal form, the figure of Egbert in *England, My England* represents a version of Englishness that is located in a premodern past.[17] Egbert's openness to the differences between human beings and his refusal to judge them according to nationality mark him as a character who exists outside the workings of the imperialist mentality. If Gerald's death points to the self-destructive nature of a means-end rationality, then Egbert's death in the First World War shows this rationality in the process of destroying an older set of values. For Lawrence, the continuity between war and imperialism lay in a common lust for political power and material gain, as his account of the Roman empire's destruction of the Etruscans makes clear.[18]

Lewis was no less critical of nationalism and imperialism. He viewed the appeal to nationhood as a sop to the mass-mind, writing that nationality "is a congealing and conventionalizing, a necessary and delightful rest for the many."[19] In *Time and Western Man* (1927), he viewed nationalist rhetorics as politically retrogressive; vilifying "the artificially fostered nationalism rampant throughout the world since the War," he argued that "while *in reality* people become increasingly one nation . . . they *ideologically* grow more aggressively separatist, and conscious of 'nationality.' "[20] Lewis maintained that empire-building had economic gain as its primary objective, although he distinguished between two kinds of imperialism, one in thrall to a desire for conquest and exploitation, the other motivated (at least in principle) by a belief in the viability of trusteeship.[21] He regarded European colonialism as opportunistic, and he saw the white man in his expansionist role as a violent buccaneer and marauder. Theorists of racial or cultural superiority, he pointed out sardonically, had to meet the charge "of having imposed a rotten, materialist civilization upon all sorts of people with great cruelty often, of having wiped out races of very high quality, such as the Indians of North America, in the name of a God who was all compassion."[22] No hierarchical conception of a unified "West" standing over and above a monolithic "East" is articulated in Lewis's thought, as his caustic review of Virginia Mayo's *Mother India* and his angry response to the editors of *transition* make abundantly clear.[23]

If Lewis refused lazy identifications between racial groups and historical achievements, this was because he was conscious of the ideological work performed by the discourses that sustained such oppositions. It was clear to him that racialist rhetorics served nationalist and imperialist interests, which obscured the role played by capital in political economy and international policy and diverted attention from the issue of class. A key argument running through *Paleface* is that the issue of race is used to distract from that of class and that workers in England and America were wage-slaves just as much as workers in the imperial dominions. For Lewis, white racial pride was misplaced not just because it gloried in dominion over others but because it misunderstood the way nationalism falsified the nature of *metropolitan* social relations. No defense of white superiority was implied. *Paleface* assaulted *all* racialist rhetorics, and in contrast to the sociocultural hierarchies such rhetorics upheld, Lewis expressed his belief in "the 'principle of an absolute value in the human person as such,' of whatever race or order" (*P*, 6). Dismissive of white justifications of colonialism and its pretensions to cultural superiority, Lewis wrote mockingly that the "Paleface . . . has fallen so low intellectually, is socially so impotent, and his standards of work and amusement are so mechanical, that he cannot be taken as an ideal by any man" (*P*, 57). Even in *Hitler* (1931), which misread National Socialism so abysmally, Lewis was skeptical about nationalism. Arguing that the Hitler Movement sought to create individuals who are "conscious of *the identity of interest between themselves and their race*," he claimed that "there is no question of the Anglo-saxon [*sic*] ever emulating this 'racialism' of the Germans," a position to which he held throughout his life.[24] What must be remarked, of course, is that although Lewis dismissed Nazi Aryanism as "ethnologically indefensible," he was drawn to National Socialism's stress on concentrating political power, which he mistakenly believed could combat postwar socio-cultural fragmentation.[25]

⁝ ⁝ ⁝

The category of race does, however, play a role in Lawrence's writing. Both *The Rainbow* and *Women in Love* engage with African art in terms that rely on dualist conceptions of culture. Toward the end of *The Rainbow*, Ursula criticizes Skrebensky's decision to go to India, but Lawrence also attributes to Skrebensky an eroticized account of Africa, in which it is associated with darkness, strangeness, blood, sensuality, fecundity, and passion. In language that seems to have strayed across from Conrad's *Heart of Darkness*—the overt sexuality apart—*The Rainbow* contrasts a hollow English society peopled by "performing puppets" (*R*, 449) with a primordial African blackness. Introduced by Skrebensky to the mysteries of a passional sexuality, Ursula is granted a visionary knowledge of her society and its inhabitants that enables her to "see, beneath their pale, wooden pretence of composure and civic purposefulness, the dark stream that contained them all" (*R*, 448). This sexual darkness is opposed to the social mechanism—civic responsibility, public conventions—and it opens up a path that leads Ursula beyond a sensual existence to an entirely different conception of subjectivity. The agency by way of which this personal regeneration takes place is that of a racially troped otherness.

In *Women in Love*, Birkin's search for a sensuality located in an unconscious center of being is opposed to Hermione's intellectual will-to-power and Gerald's mechanical will-to-action. But the novel's engagement with West African statuary suggests ambivalence about the regenerative potential of this art. The wood-carvings in Halliday's flat affect Gerald and Birkin differently; the former equates them with violent sexual desire and struggles to grant them aesthetic value, whereas the latter sees them as the culmination of an artistic tradition devoted to purely physical consciousness. Whereas *The Rainbow*'s "primitivist" discourse presents a generalized "African" sensuality as a form of germinative knowledge, in *Women in Love* it is a dead end. And this shift involves another form of racial othering. Halliday's Hindu manservant appears to have been infected by the mindless physicality associated with the sculptures in Halliday's apartment. With his pidgin English and his borrowed clothes, he appears to Gerald as "half a savage, grinning foolishly" (WL, 73), while Birkin feels "a slight sickness, looking at him, and feeling the slight greyness an ash of corruption, the aristocratic inscrutability of expression a nauseating, bestial stupidity" (WL, 80).

Halliday and his bohemian circle are the targets here, and Jack F. Stewart has plausibly argued that Lawrence is satirizing "the inherent contradictions of self-conscious primitivism" in this scene.[26] But why should he assault this group by way of references to bestiality and sensuality? Reflecting on Halliday's statues, Birkin distinguishes between two modes of consciousness. He thereby establishes a dichotomy that Lawrence was to develop in later works. The contrast in *Women in Love* between the mechanical sterility of "European" life and the visceral physicality of "African" existence has been discussed at length by critics, and most agree that the novel describes two opposed racial-cultural trajectories that are portrayed as equally disintegrative.[27] What has less often been remarked is the way in which both the "Nordic" and the "African" trajectories identified in the text offer reductive readings of complex realities. I hesitate to call them "traditions" or even "civilizations," since in Lawrence's usage they are more like abstractions that essentialize "black" and "white" as two antithetical modes of life, art, and culture. The sculptures referred to in *Women in Love* are described as "African," but it has been suggested that Lawrence may have been referring to Yoruba, Baule, or Bambara artifacts in the "Fetish" chapter and possibly to Temne, Mende, or Baule pieces in the "Moony" chapter.[28] While it is impossible to resolve such questions, what is beyond doubt is that in referring to these sculptures as "African" and then attributing to them an overarching aesthetic and cultural identity, Birkin is not only treating them in a homogeneous fashion but also positioning them as the antithesis of a "northern" European culture that is no less essentialized in this discourse. *Women in Love* works with this opposition to the bitter end. Birkin's rejection of the two paths of dissolution in favor of a third way is predicated on a prior *acceptance* of the terms he has set up and that he endeavors to transcend, but the terms themselves are not called into question. If Halliday's coterie follows the path of blind sensualism, while Gerald follows the path of a frozen negation, then Birkin tries to transcend the Nordico-African binary by advocating an individualism that values autonomy over community and sees relationships in terms of an impersonal balance between starlike selves.

⋮ ⋮ ⋮

The loss of a sense of community in Lawrence's novels is inseparable from the fragmentation they depict; it is a loss that Jessica Berman, following Raymond Williams, more broadly describes as "a key experience of the narratives of modernism."[29] It has long been understood that Lawrence's travels throughout the 1920s combined a desire to escape from an ostensibly dying civilization with a quest for a different modality of being. But this search for an unbroken mode of consciousness involved another strategy: it combined one version of a mythic past with a racially inflected view of consciousness itself. The dissociation of sensibility identified by Lawrence was conceived as a split between "white" and "Indian" forms of life, the "African" sensuality identified in *Women in Love* dropping out of view as the unnecessary third term. This tropical negation—a corrosive, corrupting physicality—is contrasted to the positive sensuousness valued in *The Plumed Serpent* and *Mornings in Mexico*, where it is linked with a lost knowledge that must be recovered.[30]

Why this particular trajectory of thought? Here Lawrence's travels are of significance. Between late 1921 and early 1922 he could not decide whether to go to Ceylon or to America, and he veered between interest in Buddhism and a belief that the regeneration he sought lay in New Mexico. In the event, his brief trip to Ceylon had an enormous impact on him, calling forth a host of negative judgments. He objected to the people, the food, the climate, and the way of life; he associated Ceylon with stagnation and apathy; and he rejected Buddhism on the grounds that the meditative inner life was a form of escapism from the social and cultural problems he wanted to confront. His revulsion came to a head in an extraordinary letter in which he asserted that the "natives are *back* of us—in the living sense *lower* than we are" and that "they're going to swarm over us and suffocate us," a fear that led him to affirm his national loyalty in anxiously defensive language: "But you don't catch me going back on my whiteness and Englishness and myself. English in the teeth of all the world, even in the teeth of England."[31]

New Mexico was the last throw of the dice. Lawrence was so primed for the trip that talismanic invocations of New Mexico appear in his letters from late 1921, and they suggest that his later account of it was colored by deeply felt preconceptions. He wrote, for example: "The Indian, the Aztec, old Mexico—all that fascinates me and has fascinated me for years. *There* is glamour and magic for me."[32] L. D. Clark comments on this attitude that Lawrence "had brought to America with him a gigantic mythic image of the Indians which he had spent years in building and which he was unsure for a while how to test against reality."[33] His first contacts with the Apaches were distinctly uneasy, and it took him some time to come round to the views he would express in *The Plumed Serpent* and *Mornings in Mexico*.[34] And although Lawrence saw the intuitive knowledge possessed by the tribes with which he came into contact as the residue of a once universally held aboriginal knowledge, he began in the 1920s to discuss it in racial terms. In his discussion of Fenimore Cooper's Leatherstocking novels in *Studies in Classic American Literature* (1923), he described aboriginal America as hostile to the "white" psyche; in *The Plumed Serpent* his critique of colonialism focused on the incommensurability of two ways of life, which he depicted in terms of racially opposed modes of consciousness; and in *Mornings in Mexico* he suggested that these two forms of thought were so opposed to one another that they were mutually annihilating.[35]

*The Plumed Serpent* and *Mornings in Mexico* concentrate on the materialism and idealism underlying colonialism, deriding its introduction of a mechanical way of life in the name of supposedly spiritual truths. *The Rainbow* offers a premonition of this critique when it mocks the white "monkey tricks of knowledge or learning or civic deportment" and refers to a "primeval darkness falsified to a social mechanism" (*R*, 448). The European colonists are "conquerors of the moment" who have brought about "a mechanical triumph," a line of argument coterminous with the critique of industrialization made in *Women in Love*, especially in its depiction of Gerald's belief in the "pure instrumentality of mankind" (*WL*, 223).[36] *The*

*Plumed Serpent* and *Mornings in Mexico* favor the metaphor of "monkey tricks" in their accounts of colonialism, a trope that combines genuine contempt for its legacy with a superficial analysis of its effects. Indeed, Lawrence's preoccupation with *consciousness* produces a marked lack of interest in the material consequences of colonial exploitation: everything is folded into a dualistic schema based on opposed modes of being. In *The Plumed Serpent,* "the old mode of consciousness, the old, dark will, the unconcern for death, the subtle, dark consciousness, non-cerebral, but vertebrate" of the "Indians" is associated with the antediluvian world and contrasted with "the mental-spiritual life of white people" that "flourishes like a great weed let loose in virgin soil."[37] This "weed" is in turn associated with externally imposed forms of governance that gain small purchase on the primeval life they seek to control. Ramón's program is apolitical, and his desire to reawaken the Mexican people is couched in organicist terms, while the struggle against the colonizers is imagined as a fight against a mechanical consciousness that is alien to the land and its indigenous people.

This way of thinking about colonialism fitted with Lawrence's sense of what was afflicting Europe. By conceiving the conflict between Mexico and its colonizers as predicated on mutually hostile modes of consciousness, he translated it into the terms that had been gradually structuring his thought since 1915. Just as a mechanical, instrumental approach to life in the metropolis gave rise to loss of contact with the natural world, so this same dominative approach in the Americas produced a surface society beneath which a dark aboriginal life clung on to truths that had once been known to other civilizations. Mark Kinkead-Weekes has argued that Lawrence displays sympathy for the Mexican "Indians," but this in no way contradicts the fact that his interest in them arose from his near obsession with healing the ills of Europe. *The Plumed Serpent* is of course a problematic work in Lawrence's oeuvre, which has been lambasted for its sexual politics, its advocacy of strong leadership, and its self-conscious mythmaking. In a lucid reading of the novel, Michael Bell argues that it should be read as "the supreme aberration, rather than the proper fulfillment, of the Lawrencean metaphysic" precisely "because it has got its mythopoeic religion 'in the head' "—in other words, it enacts the very strategy that had earlier been dismissed as unviable in *Women in Love*.[38] This may be so, but it should still be noted that despite his attempt at imaginative identification with Mexico's postrevolutionary plight, Lawrence focuses above all on educating his white protagonist, who finally realizes that she has all along wanted the fusion between two forms of life. *Her* crisis is *England's* crisis: the lost truths of an intuitionist understanding of life are required to overturn a mechanistic understanding of the world. England, Lawrence wrote, "must be juxtaposed with something that is in the dark volcanic blood of these people" because it "needs a polarity of two."[39]

What did this actually entail? And what, exactly, was Lawrence after? To these awkward questions he gave a number of answers, at times suggesting that the "white" way of life must be overturned, at others urging the viability of a double-consciousness in which the individual would be empowered to see both ways at once, and still at others urging a fusion between the two modes of consciousness he had identified. He appeared to be searching for a felt knowledge in which thought and emotion were reintegrated. He conceived his position as a recapitulation, not a retrogression, and he insisted that it was impossible, still less desirable, to try to go back to the past. Rather, he was urging the relevance to modernity of an animist philosophy against a cerebral view of existence that cut human beings off from the natural world and exalted its subjugation to instrumentalist logics. Nor should this position be understood as an assault on the conscious mind, which he sought to radicalize rather than to destroy. In "Pan in America," he restated his faith in an organic existence in terms that hint at the link in his thought between the critique of means-ends rationality and that of colonialist rapacity.[40]

Lawrence's view of two modes of consciousness associated one with the historical process and located the other in an archaic past. Johannes Fabian has argued that "a discourse employing terms such as primitive, savage . . . does not think, or observe, or critically study, the 'primitive'; it thinks, observes, studies *in terms of* the primitive. *Primitive*, being essentially a temporal concept, is a category, not an object, of Western thought."[41] For Fabian, discourses of "primitivism" are allochronic. They deny coevalness between the enunciating subject and the object of study and are oriented toward the enunciating subject, in that their concern with the "other" derives from a desire to overcome a sense of crisis associated with the metropolis. With respect to these issues, they cannot be disentangled from colonialist assumptions, however sympathetic or laudatory their accounts of other peoples might be. Although Lawrence turned to "Indians" in order to portray their culture as a source of value, his homogenizing language viewed that culture in terms of a unified worldview, presented it as an object to be surveyed, and depicted it as the antithesis to a decadent "white" culture. Lawrence's "Indians" of New Mexico seem to exist primarily as the means by which a *European* crisis may be articulated. This strategy instantiates a reductive binary and upholds a cultural hierarchy which deploys a metropolitan concept of alterity—Fabian's "primitive" as a category of Western thought—that is itself a product of European dominance. Even Lawrence's cosmopolitanism is a consequence of this dominance, for inasmuch as his traveling signals his dissatisfaction with the metropolis it also discloses the center's (and his) material power; *pace* James Clifford, the peons whose blood-consciousness he valorized were not much in evidence on the streets of London.[42]

⋮ ⋮ ⋮

Lewis's critique of Lawrence in *Paleface* might be described as a strong misreading, although given that he focused on *Mornings in Mexico*—in which Lawrence is uncompromising about the fundamental incompatibility between "white" and "Indian" modes of consciousness—the misreading was not a willful one. Lewis pushed what he took to be the logic of Lawrence's position to an extreme in order to expose its underlying sentimentalism and its racially motivated version of "primitivism." *Paleface* also derided white European and American abjection, arguing that a key cultural consequence of the First World War was an exoticism that rejected everything in a now despised civilization in order to seek redemption elsewhere, and he saw this exoticism as part of a wider "primitivism" that embraced Bergsonian thought, modernist subjectivism, and art movements such as Dada and Surrealism. Lewis prosecuted his case against this "primitivism" across various works in the 1920s, concentrating his fire in *Paleface* on those who were giving it a racial twist. But while he continued to proclaim his allegiance to a tradition he would later describe as a "wide, well-lit graeco-roman highway," he rejected unitary conceptions of it and extolled the cultural legacy of various non-European societies.[43] Seeking to inscribe an otherness he coded as "Eastern" into a "West" whose borders the likes of Massis and Spengler wished to patrol, Lewis articulated a theory of cultural belatedness in which the "West" was portrayed as a backward latecomer. Thus he claimed in *Time and Western Man* that modernist art "looks novel because it is attempting to get back to standards or forms that are very ancient, and hence strange to the European," and in response to the objection that its artifacts were "asiatic" he remarked that the real trouble with them "is in reality the opposite to that—namely, that they are not asiatic enough" (*TWM*, 24).

Useful though this is as a corrective to European cultural arrogance, it nonetheless advocates a problematic "Oriental" classicism, which may not be articulated in racial terms but still deploys a rather static East/West binary. *Paleface*, moreover, was concerned with contemporary America. What, then, of another tradition—that of the Harlem Renaissance? It is apparent that although Lewis came out in favor of the "melting-pot" (the book's subtitle) and condemned racial intolerance, he identified black American culture principally with propagandist writing on the race question and with jazz, finding little of worth in either. He absolutely failed to understand jazz (which he construed as the expression of a despised cult of sensation) and he was hostile to all propagandist art in principle. Opposed to all hierarchical views of race, Lewis argued that propagandist, consciousness-raising books were trapped by the very hierarchies they sought to overthrow; they enacted "the mere reversal of a superiority—a change in *colour*, nothing more—rather than its total abolition" (*P*, 41). In the 1920s, he saw little of value in the Harlem Renaissance. It was not until *America and Cosmic Man* (1948) that he would write: "American civilization as we know it owes more, probably, to the Negro than to anybody. The coloured people are the artistic leaven; out of their outcast state they have made a splendid cultural instrument."[44]

Lewis's and Lawrence's focus on the imperative of cultural renewal forced them to rethink Europe's relations with a variety of colonial "others," a process that led them to reject nationalist rhetorics and to develop new sustaining myths. In both cases, appeals to "primitivism" played a role, but these appeals differed in terms of their respective conceptions of the "primitive" and the uses to which it should be put in the course of revivifying European society. And if Lawrence exaggerated the flaws of European civilization and overpraised the alternative existential path represented by the "Indians" of New Mexico, then Lewis exaggerated the value of European civilization and was overly critical of those, like Lawrence, who sought to overcome its instrumentality by advocating what Bell describes as a "holistic metaphysic."[45] If "primitivism" is a category of Western thought that is elaborated in terms of antecedent intellectual assumptions and cultural imperatives, then Lawrence's and Lewis's opposed deployments of this category reveal two different conceptions of the postwar European crisis and of the direction modernist art should take in response to it. There are many ways of troping this difference—Apollonian/Dionysian, conscious/unconscious, mind/heart—and it is useful up to a point to note that Lewis and Lawrence fall on either side of such divides. Thus in contrast to Lawrence's claim that "our belief, our metaphysic is wearing woefully thin" and that there is "no future; neither for our hopes nor our aims nor our art" (*FU*, 15–16), Lewis split open the concept of "the West" in order to extend and radicalize it. By emphasizing its irreducibility to race, place, or *Geist*, he sought not only to define what Benedict Anderson describes as an "imagined community" but also to construe this community as an internally fissured and incomplete entity.[46] To Lawrence the "Western" tradition was a finished tradition, which needed to pass away before it could be regenerated; his critique sought to dismantle its prevailing assumptions and to advocate a more sensuous apprehension of the world. Lewis contended that the disengaged stance offered the best means of articulating an emancipatory knowledge and creating a value-conferring art. Yet while Lawrence did not live to witness the Second World War, for Lewis it laid to rest the faith he had once had in this concept, leaving him to welcome its demise: "I am glad the *coup de grâce* has been delivered—by itself, to itself. Western Europe, bankrupt, if possible more confused than ever, broken and apathetic, awaits the coming of the next phase. . . . No one in 1947 would be likely to give a thought to 'Western Man.' How hollow a ring the two words have, with their ironical capitals!"[47]

## Notes

1 See Koebner and Schmidt, *Imperialism*.

2 Faber, *The Vision and the Need*.

3 Eldridge, *England's Mission*, 254.

4 Bolt, "Race and the Victorians," 146.

5 Massis, "Defence of the West," 229 and 231; Spengler, *Decline of the West*, 16.

6 GoGwilt, *The Invention of the West*, 1.

7 Said, *Orientalism*, 333 and 347.

8 See Ahmad, *In Theory*, and Clifford, *The Predicament of Culture*.

9 Lewis, *The Art of Being Ruled*, 54.

10 For a useful discussion of the problematic nature of the collective term "Indians," see Mark Kinkead-Weekes, "Decolonising Imagination: Lawrence in the 1920s," in *The Cambridge Companion to D. H. Lawrence*, ed. Fernihough, 83 n. 7.

11 See "Pan in America," "America, Listen to Your Own," "Indians and an En-

glishman," and "New Mexico" in D. H. Lawrence, *Phoenix: The Posthumous Papers of D. H. Lawrence*, vol. 1, ed. Edward D. McDonald (London: William Heinemann, 1936).

12 See Lawrence, *Fantasia of the Unconscious* (Harmondsworth: Penguin, 1974), 11–16. Hereafter cited parenthetically in the main body of the text as *FU*. For more on these issues, see Clark, "D. H. Lawrence and the American Indian," and Keith Brown, "Welsh Red Indians: Lawrence and *St Mawr*" in Brown, ed., *Rethinking Lawrence*, 23–37.

13 Lawrence, *St Mawr*, 160.

14 Lawrence, *Women in Love*, ed. David Farmer, Lindeth Vasey, and John Worthen (Harmondsworth: Penguin, 1995), 55. Hereafter cited parenthetically in the text as *WL*.

15 Lawrence, *Letters*, vol. 3, 679.

16 Lawrence, *The Rainbow* (Harmondsworth: Penguin, 1979), 462. Hereafter cited parenthetically in the the text as *R*.

17 D. H. Lawrence, *England, My England*, 32.

18 See Lawrence, *Etruscan Places*, 31 and 88. For an account of Lawrence's anti-imperialist aesthetics, see Fernihough, *D. H. Lawrence*, 170–86.

19 Lewis, *Blast 2*, 72.

20 Lewis, *Time and Western Man*, ed. Paul Edwards (Santa Rosa: Black Sparrow Press, 1993), 78. Hereafter cited parenthetically in the text as *TWM*.

21 Lewis, *The Hitler Cult*, 169–75 and *The Mysterious Mr Bull*, 238–47.

22 Lewis, *Paleface: The Philosophy of the "Melting Pot"* (London: Chatto and Windus, 1929), 69. Hereafter cited parenthetically in the text as *P*.

23 Lewis, *The Enemy*, 3, 17.

24 Lewis, *Hitler*, 5, 64, and 85. See also Wyndham Lewis, *Anglosaxony: A League that Works* (Toronto: Ryerson, 1941), and Wyndham Lewis, *America and Cosmic Man* (London: Nicholson and Watson, 1948), 154.

25 Lewis, *Hitler*, 143.

26 Stewart, "Primitivism in *Women in Love*," 50.

27 See Chamberlain, "Pussum, Minette, and the Afro-Nordic Symbol in Lawrence's *Women in Love*," 415, and Morris, "African Sculpture Symbols in *Women in Love*," 28.

28 Morris, "African Sculpture Symbols," 26–27, and Lawrence, *Women in Love*, 541 and 548.

29 Berman, *Modernist Fiction, Cosmopolitanism, and the Politics of Community*, 2.

30 Lawrence, *The Letters of D. H. Lawrence*, vol. 4, 157.

31 Ibid., 234.

32 Ibid., 125.

33 Clark, "D. H. Lawrence and the American Indian," 320.

34 See Lawrence, "Indians and an Englishman" in *Phoenix*, vol. 1, 95–96. Lawrence's ambivalence is discussed in Clark, "D. H. Lawrence and the American Indian," and Kinkead-Weekes, "Decolonising Imagination."

35 Lawrence, *Studies in Classic American Literature*, 56–57; *The Plumed Serpent*, 431; *Mornings in Mexico*, 85–88.
36 Lawrence, *Mornings*, 148 and 149.
37 Lawrence, *Plumed Serpent*, 431.
38 Bell, *D. H. Lawrence*, 206.
39 Lawrence, *Letters*, vol. 4, 522.
40 Lawrence, *Phoenix*, vol. 1, 31.
41 Fabian, *Time and the Other*, 18.
42 Clifford has argued against the view that "certain classes of people are cosmopolitan (travelers) while the rest are local (natives)," suggesting that this is "the ideology of one (very powerful) traveling culture." See "Travelling Cultures," 108. My aim here is to emphasize the role that power and wealth play in who can travel and how far they may do so.
43 Lewis, *Rude Assignment*, 207.
44 Lewis, *America and Cosmic Man*, 186.
45 Bell, *D. H. Lawrence*, 166.
46 Anderson, *Imagined Communities*.
47 Lewis, *Rude Assignment*, 207.

## Works Cited

Ahmad, Aijaz. *In Theory: Classes, Nations, Literatures*. London: Verso, 1994.

Anderson, Benedict. *Imagined Communities: Reflections on the Origin and Spread of Nationalism*. London: Verso, 1991.

Bell, Michael. *D. H. Lawrence: Language and Being*. Cambridge: Cambridge University Press, 1992.

Berman, Jessica. *Modernist Fiction, Cosmopolitanism, and the Politics of Community*. Cambridge: Cambridge University Press, 2001.

Bolt, Christine. "Race and the Victorians." In *British Imperialism in the Nineteenth Century*, ed. C. C. Eldridge, 126-47. London: Macmillan, 1984.

Brown, Keith, ed. *Rethinking Lawrence*. Milton Keynes: Open University Press, 1990.

Chamberlain, Robert L. "Pussum, Minette, and the Adro-Nordic Symbol in Lawrence's *Women in Love*." *PMLA* 78 (1963): 407–16.

Clark, L. D. "D. H. Lawrence and the American Indian." *D. H. Lawrence Review* 9.1 (Spring 1976): 305–73.

Clifford, James. "Travelling Cultures." In *Cultural Studies*, ed. Lawrence Grossberg, Cary Nelson, and Paula A. Treichler. London: Routledge, 1992: 96-112.

Cromer, Earl. *Ancient and Modern Imperialism*. London: John Murray, 1910.

Doherty, Gerald. "White Mythologies: D. H. Lawrence and the Deconstructive Turn." *Criticism* 29.4 (Fall 1987): 477–86.

Eldridge, C. C. *England's Mission: The Imperial Idea in the Age of Gladstone and Disraeli, 1868–1880*. London: Macmillan, 1973.

Faber, Richard. *The Vision and the Need: Late Victorian Imperialist Aims*. London: Faber and Faber, 1966.

Fabian, Johannes. *Time and the Other: How Anthropology Makes its Object*. New York: Columbia University Press, 1983.

Fernihough, Anne. *D. H. Lawrence: Aesthetics and Ideology*. Oxford: Clarendon Press, 1993.

——, ed. *The Cambridge Companion to D. H. Lawrence*. Cambridge: Cambridge University Press, 2001.

GoGwilt, Christopher. *The Invention of the West: Joseph Conrad and the Double-Mapping of Europe and Empire*. Stanford, Calif.: Stanford University Press, 1995.

Haegert, John. "Lawrence's *St. Mawr* and the De-Creation of America." *Criticism* 34.1 (Winter 1992): 75–98.

Koebner, Richard, and Helmut Dan Schmidt. *Imperialism: The Story and Significance of a Political Word, 1840–1960*. Cambridge: Cambridge University Press, 1964.

Lawrence, D. H. *The Rainbow* (1915). Harmondsworth: Penguin, 1979.

——. *Women in Love* (1920). Edited by David Farmer, Lindeth Vasey, and John Worthen. Harmondsworth: Penguin, 1995.

——. *England, My England* (1922). Harmondsworth: Penguin, 1985.

——. *Studies in Classic American Literature* (1923). Harmondsworth: Penguin, 1977.

——. *Fantasia of the Unconscious* (1923). Harmondsworth: Penguin, 1974.

——. *St Mawr* (1925). Harmondsworth: Penguin, 1981.

——. *The Plumed Serpent* (1926). Harmondsworth: Penguin, 1966.

——. *Mornings in Mexico* (1927). London: William Heinemann, 1950.

——. *Etruscan Places* (1932). London: Martin Secker, 1932.

——. *The Letters of D. H. Lawrence*. Vol. 3 (October 1916–June 1921). Edited by James T. Boulton and Andrew Robertson. Cambridge: Cambridge University Press, 1984.

——. *The Letters of D. H. Lawrence*. Vol. 4 (June 1921–March 1924). Edited by Warren Roberts, James T. Boulton, and Elizabeth Mansfield. Cambridge: Cambridge University Press, 1987.

Lawson Walton, J. "Imperialism." *Contemporary Review* 75 (1899): 305–310.

Lewis, Wyndham, ed. *Blast* 1 (1914). Santa Barbara: Black Sparrow Press, 1981.

——, ed. *Blast* 2 (1915). Santa Barbara: Black Sparrow Press, 1981.

——. *The Art of Being Ruled* (1925). Edited by Reed Way Dasenbrock. Santa Rosa: Black Sparrow Press, 1989.

——. *Time and Western Man* (1927). Edited by Paul Edwards. Santa Rosa: Black Sparrow Press, 1993.

——. *The Enemy* 3 (1929). Edited by David Peters Corbett. Santa Rosa: Black Sparrow Press, 1994.

——. *Paleface: The Philosophy of the "Melting-Pot."* London: Chatto and Windus, 1929.

——. *Hitler.* London: Chatto and Windus, 1931.

——. *Men without Art* (1934). Edited by Seamus Cooney. Santa Rosa: Black Sparrow Press, 1987.

——. *The Mysterious Mr Bull.* London: Robert Hale, 1938.

——. *The Hitler Cult.* London: J. M. Dent, 1939.

——. *Anglosaxony: A League that Works.* Toronto: Ryerson, 1941.

——. *America and Cosmic Man.* London: Nicholson and Watson, 1948.

——. *Rude Assignment: An Intellectual Autobiography* (1950). Edited by Toby Foshay. Santa Barbara: Black Sparrow Press, 1984.

Massis, Henri. "Defence of the West 1." Translated by F. S. Flint. *New Criterion* 4.2 (April 1926): 224–43.

——. "Defence of the West 2." Translated by F. S. Flint. *New Criterion* 4.3 (June 1926): 476–93.

Morris, Inez R. "African Sculpture Symbols in *Women in Love.*" *D. H. Lawrence Review* 16.1 (Spring 1983): 25–44.

Pinkney, Tony. *D. H. Lawrence.* Hemel Hempstead: Harvester Wheatsheaf, 1990.

Said, Edward. *Orientalism: Western Conceptions of the Orient.* Harmondsworth: Penguin, 1995.

Seeley, J. R. *The Expansion of England: Two Courses of Lectures.* London: Macmillan, 1885.

Stewart, Jack F. "Primitivism in *Women in Love.*" *D. H. Lawrence Review* 13.1 (Spring 1980): 41–62.

*Vincent Sherry*

⋮

FIVE

# T. S. Eliot, Late Empire, and Decadence

From "King Bolo" to "Apeneck Sweeney": these two cartoon images might be taken to constitute the range of T. S. Eliot's imaginative understanding of colonized peoples.[1] Pictures of caricature primitives—a West Indies tribal chieftan mocked by his roly-poly name, a simian Irishman—manifest the vantage—the arrogance—of a British empire still sufficiently well-established in Eliot's sensibility, it may be supposed, to authorize the attitudes expressed here. With the sort of rough retributive justice the authors of *The Empire Writes Back* promise in their title, then, Eliot appears in their account . . . well, hardly at all. He is written out of this foundational work of postcolonial literary studies as he is dismissed, in quick passing, as an American who remakes himself wholly in the image of the imperial power—or who is, simply, unwilling to retaliate against that power.[2] Their censure is underwritten by the fact that the major phases of his writing life antedated the main events in the late process of decolonization, which culminated in the 1940s and 1950s. But if the postcolonial temperament rightly identifies, not the historical location of the poet, but an interpretive stance for the critic, Eliot's work may submit usefully to consideration within a framework of analysis that is freed from any presumptive understanding of the ideological rights of empire. In this approach, the imperial construction of geopolitical history may be taken as an establishing fact for Eliot's literary imagination. The poet's negotiations with this formative circumstance reveal far more, indeed, than the cartoon truisms a *Punch*-like critical kit uses to reduce complex circumstances to ready formulations.

The status and fate of the imperial project in the high moment of Eliot's literary activity in Britain—between 1914 and, say, the early 1940s—provided a determining awareness for this work.[3] While the Great War of 1914–18 was not identified, like the Boer War, with the specific interests and aims of empire, the global dimensions of this first world war included action in theaters relevant to old and new colonial domains. Rationales for the war included a heavy measure of argument about the need to maintain hegemony across a world-imperial compass, contesting again the question of German or British control over the channels of commercial traffic in their mercantile empires.[4] Given the massive scale of casualties in this first mass war, no degree of Victorian optimism could turn the Allied "victory" in November 1918 into a new writ of legitimacy or restored warrant of authority for British interests of any far-reaching kind. Global ownership in an old imperial program was a shaken framework of expectation.

This end-of-empire-days feeling finds an intense literary witness in Eliot's own lengthened end-of-the-war moment. He registers this sense of late imperial time with a complexity that signals the depth to which his poetic imagination has been penetrated by this historical condition, and that makes his work of this moment a chapter worth rehearsing for literary history. Here, he turns the ready conventions of elegy to an individually expressive use—with a special density of poetic presentiment, as we will see, and an exceptional measure of verse invention. His imaginative engagement with the declining fortunes of British imperial history in these years is also accompanied by his growing preoccupation with the possibilities of a poetic stance associated originally, if distantly, with the fall of another empire, the Roman: Decadence. How Eliot extends this tradition in literary history—through the models of a specifically English decadence, which flourished, if that is the word, in the mid-late nineteenth century, that is, in the incipient moment of British imperial decline—is the critical story I wish to lead to and finish on here.[5] For Eliot, the import of the fall is proportionate to the values he has invested in empire, and so this consideration of his lengthy and complex engagement with its decay may begin with an account of his specially idealized construction of the imperial project.

⁝ ⁝ ⁝

Writing as late as 1951, in "Virgil and the Christian World," Eliot reclaims an "ideal" of Roman civilization from the "reality" of its quotidian life, which, he readily concedes, was "coarse and beastly": "Virgil made of Roman civilization in his poetry something better than it really was."[6] This improvement is a function specifically of the imperial ideal, as embodied most notably in the imaginative plan of the *Aeneid*. "There, Virgil is concerned with the *imperium romanum*, with the extension and justification of imperial rule. He set an ideal for Rome, and for empire in general, which was never realized in history; but the ideal of empire as Virgil sees it is a noble one."[7] This concession to the discrepancy between the "ideal of empire" and its actual "history" calls for help elsewhere in the essay, and Eliot specifies "*labor*, *pietas*, and *fatum*"—work, devotion, and a sense of destiny—as the tonic and resolving qualities, a set of practicable values.[8] While these principles are given additional validity in being so long-lived, and are consistent with the "Christian World" of his present and particular interest, it is important to note that the trumping validation for Virgil's imperial ethos comes instead from a nondenominational quarter. What gives a controlling and organizing value to the admittedly miscellaneous elements of that imperial program is "an attitude towards all these things," specifically, a vantage, a capacity to see "a *unity* and an order among them" (emphasis mine).[9]

This propensity is the same faculty he raises to equal importance in an essay he wrote more than thirty years earlier, in 1919, in his appreciation of the "Romantic Aristocrat," George Wyndham. He cites Wyndham's various activities, some of work in service to empire, which included "a campaign in Egypt . . . service in South Africa accompanied by a copy of Virgil . . . a career in the Commons, a conspicuous career as Irish Secretary. Finally, there was a career as a landowner—2400 acres." Eliot then claims that these "apparently unrelated occupations" make sense in view of the special "*unity* of Wyndham's mind."[10] But in what particular or explicit terms is this "unity" understood by Eliot? After all, Wyndham appears in this piece as the sheerest amalgam of assigned roles and stylized impulses, which Eliot elsewhere brings under the tenuously generic heading of "this peculiar English type": as "the aristocrat, the Imperialist, the Romantic riding to hounds across his prose, looking with wonder upon the world as upon a fairyland."[11] This sense of "fairyland" is a coordinate of considerable force in the sensibility Eliot understands as Wyndham's. And when "fairyland" is seen realistically and specifically as the previously unknown regions of the globe, the various personae Wyndham projects into that dimension may be formed in accord with a single trajectory—an imperial conquest of the exotic. In fact, the ideal or ideology of empire dominates Eliot's understanding of Wyndham's importance, and this element in his interest can be seen as salient as he turns to Wyndham's Egyptian exhibition. The point of imaginative attraction on Eliot's part lies apparently in the "romantic" aspect of this travel narrative, represented here as a vehicle of self-realization, but this adventure evidences its full import for Eliot through the comparisons it discovers with the legendary precedents of several empires, Roman as well as British, Augustan, and Elizabethan:

> He was chivalrous, the world was an adventure of himself. It is characteristic that on embarking as a subaltern for Egypt he wrote enthusiastically:
>
> > *I do not suppose that any expedition since the days of Roman governors of provinces has started with such magnificence; we might have been Antony going to Egypt in a purple-sailed galley.*
>
> This is precisely the spirit which animates his appreciation of the Elizabethans and of Walter Scott; which guides him towards Hakluyt [Elizabethan cartographer] and North. Wyndham was enthusiastic, he was a Romantic, he was an Imperialist.[12]

The buccaneering wonder that Eliot attributes to this outward-bound voyager is supported strongly then by the charter rights of empire, which not only authorize an attitude to the world but, for Eliot, precede and provide for Wyndham's single, main orientation toward it. The *unity* Eliot esteems as Virgil's imperial genius thus appears also in this earlier homage, but more obviously as his added emphasis, as he uses the imperial orientation to unify Wyndham's multifarious life and idealize—at least, *romanticize*—it.

This ideal of unity locates a point of attraction in an imperial imaginary. This value suggests a regimen of authority coextensive with the regulated domains of empire. In Eliot's case, however, this quality of formal order speaks most clearly to the appeal the imperial scheme exerted for him in the circumstances of his own first exposure to it as a historical reality—not in the (ex)colonial America of the turn of the century but, beginning in late August 1914, in Britain, chiefly in London. He begins to inhabit the capital of world-empire at the moment it is being most strenuously contested as a center of reference, equally strategically and ideologically. Strategically, there is the steadily worsening circumstance of the Continental war, which extends to conditions in Ireland. Ideologically, the values of a specifically British "Civilisation"—formerly, the standard and rationale for imperial expansion—are being challenged not only by the unprecedented atrocities of this military conflict but also in the propaganda campaigns with German *Kultur*, a discourse to which Eliot's recent residence in Germany has alerted and opened him. In this circumstance, understandably, the ideals of empire are to equal degrees jeopardized and prized, so that, as the threat to their former hegemony escalates, so the intensity of his imaginative attraction to them may also rise. It is in terms of this double rhythm, each side lifting and reinforcing the other, that the major work of Eliot's first post-American phase reveals one of its integral establishing patterns.

In this story, a signal position may be taken by an incident in Eliot's biography on March 19, 1917: his taking up employment in the "Colonial and Foreign Department" of Lloyd's Bank in London. After a nearly three-year-long dry period, which had begun roughly on his arrival in England, the move to Lloyd's coincided with a revival of his ability to compose poetry. Already on April 11, 1917, he can write to his mother: "Then too I have felt more creative lately . . . I have been doing some writing—mostly in French, curiously enough it has taken me that way—and some poems in French will come out in the *Little Review* in Chicago ["Le Directeur," "Mélange Adultère de tout," "Lune de Miel," and "The Hippopotamus" appeared there in July]."[13] A subsequent rush of productivity is chronicled for Eliot's mother only nineteen days later by Vivien, who attributes the extraordinary activity she records to the happy circumstance in the bank: "not one of his friends has failed to see, and to remark upon, the great change in Tom's health, appearance, spirits, and literary productiveness since he went in for Banking. . . . No one could be more surprised than I am. . . . Only when he began to be more bright and happy and boyish than I've known him to be for nearly two years, did *I* feel convinced—and only when he has written *five*, most *excellent* poems in the course of one week, did Ezra Pound and many others, believe it possible."[14] The surge of work that Vivien references here includes the specific initiative of Eliot's quatrain art. This is a verse experiment he will extend over the next two years as a sustaining form of poetic activity, one whose development features some of the major titles we will read here, and whose brisk rhythms and witty rhymes seem to evidence the energy she identifies in palpable prosodic qualities.

The creative strength of these days echoes to a rising sense of excitement about his work at Lloyd's, where his sense of personal agency appears proportionate indeed to the ranging domain of his own "Colonial and Foreign

Department." "Lloyd's is one of the banks with largest foreign connections, and I am busy tabulating balance-sheets of foreign banks to see how they are prospering. My ideal is *to know the assets and liabilities (of every bank abroad that Lloyd's deals with)* for ten years past!"[15] "The man who taught me my job has gone on his holiday, and I have *full control* over it now. *All the money* coming in . . . *passes through my hands*. The foreign work is I believe the most interesting part of banking, especially at the present time, when one can from time to time *see very big things happening*."[16] While Eliot's personal work, which involved translation and asset and account tabulation for those various colonial and foreign banks, occurred at a level of somewhat limited consequence, his sphere of influence was steadily increasing. And if he was but a "cog in the machine of Britain's commercial empire," as Peter Ackroyd characterizes his position,[17] the machine itself obviously swept him up and augmented his sense of himself. The occasional grandiosity of personal power in his report scales it all the more accurately (if fantastically) to the order and proportion his "*Colonial* and Foreign Department" invokes through its title, which denominates not only a worldwide range of activity but an imperial orientation toward it. This is a global economy on which the capital city establishes the vantage—to Eliot's own advantage.

The point of this observation goes to an understanding of Eliot's feeling of literary empowerment in these years. He connects his cresting recognition as a man of letters to his mounting power at Lloyd's, implicitly but irresistibly, in a lengthy letter to his mother on March 29, 1919. "They are organising some new work," he begins, "a new department, in fact, of a very interesting and important kind," one whose global dimension measures the import of his own role in it: "There is a man from the Foreign Office coming in too," Eliot makes a point of noting, and his own work "will be on a large scale, with numerous assistants."[18] He proceeds then to a review of his situation as a writer, which moves to an assertion of the place he claims in literary London, indeed, in Anglo-American literary history: "I really think that I have far more influence on English letters than any other American has ever had, unless it be Henry James."[19] At this moment, Eliot's published writing adds up to one slim volume of verse, some poems appearing subsequently in periodicals, a bunch of occasional essays, and a somewhat desultory number of reviews. While he has earned considerable repute, the acclaim is less than a year old, and if his influence is registered intensely where it is felt, it is confined mainly to a microclimate of cognoscenti—hardly the sort of "bigger picture" of literary history to which the importance of a Henry James is scaled. In the rhetorical economy of the letter, however, the authority Eliot enjoys at Lloyd's is being carried over into his poetic account, and this transaction manifests more than simple wishfulness.

Consider the transatlantic dimension of reference in this last letter. The influence Eliot has earned in the "Colonial and Foreign Department" at Lloyd's, at the financial capital and emblematic center of empire, is completed in plot and complemented in motive as the (former) colonial poet comes to London. Here he gains the authority—presumably, the authenticity—which it is the (former) power's special capacity to confer. "[F]or an American," he confides to his mother in July 1920, "getting recognised in English letters is like breaking open a safe."[20] The trove in which Eliot images the literary distinction England now yields to him certainly suggests the reference of Lloyd's Bank. Further, it hints at the status he attaches silently to that institution a year earlier, when, in effect, his position as imperial financier, fantasized or not, underwrites and legitimates the power with which this American poet in Britain endows himself. No small work in service for—and by—the empire he idealizes thus.

⋮ ⋮ ⋮

Eliot's investment in this enterprise of empire shows most of its imaginative value and literary interest, however, in the poetic uses he makes of its undoing. For the assurance he draws from this structure of authority is balanced, in fact overbalanced, by an awareness of its declining condition in contemporary history. The falling away of an imperial domain is recorded in the most important poems Eliot wrote between 1917 and 1920, which register in particular the effect of the war—and the attendant situation in Ireland—on the former order of empire. The difference the war makes is crucial in this respect. It makes historically real the fall of an imperial ideal. In doing so, it makes empire available substantially for poetry in the way Eliot's discursive prose suggests it can best—or only—be availed of. For the imperial imaginary is always fallen in the application of actual history: his essay on Kipling, as well as the one on Virgil, makes this major point.[21] And so the reign of empire appears most representatively in his poetry of this first postwar moment as a record of incomplete realizations, or compromised ideals, or foregone authority, that is, elegiacally.

Consider the majestic cadenza at the end of "Sweeney Among the Nightingales":

The host with someone indistinct
Converses at the door apart,
The nightingales are singing near
The Convent of the Sacred Heart,

And sang within the bloody wood
When Agamemnon cried aloud,
And let their liquid siftings fall
To stain the stiff dishonoured shroud. (*CP*, 50)

The galloping octosyllabic that Eliot has established as the mastering pace in the quatrain stanza of these years is modified here. These perfectly iambic tetrameter lines create and maintain a sense of processional solemnity; the cadence goes strong but also strange and fateful as the atmospheric feeling lifts recognizably into the sublime—the beauty of the wooded prospect, lit synesthetically with the incandescent precipitate of the nightingale song, mingles with the terror evidenced in the memory of Agamemnon's violent demise. Yet the plentitude of feeling that is released in these final lines does not find a sufficient cause in the single appearance of the hero in this last stanza.

This reference echoes back to the epigraph to the poem, which presents, in Greek, the death-cry of the tragic protagonist in Aeschylus's *Agamemnon*. This answering pattern is established in order to feature a comprehensive parallel in the poem between Agamemnon, as the hero returning from the Trojan War to the murderous plot of his wife Clytemnestra, and Sweeney, who, surrounded in the seedy bistro of contemporary London by a mélange of menacing females, appears also as a soldier, heroic or not, who has come back from his own war. The striking sign of the "zebra stripes along his jaw" (*CP*, 49) may be taken as one more detail in the bestiary of animal comparisons for Sweeney, but these lines can also be seen to depict the creases of fat cut into his neck by the tight, stiff collar of the military dress uniforms that were worn at this time. (In 1974, Marshall McLuhan told me that Eliot had said to him that the original for Sweeney was an Irish-Canadian airman, billeted in London during the war.) Agamemnon, as the returning warrior of the Trojan campaign, provides type and model for Sweeney, a soldier taking his own precariously relaxing leave from duty in France. Whether or not Sweeney is a diminished Agamemnon (he is), the occasion of the Great War opens as surely as that figure of mythic antiquity into the dimensions and potentials of the heroic elegy. The expansive imaginative range here, the epic perspective in the last stanza, can be scaled to a magnitude of feeling all too available to Eliot from his present location. No small sense of loss attends the perception that Britain's Great War for Civilization is being fought—and lost—by this representative of the empire's unevolved, now insurgent, colony.

One indication of the critical difference the war makes in the imaginative understanding and representation of a late imperial history may be found in comparing this poem to its companion piece, "Sweeney Erect." The most evident point of resemblance between the title figures lies in their simian familiarity, the condition Eliot attributes all too predictably to these colonized primitives: "Apeneck Sweeney" looks familiarly across to his mate's—the Irish primate's—"Gesture of orang-outang" (*CP*, 34). No reference to the present war can be pressured out of "Sweeney Erect," however. The absence shows as a considerable difference in the range and quality of feeling, especially in the closural motion of this poem. Here, as in "Sweeney Among the Nightingales," the coordinate conjunction that Eliot places as the first word of the last stanza marks a kind of final pivot, a signal that some comprehensive or intensive "last turn" is being taken—or attempted:

> The ladies of the corridor
>     Find themselves involved, disgraced,
> Call witness to their principles
>     And deprecate the lack of taste
>
> Observing that hysteria
>     Might easily be misunderstood;
> Mrs. Turner intimates
>     It does the house no sort of good.
>
> But Doris, toweled from the bath,
>     Enters padding on broad feet,
> Bringing sal volatile
>     And a glass of brandy neat. (*CP*, 35)

The mechanical regularity that the quatrain style features as the effect of its heavily stressed rhymes and equally emphatic meters certainly strengthens the hand of the caricaturist, who drafts a sort of stanza-by-stanza, comic strip depiction of these ridiculous automaton figures. Such headlong measures are intercepted in "Sweeney Among the Nightingales," however, where the range of imaginative reference includes the contemporary event of the war. The change of cadence there, which admits a wholly different order of feeling, is indeed a rhythmical synonym for the dying fall of an older order of empire.

This sense of downturn in imperial fortunes in the current war also locates a moment of powerful feeling in "A Cooking Egg." The significance of this instance may be emphasized again by the break it makes from the regular cadence of Eliot's quatrain art, which is strongly evidenced here. His hurdy-gurdy rhymes and rigmarole rhythms project the dominant voice of this poem as a sort of know-nothing, know-it-all, popular gossip, as ludicrous as he is (playfully) pretentious in his references:

I shall not want Honour in Heaven
   For I shall meet Sir Philip Sidney
And have talk with Coriolanus
   And other heroes of that kidney.

I shall not want Capital in Heaven
   For I shall meet Sir Alfred Mond.
We two shall lie together, lapt
   In a five per cent. Exchequer Bond. (*CP*, 36)

This caricature-in-voice is interrupted and significantly inflected as the poem turns toward conclusion:

But where is the penny world I bought
   To eat with Pipit behind the screen?
The red-eyed scavengers are creeping
   From Kentish Town and Golder's Green;

Where are the eagles and the trumpets?

   Buried beneath some snow-deep Alps.
Over buttered scones and crumpets
   Weeping, weeping multitudes
Droop in a hundred A. B. C.'s. (*CP*, 37)

"The nightingales are singing near / The Convent of the Sacred Heart" is matched, rhythmically and even grammatically, by "The red-eyed scavengers are creeping / From Kentish Town and Golder's Green." And the change of cadence in the next verse here, the line breaking the quatrain pattern, marks a difference in aesthetic emotion that matches the shift in the finale to "Sweeney Among the Nightingales." The intensification in "A Cooking Egg" includes, too, an allusion to present conditions in the Great War, the first mass war. Its human cost is scaled to the proportion of these "[w]eeping, weeping multitudes" and imaged in the pathos of its conscripted masses' typical lives, in the figures of the "buttered scones and crumpets" that are served in a hundred public canteens, those Allied Baking Companies. This frame of war reference is sustained as projected from the earlier mention of "Sir Alfred Mond" and the "five per cent. Exchequer Bond," where this minister in the war cabinet is linked, from his former career as wealthy financier, with the instruments used to fund the war.

The softly sardonic comedy in the rhyming of "crumpets" and "trumpets" includes an ironically protected perception of the relation between these two figures: between the common food of the cannon fodder and the insignia of the imperial imaginary, "the eagles and the trumpets" of a Roman *triumphus*. This pair of images reappears—"You can see some eagles. / And hear the trumpets"—in Eliot's later (1932) poem, "Coriolan: Triumphal March" (*CP*, 125); that rite of the Roman empire, a procession of treasure and captives through the capital city, provides the fancied parallel for the regalia of a modern military parade in Eliot's poem. But the rhetorical form in which these emblems emerge in "A Cooking Egg" provides for their special import here. The rhetorical question addresses its appeal in Eliot's own version of the *ubi sunt* lament, that is, elegiacally. It is as a foregone source of order and authority that this memory and legend of the Roman triumphal march exerts its particular poetic power, which is measured, indeed, in its distance, its *ir*relevance—in the poor, bare, *un*accommodated lives of these somber conscripts in the mass army of the new empire. And if Eliot can experience the imperial episteme really only as a fallen or compromised ideal, he comes back again (and again) to the war as the event that establishes his relation to empire as *materia poetica*—that is, as a subject for the most intense moments of his quatrain art, for sublimity, for elegy.

⁝ ⁝ ⁝

Beyond elegy? The "little old man" who is the title character and speaker of "Gerontion" suggests an extended dimension of poetic resource in the overture to this poem. He stakes a now familiar situation, the end-of-empire-days feeling that the war marks, in references that bring legendary history into his own historical present:

Here I am, an old man in a dry month,
Being read to by a boy, waiting for rain.
I was neither at the hot gates
Nor fought in the warm rain
Nor knee deep in the salt marsh, heaving a cutlass,
Bitten by flies, fought.
My house is a decayed house . . . (*CP*, 29)

The "hot gates" allude to the Battle of Thermopylae (*thermo-pylae*, hot gates) in the Persian Wars, an event that marks a climacteric in the history of the Persian empire and that the speaker appropriates, accordingly, as the scene of his own challenge and crisis in the most recent imperial war. He is a member of the generation too old by 1914 to have fought in that campaign, which was characterized critically, insistently, increasingly, as a war of the old against the young, an antagonism which generated an extensive literary representation.[22] The elderly condition of the figures of the political and military establishment was used to characterize the status of their enterprise, where the lack of physical vitality was matched by an absence of moral authority, of credible rationale. If this circumstance accounts for the speaker's self-presentation entirely in negative terms, using the conjunctions "neither . . . nor . . . nor" to hinge his various *dis*abilities, it also locates diminishment as a general or systemic condition. "My house is a *decayed house.*" Given the representativeness of this speaker's identity, the "house" that is "decayed" is more than an individual's dwelling. This is the "house of England," not necessarily the *royal house*, which would play too heavy-handed an irony against the manifest depravity of the speaker's circumstances, but most certainly a comprehensive, national habitation. And where the speaker characterizes himself subsequently as a "*dull head* among windy spaces" (*CP*, 29), Eliot presents him, metonymically, as the *tired capital* of England, more suggestively, of the British empire. This is a suggestion he confirms in "Coriolan," a poem that functions, among other things, as a kind of clarifying retro-echo in 1932 on the first postwar poems' historical moment. His speaker engages here in a historical fantasy that places him among his loftier forebears, in a gallery of imperial busts: "I a tired head among these heads" (*CP*, 128). Those several references in 1919 serve then to locate "Gerontion" in geopolitical space and historical time as a moment of late empire in which the sense of extensive decay is concentrated in its political and cultural capital. A likely site for a New Decadence.

The Latin meaning at the root of this English word—de*cad*ere, "to *fall* away"—preserves a memory that helps to bridge some of the evident differences between its iterations in literary history, most notably, in the late phases of Roman and British *imperia.* A premonition of manifold collapse—in political mores, in cultural practice—is a prevailing awareness in the imagination of the Latin poets and, in his own moment and place, of Eliot, who references this apprehension to the failing imperial state of his particular time. The long fall of British imperial fortunes begins of course in the previous century. Victoria's reign, even as it marked a high point in global domain, located the moment of imminent downturn. This perception was not reserved for later ages. This condition was a matter of ready (if suppressed) recognition, and it afforded the circumstance of a decadence that was specifically English and at the same time highly conscious of its historical precedents. The literary sensibilities of Pater and Swinburne reached back to comparable circumstances in late antiquity, and a prescient memory of imminent ends entered the whole range of their imaginative activity as writers.[23] For notable instance, they "buried" their English in the crypt of its classical roots and cognates. In this elaboration of the "dead language" factor in their imaginative vocabularies, the English Decadents drafted a sort of memento mori for their own literary language and its supporting historical institutions, which included a British empire now in its own incipient decline.

The literary product of this sensibility lies far to the side of the work which an Anglo-American poetic modernism might be expected to foster—at least by the standards and values of its own nascent day in the second decade of the century. A Latinate vocabulary like that seems hardly compatible with the caution Pound uttered in his admonitory "Go in fear of abstractions," or with the aims enshrined in phrases like "Direct treatment of the thing."[24] Just so, however, the negative incentive the poetics of decadence might be taken to enclose also identifies and measures the strength of this countervailing circumstance—the present state of empire, the recognition of which will compel Eliot as well as Pound into alignment with these otherwise unlikely models. Pound's surprise lies in his *Homage to Sextus Propertius*, where, in the guise of exact translation, he recovers and indulges the Latinity of his own modern English, often in a prosodic comedy of strangling polysyllabics. This is sport with historical import, however. Pound's anachronisms and transhistorical references establish the parallel he perceives between his own moment in 1917–18 Britain and that of his title figure, a poet of Rome's waning imperial age.[25] Eliot's engagement with the circumstance he shares with Pound shows not only in a comparable prosody in some of the quatrain poems, as we will see, but also in his essays on Swinburne, where he reveals an appeal in the otherwise negative precedents of decadence.

"Swinburne as Poet" (1919) is an extraordinary performance in divided judgment, which extends to the essay's final sentence. It begins, typically, antithetically: "But the language which is more important to us is that which is struggling to digest and express new objects, new groups of objects, new feelings, new aspects, as, for instance, the prose of Mr. James Joyce or the earlier Conrad."[26] The neorealism in those "earlier" iterations of modernism identifies a root value that is also a radical character for the movement. Speaking for "us," that is, as representative of the movement now, Eliot needs to frame his assertion of this principle here at the end with a conjunction that concedes that it has not been strenuously (enough) asserted. Indeed, it is the effect (if not the intent) of the essay to bring those original and now established standards of literary modernism into adjustment, specifically, to justify their inclusion of values and practices of which Swinburne is the salient example. "[T]he words which we use to state our grounds of dislike or indifference cannot be applied to Swinburne as they can to bad poetry," Eliot opens this negotiation; he then specifies the issues on which he is willing to trade: "You may say 'diffuse.' But the diffuseness is essential. . . . His diffuseness is one of his glories. That so little material as appears to be employed in *The Triumph of Time* should release such an amazing amount of words, requires what there is no reason to call anything but genius."[27] The exceptional complexity in the syntax of this last sentence suggests the strain under which its gesture of recognition is being made.

This resistance registers all the more strongly the import of the concession he makes, and repeats, now in a passage that links this verbal excess in Swinburne with "morbidity"—a word that denominates a quality essential to this poet's *decadence:*

> The morbidity is not of human feeling but of language. Language in a healthy state presents the object, is so close to the object that the two are identified.
>
> They are identified in the verse of Swinburne solely because the object has ceased to exist, because the meaning is merely the hallucination of meaning, because language, uprooted, has adapted itself to an independent life of atmospheric nourishment. . . . Only a man of genius could dwell so exclusively and consistently among words as Swinburne. His language is not, like the language of bad poetry, dead. It is very much alive, with this singular life of its own.[28]

The sort of sickly vigor that Eliot identifies in these last sentences is of course a hallmark quality of decadent art, but, as appreciated in this description, it also locates a point of strong imaginative attraction on his part. He is expressing, in fact, the quickening wit of his own application of decadent poetics—in a counter-modernist-revolutionary turn whose evidence in verse may further our understanding of its historical content and depth, its decisive timeliness. For the great welter of events intervening between the circumstances of an "earlier" modernism and 1919 has revealed the lateness of this imperial age and so made the poetics of decadence more comprehensible, more applicable.

Thus:

> Polyphiloprogenitive
> The sapient sutlers of the Lord
> Drift across the window-panes.
> In the beginning was the Word.
>
> In the beginning was the Word.
> Superfetation of τὸ ἕν,
> And at the mensual turn of time
> Produced enervate Origen. (*CP*, 47)

Eliot's first word, which out-Paters Swinburne in its polysyllabic patter, proceeds to no Poundian rectification of names, no modernist clarity or visuality. Eliot enhances its opacity with an ultra-Decadent lexicon, offering a rarefied diction ("sapient," "sutlers") and archaic grammar (using "enervate" as an adjective), not to speak of the unspeakable Greek. But does the reader risk too much in considering seriously what appears to be comic—even pompously comic—nonsense?

It may be proposed, of course, that this poem is sheer *performance:* "Mr. Eliot's Sunday Morning *Service*." Such an understanding is reinforced with knowledge of the conditions under which it was written. One of the first pieces to emerge out of the recovery that began with Eliot's employment at Lloyd's, its truest imaginative project may be just to prove that he can do it—quatrain by quatrain. The *kind* of text he chooses to perform is nonetheless important, an index of the pressures converging on him from political and literary history. And where he features the stock-in-(verbal) trade of English literary decadence in the overture to the poem, he extends this sensibility as a center of awareness through the next several stanzas. These quatrains present a consideration of motifs of sin and forgiveness, in figures of original innocence and penitential regeneration. These are themes that the practices of artistic decadence often prompt as reactionary response. "Polyphiloprogenitive," it is thus interesting to note, finds one of its very rare appearances (in slightly shortened form) in literary English in the writing of Robert Buchanan, otherwise the author of "The Fleshly School of Poetry," a strongly moralistic diatribe against the practice of "decadent" verse by Rossetti.[29] No, the verbal surface of Eliot's poem does not present a record of consistent dialectical deliberation; it presents instead a register of the several impulses Eliot finds he can stylize to the four-line measure—impulses such as this jump from the poetics of decadence to its ready ethical redress. Even—or especially—through the superficial discontinuities of the one-quatrain-at-a-time performance standard, then, his engagement with decadence reveals the significance of persistence.

The most surprising turn in this series is the one that comes in the final stanza:

> Sweeney shifts from ham to ham
> Stirring the water in his bath.
> The masters of the subtle schools
> Are controversial, polymath. (CP, 48)

Where the "masters of the *subtle* schools" echo knowingly to those "sapient *sutlers* of the Lord" in the opening quatrain, and the poem's last word begins with the same Greek prefix as the first, this rite of verbal answer and closure returns to the overture of the poem as an orienting framework for this conclusion. Here the sudden, otherwise utterly unlikely appearance of "Sweeney" makes strong sense—in connection with the conditions underlying the dialect of decadence that Eliot inscribes in those first quatrains. The Irish caricature is not only broad, it is also "subtle"—Paddy's pig provides the basis for the wordplay in representing the character's hams, the parts to which he is reduced—and the intensity as well as the inventiveness show in ratio, arguably, to the threat his countrymen currently represent: the Easter Rising of 1916 has crested to a steady state of insurgency in that increasingly volatile colony. The apprehension of an empire unraveling at the extremities is intensified daily with reports from the theaters of war, near and far. And this presentiment of a waning imperial age underwrites, provides a contemporary relevance and (in its own way) authenticity, for the lexicon of Eliot's new decadence in the overture to which this conclusion answers.

A primary site of cultural decadence provides the location of "Burbank with a Baedeker: Bleistein with a Cigar," which features equally an end-of-empire feeling. Situated in Venice, this poem is ghosted with the memory, the material legacy, the decaying splendor that is this city's perennial identity. Museum of the booty its marine imperial power accumulated over previous centuries, Venice is seen ever to be sinking into the coastal plane that sustains its riches so unreliably, so emblematically: it presents an image at once of the grandeur of imperial domain and the precariousness, the transiency, of that status. To those potential associations Eliot's closing quatrain does customary but full justice, citing the icon of St. Mark's lion as the image of temporal devastation, of a glory already fallen, always foregone:

> Who clipped the lion's wings
> 　　And flea'd his rump and pared his claws?
> Thought Burbank, meditating on
> 　　Time's ruins, and the seven laws. (*CP*, 33)

These "seven laws" make reference probably to *The Seven Lamps of Architecture*, where Ruskin enumerates the "laws" of moral order in public construction, in general, and in Venice, in particular. Here, as in *The Stones of Venice*, the image of "ruins," "Time's" and tides' but also of "laws," that is, of ethical as well as temporal and material degeneration, holds the controlling focus. Yet the feeling in Eliot's final stanza draws on sources closer, and so deeper, than those afforded by the site of Venetian decline—imperial, architectural, or civic. Ruskin's own motives in *The Stones of Venice* included a wish to turn the story of its fall into a cautionary tale for England as a maritime imperial power.[30] And it is an apprehension of the present state of the British empire that precedes Eliot's poem and accounts for its depth of imaginative feeling, as an inquiry into one of its formative circumstances may reveal.

On November 10, 1918, Eliot corresponded with his English friend Douglas Goldring. This novelist and travel-writer had published a critique of the Irish literary revival, *Dublin: Explorations and Reflections of an Englishman*, which singled out for criticism one of the more conspicuous spokespersons of that movement, Ernest Boyd. Boyd retaliated with a review of Goldring's book in the Dublin weekly, *New Ireland*, on May 19, 1917, "Broadbent's Baedeker," which prompted a riposte from Goldring, "On the Importance of Being Ernest," which stirred a further rejoinder from Boyd, "A Boy of the Bulldog Breed."[31] Boyd accused Goldring, in effect, of cultural imperialism, an attitude that scants any capacity in Irish writers to author themselves in a fashion independent of the benefices of the literary capital of London. In his November letter to Goldring, Eliot refers to "the cuttings from *New Ireland*" and positions himself thus in relation to the exchange: "my opinions nearly coincide with yours,"[32] which, when expressed in "On the Importance of Being Ernest," presented a subironic tolerance, a patronizing and ultimately dismissive assessment of the political ambitions of Irish literary culture. Whatever difference Eliot's "nearly" might admit, the relevance of this exchange to "Burbank with a Baedeker: Bleistein with a Cigar" includes the obvious prominence of the "Baedeker" reference in the title, the conspicuous alliteration of "b"s, and the clear agreement with the English position on the issues of substance here. The Irish Question presents an essential reference for Eliot's poem and turns its representation of decadence in Venice toward this most local context and timely point. The decline over time of the Venetian marine-mercantile empire provides a shadow plot for parallel processes in British imperial history, which have eventuated in the regrettable developments of the Continental war as well as Ireland—a twofold story invoked elsewhere in the single figure of "Sweeney."

The figure of "Burbank" provides an identifiably British reference for the lessons of decadence that the Venice setting demonstrates. This patronym tags an English character as the protagonist of the fall that Eliot records in the opening quatrain—

> Burbank crossed a little bridge
> Descending at a small hotel;
> Princess Volupine arrived,
> They were together, and he fell,

—and ceremonializes in the second stanza:

> Defunctive music under sea
> Passed seaward with the passing bell
> Slowly: the God Hercules
> Had left him, that had loved him well. (CP, 32)

The reference to the abandonment of Burbank by Hercules seems a little odd, given the otherwise undistinguished nature of Eliot's character, but the allusion assumes some coherence once Burbank is understood as a figure in a poetic fiction of imperial decline. Eliot is echoing Shakespeare's representation of the god's desertion of Antony, an event coincident in the play with his imminent defeat at Actium:[33] this battle marks a decisive turn in Roman history—all in all, the end of the Roman Republic and the beginning (of the end) of the Roman empire. Shakespeare is otherwise clearly in play in this quatrain, which opens with an echo of "The Phoenix and the Turtle":

> Let the priest in surplice white
> That defunctive music can,
> Be the death-divining swan,
> Lest the requiem lack his right.[34]

Eliot complements this liturgical feeling in the repetition with variation of "Passed" and "passing," of "Had left him" and "had loved him well." And if the requiem Eliot offers his fallen Burbank seems at least a little wrong, given the discrepancy between the dimensionality of the event—by "a *little* bridge," in "a *small* hotel"—and the grandiosity of the mythic parallels, this oversizing once again identifies and measures the general or representative status of the Burbank character. A level of feeling is being generated out of the legends of this fall that is equal in degree and kind to the national scale of this protagonist, to the more than nominal Englishness of "Burbank." And this dimension represents a potential of feeling he realizes in the next stanza, where the formal order of a near state-occasion turns around the event of his "passing," his fall:

> The horses, under the axletree
>     Beat up the dawn from Istria
> With even feet. Her shuttered barge
>     Burned on the water all the day. (*CP*, 32)

The "even feet" of Eliot's meter provide for his own processional pace, which is complemented and further solemnized by the cosmic quality of the imaginative prospect here.

The frame of reference that Eliot establishes for the "passing" of Burbank in the first three stanzas, then, provides for the extended temporal perspective in the final quatrain. Here, we can now see more clearly, Eliot turns a Ruskinian meditation on Venetian time into a sort of off-angle gloss on his own English moment, which the Goldring correspondence recalls as the waning state of the British empire. Outwardly Venetian, inwardly English, this location shows its emotional proximity and poetic productivity for Eliot as he deploys the diction and tropes of literary decadence in one summary instance. "A meagre, blue-nailed, phthisic hand" goes his notation for one of the high-end denizens of Venice, "Princess Volupine" (*CP*, 33). The outlandishly rare and recherché (and unpronounceable) adjective—"phthisic" means "decay"—provides the ultimate judgment of this topos of material-social decay and the last word of English decadent poetics.[35]

If late imperial time is essentially the moment of literary decadence, it extends in the twentieth century to the era of modernism—as a New Decadence. Eliot (and Pound and Lewis and Joyce) will at once find and contest their identity in relation to the precedent group of Swinburne and Pater, Rossetti and Wilde. And the developing situation of the empire presents a circumstance in which the poetics and ethics of early modernism, to the degree that these may be understood as uniform, make some historical sense. The global framework of colonial holdings presents a condition, a sort of real-time model, for the modernist concept of a world literature, one in which the various ethnic and linguistic traditions speak in the one imaginative language (of their own literary English). Most important, the challenge and test the historical order of empire underwent through the (long) turn of the century help to establish the idea of cultural centrism and abiding tradition as the embattled and dramatic center of attention that it is in the modernist program.

Consider, in this regard, in the signature work of modernist cultural preservation, in the restoration quest that is one of the poetic plots in Eliot's *The Waste Land*, the importance accorded to the declining imperial state. There is the epigraph in the original manuscript from Conrad's *Heart of Darkness*, where Kurtz's "The horror! The horror!"[36]—uttered at the limit and verge of commercial empire—bespeaks the end and failure of the imperial project, all in all, of Western meliorism and rationalism. There is the body of the drowned Phoenician sailor, an image circulating through the text as one more memento mori on the aims and ambitions of maritime empire. The reference to the naval battle at Mylae near the end of "The Burial of the Dead" (70) invokes another moment of reversal and downturn in imperial fortunes, once again of Phoenicia, while the phantasmagoric prospect in "What the Thunder Said," of "hooded hordes swarming / Over endless plains" (369–70) in Europe and across the Mediterranean, irresistibly recalls a late imperial day in Roman history. Early and late days in the maritime empire of Britain are imaged as the context and point of a contrast pattern in "The Fire Sermon": the Thames is depicted in its current condition, in which the "river sweats / Oil and tar" (266–67), then in the young time, the sap years of marine imperial reign, through the allusion to Elizabeth and her ceremonial vessel on the "brisk swell" (284) of a sea-borne tide. These several references to the lifecycle and fate of empire's domain crest to a present climacteric and crisis in the opening scene of "A Game of Chess" (77–96), where allusions to Cleopatra and Dido summon the female figures who play so important a role, being linked to Antony and Aeneas, in the last and first turns of Roman imperial history. In this chambered space the atmospheric prospect belongs decisively, overwhelmingly, to a late imperial phase: a room loaded with stuff, artistic or not, is choked with the sheer material surfeit and clot that the references to Cleopatra and Dido may identify as the spoils of empire, here as empire spoiled. The elegies Eliot has written to empire, whether to fading ideal or failing ideology, are scripted in any case to the special sense we may stress in his joint identity as modern*ist* de*cad*ent: as a writer whose *preoccupation* with his own moment in modern time includes in its framework of greatest emotional resonance the experience of a *fall* from a former order, one which he maps to the signs of decline in the British empire.

## Notes

1 Most of the "Bolo" poems, circulated privately in Eliot's lifetime, are gathered in *T. S. Eliot, Inventions of the March Hare*, 315–21. These poems feature sexual-scatological fantasies through this figure of the colonized primitive, who is usually seen in relation to "Columbo," namesake and type of the European colonizer. The one comprehensive study of these pieces is by McIntyre, "An Unexpected Beginning." "Sweeney Among the Nightingales" (1918), *T. S. Eliot, Collected Poems 1909–1962* (1963; reprint, New York: Harcourt Brace, 1991), 49. Quotations from Eliot's poetry are from this edition and will be referenced parenthetically as *CP*.

2 See Ashcroft, Griffiths, and Tiffin, *The Empire Writes Back*, 4.

3 For a discussion of Eliot and empire, see David Trotter, "Modernism and Empire: Reading *The Waste Land*," *Critical Quarterly* 28.1–2 (1986): 143–53.

4 A comprehensive account of (French, German, and Russian as well as British) imperial aims and the developing military and political conditions of the war is provided by Kanya-Forstner, "The War, Imperialism, and Decolonization," esp. 232–33, 236–38, 239, 247–50.

5 For a discussion of modernism and degeneration in relation to empire, see Rod Edmond, "Home and Away: Degeneration in Imperialist and Modernist Discourse," in *Modernism and Empire*, ed. Howard J. Booth and Nigel Rigby (Manchester: Manchester University Press, 2000), 39–63.

6 Eliot, "Virgil and the Christian World" (1951), in *On Poetry and Poets*, 124–25.

7 Ibid., 126.

8 Ibid., 125.

9 Ibid., 127.

10 "A Romantic Aristocrat" was included as a section in "Imperfect Critics" (1919), which was gathered in *The Sacred Wood* (1920); in *The Sacred Wood and Major Early Essays*, 15.

11 Ibid., 16.

12 Ibid.

13 *The Letters of T. S. Eliot*, vol. 1, 175.

14 Ibid., 177–78.

15 Eliot to Charlotte Eliot Smith, March 21, 1917, *Letters*, 165–66.

16 Eliot to his father, June 13, 1917, *Letters*, 184.

17 Ackroyd, *T. S. Eliot*, 79.

18 *Letters*, 279–80.

19 Ibid., 280.

20 Ibid., 392.

21 "Rudyard Kipling" (1941), in *On Poetry and Poets*, 245: "his view of empire," for which Eliot's respect is evident, is "a view which expands and contracts at the same time. He had always been far from uncritical of the defects and wrongs of the British Empire, but held a firm belief in what it should and might be."

22 In the war lyrics of Ezra Pound's *Hugh Selwyn Mauberley* (1920), for instance, in *Personae*, 188: "Died some, pro patria, / non 'dulce' non 'et decor' . . . / walked eye-deep in hell / believing in old men's lies."

23 A good account of these political and historical conditions and the answering practice of nineteenth-century English decadents comes from Dowling, *Language and Decadence in the Victorian Fin de Siècle*, esp. "Romantic Philology and Victorian Civilization," 3–45, "The Decay of Literature," 46–103, and "The Fatal Book," 104–74.

24 Ezra Pound, "A Few Don'ts by an Imagiste" (March 1913), *Ezra Pound's Poetry and Prose*, 120; "Imagisme" (March 1913), ibid., 119.

25 In *Personae*, 205–25, e.g., 217, "The time is come, the air heaves in torridity, / The dry earth pants against the canicular heat," and 223: "Upon the Actian marshes Virgil is Phoebus' chief of police, / He can tabulate Caesar's great ships."

26 Eliot, "Swinburne as Poet" (1919), *The Sacred Wood*, 87.

27 Ibid., 84–85.

28 Ibid., 87.

29 Buchanan's phrase, "divine philoprogenitiveness," is cited for rebuke by Matthew Arnold in *Culture and Anarchy*, 191. See Buchanan's *The Fleshly School of Poetry and Other Phenomena of the Day*, e.g., "Mr. Dante Gabriel Rossetti," 33–55.

30 This caution is given explicitly by Ruskin in the opening paragraph, *The Stones of Venice*, vol. 1, 15; see also *The Seven Lamps of Architecture*.

31 Boyd, "Broadbent's Baedeker"; Goldring (signed "Broadbent"), "On the Importance of Being Ernest"; Boyd, "A Boy of the Bulldog Breed."

32 *Letters*, 253.

33 *Antony and Cleopatra*, 4.3.16–17; in *Shakespeare: The Complete Works*, ed. Hardison.

34 "The Phoenix and the Turtle," 13–16; in *Shakespeare: The Complete Works*.

35 The purity or sublimity of feeling that Eliot provides through the figure of "Burbank" contrasts notably, of course, with the invidiousness of his anti-Semitic view on "Bleistein," and in the tribal familiars Eliot stigmatizes with the sound-alike syllables of Volup*ine* and Kl*ein*. A similar pattern of contrast is manifest in "Gerontion." The "decayed house" of this speaker's England, which presents all the potential for poetic sentiment that we recognize from the decadent setting in Venice, features also "the Jew." As "the owner," moreover, this Semitic figure assumes responsibility for a condition he typifies at its worst, at the lower animal level, as he "squats on the window sill" (*CP*, 29). These dual decadences may be taken as opposite but complementary expressions of a single condition, one which reveals the full historicity of Eliot's attitudes and practices. The end-of-empire-days feeling generates a fashioning of lofty poetic language, whether this is the idiom of conventional elegy or the special idiolect of English decadence. These same dire circumstances also prompt a reactionary need to explain, to fix blame. In a typical fiction, given new currency in the first

postwar moments, Eliot's "Jew" appears as the usual suspect. This Semitic figure emerges at once as the emblem and the agent of decay, being understood as the source of the degeneration from which he also profits. For the development of anti-Semitism in Britain in the years during and just after the war, see Redman, *Ezra Pound and Italian Fascism*, 41–44.

36 *The Waste Land: A Facsimile of the Original Drafts*, 3. Other quotations from *The Waste Land* are to *Collected Poems*, here by line number.

## Works Cited

Ackroyd, Peter. *T. S. Eliot: A Life*. New York: Simon and Schuster, 1984.

Arnold, Matthew. *Culture and Anarchy*. Edited by J. Dover Wilson. Cambridge: Cambridge University Press, 1932; reprint, 1969.

Ashcroft, Bill, Gareth Griffiths, and Helen Tiffin. *The Empire Writes Back: Theory and Practice in Post-Colonial Literatures*. London: Routledge, 1989.

Boyd, Ernest A. "A Boy of the Bulldog Breed." *New Ireland*, June 2, 1917, 62–63.

——. "Broadbent's Baedeker." *New Ireland*, May 19, 1917, 24–25.

Buchanan, Robert. *The Fleshly School of Poetry and Other Phenomena of the Day*. London: Strahan, 1872.

Dowling, Linda. *Language and Decadence in the Victorian Fin de Siècle*. Princeton, N.J.: Princeton University Press, 1986; reprint, 1989.

Eliot, T. S. *The Letters of T. S. Eliot*. Vol. 1 (1898–1922). Edited by Valerie Eliot. London: Faber, 1988.

——. *On Poetry and Poets*. London: Faber, 1957; reprint, 1971.

——. *The Sacred Wood and Major Early Essays*. Mineola, N.Y.: Dover Publications, 1998.

——. *T. S. Eliot, Collected Poems, 1909–1962*. New York: Harcourt Brace, 1963; reprint, 1991.

——. *T. S. Eliot, Inventions of the March Hare: Poems, 1909–1917*. Edited by Christopher Ricks. New York: Harcourt Brace, 1997.

——. *The Waste Land: A Facsimile of the Original Drafts Including the Annotations of Ezra Pound*. Edited by Valerie Eliot. New York: Harcourt Brace Jovanovich, 1971.

Goldring, Douglas ("Broadbent"). "On the Importance of Being Ernest." *New Ireland*, May 26, 1917, 49–50.

Kanya-Forstner, A. S. "The War, Imperialism, and Decolonization." In *The Great War and the Twentieth Century*, ed. Jay Winter, Geoffrey Parker, and Mary R. Habeck, 231–62. New Haven, Conn.: Yale University Press, 2000.

McIntyre, Gabrielle. "An Unexpected Beginning: Sex, Race, and History in T. S. Eliot's Columbo and Bolo Poems." *Modernism / Modernity* 9.2 (2002): 283–301.

Pound, Ezra. *Ezra Pound's Poetry and Prose: Contributions to Periodicals*. Edited by Lea Baechler, A. Walton Litz, and James Longenbach. Vol. 1. New York: Garland, 1991.

——. *Personae: The Shorter Poems of Ezra Pound*, rev. ed. Edited by Lea Baechler and A. Walton Litz. New York: New Directions, 1926; reprint, 1990.

Redman, Tim. *Ezra Pound and Italian Fascism*. New York: Cambridge University Press, 1991.

Ruskin, John. *The Seven Lamps of Architecture* (1849). Reprint, Boston: Estes, 1900.

——. *The Stones of Venice* (1851). 3 vols. Reprint, Boston: Estes, 1899.

Shakespeare, William. *Shakespeare: The Complete Works*. Edited by G. B. Hardison. New York: Harcourt, Brace, and World, 1952.

*Brian May*

⋮

SIX

# Romancing the Stump: Modernism and Colonialism in Forster's *A Passage to India*

Influential postcolonial critics—most notably Edward Said and Sara Suleri—have described *A Passage to India* as an essentially colonialist, even imperialist, text.[1] Focusing on disparate aspects of the novel ranging from what have been characterized as politically patronizing and sexually exploitative representations of the human other, on the one hand, to mystifying, often nullifying descriptions of *nonhuman* Indian flora, fauna, and fields—not to mention caves—on the other, postcolonialism has been apt to see *Passage* as just another "paranoid response of . . . Orientalists."[2] It is somewhat unjust to reduce Suleri's nuances to such a formula, since her reading is among the most detailed, comprehensive, and persuasive of the more political considerations. Yet two of her basic claims may be said to undergird much of what has been alleged of India's "material world" and are therefore worthy of close attention:[3] first, that the Indian landscape or its "topography" or "geography" in *Passage* is entirely "symbolic," failing to "suggest [the] 'natural' "; second, that this landscape often signifies existential lack or a "hollow symbolic space."[4] Indian particularities and substantialities, wholly troped as they are, are but tropes of "emptiness," "irrationality," "ineffability," "inauthenticity," "terrifying docility," "engulfing unreliability"; India itself is a vast exotic "figure," an "image of profound unreality."[5]

Both of these claims are challenged in what follows. I argue that Forster's India largely frustrates symbolism while permitting, here and there, a chastened and subdued impressionism, which emerges as a potential, if only partially explored, avenue to the self-critical and the anti-ethnocentric. By way of what I call the "bathetic mode," which follows upon the disappointment of symbolist and impressionist expectations, India offers an indeed "natural," even preternatural, presence. This presence may manifest itself as solid object or substantial locale, salt of the earth or "[f]lesh of the sun's flesh" (literally), some essential, elemental thing that subsists beyond the vulgarly Orientalist and primitivist gaze, though not finally free from a subtler mode of romantic imperialist idealization.[6] At the same time, I contend that the hollowing- or "scour[ing]-out" (208) of the Indian landscape that Suleri deems exoticist and colonialist signifies, to the contrary, the anti-exoticist, the anticolonialist. Indeed, Forster's frequent depiction of India as "hollow" rescues it from that insidious imperialist idealism or "elementalism" approached by way of its naturalization, a mode resulting when the landscape has been rendered so obdurately solid that it becomes identified with a preternatural, aboriginal substantiality. Forster, in other words, conceives of India according to a complex dialectic, one that registers the land's material otherness, occasionally imbuing it with a sense of the primordial, at the same time that it resists this motive radically, even apocalyptically.

My ambition, then, is to offer a more nuanced and complicated account of Forster's politics of colonial representation. But just as central is my intention to place this account in the larger context of Forster's modernism and thereby to approach the question of how English modernism and British colonialism consort. As I will argue, the three competing modes of putatively imperialist representation at work in *A Passage to India*, the trio that I will distinguish and whose conflictual relationships I will examine—impressionism, elementalism, apocalyptism—are significantly "modernist" modes of representation. To distinguish these modes as such, and to identify the kinds of work that they do, severally and together, is to begin to redefine the relationship between modernism and colonialism as intricate and conflicted. And, certainly, this is a worthy task, given how often the complexities in this relationship have been overlooked.

Most especially I hope to add to the growing body of "new modernist" studies whose aim has been to achieve a more inclusive and expansive view of this most significant of twentieth-century movements in literature and culture. If the complexities constituting modernism-and-colonialism have sometimes been invisible, so, clearly, have been the internal complexities characterizing modernism itself, modernism considered as a political episode.[7] As I will argue, *A Passage to India* well exemplifies the capacity of modernism to constitute itself as ideological self-critique. As I mention above, *Passage* in the end proves critical not just of an obviously romantic and Orientalist symbolism but also of its own equally suspect alternative, a radically realist, indeed *modernist,* elementalism. In doing so it betokens a potential that may be found in modernism, and one that is explored not just in my own pages in this volume but also in those that precede and follow.

⁝ ⁝ ⁝

How symbolic, after all, *is* Forster's India? What Parry describes as its "polysemous symbolic resonances" sustained until fairly recently a celebratory tradition devoted to "explain[ing *Passage*] as mythopoeic and wholly detached from history," a judgment of the book also promoted by more recent and censorious critics eager to attach it to history, explaining it (away, some would say) as just "another exercise in Orientalism."[8] The humanists and the postcolonialists agree—it's a symbolic novel, perhaps even a "symbolist" one.[9] But just how substantial are its symbols and its symbolism? Study of the novel's putatively symbolic episodes reveals, I will argue, the wisdom in Parry's equivocal diction of mere "resonances."[10] The resonances come across as true "echoes," authentic symbolic episodes, only when, retreating from Forster's material India, we attain the "suitable distances" required to make the Marabar "look romantic" (126), something that may require a trek to the moon (100).

In short, there is a conflict in *Passage* between symbol and substance, between spirit and matter, mystery and muddle, and it is a conflict at which the narrator points, even when gazing (over Mrs. Moore's shoulder) upon the moon's "radiance," a radiance that stands upon the Ganges "like a luminous sheaf upon the fields of darkness" (32). For the narrator, for whom the appearance of the Indian landscape is almost always a sensitive register of circumambient vicissitudes, the typical "fields" are scarcely so poetic. They are just fields. And fields, disappointingly, usually are all we have. India is not a place of distinct symbolic presences in "definite outline" (100); even the outline of the luminous sheaf is described as "already altering" as we watch. India, typically, is a place of places, a locus not of figures (whether luminous sheaf or "bright circlet") but of grounds: "[It] is the country, fields, fields, then hills, jungle, hills, and more fields" (136). India is not a grand symbolic monad to be apprehended momentously; rather, it is a finite, humdrum series, a train of places that are discrete ("fields," for example, as opposed to "hills"), recurrent ("fields, fields . . . more fields"), and not particularly distinguished, being entirely typical (all fields are "dull fields").

Of course, this sense of India as a train of nonsymbolic nonevents is the product of a train, the "branch-line train" on which the bored Baedecker of this description is stuck, "lost on a low embankment between dull fields" (136) along with the rest of Aziz's Marabar party. That is why the narrator's sense of India could be dismissed as just another faulty projection of the tourist's or, rather, tour guide's point of view, one common in Forster even outside the two Italian novels and the travel writing (*Alexandria*, for example). Certainly Forster's Indian tourist should be distinguished from the usually comic, delicately ironic personae of the earlier work; in *Passage* the tone is, by contrast, sardonic: "fields, fields, then hills" (oh, hills!). But, given the narrator's present confinement to a railway version of the Anglo-Indian "dog-cart" whose perceptual perch Adela Quested finds both merely aesthetic and deeply frustrating, his sourness should not be taken for heightened perceptiveness. It could just as easily be dismissed as a product of fatal distance and detachment.

Yet aesthetic detachment, it turns out, is not the problem; the frustration persists even once the symbol-seeking narrator manages to go to ground. For upon closer inspection, none of those fields presents anything less atypical or more distinctive, let alone more symbolic. "The branch line stops, the road is only practicable for cars to a point, the bullock-carts lumber down the side tracks, paths fray out into the cultivation, and disappear near a splash of red paint" (136). As the branches branch, they only get thinner until they "disappear," depositing the traveler amid incongruous material no more meaningful for being colorful. That the colored material is identified as paint, and as having been splashed, would suggest a point of view alert to artifice and thus to an aesthetic, or symbolic, intention. But neither intention is in evidence here. The aesthetic material seems to have been left lying around, as if dumped or dropped, the aesthetic task abandoned or aborted. Thus the "real India[n]" landscape offers not icons and eidolons, but their opposite, vacant spaces, "void[s]" (32) in which materials have been handled without much constructive, let alone aesthetic—let alone *symbolic*—intention, without much ceremony of any kind.

It is also "without much ceremony," as the narrator comments, that the Brahmin priest Godbole "smear[s mud] on his forehead" (316) at the "climax" (315) of the Gokul Ashtami festival in Part Three. Even here, during a conspicuously symbolic event, the substance of the symbol, raw substance, is handled offhandedly. The consequence is a casual, even quizzical reception of the symbolic gesture in question. Further diminishing its symbolic force—and the force of virtually all such gestures in the novel—is the fact that the mud Godbole smears is not, after all, truly river mud, mud symbolic of the material, the corporeal. But this mud has already become part of an aesthetic composition; Godbole finds it not lying in the river bed but adhering to the model "village of Gokul." Thus it is hard to see it as "the spot of filth without which the spirit cannot cohere" (305). It is a spot of filth, rather, without which an aesthetic representation cannot cohere—and a representation, as the narrator indicates, that itself exists at a remove from the thing it represents (a "substitute for the silver image," it exists "on behalf of another symbol" [315]). Such symbolic displacements—"those 'imitations,' those 'substitutions' " (290)—fascinate the narrator, who tirelessly points them out, thereby going out of his way to dampen all symbolist enthusiasm.[11] Even Godbole's famous Gokul vision of Mrs. Moore is described as quite possibly a spurious substitution, a "trick of his memory" (290).[12] And in describing it as such, Forster's narrator is indicating his own general refusal to substitute.

It is a different example of this general refusal that is the one most likely to interest the readers of this volume. In the famous final scene of the novel, Aziz and Fielding, taking their last ride together in the Mau countryside, encounter a cobra, and the reader encounters a perfect opportunity for the narrator to say something conventional about India; as typical symbols of the Orient go, the Orient as realm of exotic threat, the cobra is hard to beat. But this particular snake is just going about its business, "doing nothing in particular," then "disappear[ing]" (317). Here too, Forster forgoes the opportunity to symbolize. We are left without an image, let alone a symbol, as the disappearing cobra, not itself remarkably colorful, is swallowed up by a colorful knot or clump ("custard apple trees"). As with the detrained narrator's disappearing branch of pathway, this (snake's) road disappears into cultivation, and "color," again, is all that remains. True, the episode has a "resonance"—there are faintly Edenic suggestions (snake, apple, two human beings in a "park-like" setting). But these serve only to reinforce our sense of the snake's undistinguished (and not very satanic) presence. Like the riders, the narrator gives the snake "elbow room," refusing to harness it with the color, mystery, and romance attached to its Marabar cousin by Adela and Aziz earlier. Indeed, here it is not the snake in the grass but the grass itself, the landscape ("jolly bushes and rocks" [317]), that attracts the narrator's attention, figure again dissolving into ground.

What we are witnessing in all these episodes of refusal may usefully be defined as a species of bathos, that "sudden slip and swoop and slither as down a well-buttered slide, from the peaks into the abyss."[13] Bathos—the experience of "only nothing particular after all"[14]—is clearly evident in Forster's earlier work, where things are usually much less exciting than we might wish. What we might call the *bathetic*, "life's daily greyness," to use the language of *Howards End,* lies unobtrusively and below the peaks of "adventure," "splendour," "Time and Judgment," "Tragedy," and "Squalor," all of which are characterized as slippery human constructions.[15] It is, for example, the featureless dawn ("a grey evening turned upside down") into which slides that most touchingly feckless of solitary walkers, Leonard Bast;[16] it is also that space in which Aziz meets an old woman rather than the enchantress of fantasy, a "fabric bigger than the mosque" falling "to pieces" (20), and it would thus appear to be a most unromantic space. Not just anti-symbolist, then, the bathetic in Forster would seem to be anti-romantic, too. Certainly that is the impression given by the Marabar snake scene in *Passage* alluded to above, the first and falsest of the novel's snake sightings and also the episode in which Forsterian bathos reaches an instructive nadir. Here Adela and Aziz share a brief serpentine "romance" (Adela sees "A snake!" and Aziz "a black cobra, very venomous" that dwindles, upon "field-glass" inspection, to the "withered and twisted stump of a toddy-palm") (140–41). The field-glasses obviously serve Forster's epistemological theme, and it is not too much to see them as Forster's small, manual trope for the entire nineteenth-century realist tradition,[17] which aims to "see the object as in itself it really is."[18] Clearly, we are being offered a little epistemological fable, and the moral may seem equally clear: the romantic imaginings of the tourist, that *flâneur* or dawdler, depend entirely on distance and detachment, being baseless, rootless. In a world in which "[e]verything seem[s] cut off at its root, and therefore infected with illusion" (140), romantic things may seem particularly illusory, and Forster in his moments of bathos may seem particularly anti-romantic.

⋮ ⋮ ⋮

Forster may also seem particularly anti-impressionist. Certainly impressionism, or "Post Impressionism" (66–67), in Aziz's phrase, is a topic in the book. Now the impressionable young Oscar Wilde, student of Whistler, is not. But note how Wilde's "Impression du Matin," like several others among his early-Nineties poems strongly influenced by Whistler ("Symphony in Yellow," for example), suggests a tendency in literary impressionism to occupy transitional moments (e.g., dawn or sunset), registering the moments-within-the-moment as changes in color:[19]

> The Thames nocturne of blue and gold
> Changed to a Harmony in gray:
> A barge with ochre-colored hay
> Dropt from the wharf: and chill and cold
>
> The yellow fog came creeping down
> The bridges . . .[20]

Wilde's poem is worth quoting because its attention to changing color provides a good impressionist norm with which to compare Forster. Consider, for example, the (bathetic) episode of the Marabar sunrise: "Colour throbbed and mounted behind a pattern of trees, grew in intensity, was yet brighter, incredibly brighter, strained from without against the globe of air" (137). Clearly, Forster's vital dawn aids and abets impressionist color; it does not efface it, as does the dawn we find in Wilde's poem. Moreover, here at the Marabar, impressionist color does not lie inert, having been "splashed" about; mounting and straining rather than dropping or creeping, Prufrock-fashion (note the catlike "yellow fog") as in Wilde, Marabar color is dynamic, eschewing those needless vehicles of fog and barge. Nevertheless, the continuous and precise notation in Forster is itself enough to suggest a strong family resemblance to Wilde, and the consequence is to characterize Adela Quested, the observer at hand, as indeed the "Post Impressionist" Aziz has imagined that she may be. How impressionism itself is here characterized is also clear. Color throbs, mounts, grows, strains—"[b]ut at the supreme moment . . . nothing occurred." "But," indeed: the "moment," itself, what Forster earlier termed "The Eternal Moment" and what may be recognized as a variety of impression—the highly charged moment fails, and the impressionist experiences a "profound disappointment" (again, bathos) foreign to the young Wildean persona (137).[21]

Forster's India, then, would seem to be no more favorably disposed to impressionism than to symbolism. Note in this regard how sharply Forster differs from Wilde on the question of the moment's durability. Wilde's observer blithely courts disappointment by continuing receptive to impressions even as the favored "nocturne" fades and is rudely supplanted ("clang") by morning; he seems to be setting himself up for a sudden swoop down the slide of bathos. But at the critical moment he is able to find one last creature of the night, "one pale woman all alone," palely loitering "beneath the gas lamps' flare / With lips of flame and heart of stone."[22] Forster's impressionist, by contrast, enjoys no such providence, "the hues" in the "east decay[ing]," the sun "trailing yellowish" and merely "touching the bodies already at work in the fields" (137–38). Forster's impressionist may seem less ready and resourceful than Wilde's, but clearly Forster's India offers fewer resources, being the very site of the bathetic, the kind of place that stimulates, when it stimulates, such observations as the following: "Most of life is so dull that there is nothing to be said about it, and the books and talk that would describe it as interesting are obliged to exaggerate, in the hope of justifying their own existence" (132). Is impressionism in *Passage*, then, simply a mode of "exaggeration"?

Perhaps, but it would be a mistake to see Forster as simply anti-impressionist, since Adela, his central impressionist in *Passage*, is not simply repudiated but is presented as herself dissatisfied by mere impressions, mere "colour" (47). "Colour would remain," she imagines early in her stay, suffering a "vision of her married life": "Colour would remain—the pageant of birds in the early morning, brown bodies, white turbans, idols whose flesh was scarlet or blue—and movement would remain" (47). Certainly color and movement, two principal constituents of the impression, would survive marriage, but it is also certain that marriage would not magically transmute this pair into vehicles of transcendence; even once married she would still be out of touch with "the force that lies behind colour and movement."[23] Forster himself shares Adela's dislike of what Conrad called "*only*" an impression,[24] the partial, merely sensory impression[25] to which one is limited by the "glass shade"[26] of marriage or by those sturdier dividers, the "echoing walls" of civil, political, social, and racial difference (43). *Passage*'s perspective on the impression is, in other words, complex. Note how Adela's mention of that "pageant of birds" brings us back to the impressions of the narrator himself, who is impressed by Chadrapore as a virtual "city for the birds" when he gazes out from the hill occupied by the Civil Station. Forster is not so anti-impressionist as to forbid his narrator impressions. Like Adela, the narrator tries to see "the real India" (26), India as "spirit" rather than as "frieze" (47), and nowhere is the attempt more dramatic than in the opening exploration of Chandrapore and environs. Exhibiting a restlessness with individual impressions and apprehensions, moving somewhat haphazardly from one to the next, the opening chapter suggests a kind of disappointment not unlike Adela's at the Marabar, and the disappointment again points to the essential futility of impressionist knowing, at least in India. Yet at the end of the novel we see signs that the narrator has accepted this fact about impressionism in India. Lounging on the "grassy slope" among "jolly bushes" with Aziz and Fielding, the narrator offers his simple impression of the Mau countryside: "There were round white clouds in the sky, and white pools on the earth; the hills in the distance were purple. The scene was as park-like as England, but did not cease being queer" (317). The narrator attaches no "adjuncts" and attempts no precise analogies, nothing that would falsely reduce the scene's "distance" from a typical English scene—nothing that would obviate its essential queerness.

If Forster thus neither endorses nor eschews impressionism, little wonder that the politics of the practice can seem equally equivocal. Impressionism is good, on the one hand, because it seems to indicate an authentic desire to connect with the other, even the colonial other, as we see when Adela complicates her impression of the punkah wallah as a "male fate," a "winnower of souls" who "seemed to control" the trial, by specifying his social and material origins ("he was of the city, its garbage had nourished him" [217]). On the other hand, impressionism is not good because, all too often, the mere impression, the surface apprehension, which is interested, is all one gets; witness Ronnie Heaslop's unfavorable "impression" of Aziz's conduct at the mosque, "the essential life" of whom lies "slain" once Ronnie is through with him (34). The question may be approached cogently, it may even be answered, by following the lead of Jesse Matz. In *Literary Impressionism and Modernist Aesthetics*, Matz delineates the pursuit of a mode of "impressionist collaboration" in which the representative of a group, traditionally associated with the body and its sensations ("women and workers," "women and lower-class people"), is allowed the impressions the author himself craves but is afraid to indulge—and is then punished for indulging them.[27] Such impressionist proxies Matz calls, adapting Geoffrey Hartman, "figures for mediation" or "*counterparts*," and Adela, for obvious reasons (being a woman and a sometime impressionist), would seem to be the novel's best candidate for this medial, and politically fraught, position.[28] Yet as we look closer we see that Adela is not a good counterpart. Note how James, for example, emphasizes the female impressionist's physical involvement in her impressions: Isabel Archer's "flexible figure turned itself this way and that, in sympathy with the alertness with which she evidently caught impressions."[29] Adela's own body, by contrast, described as insignificant and unattractive ("she regretted that neither she nor Ronnie had physical charm" 153), evidently is not so involved. After the reported attack in the cave, "her senses [have become] abnormally inert and the only contact she anticipate[s is] that of mind," suggesting that mental, rather than sensuous, contact is her dominant mode (193). Counterparts, the theory has it, typically are not very mental. Adela is "such a dry, sensible girl" (179), "hard [and] prosaic" (230) if a bit "theoretical" (151), often "go[ing] on and on as if she's at a lecture—trying ever so hard to understand" in a way that annoys Fielding (119), but also "frankly and coolly" examining difficulties as they arise (85). And if she is scarcely the impressionable young female counterpart to be found, according to Matz, in much impressionist fiction, her sensibility renders her closer to the "implied author," who "*sublates* the counterpart" in order to avoid him- or herself "giving up intellect's independence."[30] Indeed, Adela's approach to the position of the "*sublating*" impressionist author effectively displaces Forster himself therefrom, rendering him an elusive target of the kind of "vulgar Marxist interpretation" which tends to regard any assertion of "solidarity" with the object of one's impressions, or of the impressions of one's proxy, as "sham sympathy, an epistemological exploitation of otherness, [an] estrangement" created by "primitivism's distortions and condescensions."[31]

The point is that it is much more difficult to charge Forster with pernicious sublation when Adela, the mediating consciousness, is so rationalist, so desirous of understanding and "adventure" (69), so dry, hard, self-conscious, self-critical: "Her particular brand of opinions, and the suburban Jehovah who sanctified them—by what right did they claim so much importance in the world, and assume the title of civilization?" (218). Here Adela is meditating on the punkah wallah at the trial, and clearly it is an occasion to engage in the typically modernist variety, as recent criticism has it, of primitivist sham sympathy and epistemological exploitation. Yet the "impression" prompts self-"rebuke," which is accompanied by an intuition and recognition of her own "narrowness" (218)—scarcely the stereotypically modernist outcome of primitivist "idealization" and "condescension."[32] The consequence is that at the critical moment Forsterian impressionism and Forsterian modernism come across as something quite distinct from a mode of exploitative primitivism. Leading instructively to disappointment, to bathos, impressionism also leads to an apprehension of epistemological, even cultural, limitation. English culture—English "civilization"—comes into question here, and this is important to any consideration of the politics of Forsterian modernism. For cultural self-critique is a kind of practice more often associated with postmodern alternatives to modernism than with modernism itself. Thus modernism here—modernism as represented by Forsterian impressionism—emerges not as an epistemological and ethical dead-end, a blind-alley of ethnocentrism, but as a possible avenue of imperial self-critique.

⋮ ⋮ ⋮

As my discussion of Forster's impressionism and modernism has revealed, Forster does not try to hold the Victorian realist line against the encroaching perceptual and linguistic mode of impressionism and the "incipient . . . literary modernism" it betokens.[33] Forster is not, after all, consistently anti-impressionist or anti-modernist, and that is not, ideologically speaking, a bad thing. To put this claim in larger literary-historical terms, we may note that it is not a bad ideological thing that Forster's impressionism and modernism should participate in the romantic legacy whereby romanticism sustains itself well into the twentieth century in such "belated and self-critical" forms.[34] But it must also be said, and I will now say it, that there is another interesting way in which modernism in *Passage* may sustain romantic possibility, and this way is especially interesting because it is so ideologically problematic. This is a way that lies, paradoxically enough, through realism and beyond, occupying the extremity of the book's realist argument, bathos again serving as vehicle.

That the bathetic may serve the realist we have already seen. To say what the impressionist, submitting to bathos, says, that everything in the Marabar seems a mere impression, a perception infected with illusion, its object being cut off at the root—to say that is not to say that there is nothing rooted. Things cut off at the root, like this stump, "seem[ ]" infected, and may be, but nothing necessarily is, and anything may be disinfected. For the field-glasses, those agents of bathos, of instructive disappointment, provide as it were a disinfectant gaze. Through them Adela discovers a thing that is not illusory, what India uniquely has to offer, the thing as in itself it really is, disinfected of illusion, withered, reduced, and now, like a withered stump, irreducible. To be sure, the thing itself in *Passage*, like the thing itself in *Howards End* ("only nothing particular after all"), is not much of anything. Like the "stones or crystals [pressing] against the [walker's] tread," "unexpectedly rigid and sharp" (18), India's reduced and now irreducible things, those that make a sharp impression even as they erase a romantic one, tend to be small things. Smallness is the hallmark even of that other set of impressive and irruptive stones, that "group of fists and fingers . . . thrust up through the [Marabar] soil" (9); to the impressed viewer who conducts the opening chapter's famous panoramic tour of Chandrapore, they are like the "core of blue persist[ing]" in and against "distance" (9): both display a relatively small figure in what seems a limitless ground, an "endless expanse" stretching "[l]eague after league" (9). But in Forster, smallness is not equivalent to insignificance. The protagonist of Forster's second novel, *The Longest Journey*, is an "anxious little speck" riding through what seems the "infinite space" of Wiltshire Downs (a scene that reads like an early version of Adela's and Aziz's adventure in the Marabar); but he is also described as feeling "extremely important," "extremely tiny and extremely important."[35] To put it another way, Forster's small things, disclosed in moments of bathos, are fundamental things, and this is no less true for India than for Wiltshire.

This interest in the basics points to one of the narrator's most notable rhetorical responses to the Indian landscape, to the larger Indian "*quaestio*" ("subject for debate"): *partito*, or *diaeresis*, the listing of types or parts.[36] Molly B. Tinsley has studied this reaction in detail and identified some of the syntactic forms it tends to take, the most interesting being its "appositive catalogues."[37] We see precisely this form in the list of landscape types offered by the trainbound narrator (fields, jungles, hills). The narrator's will-to-list is evident: we are provided with the makings of a list even when no list is provided. For example, the narrator gives us all we need to catalogue the discrete landscape features we find within just one of the types of landscape in the list of landscape types. Of the fields, jungles, and hills, we may investigate the hills, the Marabar Hills, and find stumps, saucers, slabs, and mounds. We have a list within a list, which carries its own embedded sublist, as the stumps and mounds provoke further cataloguing. Aziz's party, entering the Marabar, encounter "some mounds by the edge of the track, low, serrated, and touched with whitewash" (140). Low, serrated, and touched: that's about all they are, though it seems worth mentioning that there are "some" of them, just as it was worth mentioning earlier that there is "something" about the soil of India, generally, "something hostile in it" ("it either yields . . . or it is unexpectedly rigid and sharp" [18]). Low, serrated, and touched, then, but also hostile, being either yielding or rigid and sharp: such are some of the things about some one among the things in the list of the Indian landscape's things. The vagueness is distinct, as is the flatness created by the very act of listing or leveling, which "relinquishe[s] two conventions of Western form—climax and closure,"[38] and by so limiting the descriptive terms in the list to this small set, while allowing none of these terms to be richly descriptive ("low," "serrated," "touched"). When the hills "shoot up" on approach, they do so in a "single slab" (137); the "inverted saucer" Adela and Aziz encounter on their way up the Kawa Dol is, similarly, merely "nicked" (152). Such flat diction is all that we have; the resources of metaphor go unexplored. Consequently, the entire definition of material India seems lacking. As Cicero writes, *"Definitio est oratio quae id quod definitur explicat quid sit"* (A definition is a statement which explains what the thing defined is).[39] What India "is" is scarcely explained by a diction so featureless, so *bathetic*, whether it be naming or modifying, unless India is indeed a place of such flatness, of such bare forms.

Bathos gets us back to basics, then, however unexciting these basics may be, and thereby seems to serve realism. But it may serve another master, too. For there is something about bathetic India's sticks, stones, stumps, and slabs that is more than merely real and that justifies the term "elemental": they are the irreducible residue of nonhuman otherness. But with this recognition of a kind of elementalism in Forster's India comes a small surprise. The relationship between bathos and romanticism in *Passage* may not be so obvious, after all; there are moments in which, the extremes meeting, the two undergo a rapprochement. India's elemental things, disclosed in moments of bathos, of realist apperception, confer upon India a distinction: the very locus of the elemental, it is the site of a particularly insidious kind of romance, the romance of realism itself. The "veritable ding an sich itself," according to Stevens, may be a "vocable thing, / But with a speech belched out of hoary darks": the utterance of Shelley's Demigorgon rather than his Jupiter, yet for all that not less Shelleyan.[40] The "last distortion of romance" is the belief that we are free from romance altogether.[41] In Forster, too, there is a "palm at the end of the mind," if but a toddy palm's stump.[42] Like Stevens's Crispin, who senses "an elemental fate, / And elemental potencies and pangs, / And beautiful barenesses as yet unseen, / Making the most of savagery of palms," Forster's characters—his readers, even more so—may find a kind of romance in bareness, in savage spareness.[43]

I spoke of this rapprochement in *Passage* between romantic and realist extremes as a small surprise; a larger one is that such moments of rapprochement indicate Forster's approach to a particular potential to be found across the spectrum of specifically modernist writing. Maybe this will be no surprise; we have just seen how well Forsterian elementalist romance aligns with that of a famous modernist poet (Stevens), and readers may also have noted how well Forster's elementalist diaeresis, which I have also discussed, resembles the kind of recognizably modernist rhetoric that has come to be called "minimalist."[44] But now it is time to approach the modernism of Forsterian elementalism directly. Douglas Mao has written persuasively of the modernist romance with the "solid," its productive preoccupation with "otherness in its most resilient opacity," its "extraordinarily generative fascination with the object . . . as object" rather than as symbol or as commodity.[45] That Forster, likewise, points at the solidity, opacity, and otherness of, among other Indian things, Marabar rocks and stones (one of which only resembles a "saucer" [168]) and Marabar sticks (one of which only resembles a snake)—such a fact distinguishes Forster's text as one that also participates in this modernist practice. It is evident how a certain sort of modernist might romance Marabar sticks and stones, whose status as mere objects, as nonsymbolic and extra-economic entities, is strongly asserted. Marabar stones "bear no relation to anything dreamt or seen"; they "are like nothing else in the world" and, thus, symbolize nothing in the world, given that the vehicles of symbols require some connection, however untenable, to their tenors (124). The Marabar hills may be said to have been "commodified" to the extent that the local villagers "willingly serve as guides," but it is clear that the Marabar excursion undertaken by Aziz is an unusual phenomenon; the caves seem as novel to the mass of locals as to Aziz's party and do not appear to be a tourist-trap. The Marabar, then, will not submit to human exigencies, whether economic, figurative, or linguistic ("there is something unspeakable in these outposts" [124]).

Now such indifference to human needs and practices may sound unappealing, even unromantic, especially when the object in question is discovered to have no needs and practices of its own. Mao describes the modernist object-qua-object "as not-self, as not-subject, as most helpless and will-less of entities."[46] Where, then, does the romance come in? The answer is that the modernist object is also typically regarded as "fragment of being"—nonhuman being.[47] And here, again, Forster's "sun-born rocks" are apposite: "[F]lesh of the sun's flesh," the Marabar hills are "older than anything in [our] world, and the sun that has watched them for countless aeons may still discern in their outlines forms that were his before our globe was torn from his bosom" (123). Among fragments of being, the Marabar is a great fragment of the otherworldly, nonhuman, variety. Perhaps therein lies the appeal. Mao's modernists prize objects that are the very "crystallization of non-human being," the fascination with such objects approaching to "something like love."[48] Note by contrast Stendahl's account of "crystallization" in *De l'Amour* as "that operation of the mind which turns whatever presents itself into a discovery of new perfections in the object of love. . . . Here is the reason that love is the most powerful of all passions. In the case of other passions, desire must come to an accommodation with cold reality; in love alone, reality is keen to model itself on desire."[49] The reality keen to model itself on *modernist* "desire" must be not merely "impersonal" but virtually inhuman, even unearthly, and the same may be said of modernist desire itself, which is less attracted to warm fuzzies than to cold reality. Modernist objects permit modernists to transcend all recognizable desires—and yet still desire. Forster's own "crystals" are not human but forms of matter, embodiments not of love but of that which challenges our capacity for it. That greatly ecumenical and most Reverend Sorley, for example, whose heaven is a big-tent affair, must exclude crystals from his heaven; they are on par with "mud," matter that has lost all form and that is no less unattractive than "the bacteria inside Mr. Sorley" (38).

What are the politics of such modernist desire? The answer is not obvious. As Mao notes, "the privileging of the solid object could be absorbed by or made to align with diverse political positions."[50] But the kind of "privileging" we find in *Passage* seems narrow in its alignment. Certainly it does not seem to line up with liberalism. Forster's liberals prize a certain kind of solidity, both in and out of India: Fielding, with Adela—one of *Passage*'s obvious liberal humanists—at one point needs "the solid ground" (197), the same epistemological ground that Forster, perhaps the most famous nineteenth-century liberal of the twentieth century, later reported feeling "crumbl[e] beneath him."[51] The image of a small patch of Arnoldean liberal solidity amid threatening flux is often found in Forster. Just as often, though, its extraliberal economic foundations are revealed; the Schlegel sisters may go on being Schlegelian year after year only because they have "piles of money" or "islands" upon which to "stand each year" above the London welter and the "abyss."[52] In any event, the solidity to be found in India should not be conflated either with "Culture" or with "coin."[53] Nor should it be aligned with the conservative, male, imperialist Wilcoxian alternative to the liberal, that "concentrated light upon a tiny spot, a little Ten Minutes moving self-contained through its appointed years."[54] Henry Wilcox's coevals in *Passage* are the Turtons, Burtons, Callendars, and Ronnie Heaslops, officials who stay away from Indian things as much as possible, sticking to convention, to approved themes, to their own kind, to the club, to the Civil Station.

The political position with which Forster's modernist desire in India best aligns is that of an illiberal formalism. India's aboriginal stones and crystals should remind us of modernism's stark distillation of experience to primary pigment and geometric form. "O Brancusi, with your chisels and hammers," writes Carl Sandburg, that great lover of "slabs" in 1922, "birds going to cones, skulls going to eggs";[55] or going to lines, squares, and squiggles, what Yeats referred to in his own work as "stylistic arrangements of experience comparable to the cubes in the drawing of Wyndham Lewis and to the ovoids in the sculpture of Brancusi";[56] or to the "planes in relation," from which Henri Gaudier-Brzeska, stuck in the trenches, will derive his "EMOTIONS SOLELY."[57] Even at Howards End, (un)safely in the English countryside ("London's creeping"), Margaret Schlegel finds "narrowing circles [encompassing a] sacred centre,"[58] and the liberal-minded Margaret prizes this "tight circle of safety and inviolability," as Wilfred Stone describes it. In question, then, is a modernism of basics, of purified, unadorned essences, and its politics has been defined numerous times. As Arthur Danto summarizes the usual indictment, the "history of modern art is the history of purgation, of generic cleansing, of ridding the art of whatever was inessential to it. It is difficult not to hear political echoes of these notions of purity and purgation . . . crash[ing] back and forth across the tormented fields of nationalist strife."[59]

To be sure, it is equally difficult not to suspect that Danto's sense of a strict historical connection between aesthetic and political programs represents a kind of grotesque simplification, itself an expression of that "great new academic mythology" that trusts to "the inevitably nefarious political nature of modernist art."[60] Yet clearly Forsterian elementalism lies open to this political charge, at least in one of its gentler forms. That Forster's India, with its "eternal" rocks (153), dull or "sparkling" (152), offers access to these forms and to the "starker, barer world" they inhabit, that India stirs such modernist desire and the "starker, barer self" to which it belongs,[61] suggests that Forster's modernist, elementalist romance depends on an Indian exotic. And any India that gives a home to the exotic thereby becomes, the argument goes, an India in the "Orientalist code."[62]

⋮ ⋮ ⋮

Scarcely, however, are we invited to build with India's elemental sticks and stones and, thereby, to become occupants of this "political position." For one thing, we soon find that it would be foolish to trust those epistemological instruments of elementalism, the field-glasses, which prove fragile, failing to survive their own encounter with the Marabar ("the eye-piece [becoming] jammed" [167]). These empiricist adjuncts of "Western education" (119)—adjuncts that figure similarly, if gruesomely, in Conrad's *Heart of Darkness*, providing an even more surprising "nearer view"[63]—these same adjuncts that enable Adela to see the toddy-stump for what it is, and that thus inculcate both Adela's bathos and the reader's modernist romance, become involved in Adela's own "terrible adventure" (212), "the climax" of which, bathetically enough, "was the falling of her field-glasses" (194). They enable acts of self-defense, yes, but also of assault, even self-assault; if Adela tries to use them to repulse the putative rapist ("I hit at him with the glasses"), they also serve the latter (it is by the "strap" that she is "pulled . . . round the cave" [193]), and things become yet more interesting if we believe that, to adapt Robinson Crusoe, "there was nothing in this cave that was more frightful than [her] self."[64]

The strap ends up "newly broken" (167), and we are reminded of the "mountaineer whose rope had broken" (152) just minutes earlier, the free-falling Adela, whose discussion of her personal life with Aziz while ascending Marabar rocks has coincided with the vexing discovery that she does not love her fiancé, Ronnie. If the implements of Western empiricist investigation prove fallible, these stays against confusion failing in critical moments, it is also the case that the foundations disclosed by elementalist adventure prove very slippery indeed. What would Adela have seen, we wonder, had she twice employed her field-glasses? Would the toddy stump have "already altered," like the Ganges' "luminous sheaf"—would it have disappeared? Perhaps not, but Forster is scarcely encouraging elementalist romance by thus indicating the unreliability of its instruments and objects. Rather, against elementalism he is pitting something formidable—the unsettling, sometimes devastating, experience of absence.

This contest between elements and absences achieves the shape of a pattern once we know to look for it. Orienting tokens of the elemental have a habit of emerging from a dim Indian miasma only to disappear, seemingly absorbed back into it. If the Indian soil is sometimes "unexpectedly rigid and sharp, pressing stones or crystals against the tread," just as often it "yields, and the foot sinks into a depression" (18), and India's cyclists have it as bad as do the pedestrians. All "adjuncts" of warning and control, lights, bells, and brakes, prove useless, India being "a land where the cyclist's only hope is to coast from face to face, and just before he collides with each it vanishes" (16). India is an either/or of impressive elemental presences and sudden absences that keeps one guessing. Consider, also, the overarching plot (the account of "rhythm" in *Aspects of the Novel* comes to mind): although "Caves," Part Two of the novel, opens with an extended description of those most famous "depressions," the Marabar Caves, the reader's feet sink in the Marabar only after having enjoyed a series of crystalline episodes (Part One), virtual stepping stones in what appears to be the usual nineteenth-century realist plot[65] (which is delineated coyly at the end of chapter 5: "Would they [Ronny and Adela], or would they not, succeed in becoming engaged to be married?" [52]). The polo matches (between Aziz and the stray subaltern; between Adela and Ronny), the mosque visit, the sick-room episodes, the play and parties at the club, even the change in the weather: each emerges into sharp relief, each constituting an element of the story, a point in a plot-line that leads into the narrative aporia of the Marabar Caves.

The upshot should be clear—these intimations of absence following hard upon the heels of the elemental suggest the contingency and partiality of the latter: "Some kites hovered overhead, impartial, over the kites passed the mass of a vulture, and with an impartiality exceeding all, the sky, not deeply coloured but translucent, poured light from its whole circumference. It seemed unlikely that the series stopped here" (39–40). The ultimate epistemological argument of the novel is clarified in several passages that similarly indicate a vantage transcending whichever one we happen to occupy, however elementally grounded, and a vantage that is itself always already transcended by another ("Beyond which again . . ." [40]).[66] It also matters that we find this beyondness not just beyond but also within.[67] Hence, the Marabar's caves and "chambers" are primordial spaces "never unsealed since the arrival of the gods," the most interesting of which lies within the Kawa Dol, "a bubble-shaped cave that has neither ceiling nor floor, and mirrors its own darkness in every direction infinitely" (125). If the kites, and so forth, call into question the sufficiency of India's elemental objects, the caves call into question their solidity. Thus the same India that seems to encourage elementalist romance prompts notions of the elements' disappearance or dissolution within a darkness that contains them and that they themselves contain. Elemental forms cannot happily orient and establish us, not in the end, since, like a circle, they give upon an absolute emptiness both beyond and within. Again, the larger argument served in such interrogative narrative moments is that of the "skeptical epistemologist" found in the works of conspicuously modernist novelists like Joseph Conrad, Ford Madox Ford, and Virginia Woolf.[68]

The mistake made in dealing with these depressions and supersessions and "nullah[s]" (89) of various kinds is to see them as grounds for an independent and "final judgment."[69] For such a reading ignores, among other things, Bombay's "thousands of coconut palms" (cousins of the toddy) that wave farewell to Mrs. Moore as she makes her "passage back" (95), laughing incredulously, "you took the Marabar caves as final?" (210). The apocalyptist, modernist passages of "topography," whether hollowing-out or superseding, serve not as a mode of finality but as a check upon the temptation to embrace the elementalist—also modernist, as we have seen—mode. They are not the last words, and they do not in the end render India a figure of Orientalist inscrutability so much as undermine its idealizations as primordially solid and substantial. Forster's India, in general, does not offer symbols of an unknowable universe so much as signs of a particular land, people, and culture still unknown—a land, people, and a culture known "not yet," "not there" (322), not in their particularity.[70] That things cannot be known fully and finally does not suggest that they are not worth knowing partially. Hence we confront the particularity of those solicitous "coconut palms" that seem to insist on being recognized in all their difference. About the caves these coconuts ask, rhetorically, "What have we in common with them?" (210). This emphasis on "differences—eternal differences"[71] is often overlooked, as is the fact that in the end Mrs. Moore transcends her singular interest in the Marabar and its echo, as she "long[s] to disentangle the hundred Indias that passed each other in [Bombay's] streets" (210).

A hundred Indias, uncommon each and every one, none the "final," the "*real* India" (24): we have come some distance from the India with which we began, that place distinguished as undistinguished, the home of bathos, with its fields and hills—some of which manage to display, after all, elemental stumps and slabs. Instead of a sense of India's repetitiveness and regularity, instead of an irreducibly elemental quality, we have a sense of Indian multiplicity and particularity. As Tinsley notes, Forster's appositive catalogues at certain crucial times become "direct object catalogues" or collages that eschew abstraction ("Noise, noise, the Europeanized band louder, incense on the altar, sweat, the blaze of lights, wind in the bananas, noise, thunder, eleven-fifty by his wrist-watch" [277]), turning a rhetoric of elementalism to the task of registering a rich and concrete particularity.[72] Thus if our sense of Forster's India has broadened, so has our sense of his aesthetic project. The refusal of singularity and finality, even at the cost of an acceptance of partiality, is an artistic as well as an epistemological phenomenon; aesthetically, too, Forster refuses finality, moving between symbolism, impressionism, elementalism, apocalyptism, and "particularism" (let us call it). As a result, none of the modes of aesthetic apperception explored in *A Passage to India* emerges, finally, as the right or wrong mode, the mode that is entirely adequate—or definitively inadequate. Even symbolism is not exactly negated; for all the diminutions and qualifications I noted above, the symbolic "resonances" still resonate, still echo, even if they do not triumph. Likewise, the famous Marabar echo itself is by no means embraced, remaining not the dominant theme, but a subdominant.

With this more complex sense of Forster's aesthetic project should come, I would argue, a similarly enlarged grasp of Forster's politics, and one that should function to obviate any quest to determine the ultimate political valence of the novel. By this I mean to point to a connection between Forster's critique of finality, with respect to the question of India and its representation, and his refusal to take up a consistent position on distinct political questions such as Indian self-rule. This is a connection that some have refused to explore. Said, for example, recognizes it and even finds it "interesting" as it has appeared in the work of Parry—only to reject it in renewed quest of a "total text."[73] But any such totalizing imperative as Said displays serves only to distract both from the richest, most capacious apprehension of the novel and from the very spirit of the postcolonial project.

The issue that needs to be addressed in what space remains is that of a similarly totalizing or finalizing view of modernism, a view of modernism as a monolithic phenomenon whose constituent forms, being so much of a piece, scarcely call for "disentangling." In disentangling several of the various forms of modernism, incipient and other, that emerge in *A Passage to India*—impressionism, elementalism, and apocalyptism, each with its own distinct rhetoric—I hope to have reinvigorated the political debate over modernism. *Passage* occasions, I have been arguing, "an extremely dense *clash* of visions": the phrase we owe to Fredrick Crews, who is describing Forster's early novel, *The Longest Journey*, but who may as well be talking about *A Passage to India*, especially its modernism.[74] The impressionism in the novel, the elementalism, the apocalyptism, the particularism: none of these "visions" is embraced or endorsed, finally; rather, each vision remains partial and provisional. In pointing to this provisionality, I hope to have contributed to the conclusion that modernist writing may display a complexity on the ideological level that is every bit as rich as the notorious complexity ascribed to its aesthetic form.

## Notes

1 See Suleri, *The Rhetoric of English India*; also see Suleri's "Geography of *A Passage to India*." Said's book is *Culture and Imperialism*. Said distinguishes between "imperialism" and "colonialism" as follows: " 'imperialism' means the practice, the theory, and the attitudes of a dominating metropolitan center ruling a distant territory; 'colonialism' . . . is the implanting of settlements" (9). My own view of colonialism–and that developed elsewhere in this collection–is, however, more capacious and includes theory and practice as part of the larger project of colonization; see the introduction to the present volume. My focus in this essay will be to relate a series of aesthetic choices in Forster to the theory and practice of colonialism.

2 Pathak, Sengupta, and Purkayastha, "The Prisonhouse of Orientalism," 200.

3 Parry, "Materiality and Mystification," 175.

4 Suleri, *The Rhetoric of English India*, 146, 145, 145, 144, and 144.

5 Suleri, "Geography of *A Passage to India*," 110, 109, 108, 109, 112, 107–8, 109, and 108.

6 Forster, *A Passage to India* (1924; London: Harcourt Brace Jovanovich, 1952), 123. All further references to this novel pertain to this edition and are cited parenthetically.

7 The analyses to be found in *Modernist Writing and Reactionary Politics*, for example, move quickly to conflate the titular phrases as the number of "reactionary modernists" grows, it being "by no means always clear" whether even Woolf and Joyce are not also reactionary modernists alongside Yeats, Lewis, Lawrence, Eliot, and Conrad. See Ferrall, *Modernist Writing and Reactionary Politics*, 11, 10.

8 Parry, "Materiality and Mystification," 177.

9 See, for example, Kermode, "The One Orderly Product (E. M. Forster)."

10 Rosecrance anticipates this reading when she notes that "Forster's symbols reiterate the major themes"—they "follow[ ] the pattern of other appeals to the god . . . the absent Krishna [who] does not respond," the appeals themselves left to "echo outward to infinity." See "*A Passage to India:* Forster's Narrative Vision," 77.

11 A final, irresistible example of such symbolic "diver[sion]" (287) is the "red-silk napkin," the "napkin [that] was God, not that it was. . . . It was just a napkin, folded into a shape which indicated a baby's" (288).

12 Forsterians will at this point hear an echo of the moment in *The Longest Journey* when Rickie Elliot regards Stephen Wonham's "trick with paper" (creating a luminous sheaf by crumpling paper, igniting it, and sending it floating down a stream at night) as a profound symbolic episode—only to be mocked by the latter (*The Longest Journey*, 292). *Pace* Malcolm Bradbury, who notes Forster's "radiating expansiveness of language" ("A Universe . . . Not . . . Comprehensible to Our Minds," 37), we may note how the radiating language sometimes constricts; the echo in this talk of "tricks" works to cut Godbole's vision down to (human) size.

13 Lewis and Lee, *The Stuffed Owl*, x.

14 Forster, *Howards End*, 88.

15 Ibid., 104, 230, 225, 226, 234, and 234.

16 Ibid., 88.

17 Constituted by continentals like Stendhal, Balzac, de Maupassant, and Zola, and by English Victorian authors like Thackeray, Trollope, Dickens, and George Eliot.

18 See Matthew Arnold, "On Translating Homer," *The Complete Prose Works of Matthew Arnold,* vol. 1: *Matthew Arnold on the Classical Tradition*, 174.

19 "Impressionism," writes Jesse Matz, "seeks generally to suggest atmosphere and mood; it subordinates plot, fixes moments, fragments form, and intensifies affective response . . . [it] fuses subject and object, finds truth in appearances, and evokes the dynamic feeling . . . of life itself" (*Literary Impressionism and Modernist Aesthetics*, 14). Though Wilde's "Impression du Matin" says nothing explicit about the "truth in appearances," a preoccupation of several of Wilde's

essays, it strictly observes the criteria of suggestion, subordination, fragmentation, intensification, fusion, and evocation.

20 Wilde, *Poems*, 85.

21 Forster, "The Eternal Moment," *The Eternal Moment and Other Stories*.

22 Wilde, "Impression du Matin," lines 13–16.

23 Quoting Herbert Howarth, Matz notes how the impression attends to movement, its ambition being to "evoke . . . the dynamic feeling—'the flow, energy, vibrancy'—of life itself" (*Literary Impressionism and Modernist Aesthetics*, 14).

24 Quoted in Matz, *Literary Impressionism and Modernist Aesthetics*, 14.

25 Matz calls it "merely a visual image or sensory phenomenon" (8).

26 Forster, *Howards End*, 184.

27 Matz, *Literary Impressionism and Modernist Aesthetics*, 33, 41, 34.

28 Ibid., 33.

29 Quoted in ibid., 105.

30 Ibid., 34, 34, 33.

31 Ibid., 148.

32 Ibid., 40. Note Matz's interpretation of literary impressionism, the entire movement, as just this ideologically complex, just this resistant to postmodern ideological dismissal (esp. 35–45).

33 Stowell, *Literary Impressionism*, 9.

34 An "intermediate phase in the process through which, in so many accounts, Romanticism becomes and even encompasses Modernism," impressionism is a "belated and self-critical Romanticism" (Matz, *Literary Impressionism and Modernist Aesthetics*, 40).

35 Forster, *The Longest Journey*, 120, 119, 20.

36 Cicero, *Topica*, 7.34. Cicero discusses *partitio* or "enumeration" as one of the two ways in which "definitions are made" (the other being "analysis"). See *Topica*, 5.28–34.

37 Tinsley, "Muddle, *etcetera*," 79.

38 Ibid., 72.

39 Cicero, *Topica*, 4.26.

40 See Wallace Stevens, "The Comedian as the Letter C," *The Palm at the End of the Mind*, I.69–71.

41 Ibid., I.76.

42 Stevens, "Of Mere Being," *The Palm at the End of the Mind*, 1.

43 Stevens, "The Comedian as the Letter C," II.37–40.

44 "Minimalism, an abstract and by some measure even a geometric art form, at best aims to do more and more with less and less" (Brater, *Beyond Minimalism*, ix). Forster's Indian "minimalism," which lists Lockean primary qualities, thus accreting small piles of abstraction, is scarcely minimalism "at its best," since it is content to suggest how little may be done with the "less" that India provides.

45 See Mao, *Solid Objects*, 4.

46 Ibid.

47 Ibid.
48 Ibid., 17, 4.
49 Stendhal, *De l'Amour*, 43, 62.
50 Mao, *Solid Objects*, 15.
51 Forster, "What I Believe," *Abinger Edition of E. M. Forster*, vol. 11: *Two Cheers for Democracy*, 72.
52 Forster, *Howards End*, 46.
53 Ibid., 85, 46.
54 Ibid., 178.
55 Carl Sandburg, "Brancusi," 301.
56 Yeats, *A Vision*, 25.
57 Pound, *Gaudier-Brzeska*, 28.
58 Forster, *Howards End*, 240, 237. "The purity of detachment strongly appeals to [Margaret]," its "attendant promise" being "decadence and brutality," the "malignancy inherent in a spiritual-esthetic withdrawal." See Stone, "*Howards End:* Red-bloods and Mollycoddles," 407.
59 Danto, *After the End of Art*, 70.
60 See Caserio, review of *Painterly Abstraction in Modernist American Poetry*, by Charles Altieri, 583.
61 Stevens, "The Comedian as the Letter C," I.61–62.
62 Suleri, *The Rhetoric of English India*, 170.
63 See Conrad, *Heart of Darkness*, 58.
64 Defoe, *Robinson Crusoe*, 183. A critical review of such readings of Adela as "haunted by sex ghosts" of her own conjuring may be found in Silver, "Periphrasis, Power, and Rape in *A Passage to India*," 87.
65 See Houghton, *The Victorian Frame of Mind*, 374.
66 See, for other examples of Forster's "rhetoric of beyondness," May, *The Modernist as Pragmatist*, 3, 13, 34, 46, 80, 90–91, and 141.
67 For a cogent discussion of the "beyond within" as modernist trope, see Levenson, *Modernism and the Fate of Individuality*, 5–13.
68 The phrase is Levenson's (*Modernism and the Fate of Individuality*, 7). Fokkema, for example, writes of modernism's preference for "hypothetical constructions expressing uncertainty and provisionality" (*Literary History, Modernism, and Postmodernism*, 15).
69 Rosecrance, "*A Passage to India:* Forster's Narrative Vision," 87.
70 Beer approaches this point in his comment on Forster's "attitude to the stability of objects": "While recognising their ineluctable presence [he] would regard any attempt to give them finality as a form of enslavement." See "*A Passage to India*," 129.
71 Forster, *Howards End*, 239.
72 Tinsley, "Muddle, *etcetera*," 78.
73 Said, *Culture and Imperialism*, 201.
74 Crews, *E. M. Forster*, 51.

## Works Cited

Arnold, Matthew. *The Complete Prose Works of Matthew Arnold.* Edited by Robert H. Super. Vol. 1: *Matthew Arnold on the Classical Tradition.* Ann Arbor: University of Michigan Press, 1960–77.

Beer, John. "*A Passage to India*, the French New Novel, and English Romanticism." In *"A Passage to India": Essays in Interpretation*, ed. John Beer, 104–31. Totowa, N.J.: Barnes and Noble, 1986.

Bradbury, Malcolm. "A Universe . . . Not . . . Comprehensible to Our Minds: *A Passage to India.*" In *Modern Critical Interpretations: "A Passage to India,"* ed. Harold Bloom, 29–44. New York: Chelsea House, 1987.

Brater, Enoch. *Beyond Minimalism: Beckett's Late Style in the Theatre.* New York: Oxford University Press, 1987.

Caserio, Robert. Review of *Painterly Abstraction in Modernist American Poetry: The Contemporaneity of Modernism*, by Charles Altieri. *Modern Language Quarterly* 54.4 (December 1993): 583–88.

Cicero, Marcus Tullius. *De Inventione, De Optimo Genere Oratorum, Topica.* Edited by H. M. Hubbell. Cambridge: Cambridge University Press, 1949.

Conrad, Joseph. *Heart of Darkness* (1899/1902). New York: Norton, 1971.

Crews, Frederick. *E. M. Forster: The Perils of Humanism.* Princeton, N.J.: Princeton University Press, 1962.

Danto, Arthur. *After the End of Art: Contemporary Art and the Pale of History.* Princeton, N.J.: Princeton University Press, 1997.

Defoe, Daniel. *Robinson Crusoe* (1719). New York: Penguin, 1965.

Ferrall, Charles. *Modernist Writing and Reactionary Politics.* Cambridge: Cambridge University Press, 2001.

Fokkema, Douwe W. *Literary History, Modernism, and Postmodernism.* Philadelphia: John Benjamins Press, 1984.

Forster, E. M. *Abinger Edition of E. M. Forster.* Vol. 11: *Two Cheers for Democracy* (1952). London: Edward Arnold, 1972.

——. *The Eternal Moment and Other Stories.* San Diego: Harvest/HBJ, 1928.

——. *Howards End* (1910). Edited by Paul Armstrong. New York: Norton, 1998.

——. *The Longest Journey* (1907). New York: Vintage, 1962.

——. *A Passage to India* (1924). London: Harcourt Brace Jovanovich, 1952. [Pre-1984 pagination.]

Houghton, Walter E. *The Victorian Frame of Mind, 1830–1870.* New Haven, Conn.: Yale University Press, 1957.

Kermode, Frank. "The One Orderly Product (E. M. Forster)." *Puzzles and Epiphanies: Essays and Reviews, 1958–1961*, 79–85. New York: Chilmark Press, 1962.

Levenson, Michael. *Modernism and the Fate of Individuality: Character and Novelistic Form from Conrad to Woolf.* Cambridge: Cambridge University Press, 1991.

Lewis, D. B. Wyndham, and Charles Lee, eds. *The Stuffed Owl: An Anthology of Bad Verse.* London : J. M. Dent and Sons, 1930.

Mao, Douglas. *Solid Objects: Modernism and the Test of Production.* Princeton, N.J.: Princeton University Press, 1998.

Matz, Jesse. *Literary Impressionism and Modernist Aesthetics.* Cambridge: Cambridge University Press, 2001.

May, Brian. *The Modernist as Pragmatist: E. M. Forster and the Fate of Liberalism.* Columbia : University of Missouri Press, 1997.

Parry, Benita. "Materiality and Mystification in *A Passage to India.*" *Novel* 31.2 (Spring 1998): 174–94.

Pathak, Zaki, Saswaki Sengupta, and Sharmila Purkayastha. "The Prisonhouse of Orientalism." *Textual Practice* 5.2 (1991): 195–218.

Pound, Ezra. *Gaudier-Brzeska: A Memoir.* New York: New Directions, 1970.

Rosecrance, Barbara. "*A Passage to India:* Forster's Narrative Vision." In *Modern Critical Interpretations: "A Passage to India,"* ed. Harold Bloom, 75–90. New York: Chelsea House, 1987.

Said, Edward. *Culture and Imperialism.* New York: Alfred A. Knopf, 1993.

Sandburg, Carl. "Brancusi." *The Complete Poems of Carl Sandburg.* New York: Harcourt Brace Jovanovich, 1970.

Silver, Brenda. "Periphrasis, Power, and Rape in *A Passage to India.*" *Novel* 22.1 (Fall 1988): 86–105.

Stendhal, Henri Martineau. *De l'Amour.* Paris: Cluny, 1938.

Stevens, Wallace. *The Palm at the End of the Mind.* New York: Vintage, 1972.

Stone, Wilfred. "*Howards End:* Red-bloods and Mollycoddles." In *Howards End,* ed. Paul Armstrong, 396–408. New York: Norton, 1998.

Stowell, H. Peter. *Literary Impressionism: James and Chekhov.* Athens.: University of Georgia Press, 1980.

Suleri, Sara. "The Geography of *A Passage to India.*" In *Modern Critical Interpretations: "A Passage to India,"* ed. Harold Bloom, 107–13. New York: Chelsea House, 1987.

——. *The Rhetoric of English India.* Chicago: University of Chicago Press, 1992.

Tinsley, Molly B. "Muddle, *etcetera:* Syntax in *A Passage to India.*" In *"A Passage to India": Essays in Interpretation,* ed. John Beer, 71–80. Totowa, N.J.: Barnes and Noble, 1986.

Wilde, Oscar. *Poems.* New York: Brentano's, 1909.

Yeats, W. B. *A Vision.* New York: Macmillan, 1937.

*Rita Barnard*

⋮

SEVEN

# "A tangle of modernism and barbarity": Evelyn Waugh's *Black Mischief*

Given Evelyn Waugh's commitment to formal experimentation, his attention to modern things like cocktails, cubism, airplanes, motor-races, and gossip columns, and his fascination with remote places from which the modern world can be seen at a strange and comical angle, it may seem surprising that his work has not loomed larger in the annals of modernist and postcolonial scholarship.[1] Part of the problem may be that critics have too often conflated the early Waugh with his later fictional character Gilbert Pinfold, who "abhorred plastics, Picasso, sunbathing and jazz—everything, in fact, that had happened in his own lifetime."[2] Waugh's relation to the modern is more complex than this. It is certainly true that he came to rail against almost every aspect of social modernity, but in his critical writings of the 1920s and 1930s, he treats the work of innovators like Picasso, Joyce, and Hemingway with respect and considerable perceptiveness. It was clear to him that they were trying to solve what he describes in a 1930 essay as "the aesthetic problem of representation . . . to achieve, that is to say, a new balanced interrelation of subject and form."[3] What Waugh scoffed at were the "terrors of the pseudo": the pretensions of rich ladies who thought that they could attain modernity by "inviting coloured people and the authors of the latest best-sellers to luncheon," or of editors who believed that they were "keeping up to date by hiring very young people to write for them."[4]

Waugh considered the challenges of the modern world to be strenuous: it was "a very arduous business" for artists to keep up with their own period.[5]

The faddish decadents of the 1890s, for example, never managed to be part of the vanguard of their time. Despite their ostensibly modern posturing, they ignored what Waugh deemed to be the truly transformative and emergent forces of the day: electricity, the automobile and the airplane, and psychoanalysis. The putatively shocking work of a Beardsley, he argued, was positively old-fashioned compared to Cézanne's "noble" experiments of the same period.[6] And while Waugh complained throughout his life about the vacuousness of mass-mediated cultural forms like radio, newspapers, and Hollywood movies, he also understood—perhaps more fully than any of his contemporaries—their social and artistic impact: cinema in particular was in his view "a genuine and self-sufficient art" and presented a new way of structuring fiction, appropriate to a world in which the nineteenth-century novel's "chain of cause and effect" no longer sufficed.[7]

Even if Waugh truly abhorred everything that happened in his lifetime, that fact in and of itself cannot explain the extent to which he has been scanted in our theoretical thinking about modernism. An opposition to social modernity is, after all, a familiar and even characteristic stance on the part of the most canonical and celebrated high modernists. What has discouraged a more rigorous consideration of Waugh's work is his apparent lack of seriousness. His conviction that the novel should be primarily "directed for entertainment" has made him seem somehow a less worthy writer than the more earnest modernist and colonial writers, whose sense of the utopian or uplifting mission of art he was too pessimistic, or perhaps too realistic, to share.[8] Waugh's comic irresponsibility presents something of a scandal. This was clearly the case at the historical moment of modernist canon formation, when Steven Marcus judged in a *Partisan Review* essay of 1956 that Waugh's attention to the "art of entertainment" marked him as a fine novelist—of the second-rate.[9] And it still remains the case today, especially given the highly ethical and political critical agenda generated by colonial discourse analysis and postcolonial studies.

This agenda (commendable for the urgency and purpose it has brought to literary studies during the past two decades) makes it surprisingly difficult to get a critical purchase on a text like Waugh's *Black Mischief*, the wicked satire that arose from his visit to various parts of Africa in 1930. Students in my undergraduate course on colonial and postcolonial fiction often try to get around this difficulty by reading Waugh's novel as the reprehensible antithesis to Sembene Ousmane's 1962 novel *God's Bits of Wood*.[10] They construct, in other words, a kind of "empire writes back" pairing. The strategy is not unproductive: it certainly sets some of the basic features of the two texts in stark relief.

Ousmane's stirring novel, based on the history of the 1947–48 strike on the Dakar-Niger railway line, remains the grand epic of African modernity. Taking the train as his central metaphor, Ousmane offers an optimistic assessment of the potential of modern technology. This optimism is expressed, at times, through the outdated tropes of socialist realism (outdated even at the time of the novel's publication), but it still has a subversive capacity in the African context in that it challenges the primitivist stereotype of the continent as a jungle or "just a garden for food," as one of Ousmane's characters puts it.[11] The novel in no way denies the homogenizing effects of industrial modernity, but it grasps these as potentially liberatory. The striking workers base their demands for raises, pensions, and family benefits on a principle of sameness: on the fact that the engines they operate "don't know the difference between white man and a black."[12] And just as the machine is presented as—potentially at least—the property of all of humanity, so too is the book. At a crucial point in the strike, one of the characters discovers new ideas and strategies for their collective action in a French novel: André Malraux's *La Condition Humaine*. This is not to say that Ousmane would urge his readership to discard traditional forms of knowledge for European imports: the presiding vision is a dialectical and progressive conception of history, of "the past and future . . . coupling to breed a new kind of man" (76)—and also, as the author is at pains to make clear, a new kind of woman.

In Waugh's novel, the very idea of modernity in Africa (or more exactly, in Azania, his satiric amalgam of Zanzibar and Ethiopia) is the stuff of farce. As in *God's Bits of Wood*, the image of the railroad is central; but the trains of the Grand Chemin de Fer D'Azanie don't run on time; the engine is likely to take off without the carriages; and the steel sleepers are constantly being stolen by fierce Sakuyu tribesmen, who forge them into spearheads. The novel's repetitive structure, moreover, suggests the impossibility of progress. A reiterated image is that of a broken-down car in the middle of a major roadway, in which an Azanian family has set up a home and where they live their squalid life, equally unperturbed by the disruption they cause to the flow of traffic and by the political havoc that goes on around them. Given the novel's strict dichotomy between civilization and barbarism, any sort of cultural cross-fertilization is undesirable, if not impossible: the source of much of the novel's satire is the ostensibly risible idea of a black man getting an idea from a European book. But one hesitates to use the phrase "black *man*" in connection to Waugh's emperor Seth, with his ludicrous One Year Plan for modernizing his territory. None of the novel's characters is fully human; they are caricatures, not only incapable of development but likely to regress, at any opportunity, to a state of unindividualized savagery. The novel thus demonstrates Waugh's fundamental conviction that "barbarism is never finally defeated" and that "we are all potential recruits for anarchy."[13]

The comparative analysis I have sketched out here demonstrates the critical potency of early postcolonial fiction. If one adopts my students' "empire writes back" strategy, one cannot but judge in favor of Ousmane's politically progressive, if technically somewhat more conventional work. But how far does such a comparative and implicitly prescriptive reading really get us when it comes to historicizing Waugh's fiction and analyzing the particular nexus of thematic and formal strategies we see in his work? I cannot help but recall Waugh's definition of a prig as "someone who judges people by his own, rather than by their, standards," and his insistence that "criticism only becomes useful when it can show people where their own principles are in conflict."[14] Though we must retain the right to read an author against the grain, we should at least consider the possibility that we are prigs when we criticize a writer like Waugh for failing to do what for him was unimaginable: writing a tolerant, serious, and politically inspirational novel.[15] We should also be alert to the fact that Waugh likes to set traps for high-minded readers, and especially for those who engage in the hermeneutics of suspicion. His fiction, as we forget at our peril, offers many cautionary tales about the folly of overinterpretation, especially overinterpretation of the politically slanted and conspiratorial kind.

It is easy—all too easy—to show that Waugh's novels are jam-packed with racial stereotypes and to demonstrate that his satires often deploy the discourses of racial taint and infection, as well as the discourse of climatic and geographical determinism (which has historically served to denigrate the inhabitants of the warmer climes or "coloured countries," as Waugh's brother Alec called them).[16] But a critic who proceeds to list his outrageous ethical lapses may be doing exactly what the novelist intends her to do: delivering an all-too-obvious rebuke, which the author, for complex and even perverse reasons, has set out to provoke in the first instance. Waugh's use of racist tropes is surprisingly multivalent and frequently verges on the parodic.[17] The same can be said of his revisiting of plots and motifs from more liberal and explicitly moral colonial novelists. Two brief examples of this practice will suffice. In his story "Incident in Azania," Waugh gives a gruesome twist to E. M. Forster's examination of the intertwined ideologies of race and gender in *A Passage to India*. Waugh's story concerns a beautiful English girl who stages her own abduction by native bandits. The incident causes a general hysteria among the denizens of the British legation, much like that occasioned by the putative rape of Forster's Adela Quested. The outrageous and purely imaginary cruelties to which the kidnapped girl's luscious body is submitted become a source of prurient interest both in the clubhouse and the London newspapers. When she finally escapes—unscathed, of course—it is revealed that her sensational story has unfortunately caused everyone to forget about the plight of an American missionary, who truly had been abducted. The arrival of his ears, followed by various body parts, and finally his dismembered trunk, is treated as a minor bureaucratic annoyance. "Incident in Azania," one might say, is an exposé of an exposé, a satire of a much gentler satire. It reveals the residual investment of *A Passage to India* in one of its critical targets: the colonial obsession with the purity of the white female body. The moral of Waugh's story, insofar as it has one, seems to be that such pious nonsense really should not claim as much moral energy and attention as it still seems to do in Forster's novel. A similarly parodic inversion of a canonical colonial text is evident in *Black Mischief*. Toward the end of the novel, a legation official criticizes Waugh's dissolute hero, Basil Seal, for talking about barbaric practices in front of "the ladies," who should be kept ignorant of any possible danger. "Oh, I like to see them scared," is Seal's unrepentant response.[18] The chivalrous scruples of Conrad's Marlow, who protects a lady from the corrosive knowledge of the heart of darkness, will not be of any use in resolving *Black Mischief*'s encounter with savagery.

These initial reflections on Waugh's shifty deployment of outrage and parody confirm Malcolm Bradbury's observation that Waugh was an anti-novelist—that his "plots and tone depend heavily on his power to look skeptically at the novel as a *genre*, at himself as a novelist . . . at the values he is inclined to uphold."[19] This critical self-consciousness, manifest in his efforts to preempt and manipulate the obvious strategies of critics, often makes for intriguing contradictions in Waugh's work.[20] These contradictions may be the most useful entry point for a fresh approach to his fiction, especially in the case of those works that operate on the borderlands of modernism and imperialism. Bearing in mind Waugh's own suggestion that a critic may productively show where a writer's principles are in conflict, I would like to trace out two of the perplexing conceptual tangles presented to us in *Black Mischief*.[21] I then try to relate them to a particular historical configuration. I suggest that the contradictions in Waugh's work, as well as the particular stylistic features they seem to generate, are a measure of the impact of the vast social fact of colonialism on the "aesthetic problem of representation": a problem which, as Waugh was well aware, confronted early-twentieth-century writers in a particularly formidable way.

⋮ ⋮ ⋮

The first contradiction concerns the question of authenticity, or the relationship between the original and the copy. A discourse of authenticity, we should note, is a pervasive and problematic one in discussions of modernism as a global phenomenon. The fact that modernism originated in European cities and was shaped by the nature of daily life in these places—by their characteristic culture of speed, spectacle, and commodity fetishism—has led many metropolitan intellectuals to assume that any manifestation of modernity or modernist artistic practice in the colonial world is necessarily an imitation. This is not the place to argue fully the various ways in which this judgment is incorrect or simplistic. Suffice it to say that, even if it were to some extent true, such a view is profoundly ideological and self-serving, in that it confirms the centrality of the center and the marginality of the margins.[22]

Much of the comedy in *Black Mischief* depends, of course, on the notion that colonial modernity is an imitation—that it involves an aping of ideas and practices that can at best attain a "galvanized and translated reality" beyond the metropolis.[23] The absurd One Year Plan that the Azanian emperor tries to implement can be decried as an imitation of an imitation: as an accelerated version of the Soviet Union's Five Year Plan to emulate and catch up with the technological modernity of the West. But Seth's conception of the modern is considerably more theatrical than Stalin's—and therefore more obviously coded as fake. The Azanian emperor is the ultimate mimic man: at one point he is described as a well-dressed blackface minstrel, ready to sing a spiritual (141). Matters of performance and display loom larger than actual social transformation in his agenda for modernization. A telling example of his priorities can be found in his efforts to reproduce a batch of Soviet propaganda posters he has received in the mail: he immediately thinks of solving the "difficulties of imitation" by getting slaves to copy the designs by hand (191). The more progressive thought of abolishing the cruel and archaic practice of slavery simply does not occur to him. Given his fascination with such things as straw hats, gloves, boots, and parades, and with the appearance (rather than the actual value) of such things as medals and banknotes, it is fitting that the novel's most important scene, from a symbolic point of view, should be a masquerade. At Seth's coronation ball, the idea of modernity and its dream of "making it new" find grotesque expression in the party novelties he has imported for the event. Costumes, false noses, and paper hats combine incongruously with the racial physiognomies of the wearers, which Waugh is at pains to emphasize: "brilliant sheaths of pigmented cardboard attached to noses of every anthropological type, the high arch of the Semite, freckled Nordic snouts, broad black nostrils from swamp villages of the mainland, the pulpy inflamed flesh of the alcoholic and unlovely syphilitic voids" (145). It is an unpleasant vision, to be sure, and one that is fraught with anxieties about cultural and racial purity and its authentic or mendacious expression.

But just as we think that we have Waugh pegged as an extreme spokesman for the colonial discourse of authenticity (a discourse which has proven surprisingly persistent), his work reveals some contrary possibilities.[24] Though its satire of the imitative modernity of the margins would seem designed to confirm the centrality of the center, *Black Mischief* also seems intent to explode any self-congratulatory notion of metropolitan cultural authority. The novel locates the fashionable center of the globe with exaggerated precision: it is the Curzon Street home of Lady Metroland (whose name is, of course, entirely to the point). The appalling celebrities who frequent her cocktail parties are shown to be no more cultured and no more in touch with their times than Seth. His faddishness and authoritarianism are fully matched by that of the publishing magnate Lord Monomark, who wants to make his brand new diet of onions and oatmeal compulsory for all. The parallel between the Londoners and Azanians becomes increasingly clear in the course of the novel. The Sakuyu family who squat in the broken-down car, for instance, have their English counterparts in the socialites Sonia and Alistair Trumpington, who are perpetually holed up in their dingy flat to avoid the bailiffs.

The conclusion of Waugh's novel, moreover, features a peculiar if not entirely unexpected shift. When the dissolute sophisticate Basil Seal finally returns to London after his stint as Seth's minister of modernization, he finds the city's wild parties to be "a bit flat" compared to the cannibal banquet that he attended at Moshu in the jungles of Azania. London comes to seem like an imitation of the "real thing" (305). *Black Mischief* thus ends with a reversal of the binary logic of the original and the imitation. In Waugh's fictional universe, "civilization" is such a vulnerable and tenuous notion that barbarism comes to seem the primary term: it is the authentic and original condition that all the various forms of contemporary misbehavior and incivility vainly emulate. This idea is elaborated in the irritable prose of the "Third Nightmare," a description of his return to London, which concludes Waugh's 1930 travelogue *Remote Places*:

> I was back at the center of the Empire, and in the spot where, at the moment, "everyone" was going. Next day the gossip-writers would chronicle the young M.P.s, peers, and financial magnates who were assembled in the rowdy cellar, hotter than Zanzibar, noisier than the market at Harar, more reckless of the decencies of hospitality than the taverns of Kabalo or Tabora. And a month later the wives of English officials would read about it, and stare out across the bush or jungle or desert or forest or golf links, and envy their sisters at home, and wish they had the money to marry rich men.
>
> Why go abroad?
>
> See England first.
>
> Just watch London knock spots off the Dark Continent.
>
> I paid the bill in yellow African gold. It seemed just tribute from the weaker races to their mentors.[25]

What strikes one here is not the jingoism, which is ironic in any case, but the way in which the usual terms of the competition have been revised. The savage culture is now the metropolitan one, and the pathetic imitator is no longer the African but the nostalgic colonial, yearning to ape the ways of the perfectly uncivilized socialites back home. If we bear in mind the pervasive anxiety about free-floating currencies, misleading symbols, and empty fiats recorded in *Black Mischief*, the implications of the yellow African gold that Waugh puts down on the nightclub table become clearer and richer. At the conclusion of a narrative of disconcerting cross-cultural encounter, the barbaric gold is offered as the ultimate token of value, as more stable and genuine than anything Waugh expects to find in London's decadent modernity.

The second contradiction I detect in *Black Mischief* is not unrelated to the first and it concerns the treatment of matters of geography and cultural location. Waugh (who confessed to an inveterate "inquisitiveness about places") was no less fascinated by maps than the young Joseph Conrad, and he often jokes in his fiction about their ideological and untrustworthy character.[26] In *Scoop*, for instance, we are told that the territory of the Ishmailia, inhabited by ruthless cannibals, has proven so resistant to colonization that the European powers decide by general consent to rule it off the map.[27] In "The Man Who Liked Dickens," by contrast, the remote Amazonian setting of the story is authoritatively mapped: the river Uraricoera is "boldly delineated in every school atlas," even though its actual course is a matter of conjecture and even though the inhabitants have never heard of the various republics—Columbia, Venezuela, Brazil, or Bolivia—of which, at various times, they were supposedly citizens.[28]

*Black Mischief* foregrounds the question of cartography even more decisively: it provides readers with a map of the imaginary island of Azania right after the title page. But despite this ostensibly helpful bit of front matter, a great deal of the novel's humor, as well as its peculiar forms of technical inventiveness, derives from and expresses the socio-geographic ineptitude of its characters. Waugh repeatedly demonstrates the delusory nature of Seth's assumption that the battle for progress, which he believes was "won on other fields five centuries back" (54), can readily be transferred to his jungle realm. A symptomatic detail is the emperor's question to a perplexed English visitor about where he might find a shop to buy an artesian well. Seth's notion of modernity is clearly devoid of any sense of local possibilities and constraints. It is no wonder that he favors architectural structures of steel and vita-glass, despite their unsuitability for tropical conditions, or that he plans a grand scheme of urban reconstruction that completely disregards the actual topography of his capital. Waugh's suspicion of modernist utopias, as we see here, is exacerbated by his dislike of the rootless and atopian style of thinking they tend to promulgate: a tendency best exemplified by the International Style in architecture, whose practitioners assumed that their abstract designs would be applicable anywhere and everywhere, like a scientific formula.[29]

Any discussion of cultural location in Waugh must consider the precise effects of one of his chief technical experiments: one that once caused an Edwardian gentleman to complain that the author's novels were not actually written, but spoken.[30] Waugh's fiction often presents the reader with passages of dialogue without the slightest hint of a conventionally novelistic mise-en-scène. A case in point is the opening of the third chapter of *Black Mischief*, which sets out to convey the collective reaction of Londoners to the news of the battle of Ukaka in far-flung Azania. It is worth quoting this bravura passage at some length:

> "Any news in the paper to-night, dear?
>
> "No, dear, nothing of interest."
>
> "Azania? That's part of Africa, ain't it?"
>
> "Ask Lil, she was at school last."
>
> "Lil, where's Azania?"
>
> "I don't know, father."
>
> "What do they teach you at school I'd like to know."
>
> "Only niggers."
>
> "It came in a cross-word quite lately. Independent native principality. You would have it was Turkey."
>
> "Azania? It sounds like a Cunarder to me."
>
> "But my dear, surely you remember that madly attractive blackamoor at Balliol."
>
> "Run up and see if you can find the atlas, deary. . . . Yes, where it always is, behind the stand in father's study."
>
> "Things look quieter in East Africa. That Azanian business cleared up at least."
>
> "Care to see the evening paper? There's nothing in it."
>
> "Randall. There might be a story in the Azanian cable. The new bloke was at Oxford. See what there is to it."

> Mr. Randall typed; His Majesty B. A. . . . ex-undergrad among the cannibals . . . scholar emperor's desperate bid for throne . . . Barbaric splendour . . . conquering hoards . . . ivory . . . elephants . . . east meets west . . .
>
> "Sanders. Kill that Azanian story in the London edition."
>
> "Anything in the paper this morning?"
> "No, dear, nothing of interest." (86–87)

Here Waugh's omission of any scenic description draws attention, ironically, to the question of geographical location. As in radio drama, the reader is called upon to imagine just where the voices are coming from: to visualize the offices, clubs, bed-sitters, and living rooms in which the conversations might be supposed to take place. The reader's disorientation also serves to underscore the geographic ineptitude of newspaper readers, most of whom do not have the foggiest idea where "Azania" might be, though they dimly suspect that it is inhabited by "niggers" or "blackamoors" and is therefore of scant interest—except perhaps as the clue in a crossword puzzle.

Metropolitan ignorance about the remote fringes of the world, comically exposed in Waugh's conversational montage, is no more excusable than Seth's ignorance of his immediate environment. Indeed, insofar as the novel can be read as a cautionary tale, its burden would seem to be that the modern world is one place and that the jungly heart of darkness is not so distant as one might think. The members of the British legation in Azania, isolated in their stockaded compound from what they consider to be the irrelevant squabblings of the surrounding natives, forget this at their peril. Their banal pursuit of romance, hobbies, and games would be the stuff of light comedy if it took place in the green and pleasant surroundings of, say, P. G. Wodehouse's Blandings Castle or Brinkley Court.[31] But in the sinister and morally challenging landscape of Azania—where hillsides are hollowed with "unexplored caverns, whence hyenas sally out at night to exhume . . . corpses" (228)—the cultural vacuity of the expatriate Brits seems more dangerous and culpable. A song with a line like "Start off with cocktails and end up with Eno's" (78), a recording of which the legation members receive in their diplomatic mailbag, might seem perfectly harmless when Bertie Wooster bangs it out on the piano at the Drones Club; but when the song is played near the ancient haunts of anthropophagi, the idea of wild parties and overindulgence seems to have more serious implications. In such a context the silly song serves as a presage of, or even as an invitation to the transgressions of, the cannibal banquet.

The socio-geographic delusions of its British characters are frequently cast in critical relief by the novel's jarring juxtapositions or cinematic cuts, which readers have often identified as one of the most striking features of its construction. In chapter 2, for instance, the legation's all-too-English teatime conversations about marmalade, public schools, knitting, and gardening, recorded in what we might think of as Waugh's atopic radio-drama style, is abruptly followed by a geographically specific description of the aftermath of a bloody battle: "Sixty miles southward in the Ukaka pass bloody bands of Sakuyu warriors played hide and seek among the rocks, chivvying the last fugitives of the army of Seyid, while behind them down the gorge, from cave villages of incalculable antiquity, the women crept out to rob the dead" (76). Without any overt authorial comment, this striking montage reminds the reader that Azania is not England, that in the island's rocky gorges, games like hide and seek are likely to assume a deadly seriousness.

But just as we think that a stable satirical point—namely, that it is important to attend to matters of location and that socio-geographic ineptitude is a bad thing—can be identified in his novel, Waugh seems intent to undermine that judgment. The figure that generates this uncertainty is Basil Seal, the sole exception to the geographical and political ignorance that afflicts the novel's characters. In contrast to average Londoners, who live secure in their lazy assumption that a revolution in Azania is so remote as not to merit any attention at all, Basil is keenly aware of the political situation there, to the point that he believes it may be "*one* place on the globe worth going to where things are happening" (112). Once he is on the spot and is essentially running the government, he becomes an expert on Azanian affairs: by the end of the novel, we find him dressed up in second-hand Sakuyu robes, holding forth on native practices, and participating as deviously as any Azanian chieftain in what members of the British legation would dismiss as "local politics." He even masters the language and oratorical styles of the Wanda, urging them to "kill [their] best meat and prepare a feast in the manner of [their] people" (296–97). What his expertise gets him, however, is a place in the circle of savages who sit down to devour his idiotic girlfriend Prudence, whose plane, unbeknown to Basil, has crashed in the cannibals' territory.

Once again we are left with a curious contradiction. What, if anything does Waugh advocate? Should we be attentive to what happens in marginal places, or should we eschew them, since, as Basil Seal's fate suggests, they seem to be morally infectious? And if we follow the latter course, do we not risk becoming as vacuous and amoral as the novel's London socialites? Geographical ignorance seems perilous and stupid, but expert knowledge, or so it seems, is not much better.

⁝ ⁝ ⁝

The contradictions I have traced in *Black Mischief* will not prove amenable to any easy resolution, but they nevertheless require some kind of critical account. In an illuminating essay on the novel, William Myers takes on this task with considerable success. He describes the contradictions and paradoxes of *Black Mischief* as the product of a peculiarly cross-grained temperament. Waugh, as he puts it, was not only at odds with the modern world but was also "at odds with himself to an extreme degree." "He had been an active homosexual; between his marriages he fornicated freely; he was an appalling bully, a drunkard, and a snob. Equally integral to his personality, of course, were his love of order, friendship, reason, good workmanship, honor and purity of life."[32] Certain issues—race, Myers argues, is one—seemed to make Waugh more aware of his own split impulses and allegiances, and they are therefore treated in his work with a curious mixture of fascination and brutality. Waugh's Catholicism, from which some critics have attempted to derive a stable frame of interpretation, is actually another problem issue: his conversion shortly before the publication of *Black Mischief* seems, if anything, to have exacerbated his sense of his self-division and ambivalence. Waugh was a profoundly contradictory Christian: the sharp moral dichotomies and austere sense of hierarchies that appealed to him are challenged rather than justified by central Christian doctrine of redemption.[33] It is therefore wiser, Myers suggests, to see the contradictory nature of Waugh's work as its defining quality: "a perversely negative capability of being in the midst of flagrant contradictions without reaching inelegantly towards ways of resolving them."[34]

But rather than settle for a semi-biographical account of the tangles in Waugh's fiction, I would like to search for a more historical explanation. I would like to suggest that the quintessential formal features of his work might be both a product and an expression of a set of cognitive and representational problems generated, in the final analysis, by global imperialism.

To propose such an account I would like to bring into play Fredric Jameson's 1988 essay "Modernism and Imperialism." This is one of Jameson's more vulnerable pieces, depending as it does on a rather baroque reading of a descriptive passage from Forster's *Howards End* and on a problematic gesture of bracketing and marginalization: he explicitly excludes colonial fiction (the work of Kipling, Haggard, Wells, Conrad, and the like) from his account, in order to focus on more properly "modernist" texts with a metropolitan setting and an ostensibly apolitical agenda. But "Modernism and Imperialism" is also a provocative and inspiring piece, in that it invites other scholars to think about the impact of imperial conditions on modernist cultural forms in new and exploratory ways.

As always, Jameson's reading relies on a periodizing hypothesis. He argues that the age of European colonialism from (roughly) 1884 to 1945 differed significantly from the post–World War Two era in terms of the capacity of metropolitan citizens to imagine the colonized world. It was only in the period of decolonization, he postulates, that the unknown and repressed "others" of imperialism began, as it were, to speak on their own behalf, and to demand recognition from the metropolitan powers, if only as a problem to be dealt with. Before that time, imperialism registered itself on metropolitan culture—and on modernist fiction in particular—mainly as a kind of spatial and epistemological disjunction: a failure of cognitive mapping, if you will. In the colonial era, Jameson explains, "a significant segment of the economic system as a whole is . . . located elsewhere, beyond the metropolis, outside the daily life and existential experience of the home country, in colonies over the water whose own life and life world remains unknown and unimaginable for the subjects of the imperial power."[35] The operations of empire, in other words, connect the metropolitan subject (whose quotidian routines may be confined to, say, a small area of London) with a multitude of invisible others; but the meaning of that connection remains, for most people, obscure. Imperialism, in this sense, creates the political unconscious of modernism: part of the social totality remains inaccessible and the missing pieces of the puzzle cannot readily be supplied: "No enlargement of personal experience (in the knowledge of other social classes, for example), no intensity of self-examination (in the form of whatever social guilt), no scientific deductions on the basis of the internal evidence of First World data, can ever be enough to include this radical otherness of colonial life, colonial suffering, and exploration, let alone the structural connections between that and this, between absent space and daily life in the metropolis."[36] The strange new artistic forms we associate with modernism (and Jameson focuses in this essay on the peculiarly rich and ambiguous stylistic effects that arise in modernist descriptions of place) are, then, the result of an unconscious and stylistic compensation for this epistemological incompleteness.

Evelyn Waugh's fictions about remote places would not immediately seem to fit Jameson's hypothesis. Though rigorously modernist in form, they *do* attempt some sort of representation of the margins of the colonial world.[37] In fact, those margins were, in the early thirties, more compelling to Waugh than the life of the metropolis. "The truth is that I am deeply interested in the jungle and only casually interested in Mayfair, and one has to write about what interests one," he once declared.[38] Despite this interest, Waugh's fiction does not escape the cognitive condition Jameson describes. But it does register the impact of this condition in different ways from those we see in a novel like *Howards End.*

It is worth recalling here Jameson's brief comments on *A Passage to India:* a novel one might also be tempted to put forward as an exception to the position laid out in "Modernism and Imperialism," because of its sympathetic representation of colonial subjects like Dr. Aziz and his friends. Jameson insists, however, that the foreclosure of the radical otherness of the colonized is nevertheless evident in the novel in the ever-deepening mystery of the Indian landscape and of Hindu characters, like Godbole, who remain essentially incomprehensible throughout. Now, the fantastic nature of its setting means that *Black Mischief* (for all its correspondences with Waugh's travel writing) cannot be approached with quite the same quasi-anthropological representational expectations we bring to a novel like *A Passage to India.* Truth-telling or knowledge of an actually existing "other" is strictly speaking rendered impossible from the start—and this may be Waugh's primary strategy of containment—a way of avoiding any consideration of relations of exploitation and domination. But the tropes through which the novel manages to distance its colonial characters are nevertheless intriguing. Seth, as we have seen, is presented as the all-too-recognizable mimic man; while the other Azanians, most notably the Sakuyu and Wanda of the dark jungles, are presented as not so much unknowable as taboo: any real knowledge of them is insistently proscribed. A single descriptive passage will suffice to make my point:

> Beyond the hills on the low Wanda coast where no liners called, and the jungle stretched unbroken to the sea, other more ancient rites and other knowledges *furtively encompassed;* green, *sunless* paths; *forbidden* ways unguarded save for a wisp of grass plaited between two stumps, ways of death and initiation, the *forbidden* places of juju and masked dancers; the drums of the Wanda throbbing in *sunless, forbidden* places. (154, my italics)[39]

This melodramatic description offers an alibi of sorts for the repression or foreclosure of anything other than a stereotypical encounter with colonized subjects and their realm. A similar argument may be made with regard to the end of the novel. Here the metropolitan subjects' ignorance of the periphery comes to seem even more intractable than it did in the "radio drama" passage from chapter 3. It is not only that Basil Seal's London friends fail to show any interest in his Azanian experiences (they urge him, in no uncertain terms, to "keep a stopper on the far-flung stuff" [305]) but also that these experiences end up corresponding exactly to the exotic melodrama a blasé, urban sophisticate would have imagined from the outset: jungle intrigue, murder, fetid romance, cannibal banquets. The possible intrusion of a radical otherness is, as it were, ruled out in advance and substituted for by the always-already familiar.[40]

But Waugh is more savvy about the metropolitan repression of the colonial world than many of his contemporaries. (We may even want to entertain the possibility of reading *Black Mischief* as a kind of parody *avant la lettre* of the cognitive condition Jameson describes.) To be sure, Waugh's conservative, ahistorical, and (at times) religious way of thinking—as well as his refusal to create a novel "fettered" by the old "chains of cause and effect"—makes him unlikely to rise to the interpretive challenge of thinking through the relationship between center and periphery in economic or politically progressive ways.[41] An interest in cartography, after all, cannot substitute for the vast representational and interpretive task of cognitive mapping on a global scale. But the structure of a novel like *Black Mischief* is marked nevertheless by a desire for a more encompassing vision than that permitted by the psychological, apolitical, geographically restricted modernist novel. The most striking and experimental aspects of *Black Mischief*'s construction—the oscillation from an invented Mayfair to an invented Azania, the recurrent symbolic parallelism between metropolitan and marginal situations, the juxtaposition of carefully located passages of description and passages of dialogue from which chronotopic cues are tantalizingly eliminated—may be seen as an attempt to foreground and resolve the representational problems that result from the spatial and cognitive disjuncture produced by the colonial world system. The effort is perhaps a failure on the thematic and conceptual level, as the various contradictions I have traced would seem to reveal. But the novel's construction nevertheless registers something which, at least in Jameson's account, is often repressed in modernist fiction: an awareness that the everyday life of the metropolis should not be severed from what is occurring on the periphery.

For this reason, if no other, Waugh cannot be dismissed (to return to Steven Marcus's opinion cited at the beginning of this essay) as a novelist of the second-rate, owing to his refusal to treat his themes with the requisite literary seriousness. I would suggest instead that most critics have failed to give first-rate attention to the impact of colonial modernity on matters of form. Waugh's very serious attempt to find "a new balanced interrelation of subject and form" in *Black Mischief*, his first colonial novel, reveals a surprisingly lucid understanding that modernism is best grasped as the culture of a wildly uneven but nonetheless singular process of global modernity.

## Notes

1 The quoted phrase in my title is from Waugh's *Remote People*, 41.

2 Waugh, *The Ordeal of Gilbert Pinfold*, 110. An exception to this trend is McCartney, who offers a detailed examination of Waugh's response to various aspects of modernism in *Confused Roaring*.

3 Waugh, "Ronald Firbank," *The Essays, Articles, and Reviews of Evelyn Waugh*, 57.

4 Waugh, "Let Us Return to the Nineties but not to Oscar Wilde," *Essays*, 123.

5 Ibid., 123.

6 Ibid., 125.

7 Waugh, "My Favorite Film Star," *Essays*, 68; and "Ronald Firbank," 57.

8 Waugh, "Ronald Firbank," 59. The word "directed" demands attention: it suggests that Waugh viewed the novelist's task as related to that of a movie director, who approaches narrative as an objective structure, rather than as a matter of subjective and organic creation.

9 Marcus, "Evelyn Waugh and the Art of Entertainment."

10 Ousmane's *God's Bits of Wood* was originally published in France in 1960 as *Les bouts de bois de dieu*.

11 Ousmane Sembene, *God's Bits of Wood*, 32.

12 Ibid., 80.

13 Waugh, "A Conservative Manifesto," *Essays*, 162. If Ousmane's emblem of

modernity is the *Smoke of the Savanna* speeding across Africa on its tracks, Waugh's emblem of modernity is an airplane doing the loop-the-loop. The latter maneuver is effective in producing a topsy-turvy, estranged vision of the world, but it doesn't exactly get anyone anywhere. See Waugh's *Labels*, 11–12, and McCartney, *Confused Roaring*, 4–5, for a discussion of modernity and stunt flying.

14 Waugh, *Remote People*, 40.

15 I should point out that for Waugh tolerance is not necessarily a good thing. In the past, he argues, it served people well: a spirit of tolerance helped to eliminate many cruel and unjust practices from the English social system. In the twentieth century, however, it has produced the belief that there is "good in everything": a well-meaning mindlessness that can only result in the short-circuiting of any ethical judgment. If there is a moral urgency in Waugh's work, it is best captured in the sentence with which he closes his essay on tolerance: "There are still things which are worth fighting *against*." See "Tolerance," *Essays*, 128.

16 *The Coloured Countries* is the title of Alec Waugh's book on the Caribbean, which appeared in the United States under the title *The Hot Countries*.

17 In an essay on the challenges that *Black Mischief* poses to the reader, Myers comments on the contradictory nature of Waugh's treatment of race. He notes that the novel's racist and yet somehow affectionate treatment of the character known as "Black Bitch" is calculated to make most readers feel queasy. But if we condemn Waugh too strenuously for this cartoonish characterization, or for the way he depicts Black Bitch's farcical marriage to Seth's military commander, General Connolly, we might "disqualify ourselves from joining in his sharp indignation at the mean-spiritedness of the Colonial administrators who finally take over Azania and justify Connolly's expulsion on the grounds that 'he's married to a wog.'" See Myers, "Potential Recruits," 42.

18 Waugh, *Black Mischief* (Boston: Little, Brown, 1977), 277. Subsequent references to this edition are cited parenthetically in the text.

19 Bradbury, *Evelyn Waugh*, 4–5.

20 Given the fact that so much of the satire in *Black Mischief* is directed at Africa, one might come away with the impression that Waugh is less evenhanded in practicing the politics of pillorying, since he is more likely to criticize liberal sentimentality or African modernization than conservative defenses of the English status quo. While there is certainly an element of truth in this view—Waugh's sensibility is conservative—a reading of his entire oeuvre suggests that his vitriol is as catholic as it is Catholic.

21 Though I confine myself to only a couple of the contradictions I see in the novel, one could profitably discuss at least one more. Consider the following paradox: though the novel sets out to demonstrate the vacuousness of modernity and the impossibility of human progress, it includes a defense of the chief achievements of the modern state. As the One Year Plan begins to reveal its full

absurdity, Basil Seal, Seth's minister of modernization, reminds the emperor of "a few things that have ceased to be modern": "constitutional monarchy, bicameral legislature, proportional representation, women's suffrage, independent judicature, freedom of the press, referendums" (168–69). The potency of this reminder is not undone by the farce that follows this exchange.

22 Herwitz, "Modernism at the Margins," 605–6.

23 Waugh, *Remote People*, 23.

24 Jameson points out that contemporary discussions of modernity, stripped of its earlier utopian impulses, still rely on a curious illusion: that the West has "something no one else possesses," but which others "ought to desire for themselves." See *A Singular Modernity*, 8.

25 Waugh, *Remote People*, 184.

26 Waugh's suspicion of maps may be one reason why he preferred to set his satires of remote places in invented countries: it allows him to exaggerate the unreliability of official mapping and metropolitan knowledge of the world at large.

27 Waugh, *Scoop*, 106.

28 Waugh, "The Man Who Loved Dickens," *The Complete Stories*, 128.

29 In a 1938 essay, "A Call to Orders," Waugh wrote of "the post-War Corbusier plague" during which "horrible little architects crept about [Europe]—curly-headed, horn-spectacled, volubly explaining their 'machines for living.' " These concrete and glass constructions, he argues, fail to take local conditions into consideration: "In a few months our climate began to expose the imposture. The white flat walls that had looked as cheerful as a surgical sterilizing plant became mottled with damp; our east winds howled though the steel frames of the windows" (*Essays*, 52).

30 Cited in McDonnell, *Evelyn Waugh*, 27. Waugh often emphasized the importance of dialogue in the modern novel and praised writers like Ronald Firbank and Ernest Hemingway for their innovations in this regard. He also recognized T. S. Eliot as a master of what I call the "radio drama" effect, noting that both *The Waste Land* and "Fragments of an Agon" encouraged the development of a "technical apparatus" useful to modern novelists.

31 Waugh was an admirer of Wodehouse's prose style but observed in a 1961 broadcast: "For Mr. Wodehouse, there has been no Fall of Man." Cited in Lane, "Can You Love P. G. Wodehouse Too Much?" *Black Mischief* conducts the narrative experiment of placing Wodehousean characters in a fallen world.

32 Myers, "Potential Recruits," 49–50.

33 See, e.g., Lodge, *Evelyn Waugh*, 12. Myers discusses Waugh's Catholicism persuasively in "Potential Recruits," 49–51.

34 Myers, "Potential Recruits," 51. A profound sense of contradiction is also fundamental to Waugh's understanding of the value of art. It is precisely because of the artist's own moral failings, Waugh argues, that he or she might do some good in society: "Humility is not a virtue propitious to the artist. It is often pride, emulation, avarice, malice—all the odious qualities—which drive a man

to complete, elaborate, refine, destroy, renew his work until he has made something that gratifies his pride and envy and greed. And in so doing he enriches the world more than the generous and good, though he may lose his own soul in the process. That is the paradox of artistic achievement." Cited in Lane, "Foreword: Waugh in Pieces," in *Complete Stories*, xxiii.

35 Jameson, "Modernism and Imperialism," 50–51.

36 Ibid., 51.

37 Myers concludes that "the art of Evelyn Waugh is not one of representation but of confrontation": an assessment for which there is much justification ("Potential Recruits," 48). I am insisting, however perversely, on treating *Black Mischief* as relevant to what Waugh calls the "aesthetic problem of representation."

38 Waugh, "Travel—and Escape from Your Friends," *Essays*, 134.

39 Waugh observed that his intention in the novel was to keep "the darker aspects of barbarism continually and unobtrusively present . . . like the continuous, remote throbbing of hand drums" (cited in Bradbury, *Evelyn Waugh*, 54–55). I like to think of the repetition of "forbidden" and "sunless" in the description of the Wanda's jungle haunts as creating this effect.

40 Nowhere is this demonstrated more humorously than in Waugh's story "The Man Who Loved Dickens." A young man announces to his faithless wife:

> "I am leaving next week for the Uraricoera."
>
> "Golly, where's that?"
>
> "I'm not perfectly sure. Somewhere in Brazil, I think. It's unexplored. I shall be away a year."
>
> "But darling, how ordinary! Like people in books—big game, I mean, and all that."

The very idea of genre is here associated with tedium, and the novel of colonial adventure is made to seem the most tedious of all (see Waugh, *Complete Stories*, 131).

41 This much is clear from the defense of colonialism he was to offer on the occasion of the Italian invasion of Abyssinia (see Waugh, "We Can Applaud Italy," in *Essays*, 162–64). But even here, Waugh's provocations are worth attending to, especially in the wake of the catastrophes of Rwanda, Liberia, and Sudan in our time. Waugh is right to consider African realities more formidable than might be imagined by sentimentalists who think of "immemorial customs" in terms of people "dancing round maypoles in their national costumes." Indeed, this kind of sentimentalism may be more pervasive in our neoliberal age in which a celebration of "cultural difference" has replaced the modernist emphasis on the new.

## Works Cited

Bradbury, Malcolm. *Evelyn Waugh*. London: Oliver and Boyd, 1964.

Herwitz, Daniel. "Modernism at the Margins." In *Blank—: Architecture, Apartheid and Beyond*, ed Hilton Judin and Ivan Vladislavic, 605–21. Cape Town: David Philip, 2000.

Jameson, Fredric. "Modernism and Imperialism." In Terry Eagleton, Fredric Jameson, and Edward W. Said, *Nationalism, Colonialism and Literature*, 43–66. Minneapolis: University of Minnesota Press, 1990.

——. *A Singular Modernity: Essay on the Ontology of the Modern*. London: Verso, 2002.

Lane, Anthony. "Can You Love P. G. Wodehouse Too Much?" *New Yorker*, April 19, 2004, 138-49.

——. "Foreword: Waugh in Pieces." In *The Complete Stories of Evelyn Waugh*, ix–xxiv. Boston: Little, Brown, 1999.

Lodge, David. *Evelyn Waugh*. New York: Columbia University Press, 1964.

Marcus, Steven. "Evelyn Waugh and the Art of Entertainment." *Partisan Review* 23 (1956): 348–57.

McCartney, George. *Confused Roaring: Evelyn Waugh and the Modernist Tradition*. Bloomington: Indiana University Press, 1987.

McDonnell, Jacqueline. *Evelyn Waugh*. New York: St. Martin's Press, 1988.

Myers, William. "Potential Recruits: Evelyn Waugh and the Reader of *Black Mischief*." *Renaissance and Modern Studies* 21 (1977): 40–51.

Sembene, Ousmane. *God's Bits of Wood*. Translated by Francis Price. Oxford: Heineman, 1995.

Waugh, Alec. *The Hot Countries* [*The Coloured Countries*]. New York: Literary Guild, 1930.

Waugh, Evelyn. *Black Mischief* (1932). Boston: Little, Brown, 1977.

——. *The Complete Stories of Evelyn Waugh*. Boston: Little, Brown, 1999.

——. *The Essays, Articles, and Reviews of Evelyn Waugh*. Edited by Donat Gallagher. Boston: Little, Brown, 1984.

——. *Labels: A Mediterranean Journey*. London: Duckworth, 1930.

——. *The Ordeal of Gilbert Pinfold*. Boston: Little Brown, 1957.

——. *Remote People* (1931). London: Penguin, 2002.

——. *Scoop* (1938). Boston: Little, Brown, 1999.

# IRELAND
# AND SCOTLAND

*Richard Begam*

⋮

EIGHT

# Joyce's Trojan Horse: *Ulysses* and the Aesthetics of Decolonization

> Is this country [Ireland] destined to resume its ancient position as the Hellas of the north some day?
>
> JAMES JOYCE, "Ireland, Island of Saints and Sages"

For roughly a thirty-year period, from the appearance of Richard Ellmann's *James Joyce* in 1959 through the structuralist and poststructuralist revolutions of the 1970s and 1980s, it was standard practice to regard Joyce as a largely apolitical writer, whose commitment to cosmopolitanism and modernism was inversely proportional to his commitment to Irish nationalism.[1] On this reading, Stephen's comment to Bloom in "Eumaeus" was seen as representative of Joyce's own attitude: "You suspect . . . that I may be important because I belong to the *faubourg Saint Patrice* called Ireland . . . but I suspect . . . that Ireland must be important because it belongs to me."[2] The revisionary criticism of the 1990s, led by Vincent Cheng, Enda Duffy, David Lloyd, Emer Nolan, and others has amply demonstrated that, Stephen's protests to the contrary notwithstanding, Joyce was profoundly engaged by questions of politics and history.[3] The work of the revisionary critics has been valuable not only for revealing the depth of Joyce's anticolonial sentiments but also for highlighting many of the social and cultural aspects of *Ulysses* that had previously been neglected. Yet, as beneficial as this criticism has proven, it has frequently pushed Joyce too far in the direction of nativism (see Nolan's and Castle's defense of the Citizen), while overlooking those innovations in literary style and technique that are most often associated with modernism.[4]

In what follows, I take an exegetical *via media*, positioning myself between earlier commentary, which tends to view Joyce as an aesthete indifferent to nationalism, and more recent interpretation, which often treats him as a nationalist indifferent to formalism.[5] Rejecting the notion that one must choose between textual autonomy and political commitment, Joyce aggressively pursues a strategy of cultural decolonization, but he does so—crucially—at the level of aesthetics. This means that to compare *Ulysses* to an IRA bomb, as Enda Duffy famously did, is to miss one of the novel's fundamental points.[6] For in confronting English colonialism, Joyce's approach is, not surprisingly, Odyssean rather than Achillean. Yes, *Ulysses* seeks to decolonize Irish literature by employing the formal methods of modernism, but it does so indirectly, obliquely, and, as it were, undercover. In other words, Joyce's novel functions as a kind of Trojan horse, which he uses to smuggle a distinctly Irish brand of literary culture into an English and internationalist canon.

Joyce makes clear his commitment to cultural decolonization in the opening scene of *Ulysses*, which self-consciously situates the modernist 1920s in relation to the Irish 1890s.[7] Evoking two of the dominant influences of the Irish Nineties, Oscar Wilde's aestheticism and Douglas Hyde's nationalism, Joyce develops radical alternative to both these traditions by constructing a modernism that is technically revolutionary in its innovations—at times even threatening its own representational limits—but that nevertheless retains an identifiably Irish character and sensibility. To illustrate this point, I examine how *Ulysses* employs two of modernism's most celebrated formal devices—stream-of-consciousness and the "mythical method"[8]—not to universalize its characters and situations but to particularize them.[9] But in advancing this position, my argument goes well beyond the self-evident claim that Joyce's novel evinces an interest in Irish history and politics, a position few would dispute today. My argument is, rather, that Joyce's formal intervention is far more extreme: that when he uses those devices traditionally associated with modernism's turn toward cultural or historical transcendence, it is *precisely to subvert and invert* that transcendence; that while "steam-of-consciousness" and the "mythical method" are typically viewed as vehicles for *escaping* cultural specificity and locality, Joyce employs them to *undermine* ahistorical or transcultural aspirations. In other words, Joyce's modernism deconstructs modernism's own universalist impulses, a deconstruction that is not surprising, given his preference for Aristotelian materialism over Platonic idealism; at the same time it demonstrates that concepts like "mind" and "myth"—so often conceived as terms of transcendence—can be used to recover national history and establish cultural identity.[10]

⋮ ⋮ ⋮

Toward the beginning of "Telemachus," as Stephen Dedalus and Buck Mulligan stand atop the Martello tower and look out over Dublin Bay, Mulligan intones a line from the *Odyssey* that would have been familiar to every public schoolboy of the day: "*Epi oinopa ponton*" (1.78), "upon the winedark sea." Of course the *pontos* in question is not the Mediterranean but the Irish Sea, and therefore presumably not winedark but, to quote Mulligan, "snotgreen," what he calls the "new art colour for our Irish poets" (1.73). The connection with the Irish poets is not incidental. As the episode unfolds, we hear those poets comment artfully, if not colorfully, on the very same sea that inspires Buck's morning afflatus. George Russell, invoked by Mulligan, apostrophizes it as "Our mighty mother" (1.85), while William Butler Yeats, remembered by Stephen, hymns it as the "white breast of the dim sea" (1.245).[11] The maternal imagery is especially important, emphasizing as it does one of the central themes of *Portrait:* Stephen's struggle as an artist to come to terms with Mother Ireland.[12] It is presumably with these associations in mind that Mulligan turns to Stephen and, dropping his mask for once, remarks in earnest: "God, Kinch, if you and I could only work together we might do something for the island. Hellenise it" (1.157–58).

Now it might seem that in 1904 "Hellenising" was the last thing that Ireland needed. Obviously what Mulligan means when he speaks of "Hellenising" the island is "aestheticizing" it, transforming it from the place where "motley is worn" into a kind of Oxbridge on the Liffey, a Republic of Letters, if not of citizens. At the turn of the century, talk of things Greek inevitably evoked the Nineties and a certain Paterian style and sensibility, one that *Portrait of the Artist* deliciously and mercilessly lays bare. But if a word like "Hellenise" looks back to the 1890s, it also looks forward to the 1920s, and more specifically to that *annus mirabilis*, 1922. For the Hellenisation that Mulligan so desired in 1904 would be realized eighteen years later when James Joyce published *Ulysses*, a novel that transforms a Dublin ad-man into an Odyssean hero, and an average Dublin day into a Homeric epic of wandering and return. The year 1922 was also memorable for another reason, one almost as prominent in Joyce's mind as the publication of *Ulysses:* it was the year that Ireland achieved her own Hellenic promise of democracy by at last securing statehood. With a single, typically overdetermined word—"Hellenise"—Joyce effectively condenses thirty years of political and cultural history, transporting the reader from the Ireland of the Celtic twilight and the Literary Revival, through the founding of the Abbey Theatre, the staging of *Playboy of the Western World*, the Easter Rebellion of 1916, when a terrible beauty was born—not to mention Joyce's *Portrait*—right up to Ireland's emergence as a nation with the establishment of the Irish Free State. How this passage of time is negotiated, how *Ulysses* moves from the aestheticism and nationalism of the 1890s to the literary modernism of the 1920s, will be the principal subject of this essay.

In taking up this subject, I'd like to begin with two quotations. The first is a remark Joyce made in 1906 in Trieste to Alessandro Francini: "Condemned to express themselves in a language not their own [the Irish] have stamped on it the mark of their own genius and compete for glory with the civilised nations. This is then called English literature."[13] The phrase "civilised nations" is especially rich, underscoring as it does Ireland's status in 1906 as "barbarous" colony. But of greater interest is the last part of Joyce's comment: "This is then called English literature"; for with these words Joyce predicted, with great prescience, his own literary fortunes. Having grappled with a language not entirely his own—a language he spoke and wrote only with "unrest of spirit"[14]—he created in *Ulysses* a novel that was destined to become one of the most celebrated monuments of English modernism. This was no accident. The establishment of *Ulysses* within the modernist canon was actively promoted by scholars, especially from the 1950s through the 1970s, who consistently portrayed Joyce as a writer who was apolitical, humanist, and universalist. More recently—and in ways that predictably respond to political forces within the academy—the pendulum has swung in the opposite direction, as Joyce's local and sectarian commitments have sometimes been exaggerated, with a view to seeing him as a narrowly, or even exclusively, Irish writer. The best evidence shows, as I have suggested, that Joyce positioned himself between the extremes of nationalism and cosmopolitanism, of particularism and universalism; that while he was committed to participating in, and helping to create, the international movement that modernism became, he did so in a way that retained a precise and unmistakable cultural specificity, one that left a distinctively Irish imprint on literary modernism.

And this brings me to my second quotation, the famous conclusion to *Portrait of the Artist:* "Welcome, O life! I go to encounter for the millionth time the reality of experience and to forge in the smithy of my soul the uncreated conscience of my race" (275–76). Early commentators tended to read this line in a straightforward manner, treating it as a stirring affirmation of the artist as cultural hero, while later commentators construed it more skeptically and ironically, seeing it as yet another instance of Stephen's inflated egotism.[15] Both of these readings are significantly qualified, however, when we attend to Joyce's buried pun—"forge" both in the sense of "shape metal" and "counterfeit coin"—a wordplay which reminds us that the mythical Dedalus is not merely a blacksmith but a cunning artificer as well, knowledgeable in the "ignotas artes." When Stephen informs Cranly that the only weapons he will allow himself are "silence, exile, and cunning" (269), he is recalling that other cunning artificer, Odysseus, who as Renaissance tradition informs us, dedicated himself not to *forza* but *froda*, not to the violence of the soldier but to the ingenuity of the artificer, with all that this last word implies concerning the artful manipulation of appearance, of tempting surfaces and hidden depths.[16] And here it is worth remembering that if the Trojans were a credulous and horse-loving people, so too are the English. With *Ulysses*, Joyce's greatest bequest to the English literary canon, he reminds us that Greeks are not the only ones who bear gifts, and that Trojan horses can be made of words as well as wood.

With this is mind, I would like to return to the opening scene of *Ulysses* and offer what will strike some as a polemical assertion: if a national conscience is created through forgery—through counterfeiting, cunning, dissembling, and deceit—then in 1904 the Irish were already well on the road to achieving their identity. At least this would seem to be Joyce's view, for "Telemachus" places before us two Irishmen, each of whom effortlessly plays three different roles. The first two pieces of play-acting are familiar to us because Joyce, leaving little to chance, provided the program notes himself: Stephen is cast as the Prince of Ithaca and the Prince of Denmark, as Telemachus and Hamlet, while Mulligan plays his antithetical other, those Usurpers of Kingdom, Antinuous and Claudius. Less immediately obvious, however, is a third set of roles, in which our heroes impersonate two English gentlemen from the Nineties, who entertain each other, and us, by trading witticisms on art and culture. Given that Homer and Shakespeare were both in the public domain, Joyce was free to steal from them with impunity. But his third author, the scene's ghost writer in more ways than one, would still require a payment of royalties, since he was only recently deceased and had been one of the most commercially successful dramatists ever to write for the English stage. I am speaking, of course, of Joyce's famous compatriot, Oscar Wilde. Consider the following exchange:

> —Look at yourself, he said, you dreadful bard!
>
> Stephen bent forward and peered at the mirror held out to him, cleft by a crooked crack. Hair on end. As he and others see me. Who chose this face for me? This dogsbody to rid of vermin. It asks me too.
>
> —I pinched it out of the skivvy's room, Buck Mulligan said. It does her all right. The aunt always keeps plainlooking servants for Malachai . . .
>
> Laughing again, he brought the mirror away from Stephen's peering eyes.
>
> —The rage of Caliban at not seeing his face in a mirror, he said. If Wilde were only alive to see you!
>
> Drawing back and pointing, Stephen said with bitterness:
>
> —It is a symbol of Irish art. The cracked lookingglass of a servant. (1.138–146)

In this exchange, Mulligan is quoting the "Preface" to *The Picture of Dorian Gray*, where Wilde famously observes, "The nineteenth-century dislike of Realism is the rage of Caliban seeing his own face in a glass. The nineteenth-century dislike of Romanticism is the rage of Caliban not seeing his own face in a glass."[17] The immediate context for Mulligan's remark is Stephen's refusal to kneel and pray for his dying mother. In citing the passage from Wilde, Mulligan suggests that Stephen's anti-Romantic posture, his fear of displaying sentiment or filial attachment, has made him into a Caliban, one who behaves brutishly toward his mother, one who is unfeeling, unnatural, monstrous. But the passage carries another, deeper resonance, for "Caliban" is not merely a neutral term of description, indicating an uncultured or loutish type; it is also part of the representational logic of empire, which routinely depicts the colonized subject as less than human, as part man and part animal. Vincent Cheng, among others, has anatomized and analyzed English racial stereotypes that identify the Irishman as a Caliban-like figure, stereotypes with which Joyce was familiar, as *Stephen Hero* makes clear "when Madden (Davin in *Portrait*) speaks of those 'old stale libels—the drunken Irishman, the baboon-faced Irishman that we see in *Punch*.' "[18]

It is presumably the insinuation that Stephen has descended to the level of rude colonial that motivates the special bitterness of his response. He quotes Wilde right back at his companion but now chooses a passage from "The Decay of Lying," the dramatic dialogue which famously asserts that "life imitates art." Stephen is making two points. On an aesthetic level, he objects—as does Wilde's alter-ego in the dialogue—to "art being treated as a mirror," an approach that would have the effect of "reducing genius to the position of a cracked looking-glass."[19] Stephen, "loveliest mummer of them all," as Mulligan calls him (1.97–98), tells his compatriot that they are both playing roles, both pretending to be something other than what they are, both functioning as instances of life imitating art. In this particular case, the art being imitated is a dialogue on aesthetics by Oscar Wilde. Stephen's Wildean epigram on Irish art raises the question of whether such imitation is desirable, for the epigram implies that the problem with Irish art is not merely that it is an imitation, but a cheap and tawdry one at that, a servile form of mimesis, the cracked looking-glass of a subjugated people.

But this is not all Stephen says to Mulligan. On a more general level, he is making a second point—this one cultural—which depends on the fact that his dialogue with Mulligan is mediated through Oscar Wilde. Here it is important to understand that "The Decay of Lying" is true to its own precept that "life imitates art." It therefore takes as its model an established art form, the Platonic dialogue, which it then recasts as the witty conversation of two English gentlemen just down from Oxford—sort of Benjamin Jowett meets Walter Pater, with a whiff of decadence added. But from Joyce's perspective there is another kind of imitation going on, one that is more revealing. Wilde is, in a sense, attempting to out-English the English, casting himself in the role of world-weary sophisticate, who is as remote from the stereotypical Irish Paddy as he can be. So far from being a rude man of the bogs, or the romanticized "noble savage" that Haines seeks and Synge delivers, Vivian smokes perfumed cigarettes, speaks in paradoxes, and abhors nature. Nothing could be further from the idea of the Irishman as a "natural." Wilde is, indeed, making life imitate art, turning his own life into a piece of play-acting in which the stage-Irishman reinvents himself as stage-Englishman. But perhaps what is most interesting about this mirror-act is the crack that Stephen detects in it, the crack which enables him to recognize that the mirror is secondhand and the imitation factitious, the smudged reflection of a servant kneeling before his master. If Mulligan has accused Stephen of being an uncouth colonial, a Caliban-like malcontent who narcissistically clutches at a looking-glass, Stephen returns the favor by accusing Mulligan of obsequiously toadying before power, of playing the Wildean aesthete as a means of denying his own Irish identity.[20]

Particularly noteworthy is the way Joyce's three different subtexts—the Homeric, the Shakepearean, and the Wildean—now converge. Remember that the dramatic situation in both the *Odyssey* and *Hamlet* involves a young and politically inexperienced prince learning to take up arms not against some existentially vague sea of troubles but against a very real—a too too solid and sullied—usurper. That call to arms is finally heeded: in both Homer and Shakespeare, closure is achieved only after Telemachus and Hamlet have resorted to combat. Wilde's theater brings another form of combat to the English stage, a purely verbal kind in which smooth-talking replaces heavy-breathing, in which if Ariel does not cast out Caliban, Odysseus certainly casts out Achilles. Still, however civilized the contest of wills may have become, executed with words not wounds, it is nevertheless at bottom still a duel that is being fought, conducted according to a logic of thrust and parry:

> —It's not fair to tease you like that, Kinch, is it? [Mulligan] said kindly. God knows you have more spirit than any of them.
>
> Parried again. He fears the lancet of my art as I fear that of his. The cold steel pen. (1.150–153)

Like any good fencer, Mulligan learns quickly and knows when to beat a tactical retreat. Realizing that his Wildean strategy has failed, he abandons it on the spot, announcing to the simple-minded Haines just a few pages later, "We have grown out of Wilde and paradoxes" (1.554).

Joyce himself had already grown out of Wilde—or at least found himself standing at some distance from him—as early as 1909, when he published his essay "Oscar Wilde: The Poet of 'Salomé.' " There he treats his countryman as a victim who was destroyed because he sought to ingratiate himself to the English. In elaborating this point, Joyce compares Wilde to a figure from—of all things—the Irish version of the *Odyssey:* "His name symbolizes him: Oscar, nephew of King Fingal and the only son of Ossian in the amorphous Celtic *Odyssey*, who was treacherously killed by the hand of his host as he sat at table."[21] For Joyce it is particularly telling that although Wilde cultivated the image of a bored and pampered member of the leisured class, the reality of his life was far more sordid, requiring frequent visits to the pawnshop and embarrassed requests for loans. He was only able to secure financial and social position by finally giving the English what they wanted; as Joyce remarks, "In the tradition of the Irish writers of comedy that runs from the days of Sheridan and Goldsmith to Bernard Shaw, Wilde became, like them, a court jester to the English."[22]

Mulligan encourages Stephen to play precisely the same role with Haines. When Stephen delivers his epigram on Irish art, Mulligan says, "Tell that to the oxy chap downstairs and touch him for a guinea" (1.154–55). And in the next chapter, when Stephen considers passing along another witticism for Haines's "chapbook," he imagines himself in precisely the terms Joyce applied to Wilde: he will be "a jester at the court of his master, indulged and disesteemed, winning a clement master's praise" (2.44–45).

The exchange on Wilde reaches its logical conclusion when, following the remembered hazing of an Irishman at Oxford, Stephen thinks, "To ourselves. . . . new paganism. . . . *omphalos*" (1.176). "To ourselves" is a variation on "we ourselves" or in Irish *sinn fein*, still in the 1890s the rallying cry for the revival of the Irish language and Irish culture. "New paganism" was an alternative slogan of the 1890s, associated with the social and aesthetic avant-garde that Wilde represented. As Joyce observed in his essay on Wilde, "He deceived himself into believing that he was the bearer of [the] good news of neo-paganism to an enslaved people. His own distinctive qualities . . . he placed at the service of a theory of beauty, which, according to him, was to bring back the Golden Age."[23] For Stephen both the nationalism represented by the phrase "sinn fein" and the aestheticism represented by the phrase "new paganism" are the deadends of the Nineties, examples of *omphalos* or navel-gazing. Yet the notion of the revival of Irish culture is clearly on Stephen's mind. What might a new aesthetic look like, one that acknowledged its Irish situation in a way Wilde's had not; one that did not play court jester to the English; one that was not the cracked looking-glass of a servant?

In taking up these questions, I will argue that *Ulysses* constructs its modernism out of an ambivalent and self-divided reaction to the Nineties. On the one hand Joyce rejects Wilde's all-too-English denial of his own Irishness; on the other he rejects, as we will see, the Revival's all-too-Irish assertion of its Irishness, especially as it is represented by Douglas Hyde and John Synge. My larger point, like that advanced by Gregory Castle, is that Joyce is not unsympathetic to the larger goal of the Revival—establishing a genuinely Irish culture—but that he is hostile to the specific means it employed.[24] The solution that Joyce proposes is implicitly stated in a question he asks in "Ireland, Island of Saints and Sages": "Is this country destined to resume its ancient position as the Hellas of the north some day?"[25] For Joyce the answer is a qualified yes, as long as "Hellenisation" consists neither of the Wildean aestheticism that Mulligan contemplates nor the Hydean revivalism that Haines collects. In other words, the revolutionary aesthetic of *Ulysses* will involve speaking the language of modernism, as represented by a universalizable, if not universalist, Greek culture, but speaking that language in a distinctly Irish register. It is that Irish register that I want to focus on, for it enables us to see how *Ulysses* transforms the Celtic twilight of the Nineties into the Celtic daybreak of modernism. In pursuing this argument, I will examine two episodes that are often seen as epitomizing two of the major innovations we associate with literary modernism: the "epistemological turn," the interest in consciousness and perception; and the "anthropological turn," the interest in archetype and myth. It will be my claim that while *Ulysses* serves as an obvious example of how these well-known modernist preoccupations are conceived, Joyce nevertheless develops them according to a logic that is insistently and consistently Irish.

⋮ ⋮ ⋮

"Proteus" is the episode in which Joyce most directly and searchingly confronts the problem of epistemology.[26] The famous opening words—"ineluctable modality of the visible" (3.1)—at once evoke and reverse the Homeric correspondence. Odysseus wrestling with the sea god, Proteus, is represented at the verbal level through the three-part etymology of "ineluctable": *in* (a negation) + *ex* (meaning "out of") + *luctor, luctari* (meaning "to wrestle"). Although Odysseus succeeds in holding Proteus fast, in gaining mastery over his phenomenological shape-shifting, Stephen cannot "wrestle out of" his own perceptual reality. For him the world of immediate experience is "ineluctable," holding him fast within the matrices of time and space, Lessing's *Nacheinander* and *Nebeneinander* (3.13, 3.15). Stephen's struggle with epistemology is dramatized as he attempts to work through various philosophical systems—materialist, idealist, metaphysical—which would enable him to step outside the ebb and flow of immediate experience, to achieve a theoretical still point or "coign of vantage" (3.71), to become a Kantian form of transcendental subjectivity.[27] Yet, although he literally closes his eyes to the "ineluctable modality of the visible," attempting to know reality as a pure category of mind, the historical and cultural facticity of his situation continues to obtrude. Thus, as he blindly stumbles along the beach, anxious about losing his footing, he is reminded of Haines's quotation from *Hamlet* ("If I fell over a cliff that beetles o'er his base," 3.14), and of the Englishman's offhand remark about the landscape ("these cliffs remind me somehow of Elsinore," 1.567). The effect of Haines's comment is to assimilate Irish nature to English culture, to convert the local countryside, literally the land itself—"these cliffs"—into a form of cultural capital. The irony is made all the more resonant by the fact that Haines has probably never been to Denmark, where Elsinore is located. His act of cultural appropriation is, therefore, the logical extension of his "anthropological" interest in Ireland, his liberal's enthusiasm—here one thinks of Adela Quested—for a quaint and backward culture. Meanwhile, as Stephen continues to move forward in his epistemological darkness, alive to his body's motions, he recalls that he is wearing Mulligan's castoff boots and trousers ("My two feet in his boots are at the ends of his legs," 3.16–17), remembers that he is, in the words of "Telemachus," the "server of a servant" (1.312). Even the simplest of acts, such as strolling along the beach—or constructing a theory of transcendental subjectivity—necessarily depends upon an elaborate domestic economy, consisting of things like boots and trousers. Stephen is here discovering what his countryman George Bernard Shaw never tired of pointing out: that at bottom everything is pounds and pence, that the ground on which one treads, indeed the very act of treading (and whether well-shod or down-at-the-heels) rests upon a material basis. Stephen closes his transcendental speculations with a question: "Am I walking into eternity along Sandymount strand?" (3.18–19). He hears by way of answer the sound of shells or cowries—that most aboriginal form of money—breaking beneath his feet ("Crush, crack, crick, crick. Wild sea money," 3.19) and is reminded of Mr. Deasy, who in "Nestor" proclaims that an Englishman's proudest boast is not "That on his empire . . . the sun never sets" (2.248) but "*I paid my way*" (2.251). Evidently the virtues of English solvency are helped along by empire's booty, just as Stephen's peripatetic philosophizing is helped along by Mulligan's boots.

It is worth observing here that so strong is the penchant to treat "Proteus" as an affirmation of transcendental subjectivity that even a Marxist critic like Fredric Jameson, attuned to the materiality of history, reads it in these terms. Thus, in his well-known essay "Modernism and Imperialism," Jameson treats Stephen's stroll along Sandymount as an exercise in pure epistemology: "The spatial poetry that has been detected in Forster has . . . no equivalent in *Ulysses*. 'Am I walking into eternity along Sandymount strand?' is thrust back into Stephen's consciousness, and marked as subjective."[28] I want to argue, to the contrary, that Joyce deconstructs the subjectivity so often associated with modernism; that as Stephen attempts, in the passages we have examined, to establish universal categories of time and space, the inescapable particularity of his situation is driven home, literally at every step, whether in the person of Haines the Englishman, Mulligan the Anglo-Irish landlord, or Deasy the West-Briton Orangeman.[29] The perceptual world that Stephen cannot wrestle free of is best represented, then, not by the figure of a Homeric Proteus but by a more specifically Irish sea god: "They are coming, waves. The whitemaned seahorses, champing, brightwindbridled, the steeds of Mananaan" (3.56–57).

Three of the principal preoccupations of the chapter are also firmly grounded in Stephen's Irish situation and are directly related to the question of Irish modernism. First, as he walks along Sandymount strand, Stephen considers paying a visit to his aunt and uncle, Sara and Richie Goulding. The Goulding household presents a mirror-image of Stephen's domestic condition: physical and spiritual disarray, poverty which is no longer merely genteel, and a father who has been "disappointed" by life and increasingly seeks consolation in drink. The portrait of the Goulding house exemplifies not only the reduced circumstances of the Dedalus family but more tellingly the reduced circumstances of Ireland as well: "Houses of decay, mine, his and all" (3.105). Second, much of the episode centers on memories of Stephen's time in Paris, where he often met the "wild goose," Kevin Egan, a character based on the expatriate Fenian, Joseph Casey.[30] The talk with Egan is "of Ireland, the Dalcassians, of hopes, conspiracies, of Arthur Griffith" (3.226–27)—in short, of Irish nationalism. Interestingly, while the portrait Joyce paints of Egan is unmistakably that of a failure, indicating that for him Fenian nationalism represents a dead end, the portrait is nevertheless surprisingly sympathetic: "in gay Paree he hides, Egan of Paris, unsought by any save me. Making his day's stations, the dingy printingcase, his three taverns, the Montmartre lair he sleeps short nights in. . . . Loveless, landless, wifeless. . . . They have forgotten Kevin Egan, not he them. Remembering thee, O Sion" (3.249–51, 3.253, 3.263–64). Third, and most crucially, there is the poem that Stephen is writing, a rehash of clichés cobbled together from the folk poetry of the Celtic twilight. We observe bits and pieces of the poem assembling itself in Stephen's mind, as he watches two cocklepickers pass by: "He comes, pale vampire, through storm his eyes, his bat sails bloodying the sea, mouth to her mouth's kiss" (3.397–98). Later, in "Aelous," we are given the finished stanza:

> On swift sail flaming
> From storm and south
> He comes, pale vampire,
> Mouth to my mouth. (7.522–25)

As commentators have long recognized, the stanza is a deliberate reworking of the conclusion to Douglas Hyde's "My Grief on the Sea," one of the best-known poems in his collection *The Love Songs of Connacht*. Here is Hyde's translation from the original Irish:

> And my love came behind me—
> He came from the South;
> His breast to my bosom,
> His mouth to my mouth.[31]

Hyde was, along with Yeats, arguably one of the two most prominent figures in the Irish Revival of the Nineties. David Lloyd describes him as follows: "founder-president of the Gaelic League [he] was a principal advocate of the Irish-language revival, a scholar, poet-translator and folklorist. His most famous single essay, 'The Necessity of De-Anglicising Ireland' (1892) resumes Young Ireland's attacks on the penetration of Ireland by English culture as well as capital, and on the consequent 'anomalous position' for the Irish race, "imitating England and yet apparently hating it."[32] Joyce's quotation of Hyde is often read as unambiguously parodic, an obvious send-up of the kind of gothicism that hovered over the Celtic twilight.[33] While there is little doubt that Stephen's stanza functions as an example of egregiously bad poetry—a point Lloyd's otherwise fascinating interpretation seems to miss—Joyce is doing more than simply dismissing Hyde. The most significant transformation he works on Hyde's "original" (which it must be remembered is itself a translation) is to change the free-floating spirit of the lover into the gothicized figure of the vampire. In so doing, Joyce brings into play a theme that is present elsewhere in his work—indeed, that is, as Michael Valdez Moses has shown, prevalent in Irish literature: the theme of Ireland as Island of the Dead, or more precisely of the Undead who threaten vampirically to possess the living.[34] Here is how Joyce puts the matter in "Ireland, Island of Saints and Sages":

> Ancient Ireland is dead just as ancient Egypt is dead. Its death chant has been sung, and on its gravestone has been placed the seal. The old national soul that spoke during the centuries through the mouths of fabulous seers, wandering minstrels, and Jacobite poets disappeared from the world with the death of James Clarence Mangan. . . . One thing alone seems clear to me. It is well past time for Ireland to have done once and for all with failure. If she is truly capable of reviving, let her awake, or let her cover up her head and lie down decently in her grave forever.[35]

Joyce's transformation of "My Grief on the Sea" presents Hyde not as a genuine revival of the Irish spirit of the past but one of those ghosts who haunts the living, much as in "The Dead," Michael Furey (note the Aeschylean name) haunts Gabriel Conroy.[36] In other words, Joyce is not so much offering a parody of Hyde's Irishness as he is exposing Hyde's Irishness as itself a parody, one that crucially plays into colonialist stereotypes. It is therefore not surprising that in "Scylla and Charybdis," the irrepressible Haines dashes out of the National Library to acquire his very own copy of *The Love Songs of Connacht*. If Wilde has played the Englishman's game by attempting to out-English the English, Hyde has played the Englishman's game by attempting to out-Irish the Irish. Seen from a certain perspective, Hyde's quaint revivalism is indistinguishable from Wilde's effete aestheticism.

⋮ ⋮ ⋮

I have been arguing that Joyce treats interiority and consciousness in specifically Irish terms. I would now like to advance the same argument regarding his handling of another modernist preoccupation: myth and archetype. In a celebrated passage from "*Ulysses*, Order and Myth" (1923), T. S. Eliot writes: "In using myth, in manipulating a continuous parallel between contemporaneity and antiquity, Mr. Joyce is pursuing a method which others must pursue after him." Eliot goes on to observe, "It is a method already adumbrated by Mr. Yeats, and of the need for which I believe Mr. Yeats to have been the first contemporary to be conscious."[37] The comment about Yeats is striking in the context of Irish modernism, for it serves to link the mythic method to the Celtic twilight. While Eliot attributes the modern fascination with myth to the emergence of psychology and ethnology as disciplines, he seems not to recognize that for a figure like Yeats it might also be connected with the Irish Revival. Of course, there is nothing new in the idea that Joyce was influenced by Celtic folklore or drew upon Irish myth and legend.[38] What I would like to suggest is something different: not that *Ulysses* borrows from the Irish folklore tradition—a claim no one would deny—but that even when Joyce uses myths that are archetypal or universal, he directly ties them to an Irish scene.

One way to illustrate the point I want to make is to examine how Joyce and Eliot handle mythic material that is transcultural, or at least non-Irish. To perform this exercise I will briefly consider *The Waste Land* alongside the "Oxen of the Sun" episode from *Ulysses*. The salient features of Eliot's poem are well known: the burial of the dead, the land laid waste, the equivocal speech of the thunder, and the question of whether the god or logos has been born. Critics have not noticed quite as readily, however, that these same elements define the narrative situation of "Oxen."[39] Patty Dignam has been buried earlier in the day, Dublin is suffering under a drought, and as the clouds gather, there is a rumble of thunder and a downpour of rain. At the same time, the Word is made flesh as Mrs. Purefoy, who has been in labor for three days, delivers her child, the gestation of English literature reaches its term, and Stephen and the medical students tumble out into the street in a parody-birth.

The affinity between the two texts becomes especially apparent when we turn to individual passages in "Oxen of the Sun." Here, for example, are the burial of the dead and the vision of the land laid waste:

> So Thursday sixteenth June Patk. Dignam laid in clay of an apoplexy and after hard drought, please God, rained, a bargeman coming in by water a fifty mile or thereabout with turf saying the seed won't sprout. . . . The rosy buds all gone brown and spread out blobs and on the hills nought but dry flag and faggots that catch at first fire. All the world saying, for aught they knew, the big wind of last February a year that did havoc the land so pitifully a small thing beside this barenness. (14.474–481)

And here are the freeing of the waters and the rejuvenation of the land:

> . . . some sheer lightnings at first and after, past ten of the clock, one great stroke with a long thunder and in a brace of shakes all scamper pellmell within door for the smoking shower. . . . In Ely place, Baggot street, Duke's lawn, thence through Merrion green up to Holles street a swash of water flowing. . . . In sum an infinite great fall of rain and all refreshed and will much increase the harvest yet. (14.486–88; 14.521–22)

And, finally, here are the speech of the thunder and the birth of the word:

> But as before the lightning the serried stormclouds, heavy with preponderant excess of moisture, in swollen masses turgidly distended, compass earth and sky in one vast slumber, impending above parched field and drowsy oxen and blighted growth of shrub and verdure till in an instant a flash rives their centres and with the reverberation of the thunder the cloudburst pours its torrent, so and not otherwise was the transformation, violent and instantaneous, upon the utterance of the word. (14.1383–90)

I will return in a moment to the "utterance of the word" and its significance, but the parallels in mythic structure between *The Waste Land* and "Oxen of the Sun" are, I believe, sufficiently clear. Certainly they were clear to Eliot, who, after reading "Oxen" in draft, expressed his admiration for the episode in a letter to Joyce, adding, "I wish, for my own sake, that I had not read it."[40] Yet, for all the similarities between "Oxen" and *The Waste Land*—and whether or not we believe that Eliot was in some sense stealing Joyce's thunder—it is remarkable how different these two texts are in approaching their mythic material.

Here I will touch upon one of these differences: how Eliot and Joyce treat the "waste land" theme. For the former, the waste land represents modernity itself, what Eliot called in his Joyce essay "the immense panorama of futility and anarchy which is contemporary history."[41] The specific setting of Eliot's poem may be London, but the unreal city encompasses all the cosmopolitan centers, from Baudelaire's Paris to Marie Larisch's Munich. For Joyce, on the other hand, the paralysis, decay, sterility, waste, and living death are not so much the generalized conditions of modernity as the specific conditions of a colonized and subjugated Ireland. Hence, although the medical students in "Oxen" discuss issues of central importance to the waste land theme—issues of fertility and sexuality—their discussion proceeds from assumptions that are manifestly Irish and Catholic. They exchange views on contraception (14.226 ff.), on whether, in the case of a difficult birth, it is better to save the mother or child (14.202 ff.), and on the idea of divine incarnation—or the "word made flesh" in a woman's womb (14.292). Even Mulligan's joking proposal to set up a national fertilizing farm on Lambay Island (14.634) raises questions concerning Irish depopulation on the one hand, and the ability of an impoverished nation to support an increased birth rate on the other (14.704). Amid all this, Stephen presents a pocket history that details how the Catholic Church sold Ireland to the English, beginning with Pope Adrian the Fourth's grant of the overlordship of Ireland to Henry II in 1155 and extending through Henry VIII's proclamation as King of Ireland in 1541 (14.578–647). But it is revealing that as critical as Joyce is of the role the Church of Rome has played in Irish history, the waste land allegory in "Oxen" is developed according to a logic that is emphatically Catholic: from the episode's use of Trinitarianism, to the talking in tongues, the Pentecostal imagery, and finally the birth of the Word. Again, while Eliot attempts to universalize the mythic material in his poem—in this regard Weston is especially useful—Joyce believes that the Catholic Church is universe enough. What is more, the birth of the Word toward the end of the episode establishes Joyce as the inheritor of the entire English literary tradition, finally placing him in a position to respond to Haines. He no longer plays the court jester or the Shakespearean fool but the Bard himself, for in becoming the Word he is both "ghost and prince" in the language of "Scylla and Charbydis" (9.1018), both father and son, and therefore the manifestation of the ultimate Catholic mystery: the Word made flesh.[42]

Of particular interest is Haines's gothicized reappearance in "Oxen" in a parody out of Walpole's *The Castle of Otranto*:

> But Malachais's tale began to freeze them with horror. He conjured up the scene before them. The secret panel beside the chimney slid back and in the recess appeared—Haines! Which of us did not feel his flesh creep! He had a portfolio full of Celtic literature in one hand, in the other a phial marked *Poison*. Surprise, horror, loathing were depicted on all faces while he eyed them with a ghostly grin. I anticipated some such reception, he began with an eldritch laugh, for which it seems history is to blame. Yes, it is true. I am the murderer of Samuel Childs. (14.1010–17)

The significance of the Childs murder as an act of usurpation is established in "Aeolus," where the fratricide is specifically equated with Claudius's murder of Hamlet (7.748–50). Childs's brother, who was accused of the crime and widely thought to have committed it, was acquitted at trial in 1899. Now, we are told, the "mystery" concerning the identity of the real murderer is "unveiled" (14.1032), as we discover that the crime was committed by a "third brother" who turns out to be Haines. In other words, lurking behind the usurpation Stephen has suffered at the hands of his fellow Irishman, Mulligan, is the man truly responsible for his fate, that "other" brother with whom he shares a common language. It seems not only is history to blame—so too is Haines. But Joyce's fun does not end here. For if he has cast himself in the role of Shakespeare, thereby appropriating the entire English literary tradition, he now completes the reversal by casting Haines in the role of Irish peasant in a parody of Synge: "Tare and ages, what way would I be resting at all, he muttered thickly, and I tramping Dublin this while back with my share of songs and himself after me like the soulth or a bullawurrus?" (14.1018–21). Haines's parting words—pregnant, as we will see—are "Meet me at Westland Row station at ten past eleven" (14.1027).

We began in "Telemachus" with a configuration that is familiar from Irish history: Haines, the imperial Englishman; Mulligan, the complicitous Anglo-Irish landlord; Stephen, the usurped Irishman. When Stephen says to Buck in "Telemachus" that Haines goes or he does (1.62–63), he is stating his *non serviam* in political and cultural terms. The final playing out of the conflict between Stephen and Mulligan/Haines over Ireland as House of Decay, over Ireland as Waste Land, occurs at Westland Row station, where Stephen at last proclaims his liberation from Mulligan.[43] It is impossible to know if Joyce intended "Westland" as a pun on "Waste Land," since the former is a real railway terminus that logically figures into the geography of the novel. But it should give us interpretive pause that an author as attuned to wordplay as Joyce locates one of the novel's decisive scenes—the confrontation between Stephen and Buck—conspicuously offstage and in an otherwise insignificant place. Especially striking is the fact that the scene at "Westland" immediately follows the "Waste Land" of "Oxen."

Whatever Joyce's intention, it is the independence that Stephen achieves from Buck that is important here; for within the terms developed by the novel it represents the necessary first step toward "Hellenising" Ireland, toward writing a work called *Ulysses*, toward constructing a uniquely Irish form of modernism. Yet in making this assertion, I do not want to claim that Joyce's modernism is in any sense insular or exclusive. While Eliot's use of myth and Woolf's handling of interiority are less culturally specific than Joyce's, *Ulysses* seeks to participate in a fully internationalized modernism, even as it undertakes to create its own vernacular modernism. Nor are these two ideas of modernism incompatible, any more than an interest in aesthetics necessarily precludes an engagement with nationalism. Obviously in arguing that *Ulysses* employs a decolonizing strategy, I have lingered over the local, sought to show how the novel develops its internal logic out of a specially Irish scene—the Nineties and the alternatives presented by Wilde and Hyde. But Joyce's commitment to a decolonizing strategy, an Ireland that might once again emerge as a Hellas of the north, never forced him into a narrow nativisim, the bellicose and bullying patriotism of the Citizen. Indeed, in imagining a Hellas of the north, Joyce might well have envisioned a country not unlike the Irish Republic of today: liberal, prosperous, cosmopolitan, modern—a country that has achieved a distinct cultural identity, while assuming its rightful place within the community of nations. We should therefore not think of Joyce's Trojan horse as an avenger's stratagem, a machine for cultural sedition or destruction.[44] To the contrary, the effect of *Ulysses*—and for that matter other colonial works like it—has been to remove the bitter irony from Joyce's remark to Alessandro Francini: "This is then called English literature." The now familiar construction "world literature in English," encompassing Great Britain, Ireland, and the Commonwealth, not only carries no stigma but serves to sell books, promote careers, even buoy departments of literature. In a globalized world, where the indigenous has become a rare and valued commodity, modernism's internationalism is increasingly assured by its vernacularism. Joyce was among the first writers to grasp this reality and to give it a distinctive and decisive shape.

## Notes

1 This critical tradition has produced many outstanding studies of *Ulysses*; among the best known are Adams, *Surface and Symbol*; Ellmann, *Ulysses on the Liffey*; Hayman, "*Ulysses*": *The Mechanics of Meaning*; Kenner, *Joyce's Voices* and *Ulysses*; Lawrence, *The Odyssey of Styles in "Ulysses."*

2 Joyce, *Ulysses*, ed. Hans Walter Gabler et al. (New York: Vintage, 1986), 16.1160-65; hereafter parenthetical citations are to this edition, by episode and page number.

3 Cheng, *Joyce, Race and Empire*; Duffy, *The Subaltern Ulysses;* Lloyd, "Adulteration and the Novel," *Anomalous States*; Nolan, *James Joyce and Nationalism*; Castle, "Joyce's Modernism," *Modernism and the Celtic Revival*; Gibson, *Joyce's Revenge*; other important studies include Attridge and Howes, eds., *Semicolonial Joyce;* Deane, *Celtic Revivals*; Fairhall, *Joyce and the Question of History*; Kiberd, "James Joyce and Mythic Realism" *Inventing Ireland*; MacCabe, *James Joyce and the Revolution of the Word;* Mangianello, *Joyce's Politics*; Tymoczcko, *The Irish Joyce*.

4 Nolan, *James Joyce and Nationalism*, 100 ff.; and Castle, *Modernism and the Celtic Revival*, 240 ff. For a perspective on "Cyclops" that is sympathetic to Nolan and Castle but approaches the question of nationalism differently, see John Nash, " 'Hanging over the bloody paper': Newspapers and Imperialism in *Ulysses*," in Booth and Rigby, eds., *Modernism and Empire*.

5 Wollaeger's "Joyce in the Postcolonial Tropics" is a splendid example of reading beyond—indeed of reading in and through—the academic categories that so often constrain interpretation in modernist and postcolonial studies.

6 Duffy, *The Subaltern "Ulysses,"* 1.

7 The novel is set in 1904, but the opening scene is highly self-conscious, as Joyce's Greek references manipulate time-frames that look back to the Nineties and forward to his own "Hellenization" of Ireland in the 1920s.

8 We might think of stream-of-consciousness as reimagining Wilde's interest in autonomy, subjectivity, and paradox as the free-flowing verbiage of interior monologue, and of the mythical method as reimagining the Celtic Twilight's commitment to legend and folklore as the narrative restructuring of chronological time.

9 "Stream-of-consciousness" and "mythical method" are, of course, terms that have generated a good deal of controversy. The relevant scholarly debates are beyond the scope of the present essay. In using these terms myself, I refer in the first instance to Joyce's use of interior monologue and in the second to his use of "myth" as a method for narratively organizing material. The term "mythical method" derives from T. S. Eliot's "*Ulysses*, Myth and Order," *Selected Prose*; the term "stream-of-consciousness" derives from William James's *Psychology* (chapter 11).

10 See the discussion of Aristotelianism and Platonism in "Scylla and Charybdis.

11 See "Who Goes with Fergus?" Gifford points out that the "poem was included as a song in the first version of Yeats's play *The Countess Cathleen* (1892). The song, accompanied by harp, is sung to comfort the countess, who has sold her soul to the powers of darkness that her people might have food" ("*Ulysses*" *Annotated*, 18). Notice that Stephen refuses, in effect, "to sell his soul"—i.e., to kneel to the church and pray for "mother Ireland."

12 The maternal theme in the novel is firmly established in "Telemachus," both through the figure of the milkmaid ("silk of kine") and Stephen's relation to his own dying mother, whose cancer is a metaphor for an Ireland that cannibalizes

itself. For an original and powerful analysis of how Joyce treats the figure of Mother Ireland, see O'Halloran, "From Boucicault to Beckett," chapter 3.

13 Quoted in Ellmann, *James Joyce*, 217.

14 Joyce, *A Portrait of the Artist as a Young Man* (New York: Penguin, 1992), 205; hereafter parenthetical page citations are to this edition.

15 For a fascinating examination of Joyce's egotism, see Rabaté, *James Joyce and the Politics of Egoism*.

16 See Frye, *The Secular Scripture*, 65–66.

17 Wilde, *Complete Works*, 17.

18 Cheng, *Joyce, Race, and Empire*, 33; also see *Stephen Hero*, 65.

19 Wilde, *Complete Works*, 982.

20 There may be a winking allusion to the scene in *Playboy of the Western World* where a dirty and uncouth Christy is caught gazing at himself in a mirror; Synge, *Playboy*, 31–32.

21 Joyce, *Critical Writings*, 201. The "Celtic *Odyssey*," as Joyce refers to it, is to be found in the so-called Fenian cycle.

22 Ibid., 202.

23 Ibid., 204–5.

24 See Castle, "Joyce's Modernism," *Modernism and the Celtic Revival*.

25 *Critical Writings*, 172.

26 For articles that deal with epistemology and "Proteus" from a variety of perspectives, see McArthur, " 'Signs on a White Field' "; Michels, "The Role of Language in Consciousness"; and Rimo, " 'Proteus.' "

27 See Gifford, *"Ulysses" Annotated*, on allusions in the opening section to "Proteus" (44–45); the possible reference to Aristotle's *On Sense and the Sensible* and *On the Soul*, taken together with the clear allusions to Jakob Boehme's *Signatura Rerum* and George Berkeley's *Essay Toward a New Theory of Vision*, suggest materialist, metaphysical, and idealist positions.

28 "Modernism and Imperialism," 61. Jameson is here distinguishing between Forster's "infinity" and Joyce's "eternity" as part of a larger distinction he wishes to draw between "First World" and "Third World" modernism. In the latter, of which *Ulysses* is Jameson's prime example, "space does not have to be made symbolic in order to achieve closure and meaning: its closure is objective, endowed by the colonial situation itself" (61). Jameson creates problems for himself by evoking traditional categories of subjectivity (here applied to Stephen in "Proteus") and objectivity.

29 Although in reality Oliver Gogarty paid the rent at the Martello tower (Ellmann, *James Joyce*, 171), in "Telemachus" Mulligan plays the role of landlord who exacts payment from Stephen, while keeping the key to the tower (1.721–24); hence the theme of "usurper" (1.744).

30 Gifford, *"Ulysses" Annotated*, 52.

31 For Hyde's "My Grief on the Sea," see Murphy and MacKillop, *Irish Literature*, 134.

32 See Lloyd, *Anomalous States*, 101.
33 See, for example, Kenner, *Ulysses*, 57–58.
34 Moses, "The Irish Vampire."
35 *Critical Writings*, 173–74.
36 It goes without saying that Joyce treats Gabriel Conroy ironically, but this does not mean that he is any less ironic about Michael Furey, who is a cliché out of the Celtic twilight. Joyce was critical of the Irish revival, as is clear from his broadside "The Holy Office." See Ellmann's *James Joyce*, 98–104, 135, 166, 193. For a more qualified view of Joyce and the Revival, see Castle, *Modernism and the Celtic Revival*, chapters 5 and 6.
37 *Selected Prose*, 177.
38 See, for example, Tymoczkso, *The Irish Ulysses*.
39 To my knowledge, Lorch was the first critic to draw a connection between *The Waste Land* and "Oxen"; see his "The Relationship between *Ulysses* and *The Waste Land*." For other discussions of the relation of Eliot's poem to Joyce's novel, see Bailey, "A Note on *The Waste Land* and Joyce's *Ulysses*"; Day, "Joyce's Waste Land and Eliot's Unknown God"; Sultan, *"Ulysses," "The Waste Land," and Modernism*; and Worthen, "Eliot's *Ulysses*."
40 See *Letters of T. S. Eliot*, 1: 455. For Eliot's views on "Oxen," see also Virginia Woolf's *Diary*, September 26, 1922, where he is quoted as saying, "The book would be a landmark, because it destroyed the whole of the 19th Century. . . . It showed up the futility of all the English styles," 2: 203.
41 *Selected Prose*, 177.
42 Joyce here plays on the notion of Stephen both as cultural redeemer (Christ) and the "last word" in English literature.
43 Kenner puts forward this argument in his contribution on "Circe" in Hart and Hayman, *James Joyce's "Ulysses"*: "Stephen, we are told more than once, becomes conscious in the brothel that he has somehow hurt his hand. . . . The likelihood is that he struck someone or something during the scuffle at the Westland Row station, and putting this likelihood together with Bloom's remark that if Stephen were to present himself at the tower he wouldn't 'get in after what occurred at Westland Row station' (619.39), we may suspect he did something of profound importance: that he asserted himself and took a swing at Mulligan," 353.
44 For a contrasting perspective, see Gibson, *Joyce's Revenge*.

## Works Cited

Adams, Robert Martin. *Surface and Symbol: The Consistency of James Joyce's "Ulysses."* New York: Oxford University Press, 1962.

Attridge, Derek, and Marjorie Howes, eds. *Semicolonial Joyce*. Cambridge: Cambridge University Press, 2000.

Bailey, Bruce. "A Note on *The Waste Land* and Joyce's *Ulysses*." *T. S. Eliot Review* 2.2 (1975): 10.

Booth, Howard J., and Nigel Rigby, eds. *Modernism and Empire*. Manchester: Manchester University Press, 2000.

Castle, Gregory. *Modernism and the Celtic Revival*. Cambridge: Cambridge University Press, 2001.

Cheng, Vincent. *Joyce, Race, and Empire*. Cambridge: Cambridge University Press, 1995.

Day, Robert Adams. "Joyce's Waste Land and Eliot's Unknown God." In *Literary Monographs*, vol. 4, ed. Eric Rothstein, 139–210. Madison: University of Wisconsin Press, 1971.

Deane, Seamus. *Celtic Revivals: Essays in Modern Irish Literature*. London: Faber and Faber, 1985.

Duffy, Enda. *The Subaltern "Ulysses."* Minneapolis: University of Minnesota Press, 1994.

Eagleton, Terry, Fredric Jameson, and Edward W. Said. *Nationalism, Colonialism, and Literature*. Minneapolis: University of Minnesota Press, 1990.

Eliot, T. S. *The Letters of T. S. Eliot*. Vol. 1 (1898–1922). Edited by Valerie Eliot. London: Faber, 1988.

——. *Selected Prose of T. S. Eliot*. Edited by Frank Kermode. New York: Harcourt Brace and Company, 1975.

Ellmann, Richard. *James Joyce*. New York: Oxford University Press, 1982.

——. *Ulysses on the Liffey*. New York: Oxford University Press, 1972.

Fairhall, James. *James Joyce and the Question of History*. Cambridge: Cambridge University Press, 1993.

Frye, Northrop. *The Secular Scripture: A Study of the Structure of Romance*. Cambridge: Harvard University Press, 1976.

Gibson, Andrew. *Joyce's Revenge: History, Politics, and Aesthetics in "Ulysses."* Oxford: Oxford University Press, 2002.

Gifford, Don, with Robert J. Seidman. *"Ulysses" Annotated: Notes for James Joyce's "Ulysses."* 2nd ed., revised and enlarged. Berkeley: University of California Press, 1988.

Hart, Clive, and David Hayman. *James Joyce's "Ulysses": Critical Essays*. Berkeley: University of California Press, 1974.

Hayman, David. *"Ulysses": The Mechanics of Meaning*. New York: Prentice Hall, 1970; rev. ed. Madison: University of Wisconsin Press, 1982.

James, William. *Psychology*. London: Macmillan, 1892.

Joyce, James. *The Critical Writings*. Edited by Ellsworth Mason and Richard Ellmann. New York: Viking, 1972.

——. *A Portrait of the Artist as a Young Man* (1916). New York: Penguin, 1992.

——. *Stephen Hero*. New York: New Directions, 1944.

——. *Ulysses* (1922). Edited by Hans Walter Gabler et al. New York: Vintage, 1986.

Kenner, Hugh. *Joyce's Voices*. Berkeley: University of California Press, 1979.

——. *Ulysses*. London: George Allen and Unwin, 1980; rev. ed., Baltimore: Johns Hopkins University Press, 1987.

Kiberd, Declan. *Inventing Ireland: The Literature of the Modern Nation*. Cambridge: Harvard University Press, 1995.

Lawrence, Karen. *The Odyssey of Styles in "Ulysses."* Princeton, N.J.: Princeton University Press, 1981.

Lloyd, David. *Anomalous States: Irish Writing and the Post-Colonial Moment*. Durham, N.C.: Duke University Press, 1993.

Lorch, Thomas M. "The Relationship between *Ulysses* and *The Waste Land*." *Texas Studies in Language and Literature* 6.2 (1964): 123–33.

MacCabe, Colin. *James Joyce and the Revolution of the Word*. London: Macmillan, 1979.

Manganiello, Dominic. *Joyce's Politics*. London: Routledge and Kegan Paul, 1980.

McArthur, Murray. " 'Signs on a White Field': Semiotics and Forgery in the 'Proteus' Chapter of *Ulysses*." *ELH* 53.3 (1986): 633–52.

Michels, James. "The Role of Language in Consciousness: A Structuralist Look at 'Proteus' in *Ulysses*." *Language and Style* 15.1 (1982): 23–32.

Moses, Michael Valdez. "The Irish Vampire: *Dracula*, Parnell and the Troubled Dreams of Nationhood." *Journal X* 2 (Fall 1997): 66–111.

Murphy, Maureen O'Rourke, and James MacKillop, eds. *Irish Literature: A Reader*. Syracuse, N.Y.: Syracuse University Press, 1987.

Nolan, Emer. *James Joyce and Nationalism*. London: Routledge, 1995.

O'Halloran, Eileen T. "From Bouciault to Beckett: Irish Modernism and the Myth of Mother Ireland." Ph.D. dissertation, University of Wisconsin, Madison, 2004.

Rabaté, Jean-Michel. *James Joyce and the Politics of Egoism*. Cambridge: Cambridge University Press, 2001.

Rimo, Patricia A. " 'Proteus': From Thought to Things." *Studies in the Novel* 17.3 (1985): 296–302.

Sultan, Stanley. *"Ulysses," "The Waste Land," and Modernism*. Port Washington, N.Y.: National University Publications, 1977.

Synge, John Millington. *"Playboy of the Western World" and "Riders to the Sea."* Arlington Heights, Ill.: Harlan Davidson, 1966.

Tymoczko, Maria. *The Irish Joyce*. Berkeley: University of California Press, 1994.

Wetzel, Heinz. "Spuren des 'Ulysses' in 'The Waste Land.' " *Germanish-Romanische Monatsschift* 20 (1970): 442–66.

Wilde, Oscar. *The Complete Works of Oscar Wilde*. New York: Harper and Row, 1989.

Wollaeger, Mark. "Joyce in the Postcolonial Tropics." *JJQ* 39.1 (2001): 69–92.

Woolf, Virginia. *The Diary of Virginia Woolf*. Vol. 2 (1920–1924). Edited by Anne Olivier Bell. New York: Harvest, 1978.

Worthen, William B. "Eliot's *Ulysses*." *Twentieth-Century Literature* 27.2 (1981): 166–77.

*Nicholas Allen*

⋮

NINE

# Yeats, Spengler, and *A Vision* after Empire

> I published a few weeks ago a book called *A Vision*. In that there is a summing-up of European history which I divide into certain epochs. I have just got Spengler's *Decline in the West*. I was writing my notes and drawing my historical diagrams in Galway while his first edition was passing through the press in Germany. I had never heard his name, and yet the epochs are the same, the theory is the same. . . . I can almost say of his book and of the historical part of mine that there is no difference in our interpretation of history (an interpretation that had never occurred to anybody before) that is not accounted for by his great and my slight erudition. Get my book from some library—it is too expensive to buy—and above all get his.
>
> WILLIAM BUTLER YEATS to T. Sturge Moore, June 26, 1926

William Butler Yeats's *A Vision* was dated 1925 but was first available to readers in a January 1926 limited edition of six hundred copies; Yeats did not expect a wide audience for his work, but he did hope for influence. The product of research in séance and spiritualism, much of Yeats's material came from his wife's automatic writing, and from Yeats's belief that broad patterns of our developing consciousness were revealed to him through mediators from beyond. But this sense of *A Vision* as occult has obscured elements of the book's cultural dynamic, particularly shading its production during a period of constant upheaval, the First World War, the Anglo-Irish and civil wars. Disturbance was felt across Europe, in Ireland, Britain, France, and, perhaps most intensely, Germany, a country defeated in both war and peace post-Versailles. In Ireland, the problem of post-imperial relations with Britain remained fraught, as Yeats reminds us in *A Vision*, partly "[f]inished at Thoor, Ballylee, 1922, in a time of Civil War."[1] In Germany, the loss of empire so recently acquired, and the total defeat of a state founded in an aggressive sense of self-destiny, was crippling. During *A Vision*'s composition, Ireland was in process of seceding from empire; at the same time, Germany lost a majority of its possessions. Both situations opened political space for experiment in democracies whose roots in civic society were violently contested, from Dublin to Berlin.

To read *A Vision* in context of such new politics, of popular democracy and its alternatives, is to illuminate the complexity of Yeats's response to his contemporary Oswald Spengler's two-volume *Der Untergang des Abendlandes*, or *Decline of the West*, published in English in 1926 and 1928. After considering Yeats's annotations to his personal library volumes of Spengler's work, I explore how Yeats's reading emerged in his poetry. In establishing connections between Yeats and Spengler, I hope to uncover the parallel structures of authority that underpin both works in reaction to the formation of new democracies and the weakening of empires following World War I. To do this, I chart the codes of modernist collage and historical fantasy that make up *A Vision* and *Decline of the West*, reading their experiments in form as preparation for replacement philosophies antagonistic to mass representation. The fragmentary narratives of Yeats and Spengler, suggesting in their scope a false totality, from astrology to archaeology, are open to multiple, even contradictory, readings that register the failure of national narratives in the face of civil war. Their theories of time, place, and society suggest an experience of modernity ineradicably marked by empire, leading to desire for newly evolved authorities that shelter in the enigmas and geometries of modernism.

Elizabeth Cullingford was an early critic to argue for *A Vision*'s political presence. To Cullingford, the dates of composition are central to our reading. "On 24th October 1917 Mrs Yeats began the automatic writing which provided the basis for Yeats' book of esoteric philosophy, *A Vision*. On 7 November the Bolsheviks seized power in Russia."[2] Yeats, as Cullingford argues, disliked the historical basis of communism and sought in *A Vision* to assert the equal validity of the opposing tradition, "the unfashionable gyre."[3] That alternative tradition we now know as fascism, a movement still unknown as George Yeats began her meditations. Terence Brown develops this political context further. To Brown, *A Vision* "is Yeats' manifesto for the new Ireland in which he himself had enthusiastically embraced controversy and conflict," "a summons to the new state to relish such conflict as a spiritual resource which would enable it to transcend the bitter divisions of civil war."[4] The sense of national address, of the author's personal connection to the general fate, is compounded in Brown's sense of the book as modernist "in its considerable investment in the potential powers of myth to apprehend and restore spiritual reality in a desacralized, materialistic age."[5] The connection between modernism and politics is crucial to a post-imperial reading of *A Vision* (and much of Irish writing of the 1920s besides). The difficulties the text offers are not only those of occult theory, or mathematical numbering; they are fluid coordinates for an Ireland in flux. The episodic character of the text has prompted Roy Foster to describe it as "a little of the best of WBY, and most of the worst. Leaps of imagination, audacious strokes, unforgettably sonorous phrases, and brilliant imagery come in flashes; he retains the ability to make the esoteric and irrational at once universal and uniquely strange."[6] It is exactly this point, between the unique and universal, which opens *A Vision* to political reading, since the sense of transition the text materially embodies is fundamental to its own appeals to historical authenticity. All three critics, Cullingford, Brown, and Foster, agree that *A Vision* is a text concerned with time as a monitor of cultural change. The visionary who claims knowledge of historical pattern, who knows the order of chronologies, can claim authority in the present by presentiment of the future. The bewildering present is recast as a necessary phase of transition. So, in Ireland, the problems of post-imperial organization recur as new forms of old questions, with a range of predetermined outcomes. The central motivation of *A Vision* is to establish this point, and by so doing make the conditions for success of its preferred destiny more likely.

In structure, *A Vision* is constructed of four books, with accompanying drawings and poetry. The first book, "What the Caliph Partly Learned," incorporates explanation of the Yeatsian system. The second book, "What the Caliph Refused to Learn," presents these findings as geometry. The third book, "Dove or Swan," is the most explicitly historical, breaking human development into epochal sections, each with its own characteristics. The fourth book, "The Gates of Pluto," offers accounts of the soul's journey after death. Composition of the work was begun shortly after Yeats's marriage to George Hyde Lees on October 24, 1917, and *A Vision*'s occult pedigree derives mainly from its genesis in intensive periods of her mediumship.[7] Messages came to her intermittently through the following years, suggesting the presence of an indeterminate consciousness, a perfect mirror, in effect, to the state of Ireland after independence. The new government's attempt to create one sense of a state grew in violence and coercion as the controversy over the Anglo-Irish Treaty's limitations increased. In the midst of civil war, the Irish government acted with a ferocity of authority embodied in the ruthlessness of Kevin O'Higgins.[8] Reading the disjunctive components of *A Vision* introduces a sense of the period's violent transitions, as we are transported from one discourse to another, at times arbitrarily.

Just as Yeats was assembling this complex, Oswald Spengler was writing his own myth of human destiny in a Germany in upheaval. Spengler's *Decline of the West* is a parallel text to *A Vision*; Yeats owned copies of both volumes of Spengler's work and read them closely. To discover connections between the two texts opens new contexts by which to read Yeats's post-imperial vision. The first volume of *Decline of the West*, *Form and Actuality*, was a translation of the corrected second German edition. Like Yeats in *A Vision* (and Standish O'Grady before him in the *History of Ireland*),[9] Spengler had many critics skeptical of his grand theories drawn, on occasion, from mistaken evidence. Unlike Yeats, Spengler's work reached an immediate audience, with ninety thousand copies printed in Germany alone. The book was published in July 1918, the majority of it written between 1914 and 1917. This last date was crucial to Yeats as his wife received messages of the kind that would inform *A Vision* at the same time. To Spengler's translator, the impulse to write the book came "from a view of our civilization not as the late war left it, but . . . as the *coming* war would find it."[10] This sense of continued conflict appealed to the Yeats of 1917–1919 and the 1920s, as did Spengler's own symbolic imagination. To Spengler, "A thinker is a person whose part it is to symbolize time according to his vision and understanding. He has no choice; he thinks as he has to think."[11]

The sense of destinies fulfilled correlates with the mathematical plotting of *A Vision*, as individuals are linked in their achievements by character type and destiny. Yeats's attention to the phases, as he perceived them, of spiritual evolution has received much critical attention; and the shortcomings, faults, and plain idiosyncrasy of many of his judgments have encouraged the reading of *A Vision* as obscure—which it is. But embedded within *A Vision* is the idea that messages are channeled through the appropriate medium, a belief so seductive to Yeats that his wife warned him not to believe everything received from the other side. To Yeats, the very appearance of messages was evidence of his own necessity to the progress of Irish culture. So the fragmentary codes of *A Vision* become the basis of a new history divined by the chosen intellect. Spengler shared this idea of threads gathered. In a passage reminiscent of H. P. Blavatsky, an earlier influence on Yeats and the Theosophist author of *The Secret Doctrine*,[12] Spengler declared his work to be "not merely a question of writing one out of several possible and merely logically justifiable philosophies, but of writing *the* philosophy of our time, one that is to some extent a natural philosophy and is dimly presaged by all. This may be said without presumption; for an idea that is historically essential—that does not occur within an epoch but itself makes that epoch—is only in a limited sense the property of him whose lot it falls to parent it."[13]

Destiny is the motivating idea. It is a concept now associated with the excesses of nationalist expansion, as new frontiers fall to aggressive states. Destiny in Spengler operates differently, allowing him to incorporate the idea of change through time into his version of history. Destiny enabled Spengler to project past findings onto the future, to attempt "for the first time the venture of predetermining history."[14] Spengler was prompted to this by a concern that his own culture was in a phase of fulfilment after which decline was imminent. A new understanding of time allowed readers to view their contemporary pressures of war and loss as short distractions from a longer scene. Destiny is a becoming whose arrival is always announced. In Spengler, "Living direction marches to the horizon as to the future."[15] "Long before the Moses of Michelangelo, the Moses of Klaus Suter's well in the Chartreuse of Dijon meditates on destiny, and even the Sibyls of the Sistine Chapel are forestalled by those of Giovanni Pisano in Sant'Andrea at Pistoia."[16] History is an echo chamber, and to recognize destiny is to give form to the outlines of a previous generation. Connected to this idea of divination is a transformation in the arts whereby portraiture comes to represent both nature and history: "a portrait by Holbein or Titian or Rembrandt or Goya, is a *biography*, and a self-portrait a historical *confession*."[17] "The whole of Northern poetry is one outspoken confession. So are the portraits of Rembrandt and the music of Beethoven."[18]

Here is a deep similarity in form between Yeats's and Spengler's visions.

Both texts compose an inner history of the individual in culture that challenges received ideas of civic agency. Their new perception allows for reconsideration of the fundamental concepts upon which their communities are built; and in this sense both *A Vision* and *Decline of the West* are modernist treatises for two states, Ireland and Germany, faced with fundamental problems of political reorganization. Both Yeats and Spengler occupy a space in these writings that has currency only in the direct moment of production, as the tangible effects of disintegration force awareness of the present as a turning point, or change of phase. Spengler acknowledges this place between times; "Western man," he writes, "lives in the *consciousness* of his becoming and his eyes are constantly upon past and future."[19] This unfolding is bound up with Spengler's version of apocalypse. "Force, Will, has an aim, and where there is an aim there is for the enquiring eye an end. . . . What the myth of Götterdämmerung signified of old, the irreligious form of it, the theory of Entropy, signifies to-day—world's end as completion of an inwardly necessary evolution."[20] Spengler's prophetic tone mimics the spiritualist texts of Yeats's early reading, and from the evidence of the books held in Yeats's library, Spengler's attention to painting, to science, and to evolution would all have been attractive. Having published *A Vision* to a largely puzzled audience, Yeats was reassured that some other minds might support him. He read Spengler's first volume some weeks after the publication of *A Vision* and to his surprise

> found that not only were dates that I had been given the same as his but whole metaphors and symbols that had seemed my work alone. Both he and I had symbolised a difference between Greek and Roman thought by comparing the blank or painted eyes of Greek statues with the pierced eyeballs of the Roman statues, both had described as an illustration of Roman character the naturalistic portrait heads screwed on to stock bodies, both had found the same meaning in the round bird-like eyes of Byzantine sculpture, though he or his translator had preferred "staring at infinity" to my "staring at miracle." I knew of no common source, no link between him and me, unless through
>
> The elemental things that go
> About my table to and fro.[21]

These last two lines appropriate part of a much earlier Yeats poem, "To Ireland in the Coming Times"; comparing the passages in which Yeats sees most connection between himself and Spengler, we can infer Yeats's sense of purpose in his own writing. Although written independently, the two texts, *A Vision* and *Decline of the West,* become commentaries on each other in context of Yeats's reading. Byzantium was a major imaginative resource for Yeats in the late 1920s and it is significant that Yeats should see common ground between himself and Spengler in their attention to it (and more so when we consider that the reasons for Yeats's attraction to Byzantium, as Roy Foster tells us, are not yet fully understood). The key passage of similarity in which both Yeats and Spengler deal with Byzantium rests upon a moment of suspended time. To Yeats in the first edition of *A Vision*, Byzantium stands at the apex of civilization where the individual becomes the mass, the mass individual:

> I think that in early Byzantium, and maybe never before or since in recorded history, religious, aesthetic and practical life were one, and that architect and artificers—though not, it may be, poets, for language had been the instrument of controversy and must have grown abstract—spoke to the multitude and the few alike. The painter and the mosaic worker, the worker in gold and silver, the illuminator of Sacred Books were almost impersonal, almost perhaps without the consciousness of individual design, absorbed in their subject matter and that the vision of a whole people.[22]

A unity between religious, aesthetic, and practical life was far from the tumult of Ireland during Yeats's researches. Such a compact symbolizes Yeats's ideal state, of mind and politics, which binds each to the other. There is a sacrifice of will to vision, as a dream world of possible destinies hovers just beyond the waking consciousness:

> The ascetic, called in Alexandria "God's athlete," has taken the place of those Greek athletes whose statues have been melted or broken up or stand deserted in the midst of cornfields, but all about him is an incredible splendour like that which we see pass under our closed eyelids as we lie between sleep and waking, no representation of a living world but the dream of a somnambulist. Even the drilled pupil of the eye, when the drill is in the hand of some Byzantine worker in ivory, undergoes a somnambulistic change for its deep shadow among the faint lines of the tablet, its mechanical circle, where all else is rhythmical and flowing, give to Saint or Angel a look of some great bird staring at miracle.[23]

As Yeats read, this final image recurs in Spengler:

> There is a patent difference of *value* between a Substance permeating the body and a Substance which falls from the world-cavern into humanity, abstract and divine, making of all participants a Consensus. This "Spirit" it is which evokes the higher world, and through this creation triumphs over mere life, "the flesh" and nature. This is the prime image that underlies all feeling of ego. Sometimes it is seen in religious, sometimes in philosophical, sometimes in artistic guise. Consider the portraits of the Constantinian age, with their fixed stare into the infinite.[24]

The correlation that Yeats felt between his work and that of Spengler can be understood as Yeats's relief in discovering a similar mind at the end of many tiring and obscure researches; but more fundamental are the conceptual similarities in structure that mutually generate *A Vision* and *Decline of the West* as narratives in search of authority in the aftermath of empire. Yeats's own personal copies of Spengler's *Decline of the West* are marked in pencil, with pages folded, in a library that contains many books by other authors with pages still uncut. Analysis of Yeats's marginalia in his copy of Spengler's work confirms his interest in historical patterns. From the first volume, Yeats's preoccupation with space and time is evident. The following passages are marked by pencil in the margins: first,

> Neither Plato nor Aristotle had an observatory. In the last years of Pericles, the Athenian people passed a decree by which all who propagated astronomical theories were made liable to impeachment (είσαγγελία). This last was an act of the deepest symbolic significance, expressive of the determination of the Classical soul to banish distance, in every aspect, from its world-consciousness.[25]

—and second:

> The Egyptian soul, consciously historical in its texture and impelled with primitive passion towards the infinite, perceived past and future as its *whole* world, and the present (which is identical with waking consciousness) appeared to him simply as the narrow common frontier of two immeasurable stretches.[26]

Consistently, Yeats focuses his attention on two modes in Spengler—the analysis of cultures in a moment of change, and the effect of time on human consciousness. This coincides with Yeats's contemporaneous preoccupations in his own writing with conflict as necessary to transition. Especially attractive were Spengler's arguments on behalf of a new history, conceived of as a challenge to established authority. Yeats marked the following in pencil, making a tick at the first sentence:

> we must not lose sight of the fact that at bottom the wish to write history *scientifically* involves a contradiction. True science reaches just as far as the notions of truth and falsity have validity; this applies to mathematics and it applies also to the science of historical spade-work, viz., the collection, ordering and sifting of material. But real historical vision (which only *begins* at this point) belongs to the domain of significances, in which the crucial words are not "correct" and "erroneous," but "deep" and "shallow." The true physicist is not deep, but *keen;* it is only when he leaves the domain of working hypotheses and brushes against the final things that he can be deep, but at this stage he is already a metaphysician. Nature is to be handled scientifically, History poetically.[27]

Spengler prompted Yeats to question in the margins, "does he use 'deep' to signify the *amount* of extension symbolized 'deep' = extension form = symbol."[28] This arcane note gives us a further clue as to Spengler's importance to Yeats. Both writers were engaged in the writing of symbolic histories; these cultural accounts communicated their coded perspectives by systematic arrangement of particular words, like "depth," "destiny," or "will." Such words gathered charge from their repetition. The minute attention that Yeats pays to Spengler's vocabulary is evidence of a mind obsessed with the position of things, an obsession that recurs in Yeats's commentary. Spengler argues, "Chronological number distinguishes uniquely-occurring actualities, mathematical number constant possibilities. The one sharpens the images and works up the outlines of epoch and fact for the understanding eye. But the other *is itself* the law which it seeks to establish, the end and aim of research."[29]

To Yeats, writing in the bottom margins of pages, this prompts the response that

> Classical man spatializes himself in Nature
> as human body (it near
> and small)
> Modern Man spatializes himself in nature
> as the Ambient (the far
> and great)
> classical man hates the infinite and contracts.[30]

An awareness of the infinite is key, and it is only modern man, in Yeats's formulation, who can accommodate it. For Spengler, the impulse to immortality drives modern culture. Yeats concurs and introduces the end of vision as achievement, "the far and great." Repeatedly we find Yeats attending to those moments in Spengler where a Western modernity is contrasted to other cultures and periods by its particular definition of time. Accordingly, Yeats marked the following in pencil: "Without exact time-measurement, without a *chronology of becoming* to correspond with his imperative need of archæology (the preservation, excavation and collection of *things-become*), Western man is unthinkable."[31] By extension, our own individual awareness of death, of the final becoming, is central to Spengler's theories of evolving society. In awareness of mortality,

> man first becomes man and realizes his immense loneliness in the universal, the world-fear reveals itself for the first time as the essentially human fear in the presence of death, the limit of the light-world, rigid space. Here, too, the higher thought originates as meditation upon death. Every religion, every scientific investigation, every philosophy proceeds from it. Every great symbolism attaches its form-language to the cult of the dead, the forms of disposal of the dead, the adornment of the graves of the dead.[32]

This passage marks a definite change in Yeats's response to Spengler. Both *A Vision* and *Decline of the West* can be categorized, in part, as a search for new authority, Yeats by experiment in the multiple voices of his modernist collage, Spengler in the assembly of his compensatory historical epic. But the connection between the two writers extends further, as Spengler's "meditation upon death" had subsequent effects on Yeats's poetry. This is particularly true of Yeats's reading of Spengler's second volume, *Perspectives of World History*, published in 1928. The book was Yeats's unlikely companion as he rested after illness in Rapallo, gathering new strength and energy in the Italian sun (Foster, memorably, has Yeats "writing in his sunny eyrie over the road to Portofino").[33] From his Hotel Reina Christina in late January and February, Yeats finished what his notebooks call "Meditations upon Death" (a phrase we know from Spengler), published first as one poem in *A Packet for Ezra Pound* and as two separate poems, "At Algeciras—a Mediation upon Death" and "Mohini Chatterjee," in *The Winding Stair and Other Poems* in 1933. The opening passages of *A Packet for Ezra Pound*, composed in this period and collected later in the revised edition of *A Vision* in 1937, summon:

Mountains that shelter the bay from all but the south wind, bare brown branches of low vines and of tall trees blurring their outline as though with a soft mist; houses mirrored in an almost motionless sea; a verandahed gable a couple of miles away bringing to mind some Chinese painting. Rapallo's thin line of broken mother-of-pearl along the water's edge. The little town described in the *Ode on a Grecian Urn*.[34]

During this time of self-reflection, Yeats found much in Spengler to make him think of his own involvement in the Irish literary movements. The first passage marked by Yeats in his copy of Spengler's second volume suggests memories of the Abbey Theatre, the Revival, and an Ireland of the past. Inscribed in conflicts that powered the Revival, from Synge to O'Casey, was the necessary arrival, in Spengler, of the great man, the author of the master narrative:

All grand events of history are carried by beings of the cosmic order, by peoples, parties, armies, and classes, while the history of the intellect runs its course in loose associations and circles, schools, levels of education, "tendencies" and "isms." And here again it is a question of destiny whether such aggregates at the moments of highest effectiveness find a leader or are driven blindly on, whether the chance headmen are men of the first order or men of no real significance tossed up, like Robespierre or Pompey, by the surge of events. It is the hall-mark of the statesman that he has a sure and penetrating eye for these mass-souls that form and dissolve on the tide of the times, their strength and their duration, their direction and purpose. And even so, it is a question of Incident whether he is one who *can* master them or one who is swept away by them.[35]

Being swept away was a destiny real enough to a Yeats who had despaired of effective activity in the Irish senate. Time, in Spengler's previous volume, was guardian of future progress. With accurate measurement, the conditions could be created for revelation. But the introduction of personality changed the equation. Spengler's second volume deals with the necessity of the great individual for society. That greatness arose from blood purity, and so the idea of race enters a philosophy previously content with a latent affiliation to a general idea of the "West." Yeats marked the following passage at mention of Napoleon:

It was because the blood of the ruling family incorporated the destiny, the being, of the whole nation, that the state-system of the Baroque was of genealogical

> structure and that most of the grand crises assumed the form of wars of dynastic succession. Even the catastrophic ruin of Napoleon, which settled the world's political organization for a century, took its shape from the fact that an adventurer dared to drive out with his blood that of the old dynasties, and that his attack upon a symbol made it historically a sacred duty to resist him. For all these peoples were the *consequence* of dynastic destinies.[36]

Ruling families embody nations; attack on those ruling families causes reaction. This is a troubling concept for Yeats in Ireland, where the new democracy consisted of so many, to him, untested representatives. The previous ruling caste, the Anglo-Irish Ascendancy, now failed, might be read as one of those castes that controlled a society by blood right (an idea, perhaps, that informed Bram Stoker's *Dracula*). But there is the alternative possibility that a new adventurer might strike at the right time and insert his own bloodline in the establishment. As Spengler claims, "That there is a Portuguese people, and a Portuguese Brazil in the midst of Spanish America, is the result of the marriage of Count Henry of Burgundy in 1095. That there are Swiss and Hollanders is the result of a reaction against the House of Habsburg."[37] Encoded in these royal successions is the possibility of hybrid transformation, of a new becoming that combines fresh elements.

Yeats was occupied, at the same time as this reading, with the debate over new forms of politics in the Irish Free State. These included fascism, and there is a residue of his reading of Spengler in his later conversation with Eoin O'Duffy, the Irish blue-shirt leader, on the potential for reaction in 1934. Yeats urged that "unless a revolutionary crisis arose they must make no intervention. They should prepare themselves by study to act without hesitation should the crisis arise. Then, & then only, their full program. I talked the 'historical dialectic,' spoke of it as proving itself by events as the curvature of space was proved (after mathematicians had worked it out) by observation during an eclipse. O'Duffy probably brought here that I might talk of it."[38] O'Duffy probably did not understand a word of it. But Yeats's promotion of crisis as opportunity was confirmed by his reading of Spengler. His markings in the second volume revolve mainly around Spengler's concept of "Caesarism," the Caesar a new form of leader who combines pedigree with opportunity. Reading the following passage, Yeats disagreed with Spengler's particular historical periodization of Western culture, observing that

Spengler "[p]uts great periods of great art and culture too late or ours too early" and "[i]gnores literature and art" but still accepts a decay of form, of which "Swift was conscious."[39] In Spengler,

> The change from the absolute State to the battling Society of nations that marks the beginning of every Civilization . . . means the transition from government in the style and pulse of a strict tradition to the *sic volo, sic jubeo* of the unbridled personal regime. . . . Great interstate and internal conflicts, revolutions of a fearful kind, interpenetrate increasingly, but the questions at issue in all of them without exception are (consciously and frankly or not) questions of unofficial, and eventually purely personal, power. . . . None of the innumerable revolutions of this era—which more and more become blind outbreaks of uprooted megalopolitan masses—has ever attained, or ever had the possibility of attaining, an aim. What stands is only the historical fact of an accelerated demolition of ancient forms that leaves the path clear for Cæsarism.[40]

This offers a radical way to understand Ireland's predicament after independence. The fragmentation of empires into warring nations is in process; the historical evidence in Spengler points to a cleared space in which the personal can now act freely. That person is particular and powerful, a Caesar. Crucially, our aims are unimportant, our actions paramount. So Yeats warns O'Duffy to be prepared, above all, to act, to know and seize the moment when it comes. Spengler expanded his philosophy of the Caesars to Yeats's continuing interest. A Caesar appears at a specific point in a cultural cycle, immediately following the moment when cities have grown and "money and intellect celebrate their greatest and their last triumphs" (throughout Spengler the city is the object of cynicism, and it is this denial of the metropolitan that most exposes him as reactionary).[41] Popular politics serves money, and not the abstract ideal:

> In the form of democracy, money has won. There has been a period in which politics has been almost its preserve. But as soon as it has destroyed the old orders of the Culture, the chaos gives forth a new and overpowering factor that penetrates to the very elementals of Becoming—the Cæsar-men. Before them the money collapses. *The Imperial Age, in every culture alike, signifies the end of the politics of mind and money.* The powers of the blood, unbroken bodily forces, resume their ancient lordship. "Race" springs forth, pure and irresistible—the strongest win and the residue is their spoil.[42]

Yeats marked from "The Imperial Age" to "their ancient lordship" in his copy. This is not to say, of course, that Yeats agreed with what he read; it is possible that he marked each passage to disagree with it (though this seems unlikely, given that he did comment when finding fault with any aspect of Spengler's system he disliked). But again and again, Yeats is drawn to the idea of the Caesar as a revolutionary transformation in Western culture. Two vertical lines mark the left margin of the following, from one of the final passages of Spengler's work: "The coming of Cæsarism breaks the dictature of money and its political weapon democracy."[43] There will be a conflict in which "[t]he sword is victorious over the money, the master-will subdues again the plunderer-will."[44] Spengler ends,

> For us, however, whom a Destiny has placed in this Culture and at this moment of its development—the moment when money is celebrating its last victories, and the Cæsarism that is to succeed approaches with quiet, firm step—our direction, willed and obligatory at once, is set for us within narrow limits, and on any other terms life is not worth the living. We have not the freedom to reach to this or to that, but the freedom to do the necessary or to do nothing. And a task that historic necessity has set *will* be accomplished with the individual or against him.
>
> *Ducunt Fata volentem, nolentem trahunt.*[45]

The testimonial quality of Spengler's pronouncements echoes the evangelism of Yeats's earlier phase, when the world might be transformed by fairy light and symbol. Now, older and frail, Yeats found that the question of one's moment, and how to act in it, was more pressing. There is no doubt that Yeats's reading of Spengler was selective, and no doubt that their theories of time and society at times fundamentally differ. But there is no doubt either that Spengler's effect on Yeats was deeper, and more lasting, than acknowledged, and that *Decline of the West* provides an informing context for Yeats's writing of the late 1920s. Both Yeats and Spengler wrote in a moment of imperial weakness; both lived through Ireland and Germany's transition to popular politics. And both wrote major prose works that attempted, amid the perceived chaos, to divine alternative national narratives. Yeats composed a modernist collage in *A Vision* and in doing so stretched modernism to the limits. Spengler assembled a fantasy of history, literature, art, and science to create what "I am able to regard, and, despite the misery and disgust of these years, proud to call *a German philosophy*."[46] The condition of national politics cannot be overlooked in either of these strange works; neither can the realization that a joint obsession with a space of clearance outside time suggests a fatigue with popular politics that prepared for a dominating response. Both Yeats and Spengler await a new era as

Grave is heaped on grave
That they be satisfied.[47]

## Notes

*Permissions*: Quotations from *A Vision*, "Mohini Chatterjee," Yeats's correspondence with T. Sturge Moore, and Yeats's annotations in his private copy of Oswald Spengler's *The Decline of the West* are reprinted by permission of A. P. Watt Ltd on behalf of Gráinne Yeats. Quotation from W. B. Yeats, "Mohini Chatterjee," in *The Collected Works of W. B. Yeats*, vol. 1: *The Poems*, 2nd edition by Richard J. Finneran, copyright © 1933 by The Macmillan Company; copyright renewed 1961 by Bertha Georgie Yeats, all rights reserved, is reprinted by permission of Scribner, an imprint of Simon & Schuster Adult Publishing Group. Quotations from W. B. Yeats, *A Vision*, copyright © 1937 by W. B. Yeats; copyright renewed 1965 by Bertha Georgie Yeats and Anne Butler Yeats, all rights reserved, are reprinted by permission of Scribner, an imprint of Simon & Schuster Adult Publishing Group.

1 Yeats, *A Critical Edition of Yeats' "A Vision" (1925)*, 117.
2 Cullingford, *Yeats, Ireland and Fascism*, 115.
3 Ibid.
4 Brown, *The Life of W. B. Yeats*, 302.
5 Ibid., 310.
6 Foster, *W. B. Yeats*, 282.
7 For details, see ibid., passim.
8 O'Higgins was Minister for Justice in the Irish Free State; he was assassinated by Republicans in 1927 in revenge for his ordering of reprisal executions during the civil war. Yeats wrote of O'Higgins's "soul incapable of remorse or rest" in "The Municipal Gallery Revisited," *Yeats's Poems*, 438.
9 O'Grady's two-volume *History of Ireland*, published in 1878 and 1880, was a master text of the Irish revival. Influenced by Thomas Carlyle, O'Grady recast ancient Irish epic in contemporary terms, as a prompt, initially, to heroic action by the landowning classes, so establishing in part the paradoxical model of reaction and radicalism that Yeats proposes in *A Vision*. For discussion of O'Grady, see Allen, *George Russell (Æ) and the New Ireland, 1905–30*, 18–20. See also McAteer, *Standish O'Grady, Æ and Yeats*.

10 Atkinson, Translator's Preface, ix.
11 Spengler, *Decline of the West*, vol. 1, xiii. Yeats's personal copy, Yeats's library, National Library of Ireland, MS 1975.
12 Similar to Yeats and Spengler, Blavatsky considered her work a "new Genesis." For discussion of Blavatsky, see Allen, *George Russell (Æ) and the New Ireland, 1905–30*, 11–21.
13 Spengler, *Decline of the West*, vol. 1, xv. Yeats's personal copy, Yeats's library, National Library of Ireland, MS 1975.
14 Ibid., 3.
15 Ibid., 263.
16 Ibid.
17 Ibid., 264.
18 Ibid.
19 Ibid.
20 Ibid., 423–24.
21 Yeats, *A Vision*, 18–19.
22 Yeats, *A Critical Edition of Yeats' "A Vision,"* 191.
23 Ibid., 192.
24 Spengler, *Decline of the West*, vol. 1, 306. Yeats's personal copy, Yeats's library, National Library of Ireland, MS 1975.
25 Ibid., 9.
26 Ibid., 12.
27 Ibid., 96.
28 Ibid. Yeats's handwriting is notoriously difficult to decipher; transcriptions are reproduced in the knowledge that mistakes may be made even after best effort.
29 Ibid., 97–98.
30 Ibid., 97.
31 Ibid., 134.
32 Ibid., 166–67.
33 Foster, *W. B. Yeats*, 385.
34 Yeats, *A Vision*, 3.
35 Spengler, *Decline of the West*, vol. 2, 19. Yeats's personal copy, Yeats's library, National Library of Ireland, MS 1975a.
36 Ibid., 181.
37 Ibid.
38 Cited in Cullingford, *Yeats, Ireland and Fascism*, 205.
39 Spengler, *Decline of the West*, vol. 2, 419. Yeats's personal copy, Yeats's library, National Library of Ireland, MS 1975a.
40 Ibid.
41 Ibid., 431.
42 Ibid., 431–32.
43 Ibid., 506.
44 Ibid.

45 Ibid., 507.

46 Spengler, *Decline of the West*, vol. 1, xiv. Yeats's personal copy, Yeats's library, National Library of Ireland, MS 1975.

47 Yeats, "Mohini Chatterjee," *The Poems*, 251.

## Works Cited

Allen, Nicholas. *George Russell (Æ) and the New Ireland, 1905–30*. Dublin: Four Courts Press, 2003.

Atkinson, Charles Francis. Translator's Preface. In Oswald Spengler, *The Decline of the West*. Vol. 1: *Form and Actuality*. London: George Allen and Unwin, 1926. (Yeats's personal copy, Yeats's library, National Library of Ireland, MS 1975.)

Bridge, Ursula, ed. *W. B. Yeats and T. Sturge Moore: Their Correspondence, 1901–1937*. London: Routledge and Kegan Paul, 1953.

Brown, Terence. *The Life of W. B. Yeats: A Critical Biography*. Oxford: Blackwell, 1999.

Cullingford, Elizabeth. *Yeats, Ireland and Fascism*. London: Macmillan, 1981.

Foster, Roy. *W. B. Yeats: A Life*. Vol. 2: *The Arch-Poet, 1915–1939*. Oxford: Oxford University Press, 2003.

McAteer, Michael. *Standish O'Grady, Æ and Yeats: History, Politics, Culture*. Dublin: Irish Academic Press, 2002.

Spengler, Oswald. *The Decline of the West*. Vol. 1: *Form and Actuality*. Translated by Charles Francis Atkinson. London: George Allen and Unwin, 1926. (Yeats's personal copy, Yeats library, National Library of Ireland, MS 1975.)

——. *The Decline of the West*. Vol. 2: *Perspectives of World-History*. Translated by Charles Francis Atkinson. London: George Allen and Unwin, 1928. (Yeats's personal copy, Yeats library, National Library of Ireland MS 1975a.)

Yeats, W. B. *A Critical Edition of Yeats' "A Vision" (1925)*. Edited by George Mills Harper and Walter Kelly Hood. London: Macmillan, 1978.

——. *A Vision*. London: Macmillan, 1937.

——. *The Poems*. 2nd ed. Edited by Richard J. Finneran. Vol. 1 of *The Collected Works of W. B. Yeats*. New York: Macmillan, 1989.

*Maria DiBattista*

⋮

TEN

# Elizabeth Bowen's Troubled Modernism

The Troubles troubled everything . . .

ELIZABETH BOWEN, *The Last September*

Is nationalism fundamentally "neighbourliness grown a bit inflated and unwieldy"?[1] This sociable notion was parenthetically, but seriously, advanced by Hubert Butler, a long-lived Protestant Irish nationalist and one of the insufficiently heralded literary chroniclers of modern Irish and European culture. Butler's belief in the unifying power of local manners and traditions has the merit of identifying the springs of national feeling not in imagined but in actual community. It is perhaps an idea that would readily, if not inevitably, occur to a member of the Anglo-Irish gentry, a class entrenched in the politics of locality and the hospitable traditions of the Big House.

These traditions of sociability were indeed unique to Ireland, as Elizabeth Bowen observed, since the Irish Big Houses, unlike their English and French counterparts, "have no natural growth from the soil—the idea that begot them was a purely social one."[2] For the idea to take root, Bowen admits, there had to pass an epoch of "greed, roughness and panic," but by the eighteenth century, "these new settlers imposed on Ireland began to wish to add something to life. . . . They began to feel, and exert, the European idea—to seek what was humanistic, classic and disciplined."[3] These local social forms that unfolded from the transplantation of the "European idea" into Irish soil might be counted as casualties of Ireland's struggle for independence. How their creators and sponsors should be regarded is a historical question not easily settled. Writing in *Bowen's Court*, Bowen contemplated the historical future of the Anglo-Irish gentry and speculated that as a class, they "may or may not prove able to make adaptations; that is one of the many things we must wait to see. To my mind, they are tougher than they appear. To live as though living gave them no trouble has been the first imperative of their make-up: to do this has taken a virtuosity into which courage enters more than has been allowed. In the last issue, they have lived at their own expense."[4]

Given the language of Irish nationalism, the word "trouble" here is not casually chosen nor idly entertained. To live as though living gave them no trouble is to persist in a virtuosity that is at once a form of self-assertion, even aggrandizement, but also a mode of self-destructive social display. It was a mode of life sorely tested in Bowen's second, most personal novel, *The Last September,* which is set, as she relates in her preface, in "the troubled times"—that is, the guerrilla conflict between the Irish, in arms for freedom, and the British troops still garrisoning the land.[5] Bowen also recalls for her readers that for the Anglo-Irish especially, "the Troubles troubled everything," immediately adding, as if in partial disbelief, "yes, even hospitality."[6] Hospitality, the refinement and ritualization of neighborliness into patterns to grace the interactions of everyday life, is for her the tradition most imperiled by modernist upheavals in customs and governments. Such cordial formalities were threatened by the brutal violence of modern insurgency and anticolonialist, then civil war. The Troubles troubled everything, indeed; yes, even and especially the mind of the novelist split between her respect for the considerate traditions and customs of her class and her artistic allegiance to that blunt, often tactless form of truth-telling called modernism.

Butler and Bowen, who were friends,[7] were writers of conservative instincts, but radical imagination, so neither should be suspected of disingenuous ideological alibis for the cultural and political dominance of their class before the Treaty of 1922. Both were aware that one person's vision of gracious society can be another's nightmare of complacent, even self-congratulatory oppression. This is the general irony attending all efforts at "humane" colonization along European lines, as the anticolonialist novels of Conrad, E. M. Forster, Graham Greene, and George Orwell (to say nothing of later postcolonial novels by Chinua Achebe, Salman Rushdie, Buichi Emecheta, and Arundhati Roy) so memorably dramatize, but it is an irony that held a particular anguish for the Anglo-Irish. The hyphenation that links their national stems is less a sign of their hybrid identity than the mark of the double allegiances that have complicated their historical existence. In her preface to *The Last September,* Bowen's elegy, as Hermione Lee aptly calls it,[8] on the last days of Irish ascendancy, she describes these split loyalties: "Inherited loyalty to England—where their sons went to school, in whose wars their sons were killed, and to whom they owed in the first place their lands and power—pulled them one way; their own latent blood-and-bone 'Irishness,' the other."[9] These complications can be radically simplified by the bitterly resentful or exculpatory rhetoric of colonialist Ireland in which, as Butler mordantly notes, Irish Protestants have been called "imperialistic blood-suckers, or, by our admirers, as the last champions of civilization in an abandoned island."[10]

It is hard to see how feelings and traditions of neighborliness survived this climate of indignant and implacable opinion, but apparently they did. They often survived, moreover, in the unlikely form of a motivating political sentiment. Hence the existence of Anglo-Irishmen (and women), like Butler, with republican nationalist convictions. Butler is a representative rather than eccentric instance of latent blood-and-bone Irishness winning out over the Britishness that had given the Anglo-Irish their lands and awarded them both power and prestige.[11] In this, as in other respects, then, the Anglo-Irish, with their hyphenated identity and divided loyalties, represent a special case in the history of colonialism. Their singular historical position and split social consciousness posed unique challenges to modernist writers determined to imagine new forms of individual and social life that would be emancipated, yet still connected to the living strains of tradition.

The customs of those bred in country things seem unlikely sources for such modern, transformative images of community. English modernism figured its most revolutionary relation to the reigning imperial orders in T. S. Eliot's "Unreal City" and Joyce's Dublin. Dublin, however, unlike Eliot's London, Proust's Paris, or Biely's St Petersburg, was a colonial capital, so that the search for a form expressive of modern realities was indissociable from the quest for national as well as imaginative sovereignty. This being said, it must also be acknowledged that national solidarity develops differently under the tutelage of Catholic universalism and the hard schooling of the Dublin streets than it does under the Europeanizing sway of the Protestant landed gentry.[12] This, after all, was a ruling class who, as Elizabeth Bowen remarks, "had begun as conquerors and were not disposed to let that tradition lapse."[13] To what extent the modern wars of liberation, wars fought on the literary as well the political front, entailed the repudiation of such persistent, local traditions is a question that unsettles even the most confidently progressive accounts of the modernist literature of empire. In these accounts, Ireland occupies a singular position in the league of aspiring nations. Geography—the location of this "oblique, frayed island moored at the north but with an air of being detached and drawn out west from the British coast"[14]—accounts for this singularity. Irish modernism complicates and enriches it.

Both the singularity and the complications that ensue intrigued Fredric Jameson, a critic of quite different ideological persuasions from Butler's or Bowen's, as he pursued an argument very much in line with the preoccupation of this volume of essays—namely, that "the structure of imperialism also makes its mark on the inner forms and structures of that new mutation in literary and artistic language to which the term modernism is loosely applied."[15] In Jameson's view, imperialism constitutes a world system that fractures the daily life of nations, leaving them "radically incomplete" and in search of a compensatory form to express their "self-subsisting totality." E. M. Forster, he contends, may be taken as a type of the modern artist responding to this need for social coherence and connection "by way of his providential ideology, which transforms chance contacts, coincidence, the contingent and random encounters between isolated subjects, into a utopian glimpse of achieved community."[16]

Jameson then proposes a thought experiment that yields interesting results, although not as startling as his coy rhetoric might lead us to expect. He asks us to presuppose "a national situation which reproduces the appearance of First World social reality and social relationships—perhaps through the coincidence of its language with the imperial language—but whose underlying structure is in fact much closer to that of the Third World or of colonized daily life":

> We may expect to find, in some abstractly possible Irish modernism a form which on the one hand unites Forster's sense of the providential yet seemingly accidental encounters of characters with Woolf's aesthetic closure, but which on the other hand projects those onto a radically different kind of space, a space no longer central as in English life but marked as marginal and ec-centric after the fashion of the colonized areas of the imperial system. That colonized space may

> be expected to transform the modernist formal project radically, while still retaining a similar family likeness to its imperial variants.

Jameson then reveals that such a "deduction finds immediate formal confirmation, for I have in fact been describing *Ulysses*."[17]

This thought experiment, however worthwhile, does not radically challenge Butler's contention that nationalism is neighborliness hoping to extend itself in an ever widening compass of civil association. Jameson looks for a family likeness between Ireland and other colonized countries because he identifies the experience of marginalized or eccentric space, the space of the modern metropolis, as a uniform as well as a transformative pressure on modernist writing. In doing so, he tends to underestimate and even disparage the vitality of nonmetropolitan life as a stimulus to modernist renovations of social and literary forms. Take, for example, his contention that Joyce's inventive modernism is compromised, linguistically if not formally, by Dublin's status as a colonial city. Joyce's Dublin, Jameson scolds, is never allowed to progress beyond its "rhetorical past" and is socially frozen as "an underdeveloped village in which gossip and rumor still reign supreme." It is not self-evident, however, that relinquishing Ireland's "rhetorical past" is a desirable end in all instances, nor that gossip and rumor are more baleful to genuine community feeling than the managed news of totalitarian regimes.

Moreover, it is even debatable whether linguistic innovation is in all instances emancipatory or even reality-responsive. Certainly Joyce revolutionized the literary language of modernism by showing how words could be forced into their own diaspora, their verbal elements separated and set adrift in the sea of daily usage, where they will mutate, recombine, or reconstitute themselves in the "new" lexical surroundings of a transformed verbal environment.[18] The retelling of the *Odyssey* as an odyssey of styles, with different chapters organized and dominated by different symbolic and stylistic regimes, is one way the adventure of modernism becomes an adventure in language, but also an adventure in what we might call narrative home-rule, with each episode, as Joyce annotated them in the Linati schema, accorded its own self-regulating system of arts and technics. Yet Joyce also transformed the increasingly arbitrary nature of modern, imperial relationships by appealing to what Molly Bloom calls "plain words,"[19] words whose meaning is ratified by the familiarity of common usage and long acquaintance, the familiarities bred and sustained by the recurring, routine encounters of people, be they country folk or city-dwellers, living in the same neighborhood. Leopold Bloom's clumsy imprecision in defining a nation as "the same people living in the same place," a definition that, when mocked, he amends to include "or living in different places,"[20] seems less inept if place entails the obligation as well as unarguable fact of neighborliness in village or metropole.[21]

If neighborliness is such an exigent part of our feelings for the nation, then First World novels of country life, even those set in the conservative demesne of the Big House, may be as modernist as the most densely populated and labyrinthine urban narrative, their provincial characters as susceptible, perhaps even more susceptible, than their urban counterparts to the Third World feelings of restlessness, resentment, and outright revolt. Few might dispute that country life breeds the restless dissatisfaction, the longing for enlarging, variegated experience that is the preeminent modern emotion, but many might wonder whether it could also engender the modernist forms to contain such insurgent and often inchoate feelings. Does, in fact, modernist originality manifest itself only within the teeming, colonized spaces of the eccentric city? Butler thought not and even went so far as to argue that there was "something self-destructive about the great congestions of originality" of the modern metropolitan, imperialist city. "A sense of doom hangs over them as over the exuberant freedom of the Weimar Republic." He then gives his reasons for unfashionably preferring the radicalism brewed in provincial cultures to the ferment of metropolitan modernism:

> In a vast society like ours, "the man of intellect and education," as Chekhov saw him, is one among several thousands, a natural solitary, in fact. His function is to be the pinch of bread-soda in the dough, and not to foregather with other ex-solitaries and for a bread-soda pudding. Yet an Irishman sees this happening every year. Feeny and Meany, drawn away from their solitude, bring with them to the city their instinct to defy. They gather together with other ex-solitaries; then they are no longer solitary and what is more they find they are no longer original. Their insights and perceptions, which surprised and often vexed their fellow-citizens, are banal and irrelevant among the exuberant heterodoxies of their new community. In place of the known neighbours whom it was their duty to challenge, there are faceless strangers who can only be met with abstractions. To get attention in such circles, the ex-solitary man may have to turn in his

tracks, to sacrifice the particular to the general, and to accept as valid some mass-produced consensus whose insufficiency he would quickly have detected among the familiar diversities of his native town. In the way the cities acquire fanatics at the same rate as the provinces lose their solitary individuals.[22]

Butler's Chekhovian view of the relation between local culture, with its "familiar diversities," and the "mass-produced consensus" of the city suggests an inherently novelistic way of thinking about how communities are formed, disturbed, depleted, and remade in times of political change. Feeny and Meany are the protagonists in this protonovelistic allegory of country life; they are the native "men of intellect and education" whose vexing insights and instinct to defy work are more productive of social good than the stale, if "modern" views fashionable in city life. The exuberance that is generally celebrated as the signature mood of a triumphant, defiant modernity fails to exalt Butler's own cultural hopes. Indeed, the effect of repeating the word "exuberant" is to link Dublin and Weimar as two metropolitan centers high on nationalist extravagances, but perhaps living too dearly at their own expense. More than exuberant heterodoxies and exuberant freedoms is required to bring a nation into being. The work of nation-formation entails a harder, often bitter labor. Irish nationalism seems at once to recognize and soften this harsh historical fact. In Ireland the times of upheaval and transformation take the local form and proper name of the Troubles, a term that seems to hover between euphemism and poetic indirection.

No one captured the complex neighborly life of the Anglo-Irish during the Troubles with more emotional precision than Bowen in her curiously serene evocation of the final days of colonialist Ireland, *The Last September*. The serenity is attributable to the tenderness with which Bowen revisits and recasts her memories of her young womanhood in Cork.[23] The curiosity, of course, was and remains historical—how could Bowen write of country visits, tennis parties, and provincial balls in the nuance-drenched manner of Proust at a time when Ireland was convulsed by violence, its countryside the site of ambushes, its estates the burial ground of rebel guns?[24] Indeed Lois Farquar, the novel's young heroine, who, Bowen carefully discriminates, "derives from, but is not, myself at nineteen" (xii), protests her being confined, until the last stunning pages of the novel release her, within a provincial comedy of manners, while all around her the world seems bent on other and bloody business. "How is it that in this country that ought to be full of such violent realness," she complains, "there seems nothing for me but clothes and what people say? I might as well be in some kind of cocoon" (56).

A cocoon is at once an image of insulated but also of gestating life. Insulation from the violent "realness" of the Troubles frustrates Lois because she can conceive very little of time outside of the present: for her, immediacy is the index of realness (a word that itself does mild violence to the more stable and euphonious term, "reality"). Bowen is immensely sympathetic to this view, since it coincides with her own driving motive as a writer: "to impart the sense of the 'now,'" she confides in the novel's preface, "has been for me one imperative of creative writing" (ix). But in the novel, the "now" to which and in which characters are exposed is summoned not just in the lyrical intensities, often approaching violence, of a character's feelings but in the more prosaic, time-sensitive description of what people say and what clothes they wear. These mundane details and unconscious habits are of great value in imparting a way of life in its lived immediacy, of equally great value as a material record of the way history infiltrates and subtly transforms the daily life of a particular time and class. To indicate as much, Bowen takes for the novel's epigraph a line from Proust: "*Ils ont les chagrins qu'ont les vierges et les paresseux* . . ." The epigraph, as John Coates has shown, refers to those "with an artistic temperament or leanings who are unwilling to undertake the concentration and labour of creation." Coates then quotes the entire source passage: "They suffer but their sufferings, like the sufferings of virgins and lazy people, are of a kind that fecundity or work would cure."[25] The epigraph thus serves notice of Bowen's intent to satirize, even as she memorializes, her own recaptured past. Her Proustian researches into the lost and innocent times of her girlhood are marked by the irony that "meaning flows in, retrospectively, where we were blind to any. We are captured by the mysterious, the imperious hauntedness of a period not understood in its own time" (x).

The time of *The Last September* is 1920, just before the Treaty of 1922 that ended the Troubles, established the Free State, but was also to lead to civil war. The novel, then, represents a narrative effort to understand a decisive period in Ireland's anticolonialist struggles through the "chagrins" of its virginal heroine and the lazy-minded, but hospitable, Anglo-Irish occupants of a fictional place, Danielstown, that, in what we might call an act full of historical chagrin, is burned to the ground on the last page of the novel. That conflagration returns the novel to the violent "realness" of history, which the narrative, in its retrospective account of a vanished past, had struggled to evade all along. Bowen's modernism restored her most personal narrative to history even as it imaginatively mobilized her divided loyalties, setting them against each other.

It was Bowen's modernism that determined that her first loyalty must be to her art, which for her meant loyalty to the emotional and not just historical integrity of what she calls "the finished time" of her story. The aesthetic closure designated by this phrase does not entail an arbitrary act of closing off the past within the autonomous realm of art, although this is often how modernist form has been described and criticized. The finished time of her story is not so much closed off in art as exposed to emotional review and imaginative inspection. Bowen's desire to represent this finished time of her own youth required her to devise a new narrative route to the past, since, as she explained, "the ordinary narrative past tense, so much in usage as to be taken for granted, did not seem to me likely to be forceful enough" (ix). Here is how Bowen describes her solution to the problem of representing an uncomprehended, and so incomplete, if departed past:

> "All this," I will the reader to *know*, "is over." Yet I wish him to *feel:* "But see, our story begins." From the start, the reader must look—and more, he must be aware of looking—down a perspective cut through the years. The fear he might miss the viewpoint, that he might read so much as my first pages under misapprehension, haunted me. The ordinary past tense, so much in usage as to be taken for granted, did not seem to me likely to be forceful enough, so I opened my second paragraph with a pointer: "*In those days . . . girls wore crisp white skirts and transparent blouses clotted with white flowers; ribbons threaded through . . . appeared over the shoulders.*" Lois' ribbons lead into history. (ix)

Bowen's pointer—"in those days"—not only points to the past but cordons it off in legend. So begins J. G. Farrell's *Troubles:* "In those days the Majestic was still standing in Kilnalough at the very end of a slim peninsula covered with dead pines leaning here and there at odd angles."[26] "In those days" serves as a "local" narrative idiom enclosing the Troubles within the wider scope of myth, but myth as it takes root and lives in local memory rather than as it is sublimated into universal narratives. History is brought back to life precisely through now outworn or defunct fashions in speech, dress, demeanor, its now quaint and "odd"-seeming ways of making or declaring love.

Thus Lois's ribbons lead us into history, but she herself is too beset by the chagrin of the living, troubled present to be a trustworthy chronicler of her own time. The disorder wrought by the Troubles on the fabric of her daily life so exasperates Lois that the narrative decides that "[s]he could not conceive of her country emotionally" (37). Nonetheless, conceiving of Ireland emotionally is precisely what the narrative will require not only of her but of itself. It is a requirement that is fulfilled not through the dogmatic or startling impositions of estranging modernist forms but through the apparently more traditional, hence reassuring, "interplay from which plot must spring" (vii)—the interplay of the mind with its immediate world, the interplay among the characters as troubled as they are excited and entertained by their proximity to each other. Interplay is the form sociable hope takes in the novel and, as such, dictates its structure. That Danielstown, the novel's presiding figure for that sociable hope and its cultural foundations, is immolated on the last page comes, then, as a kind of historical verdict on all conceptions of Ireland, and indeed all conceptions of the novel as a representation of human interplay that cannot accommodate the modern urge for national as well as personal self-development.

In striving to make these accommodations, *The Last September* shows itself the loyal adherent to the Proustian novel of remembrance. Although inspirited by an urbane sense of satire, it does not aim to deride the times and traditions it represents so much as to resurrect them through a "perspective cut through the years" (a metaphor itself cut from the broad swath of Proust's epic language of time). The metaphor insinuates that looking back on a finished time entails—both for the writer and the reader of the novel—its own violence. More than years are sliced through by the imagination taking leave of its present for the unknown "now" of another time, place, and people (including, for Bowen, a younger, altered version of herself). The novel thus opens with an exchange of wordless greetings between the Naylors, the resident family of Danielstown, and their visitors. In the mind of Lois (who will, Bowen promises, lead us into history), that moment contains a happiness so perfect that she wishes to freeze it "and keep it always" (3). She may not keep it always, but the novel will, and will do so by encasing it within the very structures that made that moment possible. Taking its emotional cue from Lois, the novel adopts as its formal model the patterns in which the Anglo-Irish imposed their conception of the social idea. Hence the three-part structure, which deceptively suggests an unobstructed pattern of comings and goings, of neighborly interplay in an untroubled land: "The Arrival of Mr and Mrs Montmorency"; "The Visit of Miss Norton"; "The Departure of Gerald."

The third and last section at once completes the pattern and upsets it. The novel's main narrative movements are presented as demonstrably social in the high Anglo-Irish style of hospitality, beginning with the arrival of the Montmorency couple who, though intimate acquaintances of the Naylors, are formally identified in the narrative as Mr. and Mrs. Their arrival is followed, in the part titles and in the narrative course of things, by the more uncertain and disruptive visit of a Miss Norton, an "experienced fellow visitor" (98) stopping on her way to London, where she will soon be married. The last narrative panel concerns the "departure" of Gerald, the British soldier who is Lois's ardent suitor. Nothing in the part titles provokes either suspicion or alarm, so it comes as somewhat of a surprise to discover that the "departure" that is advertised as the concluding movement of the novel does not involve a lover's leave-taking but Gerald's death at the hands of the local insurgents. Given how loose a hold Bowen exerts over this normally unambiguous word, it is more accurate to say that Gerald twice "departs" from the novel—the first time when Lady Naylor, Lois's guardian, informs him of his complete unsuitability as a husband with a blithe condescension that would have drawn admiring approval from Lady Catherine DeBurgh. Soon after he is ambushed and killed on patrol. This is Gerald's real and final "departure." Bluntness would seem to be called for in these circumstances, but obliqueness is what answers. The Troubles troubled everything, yes, especially the ability to speak in direct terms about the violent realness of sudden death.

Whatever Bowen loses by refusing to announce outright the "death" of Gerald, she hopes to recuperate by conceiving of the human events of her novel, as she conceives of Ireland, emotionally. It is a conception achieved by deliberately unsettling the emotional order of narrative time. The novel begins with an homage to the Proustian "moment" as a repository of meaning and life: Lois's "perfect" moment, which is experienced with the untroubled excitement one reserves for the familiar and habitual happenings of daily life (such as the arrival of the "long-promised visitors"). But this Proustian moment is doomed to vanish; it will never be graced by the later visitings of involuntary memory, releasing its wealth of secreted life. Instead this perfect moment will be invaded by a belated understanding of the violent realness it contained in embryo, as if the moment were not the privileged instant in which the richest feelings of life are deposited but a kind of temporal cocoon in which history is incubating. Into this apparently perfect moment, intimations of trouble retrospectively insinuate themselves, disclosing the narrative and historic logic by which the arrival of the Montmorencys leads to the departure of Gerald.

I am forced to this paradoxical formulation—retrospective intimation—by Bowen's own expertness and guile in reversing the emotional values of time within her chronologically ordered narrative. The "departure of Gerald" retrospectively is seen to announce a development—Gerald's death—that should have been anticipated (he is a soldier, after all, patrolling a war-torn land) but was not. The patterns of country life, its rounds of arrivals and departures, help dispel the very anxiety that would have helped the besieged community to anticipate and so possibly circumvent such violent departures. Indeed, if Irish history is a nightmare from which Bowen's novel is trying to awake, it conforms to the classic Freudian description of the anxiety dream, in which traumatic events are felt to have been insufficiently anticipated. The waking mind has been lulled into inertia by the mesmerizing rhythms of social habits, fruit of a European culture and its imposing ideas that *The Last September* so dreadfully translates into Irish cultural soil.

Of course, not all departures are mortal, as Gerald's will be, but there is something fatal about them, at least to the novel's resident host, Sir Richard, a local type who would have been at home in a novel by Maria Edgeworth. Thus it is to his consciousness that Bowen turns in order to convey the disquieting effect of departures on a mind resistant to modernity and the unsettling troubles it brings in its wake. Here is what happens when the Montmorencys take their leave:

> Indeed, the unfamiliarity of the moment made them strange to themselves, though it now seemed to have been waiting ahead of them like a trap into which they had stepped with a degree of naturalness. Sir Richard, the least affected, thought the Montmorencys unduly animated and deplored departures. Visitors took form gradually in his household, coming out of a haze of rumour, and seemed but lightly, pleasantly superimposed on the vital pattern till a departure tore great shreds from the season's texture. (169)

The imperative "now" of Bowen's storytelling now collects into itself all the force and estranging sadness of a modernist rupture in the texture of tradition. The moment of leave-taking is, like the historical period in which it occurs, little understood in its own time. Little understood, but much feared, as related in this passage with an unease approaching panic—"tore great shreds" seems especially overwrought. This is the kind of retrospective intimation in which Bowen's narrative abounds, beginning of course with its title, that both foretells and recalls a "natural" end, not for all societies or people—for other Septembers there will surely be—but the last for *some* one. This emotionally contorted narrative tense has the power not only to conflate the "now" of the past with the future that apprehends it retrospectively but to reveal the estrangements lurking behind "the degree of naturalness" affected by those who live as though living gives them no trouble. Can we not take this moment of departure into which the characters step blindly, though animatedly, as if into a trap, as signaling the arrival of the modern, with its disassociated sensibilities and lacerated consciousness of time? What is emotionally being recorded here if it is not the power of the modern to fracture the familiar and make us feel strange not only to the world but to ourselves?

Modernism generally forswears the consolidating grace of tradition, which infiltrates and imposes itself pleasantly on the vital patterns of everyday life. Modernist art excels in less amenable forms of imposition. It may borrow from tradition its foundational structures, as Bowen borrows the social patterns of arrival and departure or as Joyce borrows the structure of the *Odyssey*, but only to expose the disruptions wrought by an importunate modernity, especially in its imperial designs. *The Last September* is built up from the gaps, observed but barely acknowledged, between what Lois calls the violent realness of the present and the social habits that absorb and disguise it. The modernist idiom thus surfaces in the interstices of the novel's indefatigable comedy of manners. It announces itself by the startling, yet strangely familiar, idiomatic turns of Bowen's narrative syntax, as in this charged, conflicted moment in which contending feelings jostle for position and recognition among the amenities of the tea table:

> Five days ago, an R. I. C. barracks at Ballyrum had been attacked and burnt out after a long defense. Two of the defenders were burnt inside it, the others shot coming out. The wires were cut, the roads blocked; there had been no one to

> send for help so there was no help for them. It was this they had all been discussing, at tea, between tennis: "the horrible thing." No one could quite understand why Captain Vermont and the subalterns did not seem more appalled and interested. It was not apparent how the subject rasped on their sensibilities. These things happened, were deplored and accepted, and still no one seemed to look on David or Gerald, Smith, Carmichael or Mrs Vermont's Timmie as a possible remedy. Here they all were, playing tennis, and everyone seemed delighted. "If they'd just let us out for a week—" felt the young men. David could not look up as he stirred his tea. What was the good of them? This they felt everyone should be wondering. But the party would indeed have been dull without them, there would have been no young men. Nobody wished them elsewhere. (54–55)

With the exception of Virginia Woolf, who was her teacher in this respect, no modern novelist weaves in and out of consciousness, gives voice to the impersonal opinions of the group mind, with the ease and elusiveness of Elizabeth Bowen. Here we witness the narrative voice dissolving and even disappearing into a generalized idiom of consensus. This would not be so remarkable were it not that the terms of this neighborly consensus, indeed the location of it, are unstable, moving unsteadily from place to place. The passage begins sociably enough with the narrator's affirming of her assembled group, "Here they all were." Yet quickly there comes the admission that what unites those assembled is their bafflement before the "horrible thing." Consciousness of that horrible, but unmentionable, thing creates a social unanimity that is incontrovertible but negative. What "everyone" feels and what "everyone" wonders can only find expression in the "Nobody" that negatively defines their collective will. What unites them "all" is that not one of them can help, or, more damning, desires to dispatch help: "Nobody wished them elsewhere." The horrible thing, the outrage of an attack, fails to suggest, much less prompt, action. We are not told, so can only guess, how this subject rasps their sensibilities. What we can discern is that this convivial gathering is conceived emotionally as modern, disassociated, out of kilter with the violent realness of the actual present. A barrack has been seized and burned, two men incinerated, others shot fleeing the flames. But this is a fact whose consequences are not fully understood in its own time. Its historical and human significance only becomes available in the conflagration that rages on the last page of the novel. By its light, the Naylors "saw too distinctly" (256) the violent realness of the Troubles overtaking them. For the moment, though, this possible reckoning is not apprehended; despite the proximity in time and place of the "horrid thing" awaiting them, no one wants either men or private thought to be engaged elsewhere.

One of those not wanted elsewhere but ultimately dispatched there is Lois's importunate lover, Gerald Lesworth. His surname, which does not seem to augur well for his fortunes as a suitor and as a soldier, places him in the companionable ranks of all gently satirized lovers of the English comic novel from Austen to Forster. Gerald is certainly no paragon of male intelligence, political acuity, or even civility. A mere sentence is sufficient to dispel any illusion that he might be: "He took up the *Spectator,* read an article on Unrest and thought of the Empire" (108). This is a fine satire on Gerald's military and national reflexes—it is equal to the best of Forster's portraits of the subalterns of Chandrapore in *A Passage to India*—but there is nothing particularly modern in our finding it in a novel.

What does seem modern is the criticism Bowen mounts against him: Gerald fails to conceive not just of Lois but of Irishness emotionally. This is partly attributed to his being a soldier with an occupying force; his militant Englishness is without imagination. But Bowen also entertains the fearful suspicion that his masculinity and capacity for thoughtless but effective action also disqualify him from such imaginative connections. Lois at least seems to think so when she remarks on men in general: "Queer, she confusedly thought, how men throw off action without a quiver of severance from the self that goes into it. They remain complete, the actions hangs in the air of the place, above the grass or furniture, crystallizing in memory, eternal, massive and edged to the touch of thought as, to the bodily touch, a grand piano. She herself felt bound to all she had done emotionally" (112). Lois may be confused about masculine modes of feeling, and with good reason, but it is Bowen who remarks and clarifies her confusion, transforming it into a commentary on the sexual properties of those men of action, like Gerald, who act in untroubled and undivided consciousness, who are, that is, antimodern. As a character, this makes him monumental, but sadly inert, as blocks of eternal substance are inert. Gerald is not disposed or even required to think of and for himself; it is sufficient that he provide the massive eternal substance for thought to linger and vibrate over. Such thoughts, when they arise, come, as they do to Lois, in the form of a forlorn clairvoyance: "As she stood looking at Gerald by the privet hedge, he emerged from the mist of familiarity clear to her mental eye. She saw him as though for the first time, with a quick response to his beauty; she saw him as though he were dead, as though she had lost him, with the pang of an evocation" (60). Looking upon Gerald, Lois seems to look back upon a man she had failed to notice, only to find herself foreseeing, in that same evocative instant, his permanent departure. She sees him as if for the first time, but also as if he were dead.

Of course, Gerald, being antimodernist and colonialist, must depart because Bowen's parable of history requires it. Bowen, in fact, goes to some length to present his "departure" as providential (although not providential in the way Jameson uses this term). It is providential on two counts: his courtship of Lois, even had it overcome, in traditional comedy of manners fashion, both her own (initial?) inability to love him and Lady Naylor's Anglo-Irish prejudice against an Englishman from Surrey, would have ended in unhappiness. This Bowen expects her readers to feel and know, and so she imparts this obvious outcome in a parenthetical remark: "(what indeed was she to do with his life and hers?)" (xii). Laurence, the novel's figure of advanced modern views, even wonders whether Lois might not have ended up as "a girl wife in the Chekhov tradition" (126). But Gerald's death is providential in a more impersonal way. His departure seems a narrative judgment rendered against the colonialist regime that he unthinkingly upholds and defends, literally, to the death. In a conversation with Laurence, Gerald openly confesses his creed that "Right is Right." Such tautologies, with the ring of the proverbial about them, are the favored slogans of downright antimoderns, with their virile contempt for the subtleties of modern thought and dissenting views. Gerald, feeble in thought if mighty in conviction, defends the promotion and imposition of what Bowen has more elegantly discerned as the "European idea" of civilization on less civilized lands: " 'If you come to think,' he explained, 'I mean, looking back on history—not that I'm intellectual—we *do* seem the only people' " (114).

The gauche Laurence, for once reticent to speak, wishes only that Gerald could infer "a contrariety of notions they each had of this thing civilisation":

> As a rather perplexing system of niceties, Laurence saw it, an exact and direct interrelation of stresses between being and being, like crossing arches; an unemotioned kindness withering to assertion selfish or racial: silence cold with a com-

> prehension in which the explaining clamour died away. He foresaw it the end of art, of desire, as it would be the end of battle, but it was to this end, this faceless but beautiful negation that he had lifted a glass inwardly while he had said, "Thank God!" (115)

Laurence's notions of civilization, which strike Gerald as "having been dictated by Sinn Fein," are articulated in a language dense, even murky with complication and unexpected stresses; that is, it is articulated in the language of modernism. This is the language in which Bowen projects her civilizing ideal of interplay, here imaged forth as a structure of interrelation. The image may be architectural, but the envisioned structure is protonovelistic, relating as it does the stresses between being and being. It is a structure of social interplay that for Bowen also forms the foundation for that perplexing but enduring system of niceties known as the novel. What erodes and morally invalidates this notion of civilization as a model of novelistic right relations is the "unemotioned kindness" with which it is erected, defended, and imposed. "Unemotioned" is an awkward neologism, perhaps a deliberate solecism that Bowen hazarded in order to call attention to its grating, unaccommodating quality. No civilization promulgated in this vein can expect to survive except in the distorted forms of selfish and racial assertion. The colonialist mandate and its "civilizing" mission are articulated in this cold language of racial assertion. It is this language that underwrites that faceless but dreadful negation of a civilization called colonialism that prompts Laurence to welcome, then toast the end of art and of desire.

Laurence's "thank God," in which he seems to accept, with relief, the collapse of a system of unemotioned kindness, reverberates in the closing pages of the novel. There we finally learn that the departure of Gerald is but a prelude to the last astonishing act of the novel, the destruction of Danielstown, like the Irish House of Usher to which it is pointedly and unhappily compared, in a blaze of flames. Here is the strange, almost somnambulistic language in which the burning of Danielstown is reported in the novel's penultimate sentence: "Then the first wave of a silence that was to be ultimate flowed back confidently to the steps. The door stood open hospitably upon a furnace" (256). The "silence that was to be ultimate" pronounces a judgment without appeal. This is the novel's last and most dreadful instance of retrospective intimation—"a silence that was to be ultimate"

—before the narrative and the historic "now" converge in a conflagration that consumes them both, leaving, like the image of Gerald in Lois's keen vision of him, nothing but a pang of evocation. Adding to this moment of Proustian chagrin is the observed persistence of local traditions of neighborliness: the house, as if conscious of its role as host, hospitably welcomes the forces that will destroy it. The tenses are symptomatically confused in this moment in which inner (soon to be silenced) life and outer force meet on the threshold precariously left open. Perhaps the doors stand open because what is being admitted, not happily but without protest, is modernist violence, consuming all that lives at its own, but also at others' expense.

How expensive Bowen calculates in the carefully considered concluding remarks in her preface. In the initial version she wrote: "But so often, during the *Bad* Times, did I in my mind's eye *of agony and apprehension seem to see* it burn that that terrible concluding page of *Last September* is *to me once* something I have lived through" (italics mine).[27] Her final version reads as follows: "But so often, during the Troubled Times, did I in my agonised mind's eye see it burn that that terrible final page of *The Last September* is for me, also, something I have lived through" (xii). The corrections are not made for the effect of some higher euphony. They work to anchor the novel more firmly in historical ground, supporting her claim that "[y]es, the setting of the novel is real, and the month has its place in history." In replacing Bad Times, which can be experienced by any culture, with Troubled Times, she uses, with a pang of evocation, a native idiom that speaks to Irish history alone. The personal chagrin attached to that history is captured in the gothic intensity of her parting confidence that often "did I in mind's eye of agony and apprehension seem to see" the burning of Bowen's Court. That slightly hysterical note is purged from her final version, in which Bowen simply declares that what she saw—not seemed to see but imaginatively saw—is not something that she has "once," but something she has "also," lived through. The difference is crucial, formally as well as emotionally. The elimination of that simple word "once," a word favored by legends and fairy tales, dislocates the novel out of the realm of country tale. It firmly relocates it in modernist narrative, where history is real and never really finished. For Bowen the Troubles troubled everything, yes, especially the modern consciousness of time.

## Notes

1 Hubert Butler, "*Envoy* and Mr. Kavanagh," *The Sub-Prefect Should Have Held his Tongue, and Other Essays*, ed. R. F. Foster (London: Penguin, 1990), 88.

2 Bowen, "The Big House," 26.

3 Ibid., 27.

4 Bowen, *Bowen's Court,* 456.

5 Bowen, *The Last September*, x. Further references are to this edition and are, for the most part, cited in the text parenthetically.

6 Ibid., xi.

7 See especially his shrewd, moving testimonial to her on the occasion of "The Erection of a Memorial Table to Elisabeth Bowen in Farahy Church, 18 October 1979," *Escape from the Anthill,* 200–203.

8 Lee, *Elizabeth Bowen*, 51.

9 Bowen, *The Last September*, xi. In his 1979 remembrance of Bowen, Butler also stressed these divided loyalties and mingled traditions in remarking how Bowen's Court, her family estate, along with those other monuments to Anglo-Irish manorial culture—Edgeworthstown, Moore Hall, and Coole Park—"had all, in their day, given shelter to an attempt to blend two traditions, the imagination and poetry of the Gael, with the intellectual vitality and administrative ability of the colonist" (*Escape from the Anthill,* 201).

10 Butler ruefully speculates that such an admiring view might likely have been "the way the Roman settler may have appeared to himself and others when the legions had departed from Britain and he was left alone with the tribes he had dispossessed" (*Escape from the Anthill,* 114).

11 Eagleton captured the strange but typical paradoxes that complicated Anglo-Irish political views when he characterized Charles Stewart Parnell, champion and (eventually disgraced) leader of Irish Home Rule, as "that oxymoronic animal, a radical landlord" (*Heathcliff and the Great Hunger*, 143).

12 Eagleton's *Heathcliff and the Great Hunger* is very eloquent on this account. See especially his chapters "Ascendancy and Hegemony" and "Form and Ideology in the Anglo-Irish novel."

13 Bowen, "The Big House," 27.

14 Bowen, *The Last September*, 37.

15 Jameson, "Modernism and Imperialism," 44.

16 Ibid., 58.

17 Ibid., 60–61.

18 Jameson disputes this claim about Joyce. The "closure" in *Ulysses*, he writes, "is objective, endowed by the colonial situations itself—whence the nonpoetic, nonstylistic nature of Joyce's language." To this I can only reply that Jameson and I have not read the same book or even the same Joyce. See "Modernism and Imperialism," 61.

19 Joyce, *Ulysses*, 52.

20 Ibid., 272.

21 "Who is my neighbor?" (ibid., 66), Bloom, born a Jew, wonders earlier in the day as he visits a Catholic church. But then Bloom is, among other things, a nationalist and phenomenologist keenly aware of how proximity is never neutral but imaginatively instigates neighborly—or xenophobic—feelings.

22 Butler, *Escape from the Anthill*, 5–6.

23 See especially Foster. "Elizabeth Bowen and the Landscape of Childhood."

24 A contemporary reviewer of the novel, though praising it, made precisely this objection to its apparent neglect of the political realities of the time. Allowing that Bowen's "humor is subtle and delightful," she complained, "She does not adequately suggest the horror threatening the Naylor family or the still worse horror endured by the people whom possibly they consider 'natives' " (Meade, "The Anglo-Irish Mind").

25 Coates persuasively argues that "the novel's epigraph, from Proust's *Le Temps Retrouvé*, seems to announce the solution to discontinuity and deracination, to failures of communication between individuals and the meaninglessness of experience, on which the great Modernist works were built" ("Elizabeth Bowen's *The Last September*").

26 Farrell, *Troubles*, 5.

27 Draft, *The Last September*, Elizabeth Bowen Collection, Harry Ransom Humanities Research Center, University of Texas, Austin, Box 7, 2.

## Works Cited

Bowen, Elizabeth. "The Big House." *The Mulberry Tree*. Selected and introduced by Hermione Lee. New York: Harcourt Brace Jovanovich, 1985.

——. *Bowen's Court* (1942). New York: Knopf, 1964.

——. *The Last September* (1929). New York: Avon, 1979.

——. Draft of *The Last September*. Elizabeth Bowen Collection, Harry Ransom Humanities Research Center, University of Texas, Austin.

Butler, Hubert. *Escape from the Anthill*. Dublin: Lillliput Press, 1985.

Coates, John. "Elizabeth Bowen's *The Last September*: The Loss of the Past and the Modern Consciousness." *Durham University Journal* 51.2 (July 1990): 207–8.

Eagleton, Terry. *Heathcliff and the Great Hunger*. London: Verso, 1995.

Farrell, J. G. *Troubles*. New York: New York Review of Books, 2002.

Foster, Roy. "Elizabeth Bowen and the Landscape of Childhood." *The Irish Story: Telling Tales and Making it Up in Ireland*. London: Allen Lane, 2001.

Jameson, Fredric. "Modernism and Imperialism." In Terry Eagleton, Fredric Jameson, and Edward Said, *Nationalism, Colonialism, Literature*. Minneapolis: University of Minnesota Press, 1990.

Joyce, James. *Ulysses*. Edited by Hans Gabler et al. New York: Vintage, 1986.

Lee, Hermione. *Elizabeth Bowen: An Estimation*. London: Vision Press, 1981.

Meade, Norah. "The Anglo-Irish Mind." *Spectator*, February 9, 1929, 560.

*Ian Duncan*

⋮

ELEVEN

# "Upon the thistle they're impaled": Hugh MacDiarmid's Modernist Nationalism

The "Scottish Renaissance" of the 1920s–30s distinguished itself among contemporary modernisms, at least in the English-speaking world, by its programmatic nationalism. Hugh MacDiarmid's long poem *A Drunk Man Looks at the Thistle* (1926),[1] the showpiece of the movement, is surely unique among the major modernist works for forcing its topical preoccupation with national identity upon the reader as a linguistic problem. The problem, while most acute for English and other non-Scottish readers, poses itself for Scottish readers too, since MacDiarmid's "Synthetic Scots" does not pretend to imitate a vernacular language but brandishes archaic and exotic words, phrases, and tropes mined from dictionaries and earlier poetry. Language materializes the category of nationality that MacDiarmid insists upon as the crux of his poem, in that Scots presents itself as a dense and resistant medium that requires the reader's work. *A Drunk Man Looks at the Thistle* reminds us—as many modernist texts remind us—that language stands in a relation of materiality to literature (since language is what literature is "made of") even if that materiality, too, is ultimately figurative (not least because literature materializes language, as writing and printed text). Where MacDiarmid's poem departs from other explorations of the question is in its specification of that materiality as a national—which is to say a historical—problematic.

The nationalist problematic underwrites the strong internationalist drive of MacDiarmid's project. *A Drunk Man Looks at the Thistle* claims modernist credentials by opening onto a horizon of "world literature," in line with the general commitment of the Renaissance to a renewal of Scottish national identity through reorientation from Anglo-British to Continental European political and cultural models—witness MacDiarmid's embrace of various forms of socialism, from Social Credit to Marxist-Leninism, or the pioneering translations of modern German and East European writers (notably Kafka) by Edwin and Willa Muir. *A Drunk Man* anchors its internationalism to a linguistic and cultural bedrock of "provincial" Scots, as MacDiarmid adapts verses by Aleksander Blok, Zinaida Hippius, Else Lasker-Schüler, George Ramaekers, and Edmond Rocher into Scots (out of English translations) and calls up heroic explorers of the existential deep such as Dostoevsky and Melville ("a Scot," 135) so as to reimagine their achievement in native terms: "Burns in Edinburgh," for example, turns out to have undertaken the Dostoevskian dive into the abyss (139–40). *A Drunk Man* makes its most overt bid for participation in an emergent modernist canon by grappling with *The Waste Land*:[2]

T. S. Eliot—it's a Scottish name
Afore he wrote 'The Waste Land' s'ud ha'e come
To Scotland here. He wad ha'e written
A better poem syne—like this, by gum! (94)

This time we can make the comparison with Burns, as he matches local performance practice against a mid-eighteenth-century imperial standard:

Thought I, 'Can this be *Pope*, or *Steele*,
  Or *Beattie's* wark?'
They tauld me 'twas an odd-kind chiel
  About *Muirkirk*.[3]

The demotic and mock-heroic challenge to a high literary tradition is a convention of modern Scots poetry.

Scotland is the crux of MacDiarmid's project in a way that Ireland, for instance, is not for Yeats or Joyce, in that the formal difficulties encountered by readers of Yeats or Joyce are not determined by a linguistic difference marked as "Irish." The standard history of modern Irish literature poses nationalism as a late-romantic developmental stage (the Celtic Revival, the Gaelic League, the Abbey Theatre) which is superseded, with the formation of an Irish Free State, for the high achievements of Irish modernism (the later Yeats, Joyce, Beckett). Joyce's "Citizen" (in *Ulysses*) performs the obsolescence—Neanderthal, "Cyclopean"—of one discourse of militant nationalism, even if Irishness is transfigured, carried forward rather than cast off, in the Joycean cosmopolitan *Aufhebung*. In Scotland, by contrast, the flowering of a nationalist movement during the decades of high modernism constitutes the developmental anomaly that Tom Nairn has called "Scottish belatedness." Belatedness, in Nairn's analysis, turns out to signify "romanticism," since literary romanticism's revival of vernacular linguistic and cultural forms, in opposition to an imperial neoclassicism, had provided the ideological substance of national identity for movements of political self-determination in nineteenth-century Europe—a historical phase brought to an end with the First World War.[4]

In a judicious account of MacDiarmid's nationalism, Stephen Maxwell questions its conformity to a romantic paradigm in *A Drunk Man Looks at the Thistle*. Citing MacDiarmid's *Scottish Chapbook* slogan "Not Tradition—Precedent," Maxwell argues that *A Drunk Man* "previews the development of his nationalist ideas beyond [their] linguistic [i.e., romantic] phase" that would take place in the 1930s and 1940s.[5] MacDiarmid's nationalist thinking took its cue from "the official Allied doctrine that the First World War was a war fought for the rights of small nations, and by the international acceptance at the Versailles Peace Conference of the principle of national self-determination"—a last formal ratification, on the stage of European politics, of nineteenth-century nationalist ideology. MacDiarmid looks beyond this "nationalism of tradition," according to Maxwell, to anticipate "the second wave of progressive nationalism in the twentieth century"—the anticolonial liberation movements of the emergent Third World, which were driven less by a romantic ambition to recover a national identity based on language and culture than by a need to forge their own terms of engagement with globalizing forces of political and economic modernization.[6] It seems over-optimistic to cast MacDiarmid as a prophet of the great phase of decolonization and Third World nationalism of the post–World War II "Bandung era."[7] Nevertheless Maxwell's account usefully locates MacDiarmid (and modern Scottish Nationalism) in a historical interim between nationalist paradigms and draws attention to the vexed status of a "colonial" problematic in his work—one in which colonization assumes, after all, the romantic formations of culture and tradition. *A Drunk Man Looks at the Thistle* confirms but also complicates Nairn's diagnosis of a Scottish modernist nationalism that bears the burden of a belated or historically displaced romanticism. The complication lies in the poem's critical recognition of and struggle with its own romanticism, yielding a provisional acceptance—at once comic and melancholic—of Scots as a material condition that resists radical transformation, the terms of which are relentlessly cast as "metaphysical," produced by the poet's imagination.

*A Drunk Man Looks at the Thistle* holds fast to a national language, Scots, which tropes the historical difference between Scotland's relation to imperial England and the overtly colonial case of Ireland. There, the lack of a distinct Anglo-Irish language, an equivalent to Lowland Scots, corresponds with other symptoms of a colonial history—such as the underdevelopment of an indigenous civil society—in a linguistically as well as politically polarized terrain. Three main languages are current in modern Scotland: Gaelic, English, and Lowland Scots. (It is worth repeating here what almost every commentator on MacDiarmid feels obliged to repeat, the historical status of Scots as a distinct language rather than a "dialect" of English.) If in Scotland too, Gaelic denotes a colonized ethnicity and English an imperial hegemony, Scots is the vernacular language of the vast majority—the middle and working classes—of the population and as such represents a "national" domain of civil society and everyday life. Historically, Scotland's fall from sovereignty did not follow a colonial trajectory of conquest and occupation by a foreign power. Scotland lost its court when James VI acceded to the English throne as James I, Elizabeth's heir. The Union of Crowns was followed, a century later (1707), by a Union of Parliaments which absorbed the Scottish legislative assembly into Westminster. The Union of Parliaments was negotiated by a formal treaty between the two nations' governing classes; in return for surrendering executive autonomy, Scotland gained access to English markets and imperial trade and kept the key institutions—of religion, law, finance, and education—that sustained a relatively autonomous, national civil society in the Lowland towns. Scots settlers, soldiers, merchants, bankers, administrators, educators, and professional men flourished across the worldwide commercial and colonial networks of the British empire. The Gaelic Highlands present a very different case: their modern history exhibits all the sorry symptoms of colonization, with military repression (in 1746) followed by economic restructuring, evacuation of populations, and legislation to abolish markers of cultural distinctiveness. But the colonial difference that marks the *Gaeltacht* cut across Scotland itself, not just across Great Britain: dividing Highland from Lowland Scotland

and England (and those regions within themselves), rather than Scotland from England.

The diagnosis of "internal colonialism," sometimes applied wholesale to Scotland, thus involves a murkier state of affairs than an "English" domination of "Scotland" within the British Isles.[8] Scotland's political absorption into Great Britain reproduced, rather, a set of relations of domination and exploitation within and across the national identity, since Scottish and English interests colluded in colonizing the Highlands and in developing the British empire overseas. The linguistic difference between English (the language of imperial administration and official culture) and Scots (the language of everyday life) encoded, rather, a broad class distinction within Lowland Scotland as its economy industrialized throughout the nineteenth century. If Gaelic could be the trope of a lost ancestral nation—as it promptly became, with exquisite contradictoriness, in James Macpherson's "Ossian" translations less than fifteen years after Culloden—Scots, rife with these complicities and internal contradictions, frames the impossibility of any such purifying conception.

MacDiarmid and the "Renaissance" literati developed a version of the critique of "internal colonialism" which diagnosed its effects in the radically internal domains of psychology and culture. This is the so-called "Caledonian Antisyzygy," or "zigzag of contradictions," a term coined by G. Gregory Smith in *Scottish Literature: Character and Influence* (1919) and adopted by MacDiarmid over the next few decades. (T. S. Eliot's review of Smith's book, "Was There a Scottish Literature?" [1919], generated his own subsequent account of tradition in a critical debate which forms the theoretical context for MacDiarmid's argument with *The Waste Land* in *A Drunk Man Looks at the Thistle*.)[9] The "Antisyzygy" characterizes a schizophrenic logic of internal doubling and splitting manifest at the level of language, the medium of culture and subject-formation. In *Scott and Scotland* (1936) Edwin Muir contends that the division between English (the "technical" language of writing, reason, science) and Scots (the "organic" language of speech, song, emotion, daily life) codified a fatal "dissociation of sensibility" in modern Scottish culture, formalized in the mid-eighteenth-century discourses of Enlightenment, when the Scottish universities promoted English linguistic standards as a cultural technology of modernization.[10]

"Curse on my dooble life and dooble tongue, / —Guid Scots wi' English a' hamstrung—," growls MacDiarmid in his second long poem sequence, *To*

*Circumjack Cencrastus* (236). The aphorism reduces the predicament to a self-evident distinction between guid Scots and bad English. Elsewhere it becomes all too clear that the task of decolonization will require the expulsion not so much of an alien English presence but of a part or aspect of oneself. The "intimate enemy" (in Ashis Nandy's formulation[11]) folds Scottish subjects in a closer embrace than in stark conditions of colonization, where a binary opposition may be easier to untangle. In a frank statement of his "quarrel wi' th' owre sonsy rose" (England), MacDiarmid complains that he "[stands] still for"—at once endures and continues to represent—

> . . . forces which
> Were subjugated to mak' way
> For England's poo'er, and to enrich
> The kinds o' English, and o' Scots,
> The least congenial to my thoughts.
>
> Hauf his soul a Scot maun use
> Indulgin' in illusions,
> And hauf in getting rid o' them . . . (157)

And early on, in the most often-quoted phrase from *A Drunk Man Looks at the Thistle*, the poet repudiates the constitutional topos of moderation and compromise that has justified Scotland's partnership in the Union: "I'll ha'e nae hauf-way hoose, but aye be whaur / Extremes meet"—a positionality, the poet goes on to boast, justified not by philosophical reason (the symptom, presumably, of a post-Union, anglicizing "Enlightenment") but by "auld Scottish instincts" (87). One way of reading the phrase—in terms of a political rather than a psychic topology—is to see MacDiarmid invoking a "colonial" site for his enunciation. If the "hauf-way hoose" suggests a provisionally domestic setting (preparing its occupant for reentry to home life), then the site where extremes meet suggests a site radically exterior to domestic norms—one governed, for example, by the "extreme" political relations of colonialism.

⋮ ⋮ ⋮

*A Drunk Man Looks at the Thistle* is not always perspicuous in its rendering of the imperial force field of Scottish identity politics. Even through its blind spots and dark passages, the poem apprehends the symbolic violence that attends the formations (which are always deformations) of national identity. In an opening diatribe against the popular ceremony of Burns Night (commemorative suppers held on January 25, Robert Burns's birthday), the poet attacks the inauthentic, sentimental modality of cultural nationalism that historians have labeled the "invention of tradition,"[12] applied in the nineteenth century as key ingredient of a Tory Unionist ideology of empire:

You canna gang to a Burns supper even
Wi'oot some wizened scrunt o' a knock-knee
Chinee turns roon to say, 'Him Haggis—velly goot!'
And ten to wan the piper is a Cockney

No' wan in fifty kens a wurd Burns wrote
But misapplied is a'body's property . . .

Croose London Scotties wi' their braw shirt fronts
And a' their fancy freen's, rejoicin'
That similah gatherings in Timbuctoo,
Bagdad—and Hell, nae doot—are voicin'

Burns' sentiments o' universal love,
In pidgin English or in wild-fowl Scots,
And toastin' ane wha's nocht to them but an
Excuse for faitherin' Genius wi' *their* thochts. (84–85)

The vision of Burns Night celebrated by Chinese and Cockneys, from London to Timbuctoo, Bagdad and "Hell," displays a profane traffic of Scottish national identity in the symbolic economy of empire, with the debasement of Burns's poetry to an ideological currency of "sentiments o'universal love" bamboozling colonial subjects. The mention of "London Scotties" and a Cockney piper at once exposes and blurs the historical agency of Scots themselves in this system. *Blackwood's Edinburgh Magazine*, the main literary apparatus for processing Scottish cultural nationalism into a trope of British imperial identity throughout the nineteenth century, had coined the phrase "Cockney" as a term of Scots contempt for low-bred Englishmen—only it was a Tory Unionist epithet aimed against radical romantic writers such as Keats, Hazlitt, and Leigh Hunt, whom one would suppose to have been MacDiarmid's precursors in a genealogy of anti-imperialism. As in *Blackwood's*, satiric scorn holds hands with nostalgia, as

MacDiarmid's verses put Scots, via Burns, in the figurative position of an original property and paternity adulterated by promiscuous sentimental exchange and intellectual "fathering." (The very dynamic, in other words, that a postcolonial criticism will celebrate under the title of "hybridization.") The sneer at the degenerate "Chinee" adds racial purity to the phantom of a traduced pure Scotland, even as it blocks critical thinking about the actual history of Scottish interests in the China trade (Jardine Mathieson in Hong Kong, and so on).

The passage may represent the default setting of a "vulgar" romanticism which MacDiarmid discards as he warms to his theme—a kind of ideological throat-clearing. Critics of *A Drunk Man Looks at the Thistle* generally agree that the poem eschews the nostalgia that infects this early polemic, although not its high-flying individualism. MacDiarmid presses for a renovation of Scots that looks forward and upward, rather than back down to an origin. Before he blasts Burns Night, the poet issues the first in a series of manifestoes:

> To prove my saul is Scots I maun begin
> Wi' what's still deemed Scots and the folk expect,
> And spire up syne by visible degrees
> To heichts whereo' the fules ha'e never recked. (84)

Here, as so often in *A Drunk Man Looks at the Thistle*, ambiguity hollows out the poet's bravado, begging the question of what exactly the poetic restructuring of Scots will entail. Does proof of a Scots soul consist in the transcendence of debased conventions of Scottishness (such as Burns Night)—or, ironically, in the invocation of them to begin with? The "heichts" are, presumably, that rarefied space "whaur / Extremes meet"—although the trope of visionary ascent traditionally promises an arrival above and beyond dialectical strife. When extremes meet, what happens—will they neutralize or suspend each other, or spark off further turbulence? Will poetic elevation bring a transcendence of Scots (sloughing it for some other, as yet unimagined condition) or a dialectical sublation (carrying it forward, in an improved variant, some sort of Super-Scots)?

The poem's linguistic retention of Scots would appear to give a decisive answer to the question. (The only stanzas in English mark its fitness for second-remove burlesque—of Eliot's "Sweeney Among the Nightingales," 150–51.) Whatever else it may knock down or throw out, *A Drunk Man* continues to offer its reader Scots, in full if not overflowing measure. Yet the question keeps asking itself throughout *A Drunk Man Looks at the Thistle*, and it probes to the quick of MacDiarmid's great invention, the stylistic medium that makes it one of the great modern poems in any language (rather than a rambling nationalist rant), "Synthetic Scots." "Synthetic" carries several different meanings. It can denote an artificial product, neither original nor organic, forged out of disparate elements. It can denote a higher unity that resolves and unifies the dialectical forces of its production; or, alternatively, a stage that remains subject to those forces, and thus one that will yield further, provisional syntheses. These distinctions inform the accounts of Synthetic Scots, and of the poetic and nationalist enterprises it underwrites, offered by MacDiarmid's critics. A single collection of essays, for example, proposes Synthetic Scots as, variously: the linguistic foundation of a renovated national culture, analogous to Dante's invention of a Tuscan-based Italian (Carl Freedman); the medium of a liberal, multicultural "dialogism" (Nancy Gish); and a deconstructive antidote to the imperial model of a "standard" language, enacting a fragmentation and dispersal of national identity rather than its reconstruction (Rena Grant).[13]

Of these accounts, Grant's best keeps faith with the fierce (sometimes truculent) contradictoriness (in his own phrase, "nocht but cussedness," 133) of MacDiarmid's performance, although Grant tends to standardize the deconstructive impulse into a governing strategy. The emphasis on the site "whaur / Extremes meet" as one of ever-breeding contradiction underrates the poem's repeated investments in a rhetoric of messianic rescue, transcendental altitude, visionary revelation, and symbolic totalization, announced in that early promise to "spire up" to unreckoned heights. Quite late in *A Drunk Man Looks at the Thistle*, the poet asks:

> Is Scotland big enough to be
> A symbol o' that force in me,
> In wha's divine inebriety
> A sicht abune contempt I'll see?
>
> For a' that's Scottish is in me . . .
> And I in turn 'ud be an action
> To pit in a concrete abstraction
> My country's contrair qualities,
> And mak' a unity o' these . . . (145)

The ambition to forge a "concrete abstraction" which will unify Scotland's contradictions expresses itself in the idiom of a rhapsodic transcendentalism. And in several sequences MacDiarmid anticipates the programmatically sublime Wallace Stevens of *Notes toward a Supreme Fiction* and *The Auroras of Autumn*. W. N. Herbert has parsed the project of "synthesis" in *A Drunk Man Looks at the Thistle* as one of symbolic totalization, fatally compromised, however, by what he calls "the solipsistic nature of [the poet's] vision."[14] MacDiarmid's symbolic technique consists "of establishing exteriorized symbols of the self, in order to reincorporate them into an aggrandized persona." In such terms, the synthesis would seem bound to fail. "MacDiarmid's inability fully to resolve his symbolic structure at any given point" ensures that the poem can only "resolve one set of paradoxes momentarily, only to create more. . . . The real energy the poem displays is caused by the poet's partial resolutions and continued bafflement."[15] This evaluation comes close to Grant's final appraisal of the poem's "recognition that it *does* encounter contradiction—though it does not seem always to recognize the logic of it—and its refusal at least to rewrite it into a nineteenth-century paradigm."[16]

Both critics, then, read the impasse of a late or residual romanticism in MacDiarmid's project of synthesis, although one interprets it, in the mode of irony, as the poem's refusal (of an organic form of national identity) and the other, in the mode of pathos, as a failure (of symbolic totalization). The recognition of a romantic poetics in *A Drunk Man Looks at the Thistle* should remind us, at least, that failure is written into the protocols of the "egotistical sublime," the formal term for what Herbert (insisting on an ethical vocabulary) calls solipsism. As Marc Redfield has put it, it seems that "any entity marked as romantic will turn out to resist its own romanticism."[17] This recognition should help us think through Nairn's diagnosis of "Scottish belatedness"—the anomalous, anachronistic appearance in Scotland of a romantic cultural politics at the European moment of high modernism. Such terms as "romanticism" and "modernism" identify loose sets of rhetorical and aesthetic strategies under the long-durational historical conditions of modernization, and they are variably rather than strictly tied to a periodizing chronology. The meditation on a "romantic" national theme in *A Drunk Man Looks at the Thistle* together with (and through) its modernism reveals, for one thing, the romanticism residual in a modernist poetics that holds onto visionary and totalizing ambitions (the "mythical method" and its analogues), even while that poetics may end up confirming the loss of an authentic origin, the ruin of a universal symbolic order.

Nairn correlates the belated appearance of Scottish nationalism in the 1920s with the absence of a genuine romantic movement, the cultural crucible of a nationalist politics, in Scotland during the early-nineteenth-century epoch of European romanticism. That absence was a consequence, in turn, of the precocious or premature development of the Scottish Enlightenment, the cultural form of post-Union civil society.[18] Although Nairn's argument is in several respects problematic (ignoring much of what was actually going on in Scottish literature in the first third of the nineteenth century), it reflects the analysis of Scottish cultural history made by the intellectuals of the Renaissance themselves, and so helps bring MacDiarmid's project of synthesis into focus as a realization or reclamation—under the formal protocols of modernism—of that absent Scottish romanticism. The void of the genuine article, in Nairn's account, was covered up by the Victorian-era industrial production of an imaginary Romantic Scotland, the debased currency of Scots kitsch denounced in the "Burns supper" sequence early in *A Drunk Man Looks at the Thistle*. As we saw, MacDiarmid's polemic clings to the idea of an authentic Burns—an original poetry buried under the rubble of vulgar misappropriation which a true reading might rescue. Elsewhere, under the slogan of the "Caledonian Antisyzygy," MacDiarmid and his cohort articulated a more thoroughgoing critique of a modern tradition of Scottish literature fatally compromised by its Unionist historical production—a critique that tended to invest all the more powerfully in the romantic fantasy of a lost, pure, prelapsarian Scotland. In *Scott and Scotland*, Muir ended up pushing back the onset of the "dissociation of sensibility" from the Enlightenment and Union to the Reformation, reiterating MacDiarmid's denunciation of the "foul trap" in *To Circumjack Cencrastus* (213).[19] That poem rejects Burns, Scott, Carlyle, and "R. L. S." altogether as representatives of a "false Scotland" (208) and identifies the true one with the occluded Gaelic realms of "Alba and Eire" (213), in a gesture that reprises the vexed Scottish origins of European romanticism in Macpherson's "Ossian" poetry, the very archetype of the inauthentic representation of national origins.

*A Drunk Man Looks at the Thistle* resists its own romanticism most productively, perhaps, in its complex evocation of Burns, who remains the metonymic representative of a modern Scots poetry and national tradition.[20] Rena Grant notes that Burns's poem about a drunk man who stays out late and has a vision provides a touchstone for MacDiarmid's, which alludes to "Tam O'Shanter" as the national model it must overgo. *A Drunk Man* makes its most explicit claim "to exceed the limits of the Burns poem and to evade [its] return to 'normality' " in a citation of the climax of Tam's adventure.[21] Spying on a witches' coven, unable to control his excitement, Tam gives himself away and scampers homeward with the witches in pursuit. MacDiarmid's drunk man boasts:

> I canna ride awa' like Tame,
> But e'en maun bide juist whaur I am.
>
> I canna ride, and gin I could,
> I'd sune be sorry I hedna stude,
>
> For less than a' there is to see
> 'll never be owre muckle for me. (109–10)

This declaration fixes Burns's role in Scottish poetry as representative of a national failure of romanticism—the failure to advance, that is, from a sentimental and satiric poetry of common life to a romantic project of visionary totalization. "Tam O'Shanter" casts visionary rapture in a materialist bathos of domestic and erotic comedy—the hero's act of seeing is at once prurient and phobic, registering its banal transgressiveness in an anthropological idiom of black magic and taboo, and shut off by his flight back home to bed; while the loss of his mare's tail burlesques the sacrifice required of the adventurer into the contact zones of romance. The poet of *A Drunk Man Looks at the Thistle*, in contrast, declares his superior readiness to stand and see all—and pay the price of that revelation, presumably, in sustaining the messianic role he elsewhere lays claim to.

In poetic terms, what would seeing all entail? MacDiarmid summons an alternative model for this visionary ambition from deeper in the Scots tradition, from the pre-Reformation past. This is the early-sixteenth-century makar William Dunbar. Early in *A Drunk Man*, MacDiarmid blasts the Scots tradition for having flung Dunbar "owre the kailyard-wa' " (106: the domesticated "cabbage-patch" of the modern literary canon). Elsewhere, in his manifestoes, he exhorted modern Scots poets to follow "not Burns but Dunbar" as their native example. Dunbar's poetry offers something more than a Burnsian vein of demotic satire; it realizes the allegorical dream-vision, fusing a fallen temporal condition with its mystic transfiguration, of which MacDiarmid's drunken rhapsody aspires to be the modern analogue.

The appeal to Dunbar, then, is quintessentially "romantic": not least in the imaginary failure that attends it. Dunbar's visionary performance employed an allegorical technique underwritten by the culture of its production and reception. Allegory works by mobilizing a communally recognized system of schemes and figures that gives cognitive access to a communally recognized metaphysical order. A modern reinvention of ancient allegory is bound to fail because it cannot summon around itself that vanished social universe of shared doctrines, conventions, and associations from which the allegorical web was woven. Instead of allegory, the modern poet—which is to say the romantic poet—must work with symbolism: the prosthesis of a severed organic bond with reality, an instrument that recovers a numinous totality all by itself, in isolation from a fallen social language, by virtue of its access to a precognitive (mystical or unconscious) ground of being. Paul de Man, in a powerful critical reversal of Coleridge's privileging of symbol over allegory as *techne* of the romantic imagination, identifies the metaphysical nostalgia attending the claims of the symbolic in historical time—to which condition, paradoxically, the allegorical can give authentic access, precisely by virtue of its "inauthentic," historically ruined status.[22]

*A Drunk Man Looks at the Thistle* thematizes the attempt and failure of symbolic totalization through a series of tropes: the visionary access of light that dialectically intensifies a cognitive darkness, the succession of poetic elevation by a comic or ironic bathos, the figural role of woman as at once mute, pure object of transcendental desire (the "silken leddy" of the interpolated Blok verses), and material speaking subject, contaminated by historical and biological existence, that refutes the poet's idealizations. Scotland becomes the topical focus of this push and pull of totalization and resistance, the decisive manifestations of which take place poetically, linguistically, as a function of MacDiarmid's Scots:

I wad ha'e Scotland to my eye
Until I saw a timeless flame
Tak' Auchtermuchty for a name
And kent that Ecclefechan stood
As pairt o' an eternal mood (144)

The lines parody in advance the T. S. Eliot of "Little Gidding." Their optative mood is at once confirmed and mocked by the phonetic resistance —dirty, sensuous—of the place-names "Auchtermuchty" (a comic shibboleth) and "Ecclefechan" (Carlyle's birthplace) to a visionary sublimation: yielding Scots as what sticks in the throat, the phoneme 'x.'[23]

Bathos defines the closing movement of *A Drunk Man Looks at the Thistle.* The poem's culminating sequence, "The Great Wheel," turns beyond Dunbar to Dunbar's master, the European supremo of visionary allegory who licenses MacDiarmid's epic ambition, Dante. As a sublime figure which joins the poet's vision with the dynamic mechanism of the cosmos, the Wheel evokes the mystical exaltation of the *Paradiso* only to deny its transcendental content—the presence of his fellow Scots ("on a birlin' edge I see / wee Scotland squattin' like a flee," 159) provokes the poet's recognition that "I micht ha'e been in Dante's Hell" (164). Rather than realizing a symbolic totalization, then, the Wheel represents that totalization as a metaphysically empty formal principle. It signifies the astronomical cycle of twenty-six-thousand years in which all of human history is stuck, from the War in Heaven to World War I (159). The poet looks down on his own national tradition:

> I felt it turn, and syne I saw
> John Knox and Clavers in my raw,
> And Mary Queen o' Scots ana,'
>
> And Rabbie Burns and Weelum Wallace,
> And Carlyle lookin' unco' gallus,
> And Harry Lauder (to enthrall us). (164)

"They canna learn, sae canna move," says the poet's ghostly interlocutor (a Virgil rather than a Beatrice):

> *But stick for aye to their auld groove*
> *—The only race in History who've*
>
> *Bidden in the same category*
> *Frae stert to present o' their story,*
> *And deem their ignorance their glory.* (165)

The effect of sticking in a groove is reproduced in MacDiarmid's formal imitation of terza rima, which rhymes all three lines of the stanza instead of reproducing the delicate onward-locking movement of Dante's rhyme-scheme. The poet protests (in a dominie's blustering English):

> 'But in this huge ineducable
> Heterogeneous hotch and rabble,
> Why am *I* condemned to squabble?'

And is answered with a last gloss on the messianic role he has intermittently claimed:

> '*A Scottish poet maun assume*
> *The burden o' his people's doom,*
> *And dee to brak' their livin' tomb.*
>
> *Mony hae' tried, but a' ha'e failed.*
> *Their sacrifice has nocht availed.*
> *Upon the thistle they're impaled.*

Unless he make a greater sacrifice:

> *You maun choose but gin ye'd see*
> *Anither category ye*
> *Maun tine your nationality.*' (165)

The poet confronts a stark choice between a categorical surrender of nationality, or a fall back into its worldly, squalid, untransfigurable state. The third, "synthetic" way, of a radical reformation of Scots, has disappeared from view. The poet will remain impaled on the thistle, the symbol now for an obdurately historical and material reality that outwears symbolic transformations.

The closing lyric of *A Drunk Man Looks at the Thistle* repeats the movement of exaltation and bathos in an aesthetic rather than didactic key. Emptied, so he says, of metaphysical desire, the poet claims a last, inalienable property: "Yet ha'e I Silence left, the croon o' a' " (166). "Silence," however, is not really silent, not least in its being a noisy literary echo (of dying Hamlet). The poem's last turn evacuates this last-ditch Romantic plenitude:

> —'And weel ye micht,'
> Sae Jean'll say, "efter sic a night!" (167)

Silence means exhaustion rather than a refuge of the numinous. Jean's rebuke, projected by the poet as a rejoinder to his own garrulousness, confirms the poem's resistance to its own transcendental drive and locates that resistance in the (ventriloquised) speech of the wife. The wife's speech, as figurative source of the everyday idiom of vernacular Scots, reiterates a Burnsian poetic: Tam O'Shanter comes back home from his visionary adventure, like MacDiarmid's drunk man, although Burns does not directly represent the wife's speaking voice. The quality of that return—is it a defeat or a victory?—remains as ambiguous as it is in Burns's poem; or rather, MacDiarmid reprises Burns's comic ambiguity at a metapoetic remove, coding the allusive fall back to Burns as a poetic triumph at the same time as it is a metaphysical defeat. The end of *A Drunk Man* reasserts Scots as the medium of a material historical existence that shows its strength, as well as its limitation, in a sensuous resistance to transcendental schemes, in addition to its being the medium of the poem's formal and aesthetic achievement, its shimmering exhibition of the material resources of a national literary tradition (Burns, Dunbar, the ballads) for future performance.

⋮ ⋮ ⋮

After *A Drunk Man Looks at the Thistle*, MacDiarmid turned his poetic career in two major directions, both of which involved a creative rethinking of the anachronistic configuration—typified by an "absent" or "belated" romanticism—of modern Scottish literary history. MacDiarmid resumed, with amplified urgency, the romantic quest for national origins, reaching beyond Dunbar to a deeper source, and then—in an apparently antithetical move—he invested his late career in a spectacularly deconsecrated and contaminated version of English as "world language." In both cases we can read MacDiarmid as troping the "place" of these languages—Gaelic, English—in a Scottish tradition, in an experimental aesthetic that augments the exploration of Scots in *A Drunk Man* and other works of the 1920s and 1930s.

In *To Circumjack Cencrastus*, the poet excoriates "Oor four universities" as "Scots but in name," with professors fluent "in Sanskrit / Or Czech—wi' a leaven / O' some kind o' English" but ignorant of indigenous language and tradition. The poet roars: "in Hell here there isna / A Scotsman amang you!" (203–4). The Scottish history and culture so outrageously neglected turn out to be Gaelic: "Where Tremnor triumphed / Or Oscar fell . . . Muireadhach Albannach, / Lachlan Mor of his stem, / And Finlay Macnab" (204). MacDiarmid affiliates *Cencrastus* with the earlier Irish Celtic Revival to proclaim a new nationalist ideal of "Gaeldom regained" (188). In "The Irish in Scotland," the poet conducts his foreign guest—after brushing aside the false tradition of Burns, Scott, Carlyle, and Stevenson—to "the islands / Where the wells are undefiled / And folks sing as their fathers did / Before Christ was a child" (208). What looks like a full-blown romantic regression is qualified, however, by MacDiarmid's glancing acknowledgments of his project's Ossianism—the constitutive inauthenticity of a modern recovery of "the Gaelic Idea" through English translation. "Where Tremnor triumphed, / Or Oscar fell" evokes the mist-wreathed mise-en-scène of *Fingal* and *Temora* more suggestively than a scientifically verifiable historical geography; while "the wells are undefiled" alludes to Spenser's tribute to Chaucer, a topos of the English construction of a national poetic tradition.[24] MacDiarmid's own lustrous translations, "The Birlinn of Clanranald" (1935) and "The Praise of Ben Dorain" (1940), render into English the great poets of the eighteenth-century Gaelic revival (Alasdair MacMhaighstir Alasdair, Duncan Bàn MacIntyre) whose work was eclipsed in literary historiography by the sensational career of "Ossian." The alternative path to a "Gaeldom regained" would be that taken by Sorley MacLean, and others who followed him, in writing a modern poetry in Gaelic after the example of those eighteenth-century masters. MacDiarmid's role, then, can be viewed as undertaking a redemption of Macpherson's, in which his own translations encourage a modern Gaelic revival rather than usurping its place: reopening the case of "Ossian" as a seedbed for new poetry, rather than reiterating its invention of cultural origins.

The next major turn in MacDiarmid's development, the assumption of "a poetry of facts" (630) and a "World Language," that is, English, as the global medium of scientific knowledge, is the step that has confirmed his status—even more than his work in Scots—as the unreadable monster of anglophone modernism. Seamus Heaney attempts to put an optimistic spin on the consensus, calling on MacDiarmid's critics to "make a firm distinction between the true poetry and what we might call the habitual printout . . . [W]hat happened to Wordsworth will happen to MacDiarmid: the second phase of his career will be rendered down to a series of self-contained, self-sustaining passages of genuine poetry."[25] Against the explicit romanticism of this call for salvage, other commentators defend the continuing avant-gardism of MacDiarmid's late phase in such works as the enormous *In Memoriam James Joyce* (1955). Carl Freedman argues that the invention of "a world language based on *and against* normative English," with its immense accumulations of data transcribed (or "plagiarized") from miscellaneous sources, dissolves the ideological categories of property and identity that sustain a traditional work of reading.[26] Robert Crawford, in the most imaginatively compelling account of this poetry, redeems the trope with which Heaney dismissed the bulk of it: "tracts of the later poet seem like nothing so much as material turned out by a computer database, bibliographical printout, cyber-text language that . . . closely [resembles] the kinds of information today most commonly held in machine-readable form."[27] This constitutes the radical project Crawford calls "Modernist Cybernetics," in which MacDiarmid's late poetry imaginatively apprehends the postliterary—genuinely postromantic—linguistic environment of digital information storage and retrieval systems that has only very recently become naturalized by the saturation of everyday life with computer technology.

More surprisingly, in fact, Crawford's analysis illuminates MacDiarmid's late poetry as a recapitulation and hyperbolic expansion of the linguistic project of the eighteenth-century Scottish Enlightenment: the achievement that, simultaneously with the work of Burns, "Ossian," and the Gaelic poets, constituted "Scotland's absent Romanticism" as the first of the modern movements in European literature. Enlightenment discourse reinvented English, the written dialect of imperial administration, as the universal medium of a new science of man. MacDiarmid's World English, an experimental variant of that Enlightenment invention for a posthuman age, thus represents the most audacious of his attempts to reimagine a "national" language in relation to its world-historical horizon.

## Notes

1 Christopher Murray Grieve (1892–1978) assumed the penname "Hugh MacDiarmid" in 1922, before the appearance of his book-length collections of poetry. In this essay I follow the convention of using "Hugh MacDiarmid" to refer to Grieve's poetic identity and persona(e). Citations of *A Drunk Man Looks at the Thistle* and other poems refer by page number to *The Complete Poems of Hugh MacDiarmid*, ed. Michael Grieve and W. R. Aitken, 2 vols. (Harmondsworth: Penguin, 1985).

2 See Crawford, "A Drunk Man Looks at *The Waste Land*"; Riach, "T. S. Eliot

and Hugh MacDiarmid"; Gish, "MacDiarmid Reading *The Waste Land:* The Politics of Quotation," in *Hugh MacDiarmid*, ed. Gish, 207–29.

3 Burns, "Epistle to John Lapraik."

4 Nairn, *The Break-Up of Britain*, 94–95, 103–5.

5 Maxwell, "The Nationalism of Hugh MacDiarmid," 207.

6 Ibid., 209.

7 For this designation, referring to the 1955 Bandung Conference of newly independent Asian and African states, see Larsen, "Imperialism, Colonialism, Postcolonialism," 12–14; citing Aijaz Ahmad, *In Theory*, and Amin, *Empire of Chaos*.

8 The standard analysis, coining the phrase, is Hechter, *Internal Colonialism*. McClintock lists "internal colonization" ("where the dominant part of a country treats a group or region as it might a foreign colony") as one among "a variety of forms of global domination": "The Angel of Progress." This description applies to the Gaelic Highlands, as in Hechter's account, but scarcely to Lowland Scotland, unless "colonialism" is to be understood in so broad a sense as to dull its analytic edge.

9 The primary texts by Smith and Eliot are reprinted in McCulloch, ed., *Modernism and Nationalism*, 6–10. See Gish, "MacDiarmid Reading *The Waste Land*," 208–20; Crawford, "Scottish Literature and English Studies."

10 Muir, *Scott and Scotland*. On the eighteenth-century "Scottish invention of English literature," see Crawford, *Devolving English Literature*.

11 Nandy, *The Intimate Enemy*.

12 See Hobsbawm and Ranger, eds., *The Invention of Tradition*, and especially Hugh Trevor-Roper's (problematic) contribution, "The Invention of Scotland: The Highland Tradition of Scotland," 15–42. For a more detailed consideration of the Scottish case, see Pittock, *The Invention of Scotland*.

13 See in Gish, ed., *Hugh MacDiarmid*: Carl Freedman, "Beyond the Dialect of the Tribe: James Joyce, Hugh MacDiarmid, and World Language," 253–73; Nancy Gish, "MacDiarmid Reading *The Waste Land*"; Rena Grant, "Synthetic Scots: Hugh MacDiarmid's Imagined Community," 191–206.

14 Herbert, *To Circumjack MacDiarmid*, 47.

15 Ibid., 55, 57–59.

16 Grant, "Synthetic Scots," 206.

17 Redfield, *The Politics of Aesthetics*, 32.

18 Nairn, *The Break-Up of Britain*, 114–18.

19 For the critique of Muir and "Antisyzygy" historiography, see Nairn, *The Break-Up of Britain*, and Craig, *Out of History*, 82–118.

20 See Riach, "MacDiarmid's Burns." See also Finlay, "The Burns Cult and Scottish Identity in the Nineteenth and Twentieth Centuries."

21 Grant, "Synthetic Scots," 191–92, 197. Kenneth Buthlay, however, finds the parallels between "Tam O'Shanter" and *A Drunk Man Looks at the Thistle* "to be

weak and in fact trivial": see MacDiarmid, *A Drunk Man Looks at the Thistle,* ed. Buthlay, 1.

22 De Man, "The Rhetoric of Temporality."

23 Edwin Morgan, a fellow poet, notes that the nationalist trope of the place-name confirms MacDiarmid's rural rather than urban cultural identity: "MacDiarmid and Scotland," in *The Age of MacDiarmid,* ed. Scott and Davis, 198. See also MacDiarmid's poems "Water Music" (1932) and "Scotland" (1934).

24 Edmund Spenser's tribute to Chaucer, in *The Faerie Queene* (4.2. 32); cited by Walter Scott in the "Dedicatory Epistle" to *Ivanhoe*—the great Scottish romance of English national origins, 19.

25 Heaney, "A Torchlight Procession of One," 321, 336.

26 Freedman, "Beyond the Dialect of the Tribe," 264, 269–72.

27 Crawford, *The Modern Poet,* 212.

## Works Cited

Ahmad, Aijaz. *In Theory: Classes, Nations, Literatures.* London: Verso, 1992.

Amin, Samir. *Empire of Chaos.* Translated by W. H. Locke Anderson. New York: Monthly Review Press, 1992.

Burns, Robert. "Epistle to John Lapraik, A Scots Bard" (1786). *Burns: Poems and Songs.* Edited by James Kinsley. Oxford: Oxford University Press, 1969.

Craig, Cairns. *Out of History: Narrative Paradigms in Scottish and British Culture.* Edinburgh: Polygon, 1996.

Crawford, Robert. *Devolving English Literature.* Oxford: Clarendon Press, 1992.

——. "A Drunk Man Looks at *The Waste Land.*" *Scottish Literary Journal* 14.2 (1987): 62–87.

——. *The Modern Poet: Poetry, Academia, and Knowledge since the 1750s.* Oxford: Oxford University Press, 2001.

——. "Scottish Literature and English Studies." In *The Scottish Invention of English Literature,* ed. Robert Crawford, 233–37. Cambridge: Cambridge University Press, 1998.

de Man, Paul. "The Rhetoric of Temporality" *Blindness and Insight.* 2nd ed. Minneapolis: University of Minnesota Press, 1983.

Finlay, Richard. "The Burns Cult and Scottish Identity in the Nineteenth and Twentieth Centuries." In *Love and Liberty: Robert Burns: A Bicentenary Celebration,* ed. Kenneth Simpson, 69–78. East Linton: Tuckwell, 1997.

Gish, Nancy, ed. *Hugh MacDiarmid: Man and Poet.* Edinburgh: Edinburgh University Press, 1992.

Heaney, Seamus. "A Torchlight Procession of One: Hugh MacDiarmid." *Finders Keepers: Selected Prose, 1971–2001.* New York: Farrar, Straus and Giroux, 2001.

Hechter, Michael. *Internal Colonialism: The Celtic Fringe in British National Development, 1536–1966.* Berkeley: University of California Press, 1975.

Herbert, W. N. *To Circumjack MacDiarmid: The Poetry and Prose of Hugh MacDiarmid.* Oxford: Clarendon Press, 1992.

Hobsbawm, Eric, and Terence Ranger, eds. *The Invention of Tradition.* Cambridge: Cambridge University Press, 1983.

Larsen, Neil. "Imperialism, Colonialism, Postcolonialism: An Introduction." *Determinations: Essays on Theory, Narrative and Nation in the Americas.* London: Verso, 2001.

MacDiarmid, Hugh. *The Complete Poems of Hugh MacDiarmid.* Edited by Michael Grieve and W. R. Aitken. 2 vols. Harmondsworth: Penguin, 1985.

——. *A Drunk Man Looks at the Thistle: An Annotated Edition.* Edited by Kenneth Buthlay. Edinburgh: Scottish Academic Press, 1987.

Maxwell, Stephen. "The Nationalism of Hugh MacDiarmid." In *The Age of MacDiarmid*, ed. Scott and Davis, 202–23.

McClintock, Anne. "The Angel of Progress: Pitfalls of the Term 'Post-Colonialism.' " *Social Text* 31/32 (1992): 1–15.

McCulloch, Margery Palmer, ed. *Modernism and Nationalism: Literature and Society in Scotland, 1918–1939.* Glasgow: Assocation for Scottish Literary Studies, 2004.

Muir, Edwin. *Scott and Scotland: The Predicament of the Scottish Writer.* London: Routledge, 1936.

Nairn, Tom. *The Break-Up of Britain: Crisis and Neo-Nationalism.* London: New Left Books, 1981.

Nandy, Ashis. *The Intimate Enemy: Loss and Recovery under Colonialism.* New Delhi: Oxford University Press, 1983.

Pittock, Murray J. *The Invention of Scotland: The Stuart Myth and the Scottish Identity, 1638 to the Present.* London: Routledge, 1991.

Redfield, Marc. *The Politics of Aesthetics: Nationalism, Gender, Romanticism.* Stanford, Calif.: Stanford University Press, 2003.

Riach, Alan. "MacDiarmid's Burns." In *Robert Burns and Cultural Authority*, ed. Robert Crawford, 198–215. Edinburgh: Edinburgh University Press, 1997.

——. "T. S. Eliot and Hugh MacDiarmid." *Literary Half-Yearly* 29.2 (1988): 124–37.

Scott, P. H., and A. C. Davis, eds. *The Age of MacDiarmid.* Edinburgh: Mainstream, 1980.

Scott, Walter. *Ivanhoe.* Edited by Ian Duncan. Oxford: Oxford University Press, 1996.

# TOWARD
# THE POSTCOLONIAL

*Declan Kiberd*

⋮

TWELVE

# Postcolonial Modernism?

The great modernist writers all felt that they were living through the ends of an old order. Hence the strong element of "post mortem" in works as varied as *The Waste Land, Women in Love*, and *Michael Robartes and the Dancer*. But such writers also sensed with excitement the contours of a new order yet struggling to be born, presaged in the hooded hordes of Eliot, the African statues described by Lawrence, or the rough beast of Yeats. Even milder-mannered authors like E. M. Forster were typical of the prevailing mood: though his books offered shrewd critiques of the closing days of nineteenth-century liberalism, they seemed unable to move beyond it. *A Passage to India* (1924) is founded on the ideal of a restored friendship between the humane Englishman Fielding and the Indian nationalist Dr. Aziz. Though good relations between them are resumed after a near-lethal sundering, the men are nonetheless separated by the rocks as they ride their horses out of the narrative—a signal that whatever international order is to emerge after the age of empire has not taken a clear shape just yet. Forster's novels terminate with a sort of helpless shrug at the intractability of political problems, a retreat into an idealization of personal relations, and some vague imitation of a supernatural force which might or might not be shaping better ends. Yet his motto—"Only connect!"—bespeaks a conviction that only a reexamination of the fundamental one-to-one relationships can lead to a new integrity in political life.

The problem with English modernism was that, with very rare exceptions like George Orwell or Christopher Caudwell, its artists did not get beyond that shrug. Even the poets of the 1930s, Auden and Spender, though enjoying a profile as social radicals, subsequently admitted that they had employed the ideas of Marx and Freud not for a liberation of the masses but rather in the more restricted campaign waged by so many bourgeois children of the period to unmask the self-deception and unexamined presumptions of their hidebound parents. Though some writers braved bullets in revolutionary Spain, few ever carried their radicalism so far as to endorse George Orwell's critique of British imperialism, that same imperialism whose vast profits had subsidized their privileged educations and permitted them the luxury of toying beautifully with their political scruples in well-advertised essays. Some of these writers eventually came out as homosexuals, but not in a fashion calculated to imbue them with a sense of solidarity with other repressed social groups: it was more a matter of style, of learning further how to *épater le bourgeois*.

There were of course some modernists who had no scruples about the imperial project: one was the poet and playwright T. S. Eliot. In 1919 he praised order, empire, and racial purity and proceeded to cite Rudyard Kipling in a denunciation of Joseph Conrad's attack on these "values."[1] Eliot could see no admirable system emerging from the breakup of empires or from the forces of international revolution: and so in his later years he turned to the British empire and Anglican church as forces which might stave off this ruin. "I am all for empires," he told Ford Maddox Ford in 1924, "especially the Austro-Hungarian Empire, and I deplore the outburst of artificial nationalities, constituted like artificial genealogies for millionaires all over the world."[2] This may have been an occluded reference to the newly independent nation-states such as Ireland, officially a Free State in 1922. In his signature poem of the same year, Eliot foresaw hooded hordes swarming from the east to destroy European humanism:

> Falling towers
> Jerusalem, Athens, Alexandria,
> Vienna, London,
> Unreal.[3]

Eliot called for European Christian empire to hold back the Bolsheviks and insisted that it should submit to the leadership of Britain, the only European nation that had established a global empire on the same lines as the old Roman empire. In his critical essays of the 1920s, Eliot explored the notion of a European mind whose thinking might underwrite this order—a tradition stretching back from Goethe through Shakespeare and Dante all the way to Virgil, that ultimate link between ancient and modern worlds. "Destiny for Virgil," wrote Eliot, "means the *imperium romanum.*" But then, in a deft and candid disclosure, Eliot admitted that this classic author's empire was largely utopian: "He set the ideal for Rome, and for empire in general, which was never realized in history. . . . We were all, so far as we inherit the civilization of Europe, still citizens of the Roman Empire."[4]

Eliot was honest enough to admit that the institution imagined by a gifted civil servant such as Virgil was not quite the sordid affair of scheming proconsuls and parasites that features in the history books. Though nominally opposed to modern profiteers (especially if they happened to be Jewish), he nonetheless saw the British empire as a good thing and toward the end of his old days he happily became a British subject, a T. S. instead of a Tom Eliot indeed. As a young man he had been a great admirer of Conrad and especially of *Heart of Darkness.* At one stage he had proposed to make its terrible line "The horror, the horror" the epigraph to *The Waste Land*, and he did quote another line, "Mistah Kurtz, he dead" as a lead-in to a subsequent work, "The Hollow Men."[5] In short, he seemed to endorse the Conradian diagnosis of a sickness afflicting Europe, and by 1924, just two years after *The Waste Land*, he described Conrad as a great novelist. But in the decades that followed he revised that opinion and by 1958 he was calling Kipling the greatest English man of letters of his generation.[6] In the intervening years, Eliot had used his authority to re-jig the English literary tradition as royalist, Anglo-Catholic, and imperial. So Conrad was forgotten, Kipling affirmed, as were nineteenth-century poets such as Keats and Coleridge who devoted themselves to purifying the English language as a register of the greatness of the English national character. Milton, on the other hand, came under severe attack, accused of lacking visual imagination but really guilty of republican politics, unlike the more cavalier metaphysical poets whom Eliot helped bring back into fashion.

English studies as practiced under the sign of Eliot had its origin in a crisis of empire—and in this last-ditch attempt by an immigrant American empire-lover to shore selected fragments of European tradition against the collapse of the political power of Europe. Even after World War II, when an exhausted Britain was overtaken by the United States as the new world power, this account of literary culture remained relatively undisturbed, and as a distinguished Anglo-American, Eliot might even be said to have emblematized the growing rapport between the old imperialists and the new.

Practical criticism, though invented by the English poets, was perfected in the American academy. It fitted perfectly with the notion of "an end to ideology" then sponsored by establishment intellectuals in Washington—this was the idea that U.S. politics was based on pragmatism and consensus rather than class conflict. Moreover, U.S. imperialism was quite different from its English predecessor in one respect. It did not overextend itself trying to run its client states, being quite content to own them (in the sense of controlling them financially). A criticism that raised no embarrassing questions of ideology proved attractive, especially when it proclaimed that in any great text there was for every prevailing idea an equal and opposite idea which might neutralize it. So American liberalism learned how to congratulate itself on a permanent suspension of judgment, a refusal to note the political and social matrices out of which so many texts spring.

The texts of English modernism, because they tried to balance the new and old worlds, and because so many asserted the primacy of the personal over the political, were endlessly debated in U.S. courses; just as in England romantic poets such as Wordsworth and Coleridge were cited as examples of radical youths, momentarily beguiled by the French Revolution, who settled—in a move proleptic of Auden and Spender—for sturdy English common sense and patriotic tradition. Wordsworth evoked, for the landscape of Cumberland, feelings akin to those of a British Tommy asked to die for his country. Keats, the man who hoped to be numbered among the English poets after his death, was hailed as a patriot of language, as was the Coleridge who wrote in *Biographia Literaria:* "Few have guarded their native tongue with the jealous care which Dante declared to be the first duty of the poet. . . . For language is the armoury of the mind, and at once contains the trophies of the past and the weapons of its future conquests."[7] The blend of military metaphor and imperial conquest explains just how a course in English romantic poetry became all too often a study in national-imperialist tradition. Indeed, Eliot on one notable occasion admitted as much when he wrote in *The Sacred Wood* (1920), "It would be of interest to divagate from literature to politics and inquire to what extent Romanticism has possessed the imagination of Imperialists."[8]

The answer is in another of Eliot's books, *The Use of Poetry and the Use of Criticism*—yet there the word "imperialist" need never be used, because the underlying assumption is that everybody thinks in exactly the same way—or at least can be made to do so. One of the primary machines for the manufacture of such consensus among the administrative classes of the colonial peoples has been the university English department, a truth well if sourly exposed by James Joyce in a telling scene from *A Portrait of the Artist as a Young Man* (1916), in which a fat young man lists off the examination results for "the home civil" and "the Indian."[9] This emerging bourgeoisie did not see literature as a means to a visionary culture but rather as a mechanism to be mastered for the securing of plum posts in the civil and imperial service. The fat young man was for Joyce the epitome of those forces which made it imperative to emigrate.

Classic accounts of Euro-modernism never took any interest in such a passage from *Portrait*, preferring to assimilate Joyce to Eliot as an exponent of the mythical method which allowed them both to manipulate in their works a parallel between ancient narratives and the modern world. In that process *Ulysses* was somewhat domesticated since the parallel was taken to be, in Eliot's words, a way of imposing order on contemporary chaos.[10]

The domesticators were in the main a succeeding generation of scholars, charged with the daunting task of explaining the texts of high modernism to baffled students who crowded the universities after World War II. These critics, in their yearning for a humane and secure world after the long concussion of totalitarian creeds, tended to recast the modernists as cosmopolitans *avant la lettre*. Hugh Kenner wrote a book called *The Pound Era* which sought to connect cultural moments in the United States, London, and Paris, while Richard Ellmann gamely argued that Yeats, Joyce, and even Wilde had "become modern" to the extent that they had ceased to be knowingly Irish. This might have been easier to demonstrate with regard to Wilde, a mind utterly untranslatable, but Ellmann felt able to effect a similar reading of the Yeats who had made of Wilde's lack of locality a grand complaint. In "Yeats without Analogue," he pronounced himself willing to admit that Irish nationalism was perhaps an absurdity (Eliot's line again), but he added (rather charitably) that Yeats himself didn't think it so. Still, Ellmann insisted, it was not very helpful to consider Yeats as one of a group who simply freshened up Celtic legends. "When he wrote *A Vision*," said Ellmann, "he forgot that he was an Irishman. And while he calls the fairies by their Irish name of Sidhe, I suspect that they too are internationalists."[11] So, in this scheme of things, even the little people transcend mere Irishness and turn out to have been subscribing members of the Fourth International.

However, even as he wrote these lines, Ellmann was forgetting that Yeats had created *A Vision* as a sort of Celtic constitution, which might underpin and inform the laws and practices of the emerging Irish state.[12] And Kenner was discounting Eliot's wistful regret that the empire of Europe was but an aspiration. There was to be a new international order in due course, but one devoted to ratifying through the United Nations the claims of an ever-increasing number of nation-states (less than fifty in 1945 but over two hundred by the year 2000). The separatist claims of an Ireland or an India, far from being anachronisms based on a mythical past, turned out to be prophetic for the future. The rocks were still separating men like Fielding and Aziz.

There had always been something strained about the attempt to recruit modernists to a mid-century internationalist project: and the critics who dreamed of such integration were never themselves fully at ease with that project. There was for one thing the obvious embarrassment of the fact that the actual, as opposed to utopian, attempt to forge a European empire had resulted in the nightmare of fascism, and that the concomitant search for a socialist international had resulted in the sufferings of many peoples under the Soviet form of imperialism. Insofar as there were some continuities between the thinking of Eliot, Pound, and the fascists, they were distressing. As an American humanist of Jewish background, Ellmann had always been attracted by the high art of Europe. But participating in the liberating armies of World War II made him painfully aware of just how many great modernists submitted to one totalitarianism or another. His lifelong project with Irish writers had an understandably ethical motive: to cast their artistic achievement in European terms, to make *Ulysses* look more like *Der Zauberberg* or *A la recherche du temps perdu*, and to rescue the humanist elements of modernism after the Holocaust.

Yet there was something paradoxical about Ellmann's achievement. His books were always bestsellers at Dublin Airport's shop and he played a definite role in bringing Ireland closer to "the idea of Europe" in the formation period of the European Union—but, by the detached integrity of their analyses, they also analyzed some of the great texts of modernism along lines which helped Irish readers more fully to know themselves. Taken all together, they provide many of the keys to an understanding of a distinctly Irish modernism—these would include the significance of the father-son relation, the emergence of androgynous heroism, a mingling of vernacular traditions with high art, and so on. These were all keys which Ellmann cut but often chose not to turn. They have since been turned by many others.

At the time of his death in 1987, it may have seemed to Ellmann that the dreams of his generation were being fulfilled. The 1980s was a decade of compulsory internationalism among the young, with world music, globalized novels, and the United Colors of Benetton. This international style was less a synthesis of national identities than a real alternative to any such particularisms, all of which it claimed to displace. Two years after Ellmann's death, however, the Berlin Wall came crashing down among the ruins of Soviet imperialism and with it crashed the shadow-Stalinism of compulsory internationalism in the capitalist West. The decade which followed saw not only the assertion of claims by the suppressed nationalities of Eastern Europe but the recovery of national and vernacular particularisms by literary critics.

What Ellmann would have made of all this is anyone's guess. His persistent refusal to make much of the Irishness of Yeats or Joyce was in some ways and in its particular time refreshing and exemplary, in keeping with the critique of narrow-gauge nationalism announced after the Irish Renaissance by writers like Patrick Kavanagh ("Irishness is a form of anti-art—a way of posing as an artist without being one"[13]) and Flann O'Brien (who castigated all exponents of "the national bucklep"[14]). Yet it was also a little disingenuous. For Ellmann's major biographies deal solely with Irish artists, yet he steadfastly rejected any possibility of using Ireland as a helpful explanatory category. So, in their earlier critical works, did such distinguished contemporaries of Ellmann as Denis Donoghue and Hugh Kenner. Donoghue published in 1969 a powerful study of Jonathan Swift with no great play made of the Irish backdrop, and Kenner did more than anyone to create the notion of an intercity modernism. Yet even before 1989 arrived, both men published collections of essays gathered around the nation as explanatory category—Donoghue in *We Irish* and *England, Their England* and Kenner with *A Colder Eye* and *A Sinking Island*.

Kenner had begun this retreat from internationalism with a dazzling reconfiguration of American modernism in *A Homemade World*. What he did for William Carlos Williams or Marianne Moore, a later generation of postcolonial critics (not all of them Irish, for we should include major texts by Andrew Gibson and Vincent Cheng) has done for Joyce, restoring to texts like *A Portrait* or *Ulysses* the integrity of the local moment.[15] And, through the same period, Homi Bhabha has begun to outline the elements of an Indian modernism as filtered through Bombay in the first decade of the twentieth century, just as Ann Douglas has delivered a magnificent analysis in *Mongrel Manhattan* in the same era. What emerges in many of these studies are the neglected elements (native traditions and local meanings) which do not fit easily into the narrative of international modernism. Of all the texts assimilated to that narrative, *Ulysses* stands supreme in both its international authority and its breadth of cultural reference. Yet, over the last ten years or so, major studies have helped readers relocate it in its original cultural and political contexts. Emer Nolan has shown, for instance, how the sympathies of the men in the Cyclops chapter extend well beyond the European humanism sponsored by Ellmann—and the brilliant English critic Andrew Gibson has, by patient recreation of the pedagogical and disciplinary contexts of so many chapters of *Ulysses*, demonstrated just how deep was Joyce's desire to avenge himself on English ways, and thereby suggested that Joyce's masterpiece exists at an acute angle not only to Irish nationalism and British imperialism but also to the project of Euro-modernism itself.[16]

⋮ ⋮ ⋮

According to Richard Ellmann, James Joyce set *Ulysses* on June 16, 1904, to commemorate the occasion on which he first walked out with Nora Barnacle and she made a man of him. As anniversary presents go, *Ulysses* must count as one of the most spectacular, but Nora Barnacle, had she ever walked through the text, could have been forgiven for wondering just how it constituted an act of commemoration. For the climax of *Ulysses* is a meeting between two men, the young poet Stephen Dedalus and the older ad-canvasser Leopold Bloom. Although attempts have been made to portray Molly Bloom's closing soliloquy as the secret life of Nora Barnacle, it is really a coda to the completed book and in most respects a glimpse into the anima of James Joyce. Writing at that depth, he could draw on nobody's consciousness but his own.

The meeting of Dedalus and Bloom is one of the oddest climaxes in the history of modernism, since it violates the convention that there must be war between bohemian and bourgeois. Instead, the poet and businessman sit down for late-night food and a friendly chat. What was Joyce's real agenda? It is possible that he was one of Ireland's first revisionists, in the sense of someone who wished to restore to a past moment the openness it once had, before subsequent events took on the look of inevitability. In rewinding the reel back to 1904, he sought to consider one other possible scenario that might have developed from the moment when he was rescued from a fracas by a kindly older man. It's well known that *Ulysses* began as a short story about just such an event, "Mr. Hunter's Day," and that it grew and grew into the assemblage we now have.

An author who finds a short story turning into an inadvertent epic could be forgiven for making the mysterious openness of past moments a central theme. And that is what Joyce does, finding in Homer's *Odyssey* a series of artistic potentials which cry out for fuller elaboration than they were given in the source text. Indeed, the fear of lost opportunities shadows the entire narrative: those scenes in "Aeolus" and "Scylla and Charybdis" when Leopold and Stephen cross paths but fail to meet are as paradigmatic as the handbill which announces the coming of Elijah but floats seemingly downriver out into Dublin Bay. The many false leads (a different Mr. Bloom who is a dentist, a boiling pot that contains not food but shirts) become a sort of ugly inversion of real potentials which have been "ousted."

All of this has implications for the ways in which we now read *Ulysses*. After so may decades of exegesis, there is a poignant desire to recapture the innocence of a 1922 reading, before the Joyce industry congealed interpretations around certain obsessive themes (the son's search for a father, and so on). What if Homer's tale were just another source text, along with the Bible and *Hamlet*, and not the ultimate key? The publication of a 1922 facsimile edition—a "people's *Ulysses*"—suggests a desire for a less knowing experience.

Is *Ulysses* a novel at all? Novels tend to deal with made societies and Ireland in 1904 was still a society in the making. The short story is designed to describe a submerged people, as Frank O'Connor argued in *The Lonely Voice*, whereas the novel seems more suited to a settled world of calibrated social classes.[17] *Ulysses* is clearly something more than an exfoliation of short stories and may in fact be written in an evolving Irish genre for which as yet there is no name. This form might best be explained by the notion of "latency."[18]

The old Gaelic aristocracy fell after 1600 but was not fully replaced by a confident native middle class until the middle of the twentieth century. In between these dates, the key works of Irish writing were collections of micronarratives cast in the form of the novel but without its sense of a completely developmental narrative. Swift's *Gulliver's Travels* is really four short *contes*, in each of which the protagonist begins a new voyage as if he has learned nothing from the previous ones. In *Castle Rackrent*, Maria Edgeworth describes many generations in just sixty pages; and the prose trilogy of Samuel Beckett, like Flann O'Brien's *At Swim-Two Birds* or Máirtin Ó Cadhain's *Cré na Cille*, is structured around anecdotes which never quite shape themselves into a novel. If epic was the genre of the aristocracy and the novel the genre of the bourgeoisie, then it is in the troubled transition period between these orders that the forms of literature go into meltdown and a radical innovation becomes possible. In countries like England, France, and Germany that transition was managed fairly speedily, but in Ireland it lasted more than three centuries.

Joyce's first prose work, *Dubliners*, had been a collection of short stories with sufficient interconnection to suggest to Yeats the promise of a novelist of a new kind,[19] but *Ulysses*, when it came, was also caught in the interstices between the short story and the novel. Joyce couldn't produce a conventional bildungsroman (the Dedalus section is aborted after three episodes) because his youth does not have his hands on the levers of power. Such a bildungsroman would typically conclude with a youth who had come in from the provinces, made all the right conquests, and now gazes over the rooftops of the capital with a feeling of having arrived at the center of things. But in *Ulysses*, as in *Dubliners*, the city is a place of paralysis. It is less a centrally-planned singular entity than a collection of villages that got amalgamated; and liberation for any protagonist can only be imagined as movement out, away from the center of paralysis.

The classic novels of Europe written before Joyce were propelled almost invariably by dialogue. Tolstoy (one of Joyce's models) knew how to attribute a sentence or two of interior monologue to his major characters in a given scene, but he saw to it that such brief interludes were well subordinated to the surrounding dialogue. In Joyce's Dublin, however, a place where everyone can talk but few know how to listen, dialogue is ineffectual, thin, and does little to advance the plot, whereas the interior monologues are usually so gorgeous in detail as to overwhelm the social world entirely.

These monologues of Stephen, Leopold, and Molly are perhaps the greatest technical achievements of Joyce's oeuvre. Taking their cue from Molly's closing "Yes," most critics see them as an affirmation of everyday life, but there is something suspect and disproportionate about their gorgeousness. Each of these characters is driven back into his or her head as a consequence of frustration and defeat in the outer world. Yeats once said that people are happy only when for every something inside them there is an equivalent outside: read in that light, the monologues can often seem pathological, a defensive tactic of the marginalized. Listening to the latest excellent CD-version of *Ulysses*, I recalled my father's question after he had listened to the fine RTE broadcast of 1982: "Don't you think it might be better not to have quite so rich an inner life?"

This is particularly true of Molly Bloom's closing soliloquy, which may end on a "Yes" but is tragic in its implications. Here is a wakeful woman, beside her sleeping husband, left with nobody to talk to but herself. After an afternoon assignation with her lover, she feels compelled to masturbate repeatedly in the bed, because her visitor came too soon and took all the pleasure for himself. The blank pieces of paper which she posts to herself seem like emblems of her lonely condition, just as her "Yes" seems a desperate tactic to convince herself that life is better than it is. When the Irish actress Fionnuala Flanagan performed the monologue in this way on a U.S. campus in the 1980s, some elderly professors handed back their membership cards to the Joyce Association in disgust at her alleged blasphemy against the sacred text.[20]

Joyce's discovery and development of interior monologue might have been predicted, for long before most other peoples, the Irish of the nineteenth century suffered from that most modern of ailments, a homeless mind. After the Great Famine, many who had started life in a windswept village found themselves ending it in Hammersmith or Hell's Kitchen, and even those who stayed at home changed languages with the result (as Friedrich Engels wrote in a letter to Karl Marx) that they began to feel like strangers in their own country. Living without a key in a suddenly strange environment, they felt removed from the past, from their language, and their very setting—which is to say that they were living in a sort of involuntary bohemia.

The more conventional bohemia of North America and Western Europe was a voluntary zone, occupied by dissident artists or the impoverished young awaiting employment. There these groups set out to improvise new forms of art and life, before carrying the revolutionary message back to the wider society. They had entered this special enclave under the pressure of architectural redevelopment or raised rents.[21]

Joyce's Dublin had some things in common with such places, being (as he said himself) "the last of the intimate cities,"[22] that is, one with a villagey feel wherever you went in it. It was filled with "aging youths" of about thirty, such as the character called Lenehan, and broken older men, like Simon Dedalus, hanging around in hopes of a job and filling the time of idleness with bouts of drinking, song, and story. But Joyce fled this Dublin and accordingly showed little interest in moving to the voluntary Bohemia or Monmartre or Montparnasse. Even as a young medical student in Paris, he appalled the visiting Anglo-Irish playwright J. M. Synge by insisting that they picnic like any bourgeois in the St. Cloud parks.[23] In the later days of his fame, his Parisian neighbors found it hard to reconcile his reputation as a daredevil artist with the uxorious familyman in dapper suits who came and went from his apartment. The famous meeting with Marcel Proust set up by admirers keen for bon mots on "the ache of the modern" resulted in nothing more than a stiff, uneasy exchange on the merits of dark chocolate truffles.[24]

In modernist Paris, most self-respecting intellectuals despised the bourgeois as a soulless money-grubbing automaton. That had not been the case in 1789, when writers had celebrated the moment when meritocrats of a new middle class were finally replacing a parasitic aristocracy. Only much later did the intellectuals begin to detach themselves from that class, becoming its first and foremost critics. In Ireland, however, although the old Gaelic aristocracy had fallen after 1600, it had been replaced by English *arrivistes* who posed as a new gentry. A native middle class was only emerging as a full social formation in the lifetime of James Joyce.

This may be one reason why those intellectuals who led the Irish Renaissance between 1890 and 1921 were so convinced of the link between cultural self-confidence and business success. The Gaelic League, for instance, not only sought to revive the Irish language but to advertise Irish manufacturers in parades initiated throughout the world on St. Patrick's Day. Joyce's own first published stories were in a farmer's journal, *The Irish Homestead*, edited by George Russell, who believed in connecting "the dairies of Plunkett" with "the fairies of Yeats."[25] Most Irish writers of the time showed a marked talent for business. Wilde edited a woman's magazine and wrote his plays to make a lot of gold. Shaw would complain to a film mogul who wished to buy rights to his play: "you keep talking about art and all I'm interested in is the money." Yeats ran two publishing houses and a self-sufficient theater company.

Joyce was, if anything, the most entrepreneurially inclined of them all. Acting for a continental backer, he set up the first cinema in Dublin in 1909. He won a franchise from Dublin Woollen Mills to sell Aran sweaters on the Continent. His most ambitious project was the setting up of a Dublin broadsheet newspaper to be called *The Goblin*.[26] It never took off, for want of cash, but it could be argued that *Ulysses* is an attempt by art to trump the modern newspaper with an even more detailed account of the life of a city on a single day. Its surreal juxtaposition of clashing styles and topics recalls that of *The Irish Homestead*, in which Joyce's epiphanies appeared alongside the week's manure prices (he was so humiliated by this location in "The Pigs' Paper" that he took cover under the pseudonym Stephen Dedalus). On more than one occasion, the writer of *Ulysses* called himself "only a scissor-and-paste man."[27]

If Joyce was impressed by business people, that was because they were, like all artists, brokers in risk, willing to back an initial hunch with long years of hack work. So it isn't at all surprising that he should have made an ad-canvasser like Bloom the central figure of his modern masterpiece. Throughout the book, Bloom is portrayed as someone well aware of the ways in which the advertisement maps the dream-world of the unconscious onto everyday settings. Seeing the communicants at All Hallows Church, he remarks on the value of the accompanying slogan: "Good idea the Latin. Stupefies them first."[28] Bloom is forever alert to a practical business opportunity, whether it be a new tramline to the city docks or a free railway pass to visit his daughter Milly in Mullingar.

Stephen Dedalus has inherited his father's wastrel habits and stands in some need of Bloom's practicality. Stephen's fellow-occupant of the Sandy Cove Tower, Malachi Mulligan, senses a rival for Stephen's good opinion in the figure of Bloom and warns that he may lust after the youth: "he is Greeker than the Greeks" (271). But perhaps it is Mulligan's interest which is more directly sexual, hinted in his early invocation of Wilde. If so, the relationship which develops between Dedalus and Bloom might be seen as a more Platonic classical substitute—the willingness of an older man, wise in the ways of the world, to advise a callow but promising youth.

Although Bloom is a surrogate father to Stephen (and one far superior in that parental role than the biological father, Simon), his stronger tendency in the later episodes is frankly *maternal*. He haunts the Holles Street Hospital out of sympathy for Mrs. Purefoy in her three-day labor. In the "Circe" episode, his fantasy of becoming a mother is realized not just in the dream-play section but more importantly when he rescues Stephen. As May Dedalus's voice-over recalls the ways in which she protected her errant eldest son, it seems as if her ghost is prompting Bloom to take over her vacated role. There is—despite Mulligan—no hint that the relationship might have a sexual dimension. Bloom in fact suspects that Stephen is muttering something about a girl named Ferguson and thinks that this could be "the best thing that ever happened to him" (702). At this stage, he is simply anxious to protect his friend's son; and the final image in the episode of Bloom's dead son Rudy reading a Jewish text seems a version of Stephen "*lisant au livre de lui-même*" (239).

The Bloom who had earlier mocked the communicants at All Hallows now recreates the sacramental moment in literal earnest by sharing coffee and a bun with the hungry young poet. That communion between bourgeois and bohemian is the true climax of the book in the course of which Bloom worries about cases of early burnout among "cultured fellows that promised so brilliantly." When he suggests that Stephen find work, however, he is rudely told, "Count me out" (747). Bloom hastens to assure his friend that there is no conflict between their definitions of what such work might be. It would be "work in the widest possible sense" "for you have every bit as much right to live by your own pen in pursuit of your philosophy as the peasant has" (747–48).

Leaving the cabman's shelter, Bloom tells Stephen that if he walks with him, he'll "feel a different man"; and, sure enough, linking arms, Stephen "felt a strange kind of flesh of a different man approach him, sinewless and wobbly and all that" (769). It is as if a guru has got on a wavelength with an adept. Bloom's prophetic role with Stephen is not to communicate in words any particular philosophy but to sacralize the everyday as a way of feeling at home in the world.

Joyce pokes tender fun at his own climax, citing lines from a popular song in describing the pair leaving "in a low-backed car" to be "married by Father Maher" (775).

That understanding is reinforced by the fact that the cabby's horse shits as they leave. The rapprochement between bohemian and bourgeois is purely temporary: if both were fully sober and less fatigued, how much would they have in common?

The scene in which Bloom shows Dedalus a photograph of a rather younger Molly might be interpreted in various ways. In one sense, the picture completes the image of the new "holy family" Stephen had joined (while also reassuring him that the invitation is not homosexual). Not homosexual—but homosocial perhaps. All through *Ulysses*, Bloom has shown a need for the company and ratification of other men. He attended the funeral of a man he scarcely knew, as if anxious to join a ritual with other males on a sacred occasion. In "Sirens," as he sat next to Richie Goulding, the two men were described as "married" by the silence of the pub (347). There may be in Bloom's gesture a homosocial desire to share the contemplation of his wife with another man: in "Ithaca" he appears to be excited by the possibility that many men have been lovers of Molly.

In the company of Stephen back at home in Eccles Street, Bloom becomes ever more balanced and androgynous. He is undisturbed by the absence of light in the dark house because of "the surety of the sense of touch in his firm full masculine feminine passive active hand" (788). The two men appear to have the polar makings of a whole person, with Stephen epitomizing the artistic and Bloom the scientific. Yet their prior psychic marriage turns out to be a little like the sexual union of Leopold and Molly—a zone of nonintersection and nonfriction in which each is haunted by the other, can share the other's solitude, but no more than that.

Bohemian life was often just a means by which failed medical students or lapsed lawyers sought to live artistically. Joyce, however, was a serious worker who fled all that in order to produce a mighty book. He never sought fashionable poverty but rather the money with which to escape it. Far from staging the bohemian's tactical withdrawal from ordinary life, he tried to emphasize the redemptive strangeness of the quotidian. *Ulysses* was published at just that moment in the history of surrealism when bohemia, through advertising, was about to become an avant-garde form of publicity.[29] In his love of advertising jingles, his openness to art as productive work, his desire to savor Nighttown, Bloom condenses all these tendencies. In a somewhat similar way, Joyce used the immense resources of money, books, and magazines to publicize *Ulysses*, while maintaining a very bourgeois pose (he never used bad language in speech, only in writing) to protect his own privacy.

Indeed, by 1922, when *Ulysses* went on sale in the streets of Paris, the war between bohemian and bourgeois in that city was already drawing to an end, as commercial art employed more and more of the techniques of the surrealists. In the decades after that, the bohemians of France, England, and the United States broke out of their old confines and helped to create the consumerist lifestyle of the new middle classes (what would later be called "modernism in the streets").[30] Joyce's own assumption, working out of the special Irish conditions, that there had never been any deep-rooted conflict probably helped to secure his rapid assimilation into the canon. One strange result is that the book which begins by satirizing the Oxford student Haines as an example of the English literary tourist had thousands of such visitors checking into hotels for the celebration of the hundredth Bloomsday in 2004.

Irish modernism had always been about hard work and serious literary production. Though Yeats liked to talk of *sprezzatura*, he really believed in Adam's Curse and the "fascination of what's difficult"[31]—as did those predecessors from Swift to Shaw, from Goldsmith to Wilde, whom Yeats liked to call Anglo-Irish but who were in fact bourgeois Protestants with a strong work ethic. Joyce, for his part, only seemed French-bohemian on the surface—Stephen's walking-cane is less that of a Parisian *flâneur* than the ceremonial rod carried by the "youthful bard" (337) of Gaeldom; and Joyce's much publicized habit of writing while stretched out on a bed drew less on Oblomov than on the traditions of the ancient *filí*. To Joyce the bourgeoisie was something which, like the proletariat itself, had yet to be fully created in Ireland. In Leopold Bloom, he created his dream of an absolute Irish bourgeois, one who can enjoy chance encounters with others and feel the streets to be his home.

But that bourgeois figure was already doomed in 1922, to be replaced in a few decades by the middle class. Bloom's was an unplanned, ruralized but civic city. Soon the middle class would urbanize an entire civilization, whose architecture and shopping malls would be so completely planned that chance encounters became less and less possible. The seeds of this degeneration are carried, in fact, by Bloom himself, in his adman's daydream of suburban life in Dundrum: "Bloom Cottage. St. Leopold's. Flowerville" (841).

Like all other characters of *Ulysses*, Bloom is a "street person," but not in today's degraded sense. As Jane Jacobs has shown, today not only the civic street but also the crowd have been done away with.[32] Dublin's current celebration of Bloomsday is really a lament for lost days when the city still seemed negotiable on foot rather than gridlocked by a hundred-thousand private cars. The citizens in Joyce's Dublin circulated in unpredictable ways, which allowed Joyce to renew his narrative styles in each episode, to keep a sense of possibilities open rather than ousted. What Joyce showed is that growth—the encounters with others—is more a matter of happy accident than deliberate design. It is what happens to the older Leopold as well as the younger Stephen, when the desire for mastery is ablated, when old routines are challenged, and the new practices which might replace them have not yet hardened into a system.

## Notes

1 Eliot, "Kipling Redivivus," 30.
2 Ibid.
3 Eliot, *The Complete Poems and Plays*, 73.
4 Raskin, *The Mythology of Imperialism*, 32.
5 Eliot, *The Complete Poems and Plays*, 81.
6 Eliot, quoted in Raskin, *The Mythology of Imperialism*, 34.
7 Coleridge, *Biographia Literaria*, 73.
8 Eliot, *The Sacred Wood*, 32.
9 Joyce, *A Portrait of the Artist as a Young Man*, 228.
10 Eliot, "*Ulysses*, Order and Myth," 25.
11 Ellmann, *Along the Riverrun*, 25.
12 Ellmann, *Yeats*, 249–53.
13 Kavanagh, quoted in O'Brien, *Patrick Kavanaugh*, 64.
14 Micheál Ó Nualláin, conversation with author, December 12, 2003.
15 Gibson, *Joyce's Revenge*; and Cheng, *Joyce, Race and Empire.*
16 See Gibson, *Joyce's Revenge*, passim, and Nolan, *James Joyce and Nationalism.*
17 O'Connor, *The Lonely Voice.*
18 Jameson, *Marxism and Form*, 38–59.
19 Ellmann, *James Joyce*, 403.
20 Fionnuala Flanagan as Molly, in performance soliloquy from Joyce's *Ulysses*, University of Minnesota, Minneapolis, April 1983.
21 Graña, *Bohemian versus Bourgeois*, 21–60.
22 Joyce, quoted in Ellmann, *James Joyce*, 523.
23 Ibid., 128.
24 Ibid., 523–24.
25 Mathews, *Revival*, passim.
26 Mary and Padraic Colum, *Our Friend James Joyce*, 55–56.

27 Ellmann, *James Joyce*, 470.
28 Joyce, *Ulysses*, annotated student's edition, ed. Declan Kiberd (London: Penguin, 1992), 99. Further references are cited parenthetically in the text.
29 Seigel, *Bohemian Paris*, 389–97.
30 That phrase is usually credited to Lionel Trilling but the underlying concept is spelled out most fully in Bell, *The Cultural Contradictions of Capitalism*, especially 1–95.
31 Yeats, *Collected Poems*, 104.
32 Jacobs, *The Death and Life of Great American Cities*.

## Works Cited

Bell, Daniel. *The Cultural Contradictions of Capitalism*. London: Heinemann, 1979.
Cheng, Vincent. *Joyce, Race and Empire*. Cambridge: Cambridge University Press, 1995.
Coleridge, Samuel Taylor. *Biographia Literaria*. London: Dent, 1956.
Colum, Mary, and Padraic Colum. *Our Friend James Joyce*. New York: Doubleday, 1956.
Eliot, T. S. *The Complete Poems and Plays*. London: Faber, 1969.
——. "Kipling Redivivus." In Jonah Raskin, *The Mythology of Imperialism*. New York: Dell, 1973.
——. "*Ulysses*, Order and Myth." In *The Modern Tradition*, ed. Richard Ellmann and Charles Fiedleson, 679–81. New York: Oxford University Press, 1967.
——. *The Sacred Wood*. London: Methuen, 1960.
Ellmann, Richard. *Along the Riverrun*. New York: Penguin, 1990.
——. *James Joyce*. New York: Oxford University Press, 1959.
——. *Yeats: The Man and the Masks*. London: Faber, 1961.
Flanagan, Fionnuala. Performance of Molly's soliloquy from Joyce's *Ulysses*. Minneapolis, University of Minnesota, April 1983.
Gibson, Andrew. *Joyce's Revenge*. Oxford: Oxford University Press, 2002.
Graña, César. *Bohemian versus Bourgeois: French Society and the French Man of Letters in the Nineteenth Century*. New York: Basic Books, 1964.
Jacobs, Jane. *The Death and Life of Great American Cities*. New York: Random House, 1961.
Jameson, Fredric. *Marxism and Form*. Princeton, N.J.: Princeton University Press, 1974.
Joyce, James. *A Portrait of the Artist as a Young Man*. London: Hammondsworth, 1992.
——. *Ulysses*. Annotated Student's Edition. Edited by Declan Kiberd. London: Penguin, 1992.
Mathews, P. J. *Revival*. Cork: Cork University Press, Field Day, 2003.
Nolan, Emer. *James Joyce and Nationalism*. London: Routledge, 1994.
Nualláin, Micheál Ó. Conversation with author. December 12, 2003.

O'Brien, Darcy. *Patrick Kavanaugh*. Lewisburg, Pa.: Bucknell University Press, 1975.
O'Connor, Frank. *The Lonely Voice*. Macmillan: London, 1962.
Raskin, Jonah. *The Mythology of Imperialism*. New York: Dell, 1973.
Seigel, Jerrold. *Bohemian Paris: Culture, Politics, and the Boundaries of Bourgeois Life, 1830–1930*. Baltimore: Johns Hopkins University Press, 1986.
Yeats, W. B. *Collected Poems*. 2nd ed. London: Macmillan, 1950.

*Jahan Ramazani*

⋮

THIRTEEN

# Modernist Bricolage, Postcolonial Hybridity

I arise and go with William Butler Yeats
to country Sligoville
in the shamrock green hills of St. Catherine.

So begins a recent homage by the Jamaican poet Lorna Goodison.[1]

We walk and palaver by the Rio Cobre
till we hear tributaries
join and sing, water songs of nixies.

Dark tales of Maroon warriors,
fierce women and men
bush comrades of Cuchulain.

We swap duppy stories, dark night doings.
I show him the link of a rolling calf's chain
And an old hige's salt skin carcass.

This Afro-Caribbean poem for a Euro-modernist traverses cultural, racial, and gender boundaries via intersections of place names—Sligo, Sligoville—mythical heroes—Ireland's Cuchulain, Jamaica's ex-slave rebels—and premodern magic—Yeats's mysticism, Jamaica's skin-shedding witches and neck-chained, calf-like ghosts. Goodison Irishes Jamaica—its hills become "shamrock green"—and Jamaicanizes Ireland—Cuchulain now has Afro-Caribbean "bush comrades." Apostrophizing a dead poet who often discoursed with the dead, Goodison writes:

William Butler, I swear my dead mother
embraced me. I then washed off my heart
with the amniotic water of a green coconut.

Conjoining myths and magic, topography and words across hemispheres, Goodison figures her intercultural relationship with Yeats as reciprocal exchange ("We swap duppy stories"): his work has changed hers, and, notwithstanding chronology, her postcolonial reception of his metaleptically transforms it. Poetry, she suggests, is for crossing boundaries between the living and the dead, between times, places, cultures. The space of a poem is neither local—a securely anchored signifier of Jamaican authenticity—nor global—a placeless, free-floating noumenon. It is a translocation, verbally enabling and enacting—between specific times and places—cross-cultural, transhistorical exchange.

This intercultural conception of poetry is central to both Euro-modernism and to what the Martinican theorist and writer Edouard Glissant has called the cross-cultural poetics ("poétique de la Relation") of the Caribbean.[2] Yet postcolonial criticism has sometimes represented the relation between postcolonialism and Euro-modernism as adversarial. Now that the postmodern is no longer seen as an outright rejection of the modern, we also need to reconsider whether and to what extent postcolonial literatures repudiate—"write back to"—an imperial Euro-modernism. In his pathbreaking analysis of Afro-Caribbean fiction, Simon Gikandi offers a nuanced statement of the agonistic position: "Caribbean modernism is opposed to, though not necessarily independent of, European notions of modernism." Gikandi thus proposes a "Third World modernism distinct from the prototypical European form, which in Houston Baker's words, 'is exclusively Western, preeminently bourgeois, and optically white.' "[3] The authors of *Toward the Decolonization of African Literature* assert a sharper divide: "African literature *is* an autonomous entity separate and apart from all other literatures. It has its own traditions, models and norms." The influence of Euro-modernist "privatism" can only obscure authentic African expression under "dunghill piles of esoterica and obscure allusions."[4] Bill Ashcroft and John Salter represent modernism's influence beyond the metropole as unambiguously imperialist: "The high-cultural discourse of modernism, with its imposition of a set of largely uncontested parameters upon a non-European cultural reality, may be seen to be metonymic of the operation of imperial domination. Modernity and modernism are rooted in empire."[5]

But far from being an obstruction that had to be dislodged from the postcolonial windpipe, Euro-modernism—in one of the great ironies of twentieth-century literary history—crucially enabled a range of non-Western poets after World War II to explore their hybrid cultures and postcolonial experience. For these poets, the detour through Euro-modernism was often, paradoxically, the surest route home. In his *History of the Voice*, Kamau Brathwaite offers one of the most vivid testaments to the importance of Euro-modernism for the postcolonization of postcolonial literatures. T. S. Eliot, he asserts, was the primary influence on Caribbean poets "moving from standard English" to creolized English, or "nation language": "What T. S. Eliot did for Caribbean poetry and Caribbean literature was to introduce the notion of the speaking voice, the conversational tone. That is what really attracted us to Eliot." Emphasizing the oral/aural medium of transmission and thus assimilating Eliot to West Indian orature, Brathwaite further explains in a footnote: "For those who really made the breakthrough, it was Eliot's actual voice—or rather his recorded voice, property of the British Council (Barbados)—reading 'Preludes,' 'The love song of J. Alfred Prufrock,' *The Waste Land* and later the *Four Quartets*—not the texts—which turned us on. In that dry deadpan delivery, the 'riddims' of St. Louis (though we did not know the source then) were stark and clear for those of us who at the same time were listening to the dislocations of Bird, Dizzy and Klook. And it is interesting that, on the whole, the establishment could not stand Eliot's voice—and far less jazz!" Brathwaite cites the parallel influence of a BBC cricket commentator's "natural, 'riddimic' and image-laden tropes in his revolutionary Hampshire burr": "he subverted the establishment with the way he spoke and where: like Eliot, like jazz."[6]

Brathwaite hails Eliot for his conversational orality and jazz dislocations, his nonstandard diction and improvisatory rhythms. That a revolutionary Afrocentrist could hear the flat British monotone of an Anglo-Catholic Royalist as subversive, could embrace Eliot as an anti-establishment poet for the 1950s and 1960s, might well seem bizarre, especially since for many North American poets of the time, Eliot *was* the establishment. When Robert Creeley, Allen Ginsberg, and Amiri Baraka turned to jazz as a model for improvisatory rhythms and phrasing, they were repudiating Eliot's academic embodiment in New Critical, formalist norms of coherence, polish, and impersonal wit. In a manifesto for the new American poetries, "Projective Verse" (1950), Charles Olson implicitly mocks "O. M. Eliot" (that is, Order of Merit) for his imperial affinities.[7] Meanwhile, in Britain, Philip Larkin and other poets of the Movement were also renouncing Eliot and Pound, put off by their polyglossia, syntactic dislocations, and arcane mythologies. But while the Beats, the Black Mountain poets, poets of the Black Arts Movement, as well as poets of the Movement in Britain, saw a stiff-necked modernism—aestheticist, elitist, writerly—as the dominant mode needing demolition, many leading poets of the "developing world," including the Barbadian Brathwaite, the Saint Lucian Walcott, the Indian A. K. Ramanujan, the Ugandan Okot p'Bitek, and the Nigerians Christopher Okigbo and Wole Soyinka, seized on Euro-modernism as a tool of liberation. These postcolonial poets, all born in a five-year span from 1929 to 1934 and thus initially educated under British colonial rule, came of age during the formal breakup of much of the British empire from the late 1940s through the 1960s. They leveraged Euro-modernism against British romantic, Victorian, and other imperial norms calcified in their local educational and cultural establishments—norms that resulted in the stilted, neoromantic poems enshrined by organizations such as the Jamaican Poetry League.[8]

For the young Brathwaite, Eliot's impersonality and unpredictability seemed an emancipatory alternative to the closed, emotive, monologic voice of the canonical English lyric purveyed in the schools. For Ramanujan, modernist astringency served as an antidote to the mawkishness and monologism of much postwar Indian poetry in English. Though often seen as a nativist, Okot p'Bitek employed brisk, modernist free verse and defamiliarizingly literal translation to satirize the hypocrisy and pomposity of African missionaries and politicians. Against the restrictive "platform poetry" of negritude, Okigbo and Soyinka unleashed an intercultural polyphony they derived in part from modernism. The opening lyric of Walcott's *Collected Poems* redeploys the agonized self-divisions of "Prufrock," with auxiliary echoes of *The Waste Land:*

> I go, of course, through all the isolated acts,
> Make a holiday of situations,
> Straighten my tie and fix important jaws. . . .

The modernist topos of self-alienation, far from being "metonymic of the operation of imperial domination," serves to contest the imperialist image of West Indians found

> In tourist booklets, behind ardent binoculars;
> Found in the blue reflection of eyes
> That have known cities and think us here happy.[9]

The choice for Walcott, Brathwaite, Ramanujan, Okot, Okigbo, and Soyinka was not between an imported Euro-modernism and a pristine native culture, since the forms of cultural dominance against which they struggled were often local instantiations of the imperium—Victorian sentiment and monologue, missionary prudishness and hypocrisy, colonial education and racism, a tourist industry complicit in the production of imprisoning stereotypes, and nationalisms and nativisms that mirrored European norms in reverse. To insist, in the name of anti-Eurocentricism, that Euro-modernism be seen as an imperial antagonist is to condescend to imaginative writers who have wielded modernism in cultural decolonization and, ironically, to impose as universal a Eurocentric standard: the antimodernism of postwar American and British poetry.

The intercultural poetic forms of modernism, in particular, have been especially attractive to so-called Third World poets in their quest to break through monologic lyricism, to express their cross-cultural experience, despite vast differences in ethnicity and geography, politics and history from the Euro-modernists. Modernist bricolage—the synthetic use in early-twentieth-century poetry of diverse cultural materials ready to hand—has helped postcolonial poets encode aesthetically intersections among multiple cultural vectors. Writing in the metropole at a time of imperial and ethnographic adventure, massive immigration, world war, interlingual mixture, sped-up communication and travel, the Euro-modernists—many of them exiles and émigrés themselves—were the first English-language poets to create a formal vocabulary for the intercultural collisions and juxtapositions, the epistemic instabilities and decenterings, of globalization.[10] By contrast with the disjunctiveness and perspectivism of the modernist poem, the premodern English lyric was, Brathwaite suggests, a model that risked suppressing the cultural complexity of postcolonial experience, because it could not adequately articulate such intercultural discordance as being schooled to write poems about unseen snowfall while living in the hurricane-swept tropics.[11] In short, for many postcolonial poets, though on the receiving end of empire, more important than the modernists' complicity in a waning imperialism and in Orientalist fantasy, or their imbrication in European literary tradition, was their creation of answering forms and vocabularies for the cross-cultural juxtapositions, interreligious layerings, and polyglot interminglings of cross-hemispheric experience.

But while postcolonial poets emergent in the 1950s and 1960s weren't antimodernists, neither were they Euro-modernist wannabes. If postcolonial criticism has often been too eager to depict postcolonial writers as revolutionary Calibans struggling heroically against hegemonic, Euro-modernist Prosperos, modernist criticism has at times been perhaps too eager to assimilate postcolonialism to Euro-modernism as "part of the same movement."[12] Yet the contrasts should not be bleached out, since Euro-modernists, even if marginal to the British cultural and political center by virtue of nationality (e.g., Irish or American), class, sexual orientation, or aesthetics ("épater le bourgeois" avant-gardism), were finally less marginal than non-European poets growing up in Castries, Bridgetown, Kingston, Mysore, Srinagar, Ojoto, Ibadan, or Gulu. Postcolonial hybridity and modernist bricolage are thus, in James Clifford's phrase, "*discrepant cosmopolitanisms.*"[13] The conditions of possibility for postcolonial hybridity are violent occupation and cultural imposition at home, across immense differences of power, topography, culture, and economics. Its non-West is primary and profoundly experiential, not the object of extraterritorial questing via tourism and museums, books and ethnography, friendships and translations. By contrast, Euro-modernists make use, as Lévi-Strauss says of the "bricoleur," of a limited heterogeneity,[14] their materials often made available by imperial and ethnographic forays. Even the most boldly cross-hemispheric Euro-modernist poets occasionally import a subaltern text or artifact or genre and embed it within a Western literary universe. Since the postcolonial writer inhabits the multiple cultural worlds forcibly conjoined by empire, hybridity—the knotting together of countless already knotted together indigenous and imposed languages, images, genres—is not an aspect but the basic fabric of the postcolonial poem. In redeploying modernism across these differences, postcolonial poets have had to refashion it for resisting local and imperial monisms, for articulating a cross-culturalism still more plural and polyphonic than

Euro-modernism. They have reshaped it through indigenous genres and vocabularies, have recentered it in non-Western landscapes and mythologies, and have often inverted its racial and cultural politics.

⋮ ⋮ ⋮

Among the hybridizing literary strategies of postcolonial poetry that can be traced in part to Euro-modernist bricolage are translocalism, mythical syncretism, heteroglossia, and apocalypticism. Translocalism, the mode of intercultural syncretism with which I began, is key to A. K. Ramanujan's "Chicago Zen":

> Watch your step. Sight may strike you
> blind in unexpected places.
>
> The traffic light turns orange
> on 57th and Dorchester, and you stumble,
>
> you fall into a vision of forest fires,
> enter a frothing Himalayan river,
>
> rapid, silent.
>
> On the 14th floor,
> Lake Michigan crawls and crawls
>
> in the window.[15]

In this morphing of Lake Michigan into a South Asian river, of the traffic light by Hyde Park into Indian forest fires, Ramanujan adapts the modernist technique of translocal "super-position," as Pound called it—Eliot's layering of the Thames and the Ganges, Pound's of a mountain near the Disciplinary Training Center in Pisa and Mount Taishan. He renews both Euro-modernist technique and its indigenous counterpart, fusing superposition to what he termed the "montage" and "dissolve" effects of Dravidian poetry, as well as the startling paradoxes of Zen.[16] As in Goodison's melding of Ireland's Sligo and Jamaica's Sligoville, Walcott's of the Greek islands and the Antilles, distances between North and South collapse: "you drown," Ramanujan writes in an echo of "Prufrock," "eyes open, / towards the Indies, the antipodes." Not that postcolonial and modernist translocalisms are identical. The Euro-modernist superpositional poem imports into an experiential Western place (the Thames, Pisa) an "other," exoticized, Eastern place (the Ganges, Mount Taishan), whereas in "Chicago Zen," the speaker "falls" from one floor of his migrant experience—Chicago—to another—India, two worlds that he has lived and that now live him. And whereas the Euro-modernist poem often de-realizes the local (Eliot's London, Pound's Pisa) by silhouetting it against an Eastern alterity, Ramanujan's poem revises this modernist strategy by oscillating between fully real but discrepant locations. Ramanujan assimilates modernist translocalism to what Salman Rushdie calls the "migrant's-eye view of the world"—born of a more fully interstitial migrancy than that of the modernists, because of its layering upon a prior postcolonial dislocation, and thus a more thoroughgoing "experience of uprooting, disjuncture and metamorphosis (slow or rapid, painful or pleasurable)."[17]

Postcolonial poets have also adapted mythical syncretism from the modernists as a key device for their intercultural poetics—like Cuchulain, so Goodison's maroon warrior; like Shango—Yoruba god of lightning—so electricity in Soyinka's "Idanre." The modernists helped make the high art poem a space for the cross-religious syncretism that was basic to life in the colonies and postcolonies, so that, once again, an imported modernism paradoxically serves as a means for transmuting into literary discourse "postcolocal" experience, to propose a portmanteau word that, combining "postcolonial" with "local," also highlights the translocalism—"colocal"—of the postcolonial. Having in modernist fashion developed his "own personal religion," out of Christian, classical, and Igbo sources, Christopher Okigbo said in an interview: "The way that I worship my gods is in fact through poetry."[18] Yeats also thought of poetry as a syncretic rite, and Okigbo delivers an appropriately ritualistic homage to Yeats as "the archpriest of the sanctuary" in his "Lament of the Masks," published by the University of Ibadan in a book celebrating Yeats's centenary, in 1965.[19] In this late poem, which has been described as marking Okigbo's shift to a more African aesthetic,[20] Okigbo paradoxically Africanizes his poetry in the act of praising a Euro-modernist. Indigenization and aesthetic modernization, for Okigbo as for Ramanujan, are not polar opposites but closely linked. Direct references within the poem to classical panegyric and to praise song indicate Okigbo's remaking of European genres within an African framework (the contributor's note also states the poem "is based on a traditional Yoruba praise-song").[21] Drawing on the traditional praise song's ritualistic imagery of the hunt, animals, and heroic action, Okigbo arrays an African elephant, jungle, plaintain leaf, and giant iroko tree alongside symbols adapted from the temple of Yeats's poetry—iron-throated singers in bird-masks—and from classical myth—"Waggoner of the great Dawn." He reterritorializes Yeats, Africanizing him as an elephant hunter, his masks as ritual objects, while deterritorializing the praise song, centering it on a European subject. It is hard not to hear a wry pun on "canon" in Okigbo's modest self-representation:

> Warped voices—
> For we answer the cannon
> From afar off—
>
> And from throats of iron—
>
> In bird-masks—
> Unlike accusing tones that issue forth javelins—
> Bring, O Poet,
>
> Panegyrics for the arch-priest of the sanctuary . . .

Having spent much time in an "ethereal ivory tower," Yeats comes across as a perhaps too idealistic—if tireless and heroic—chaser of "the white elephant." Still, on balance, the relation of Okigbo's poem to Yeats's verse is more affiliative than corrosive: like Goodison, Okigbo credits Yeats with having helped to translate lived, "postcolocal," transreligious feeling into poetry. Elsewhere, Okigbo's poetry of polymythic syncretism draws extensively on the intercultural amalgamations of Pound's poetry—from *The Cantos* he even adapts archaisms, shifting cadences, and the refrain, especially resonant in 1960s Nigeria, "& the mortar is not yet dry."[22] Okigbo remarked that he "never felt" a "conflict" between his European and his African cultural inheritances, and his praise song for Yeats synthesizes mythologies of Euro-classical ("rumour awakens"), Christian ("Water of baptism"), and precolonial African ("Thunder above the earth") origin.

Although Walcott sometimes highlights the tensions among the various points on his religious and cultural compass (e.g., the early "A Far Cry from Africa"), he, too, is often an organic syncretist, to draw on Bakhtin's distinction between "organic" and "intentional" modes of hybridity.[23] In an especially high-spirited scene of *Omeros* that humorously pumps up modernist comparativism, Walcott imagines a cyclone pounding Saint Lucia as a raucous party to which he invites European, African, and Caribbean gods. They play Yoruba and Afro-Caribbean "Shango drums" that "made Neptune rock in the caves," while the Haitian love goddess Erzulie rattles "her ra-ra," the Afro-Caribbean snake god Damballa winds, and the Yoruba and Afro-Caribbean blacksmith Ogun fires drinks with "his partner Zeus."[24] Unlike Okigbo or Soyinka, Walcott aestheticizes the transreligious, displaying his intercultural groupings as artifacts. Still, his compression of deities from diverse pantheons into one polyphonous space energizes both party and poem. Like Okigbo's, the later Walcott's syncretism tends to be more exuberant than elegiac—a celebration of transregional inheritance in the Caribbean—unlike Eliot's "mythical method," where the parallels often encode a narrative of degeneration, a Eurocentric lament over decline and dissipation.[25]

More nearly affiliated with Eliot's elegiac syncretism, if still distinct, is the work of a poet of the next generation, the Kashmiri American Agha Shahid Ali. In "Ghazal" ("Where are you now? Who lies beneath your spell tonight"), the different faiths of Ali's youth jostle alongside one another, in references to biblical stories, a Hindu temple, a Shi'a God.[26] Repulsed by violence in the name of religion—executions, smashed statues and idols—"A refugee from Belief seeks a cell tonight," perhaps in the discontinuous two-line cells of the ghazal itself:

Executioners near the woman at the window.
Damn you, Elijah, I'll bless Jezebel tonight.

*Lord,* cried out the idols, *Don't let us be broken;*
*Only we can convert the infidel tonight.*

Has God's vintage loneliness turned to vinegar?
He's poured rust into the Sacred Well tonight.

In the heart's veined temple all statues have been smashed.
No priest in saffron's left to toll its knell tonight.

He's freed some fire from ice, in pity for Heaven;
he's left open—for God—the doors of Hell tonight.

And I, Shahid, only am escaped to tell thee—
God sobs in my arms. Call me Ishmael tonight.

In the echo chamber of this final couplet, Ali commingles Job ("only am escaped [alone] to tell thee"), *Moby-Dick* ("Call me Ishmael" and the Job quotation), and Islamic tradition (Ishmael as Ur-ancestor). In this further example of what I term the dialectics of indigenization, Ali reinvigorates both the "native" and the foreign, both the Urdu-Arabic-Persian form of the ghazal and the Euro-modernist mode of mythical syncretism, bracing them together through their homologous conjunctures and fissures. Hardly a disabling, imperial influence, modernist syncretism, ghazalified, functions for Ali as a counterweight to tyrannies closer to "home"—the religious and nationalist absolutisms that have ravaged Kashmir. As required by the ghazal, the poet names himself (the *takhallos*), but he then gives himself another name, Ishmael—an intercultural node in which Judaism, Christianity, and Islam intersect, as they have in the poem's formal junctures and syncretic layerings. This *takhallos* may also recall the strange fusion of self-reference and scattershot quotation in a famous retrospective coda—"These fragments I have shored against my ruins"—particularly in view of Ali's discussion, in his dissertation-turned-monograph, *T. S. Eliot as Editor*, of the "sense of loss and desolation" in *The Waste Land*.[27] Lamenting exile, linguistic displacement, and political violence in his poems, Ali is drawn to Eliot's work by its resemblance to the melancholy of Urdu poetry, to the disjunctive collage and impersonal personality of the ghazal. Yet whereas Eliot grieves in the gaps between one version of a myth and its successors, in the instabilities and ruptures of cultural multiplicity, Ali freely moves among intimately felt inheritances from English, American, and Urdu literatures and from Buddhism, Hinduism, Islam, Judaism, Christianity, mobilizing these against both public and private losses, and against monistic structures of recuperation from such losses. The differential appropriations of Eliot by a poet of Shi'a Muslim and of Afro-Caribbean origin—that is, the differences between Ali's Eliot and Brathwaite's satiric, jazzy, creolized Eliot—again instance the diverse postcolonial indigenizations of modernism. For Ali, as for Brathwaite, Goodison, Okigbo, and Ramanujan, modernism represents not an "imposition of a set of largely uncontested parameters upon a non-European cultural reality" but a multifaceted and mutable resource, amenable to different localizing strategies and syntheses.

Modernist heteroglossia—rapid turns from high to low, standard to dialect, English to Sanskrit or Chinese, preeminently in Eliot and Pound—is another form of literary bricolage submitted to the dialectics of indigenization by postcolonial poets, especially in the Caribbean. Whereas Eliot and Pound, as Michael North has shown, made ambivalent use of African-American vernacular as vital yet debased,[28] Brathwaite, Walcott, and Goodison have adopted heteroglossia as a poetic structure to figure the code switching of Barbados, Jamaica, and Saint Lucia—an everyday practice that was, nevertheless, largely absent from earlier West Indian poems, which were usually written in Creole, Standard English, or a comic medley of the two. Although Brathwaite hears a hint of nation language in a voice recording of Claude McKay's Standard English poetry,[29] he suggests that the English lyric had rendered largely inaudible the poet's Afro-Euro-American creolization. In "Calypso," a signature poem of Brathwaite's *Rights of Passage*, the first part of *The Arrivants*, his echo of *The Waste Land* makes clear the literary template for his criss-crossing voices: Black Sam "carries bucketfuls of water / 'cause his Ma's just had another daughter" (the moonlight shines on Eliot's "Mrs. Porter / And on her daughter / They wash their feet in soda water").[30] Like Eliot, whose irregularly placed rhymes and shifting rhythms he redeploys, Brathwaite plays various Englishes against one another—in "Calypso," a prophetic voice intoning a creation myth of the Caribbean ("curved stone hissed into reef / wave teeth fanged into clay"); a satiric ode on white plantation life, built on Eliot's "so elegant / So intelligent" Shakespeherian rag ("O it was a wonderful time / an elegant benevolent redolent time—"); calypso itself ("Steel drum steel drum / hit the hot calypso dancing"); and West Indian Creole ("please to take 'im back"). Brathwaite's early heteroglossia, like Eliot's, exemplifies Bakhtin's "intentional hybridity," a poetry of satiric tensions and incongruities among voices, languages, sociolects. By the time Walcott is publishing "The Schooner *Flight*" in 1977–1979 and Lorna Goodison her first volumes of poetry in the 1980s, they, Brathwaite, and other West Indian poets are more nimbly and pervasively switching between Standard and dialectal codes, even as they have altered, abandoned, or inverted the linguistic hierarchies of modernism.

Modernist apocalypses have also served poets from different parts of the postcolonial world, and the apocalyptic is intimately tied to the intercultural in *The Waste Land* and other modernist poems, the crossing from West to East affording an extrinsic vantage point that reveals or uncovers (*apokalypsis*) the crisis of modernity. Indeed, the apocalyptic mode evinces the intense ambivalence toward modernity both in Euro-modernist and in postcolonial writing. At the end of "The Fire Sermon," inveighing against the West's unhinging of sex from religion, Eliot fuses the Buddha and Augustine—"Burning burning burning burning"—in what his note names "this collocation of these two representatives of eastern and western asceticism."[31] In "Irae," Brathwaite reroutes Eliot's moral apocalypse into a postcolonial confrontation with the West, intoning "burning burning from tomorrow" in an early version of the poem.[32] In this instance of the dialectics of indigenization, of the transformative twinning of the Euromodernist with the postcolocal, Brathwaite fuses Eliotic and Rastafarian apocalypses, as he earlier had in the vision of Babylon burned in "Wings of a Dove." Aggressively dislocating "Dies Irae" to address contemporary circumstance—a dislocation that also recalls Eliot's violent decontextualization of traditional material to simulate crisis—Brathwaite pounds out a prophecy of doom in the insistent rhymes and rhythms of the thirteenth-century hymn: "dies irae dreadful day / when the world shall pass away." In two of the tercets' middle lines, he chillingly compacts the names of massacres—"mi lai sharpville wounded knee"—and weapons—"poniard poison rocket bomb"—that occasion the poem's distress and rage. The poet sees divine retribution in the violent resistance of Jamaica's Maroon leaders—"nanny cuffee cudjoe." Brathwaite thus remakes Eliot's fiery apocalypse to condemn an imperial West that—technologically superior but ethically insane—is responsible for unspeakable injustices and atrocities and thus deserves its imminent implosion:

> day of fire dreadful day
> day for which all sufferers pray
> grant me patience with thy plenty
> grant me vengeance with thy sword

The political implications of Brathwaite's poem could hardly be more different from those we usually associate with Eliot's. Even so, in translating Eliot's apocalypse across the North/South divide and melding it, via a medieval hymn, with Rastafarian chant, Brathwaite renews the apocalyptic mode: like the Euro-modernists, he uses religious language for a compressed, visionary evocation of modernity as cataclysmic violence, a modern history trembling on the verge of dramatic and perhaps ultimate transformation.

Another poem of cosmic symbolism, including the thunder and lightning mythologized in West Africa, Christopher Okigbo's "Come Thunder" also adapts modernist apocalypticism—especially Yeats's—to bespeak a liminal moment in "Third World" history, the first of numerous civil wars that have ravaged postcolonial Africa. Okigbo presents as a second coming, complete with birds that seem almost Byzantine, the events leading up to the Nigerian civil war, in which he was to fight and die:

> Magic birds with the miracle of lightning flash on their feathers . . .
>
> The arrows of God tremble at the gates of light,
> The drums of curfew pander to a dance of death;
>
> And the secret thing in its heaving
> Threatens with iron mask
> The last lighted torch of the century . . .[33]

As in Yeats's prophecies, the violence of modernity inspires a troubled joy—"laughter, broken in two, hangs tremulous between the teeth"—and a joyous terror—the threat of an unknowable, iron-masked future. Okigbo, again like Yeats, lexically achieves the apocalyptic by combining the concrete ("The smell of blood," "myriad eyes of deserted corn cobs") with the indefinite ("immeasurable," "unnamed," "unprintable"). He Africanizes the affective and formal structures of the modernist apocalypse—his title evoking also "What the Thunder Said"—for a postcolonial vision of a rough beast about to be born. Since modernist apocalypses are thought to represent a Eurocentric response to the decline of a Western imperium, such adaptability may well seem surprising, but British poets of the 1930s, as Stephen Spender indicates, already believed that, "Considered as an apocalyptic vision, the Communist view coincides with that of T. S. Eliot in *The Waste Land* or Yeats in *The Second Coming.*"[34] Postcolonial poets have been no less ready to remake Euro-modernist apocalypses for their ambivalent visions of the historical rupture of modernity.

⋮ ⋮ ⋮

Having explored how "Third World" poets postcolonize Euro-modernism and Euro-modernize the postcolonial, I reverse the lens, reconsidering the cross-cultural bricolage of a few of the most canonical modernist poems, in view of this postcolonial reception. As I've already suggested, the North-South syncretism and transhemispheric interstitiality in Euro-modernist poems differ from the often more thoroughly hybridized language, mythology, genres, and geography of postcolonial texts. The primary transhemispheric current in Euro-modernist poems is the importation of East and South Asian materials. These poems invoke Asian religious texts, such as the Upanishads and the Fire Sermon, as well as literary genres or visual artifacts, such as haiku or a lapis lazuli carving, as potential solutions to Eurocentric crises of faith, war, literature, and tradition. They often exotically construct the East as spiritual other, as site of ancient wisdom, frozen in an archaic state, voided of a contemporary history with real human beings.[35] In keeping with other familiar patterns of circulation and long-lived Orientalist assumptions, the literary West, as site of artistic and epistemic production, mines and arrogates to itself raw materials imported from Asia and makes of them new elite forms of literary capital.

If so, how could Eliot, Yeats, and Pound furnish enabling examples for postcolonial poets? Aren't the Euro-modernists, as Neil Lazarus writes of such Western musicians as Paul Simon, guilty of a "profound insensitivity to the politico-ethical implications of cultural appropriation across the international division of labor," of a "distressing unilateralism of influence," a "complete lack of cultural dialogism"?[36] In an essay on *The Waste Land* and empire, Paul Douglass has argued that Pound and Eliot's "aesthetics of the jagged and the juxtaposed," the "fragmentary and syncretic," is inherently "reactionary," part of a larger project in "defense of . . . empire": such literary wreckage demands the imperial, reconstructive labor of a learned elite.[37] More generally, these modernist texts are increasingly thought to belong seamlessly to the Orientalist project of fabricating, managing, and disciplining the East. But the postcolonial poetic response compels us to ask whether such views are fully adequate to the cross-cultural dimension of Euro-modernist poetry, whether the manner of its assimilation of non-Western texts and artifacts—often inorganic, incomplete, self-conscious—might enable these to interact dialogically with the predominantly Western texts into which they are imported.

In my view, because of *The Waste Land*'s and *The Cantos'* heteroglot representation of the East in its languages, these indigenous texts retain at least some capacity to question both their Western host texts and the ways in which the non-West is represented. In an essay on the uses of India in *The Waste Land*, Harish Trivedi argues that "for Eliot, there aren't in this poem, there never were and never would be, any solutions outside Christianity.

Here, near the climax of his poem ["What the Thunder Said"], he takes up, in order to interrogate, the traditional claim of Eastern spiritual efficacy, and finds it wanting."[38] But in Eliot's collage of his own poetry with the text of the Brihadaranyaka Upanishad, the discordance between the ethical injunctions *Datta, Dayadhvam, Damyata* and the English responses shows up not the East's but the West's spiritual inefficacy, its helplessness to redress its crisis. The Sanskrit texts—though perhaps framed like objects in the British Museum—nevertheless write back to an empire that in the early 1920s continued to assert its superiority and mastery over these texts' site of origin. By way of an imperfect analogy, imagine if during the U.S.-led occupation of Iraq, John Ashbery or Jorie Graham embedded Koranic verses in their poetry as signifiers of spiritual wisdom. "Shantih shantih shantih," normally the closing benediction of an Upanishad, suggestively reframes *The Waste Land*, as if to say, this poem aspires to the peacefulness of an ancient, sacred, meditative text from still-colonized India, but, as perhaps indicated by Eliot's omission of the standard prefix "Om," again shows the West to fall short. Ultimately, even the poem's critique of the West, though offered in the voice of the other, can be seen as problematically appropriative, since Eliot is using Eastern materials to Western ends—Eastern supplements that are, finally, appendages to a fundamentally Western project. But we should be wary of the naive presupposition that a poetic text could, as if released from all ethnocentric moorings, engage a text from another hemisphere without assimilative pressure, without using it for its own cultural ends. Moreover, the poem's shadowing of a non-Western religion with a Christian intertext—Trivedi cites the translation of the poem's last line as the biblical "Peace which passeth understanding"—is common to some of the most celebrated postcolonial works (Achebe reshapes Igbo stories to fit Christian paradigms in *Things Fall Apart*, and Okigbo returns in *Heavensgate* to Igbo myth and culture through the story of the prodigal son).[39] While Christian yearning plays a part in *The Waste Land*, to read back into the poem the logic of the salvific Christianity Eliot later embraced is to allow this telos to evacuate the melancholic specificity, the painful splaying across hemispheres, of this literary moment. We do violence to its intercultural dialogism and disjuncture, its textual "fragments" and personal "ruins," if we overemphasize the recuperative clause wedged between these two substantives—"I have shored against." *The Waste Land*, while not escaping the Orientalism of modern Western representations of the East, also sets Eastern and Western texts in dialogic relation with one another, and in this double-voicedness, in the seams between the pieces of the transhemispheric collage, in the cross-cultural slippage between text and embedded text, the Eastern quotations retain at least some capacity to make themselves heard.

Yeats's "Lapis Lazuli" also both participates in and questions Orientalist assimilation, exoticism, and supplementarity. Like *The Waste Land*, the poem enacts a psycho-geographical movement from a Western panorama of destruction to an Eastern alterity. Here again, the onset of large-scale terror and destruction occasions the poet's cross-cultural excursion to the Orient, where Yeats stages the last in a series of rejoinders to the view that artistic gaiety is frivolous in wartime—fiddling while the metropole burns. Henry Clifton, donor of the lapis lazuli carving, had written Yeats that he feared London would be bombed, and in 1936, Hitler, Mussolini, and Spanish generals were indeed mobilizing for war. The eighteenth-century Chinese carving, arrived at in the poem after a typically modernist leap across hemispheres, seems at first to offer an exotic refuge:

> Two Chinamen, behind them a third,
> Are carved in Lapis Lazuli,
> Over them flies a long-legged bird
> A symbol of longevity;
> The third, doubtless a serving-man,
> Carries a musical instrument.[40]

After the scenes of death and ruin in the earlier stanzas, the calm enumeration of hierarchical social roles, twinned with signifiers of hermeneutic certainty (the bird "A symbol of longevity"), suggests a timeless, Oriental world of order, harmony, and stability. But in the ensuing lines, East-West binaries begin to collapse, as time and ruin invade the scene:

> Every discolouration of the stone,
> Every accidental crack or dent. . . .

If the poet has tried to displace Western war and chaos with an atemporal, Eastern security, the carving's surface fissures this Orientalist presumption. Although Yeats's poem isn't, like Eliot's, heteroglot, his modernist close reading of the artifact enables its surface to assert a reality that contravenes the Orientalist abstractions with which he began: the poem self-correctively pivots, undoing its reified image of the Chinese stone. Here, as in Eliot's poem, this slippage, though limited, creates a space for a counterdiscourse to be heard: the East is not the timeless haven the poet hoped for.

But no sooner has Yeats established the stone's fractured surface as primary than he begins to project onto it his poetic fantasies, troping each mark as

> . . . a water-course or an avalanche,
> Or lofty slope where it still snows
> Though doubtless plum or cherry-branch
> Sweetens the little half-way house
> Those Chinamen climb towards, and I
> Delight to imagine them seated there. . . .

His poetic self-consciousness foregrounded by the second use of "doubtless" and the enjambment that suspends the lyric "I" at the end of a line, the poet shows us a Western mind at the moment of its interplay with an Eastern artifact, of inspiration by and transformation of Chinese art into something other than itself. Although these lines belong to the discourse, in Edward Said's words, "by which European culture was able to manage—and even produce—the Orient," they also open a reflective space within that discourse, because they thematize the literary work of producing the Orient.[41] Instancing the imaginative joy of building again out of things that fall, the poet indulges Orientalist fantasy, writing over the stone's surface with stock plum- or cherry-branches and an imagined trek halfway up the mountain. Yet set off by the stone's corrective, his construction of a self-affirming Western lyric moment out of the fissures and interstices of an Eastern artwork is shown to supplement, twist, and distort. While the poem assimilates the Chinese Other to Nietzschean tragic joy, and while the poet is returned to himself through the wrinkle-eyed gaze of the other, this assimilation also impedes itself; after all, the poet needs the other to remain at least somewhat other, if only so that he can use the Orient as an alternative space from which to look back critically at the anguish and terror gripping the contemporary Occident. That he imagines the Chinamen climbing not to a transcendental site atop the mountain but to a halfway house figures their in-betweenness as part-Chinamen, part-figments of a Western imagination. Indeed, in a letter about the carving, Yeats similarly interrupts himself, unable to decide whether to write about the East as Other or as assimilable to Western tragedy: "The heroic cry in the midst of despair. But no, I am wrong, the east has its solutions always and therefore knows nothing of tragedy."[42] Self-interrupting, self-thematizing, the poem foregrounds what we might call the Orientalist wobble, caught as it is between assimilation and acknowledgment, between exoticism and historicity.

Another key poem in the Euro-modernist canon, Pound's "In a Station of the Metro" also crosses from West to East, but dramatically miniaturizes the journey:

> The apparition of these faces in the crowd;
> Petals on a wet, black bough.[43]

The poem's imaginative leap—often celebrated for its modernist compression and ellipsis—is again transhemispheric, from an urban Western scene, specifically located by the title in a Parisian Metro station, to an unmistakably East Asian, painterly image of flower petals against a branch. In his well-known account of composing the poem, Pound writes of "trying to record the precise instant when a thing outward and objective transforms itself, or darts into a thing inward and subjective."[44] His implicit association of the East with the "inward and subjective," as contrasted with the historicized, materialized objectivity of the urban crowd scene, accords with the Orientalist abstraction of the East as spiritual and immaterial that we also saw in *The Waste Land* and in "Lapis Lazuli." Also like Eliot and Yeats, Pound turns to Asia in a moment of crisis or, in his own word, "impasse," seizing on Japanese haiku as a literary model that enables his breakthrough—a mirror-image of the later postcolonial importation of Euro-modernism to shatter the impasse of a colonial poetics. Pound famously recounts how he reduced the poem from thirty lines to two under the influence of the compression and "super-position" of haiku, suggesting that an Asian literary structure helped engender the starkly juxtapositional poetics of modernism and, insofar as this is an intercultural formation, again complicating the view that such jaggedness is inherently imperialist.[45] With its title seen as integral, the poem is still more closely linked to the three-line structure of haiku (short to long to short line).[46] Pound's prototypically Imagist poem thus encrypts and enacts within its split, transhemispheric textual body a miniaturized psycho-biographical narrative of its genesis out of a cross-cultural imaginative passage from West to East. By at once internalizing and displaying the logic of its East-West dislocation, by refusing connectives that would discursively paper over the gap between the Western urban scene and Eastern ideality, by formally alluding to the three-line haiku without flattening its differences from this generic paradigm, the poem represents an Orientalism that is also anti-Orientalist, that is cross-cutting and counterdiscursive. Pound's later free translations of *Cathay* will—through the use of Japanese for Chinese names of places and poets—also foreground a densely mediated reception history that similarly impedes, even as other features of the texts advance, Orientalist transparency and penetration.

In sum, these three poems exemplify Orientalist appropriation, exoticism, and misreading, but the intercultural crossings they enact are also self-divided, self-impeding, and self-critical. While inserting a non-Western text, artifact, image, or genre into an Orientalist discourse, they also make audible the friction between figure and frame, foreground the wobble of assimilation or alterity. Monologic imperialism is thus inadequate as a description of their intercultural work—their jagged cross-cultural juxtapositions, their dialogic counterpointing of here and there, their leveraging of the East in their critique of the West, ultimately their openness, if only partial, to the potentially transformative impact of the voice of the other.

A later generation of poets on the margins of empire can thus help us reconsider what we think we know about modernist poetry. Not that the modernists in their own time are identical with their subsequent reception. The postcolonial uncovering of generative potentiality in modernism does not literally change the historical reality of the poets' words or actions. By the same token, Pound's profound influence on the second-generation Jewish modernists—the Objectivists Reznikoff, Zukofsky, and Oppen—does not make some of his poetry any less virulently anti-Semitic. Nevertheless, that later poets have been able to read the poetry of Eliot, Yeats, and Pound against the grain of its limitations should indeed shape our understanding of the potential of Euro-modernist aesthetics. Eliot's uses of Donne's forced, cerebral conjunctions; Yeats's transmutation of Shelley's and Blake's visionary poetics; Langston Hughes's and Sterling Brown's adaptations of Whitman's omnivorous personae—in such cases, the transumption releases and revitalizes aspects of a precursor's work. "The words of a dead man," in Auden's aphorism, "Are modified in the guts of the living." The Language poets, as Marjorie Perloff has argued, take up and expand certain features of modernist poetry that make us see it anew—constructivism, anti-absorptive artifice, the poetics of adjacency and surface fragmentation.[47] This modernism is by and large the reverse of the witty, paradoxical, ironic modernism that the midcentury American formalists—the early Robert Lowell and

Richard Wilbur—made the foundation of their poetry. In what we might term the postcolonial metaleptic, modernism's relation to postcolonial poetry illuminates yet other features—translocalism, polymythic syncretism, heteroglossia, ambivalent modernity, apocalypticism, interstitial migrancy, cultural self-alienation and self-critique and dialogism—that otherwise might risk being obscured.

Modernism is often praised or blamed for its cross-cultural appropriations with scant awareness of its postcolonial afterlives—Goodison's swapping duppy stories with Yeats, Brathwaite's hearing his own Creole rhythms in Eliot's poetry, Okigbo's Africanizing of Yeats's masks and of Pound's cross-religious syncretism, Ali's use of modernist disjunctiveness and melancholy to translate the ghazal. But these afterlives are vital in reconceptualizing the cross-cultural forms and languages of modernism, while dialectically yielding new insight into the still more vividly cross-cultural poetries beyond the Euro-American metropole. In an important essay, Ramanujan cites Eliot's famous description of European texts as forming " 'a simultaneous order,' where every new text within a series confirms yet alters the whole order ever so slightly, and not always so slightly."[48] Indigenizing and pluralizing Eliot's theory of literary tradition, he argues that Indian texts reflect and refract, invert and subvert one another, that in India "a whole tradition may invert, negate, rework, and revalue another." The same holds for the relation of his own and other postcolonial poets' work to Euro-modernism: postcolonial hybridity "confirms yet alters," reworks yet re-values modernist bricolage. It thus re-begets a poetic mode that helped beget it. Only by breaking out of exclusionary models of tradition as either Eliot's "mind of Europe" or its postcolonial obverse ("an autonomous entity separate and apart from all other literatures") can we begin to grasp the continuous remaking of "traditions" by one another across the twentieth century and beyond, the mutually transformative relations between the poetries of metropole and margin.

## Notes

1 Goodison, "Country, Sligoville," 47.

2 Glissant, *Caribbean Discourse*, xii, 134–44.

3 Gikandi, *Writing in Limbo*, 4–5. In subsequent work, Gikandi has seen more continuity between modernism and postcolonialism; see his *Maps of Englishness*, 158–62.

4 Chinweizu, Jemie, and Madubuike, *Toward the Decolonization of African Literature*, 2–3; on the necessity of freeing African poetry from Euro-modernism, see chapter 3, 163–238.

5 Ashcroft and Salter, "Modernism's Empire," 293.

6 Brathwaite, *History of the Voice*; reprinted and slightly altered in *Roots*, 286–87. Discussions of Brathwaite's statement include Gikandi, *Maps of Englishness*, 158, and Bernstein, "Poetics of the Americas."

7 Charles Olson, "Projective Verse," 248.

8 As Xiaomei Chen argues in another context—that of post-Mao China—Occidentalist affiliations can "sometimes be used as a locally marginal or peripheral discourse against the centrality of the internal dominant power." See her *Occidentalism*, 8–9.

9 Walcott, "Prelude," in *Collected Poems*, 3–4.

10 On modernism's continuities with postcolonialism, see Gikandi, *Maps of Englishness*, 158–62; Boehmer, *Empire, the National, and the Postcolonial, 1890–1920*, 169–77, and her *Colonial and Postcolonial Literature*, 123–33, 144–47; and Dasenbrock, "Why the Post in Post-Colonial." Two recent books on Caribbean poetry further explore the continuities: Pollard, *New World Modernisms*, and Jenkins, *The Language of Caribbean Poetry*.

11 Brathwaite, *History of the Voice*, 263–64, 297.

12 Dasenbrock, "Why the Post in Postcolonial," 115; in other respects, I agree with Dasenbrock's excellent piece.

13 Clifford, *Routes*, 36.

14 Lévi-Strauss, *The Savage Mind*, 17.

15 Ramanujan, *The Collected Poems of A. K. Ramanujan*, 186.

16 Ramanujan, Afterword, *Poems of Love and War*, 246, 287; Pound, *Gaudier-Brzeska*, 89. Pound layers Mount Taishan and a Pisan mountain near the Disciplinary Training Center in *The Pisan Cantos*.

17 Rushdie, "In Good Faith," 394. As migrants, the Euro-modernists traversed lesser inequities of power or differences of culture in the Northern Hemisphere.

18 Whitelaw, "Interview with Christopher Okigbo," 55.

19 Okigbo, "Lament of the Masks," xiii-xv.

20 See Ogundipe-Leslie, "The Poetry of Christopher Okigbo," 185–86.

21 *W. B. Yeats*, 245.

22 Okigbo is echoing Canto 8 in "Limits 3," *Labyrinths*, 25–26. See Egudu, "Ezra Pound in African Poetry," 337–48.

23 Bakhtin, *The Dialogic Imagination*, 258–62. Bakhtin associates all artistic hybridization with the "intentional" mode.

24 Walcott, *Omeros*, 1.9.3, 51–54.

25 Eliot, "*Ulysses*, Order and Myth," 177–78.

26 Ali, "Ghazal," 40.

27 Ali, *T. S. Eliot as Editor*, 1. Eliot, *The Waste Land*, line 430. Ali discusses the ghazal as a form in his introduction to *Ravishing DisUnities*.

28 North, *The Dialect of Modernism*, 77–99.
29 Brathwaite, *History of the Voice*, 275–77.
30 Brathwaite, "Calypso," 48–50; Eliot, *The Waste Land*, lines 200–201.
31 Eliot, *The Waste Land*, line 308.
32 Brathwaite, "Dies Irie," 37–39; "Irae," 90. See also Tuma, *Fishing by Obstinate Isles*, 256–58.
33 Ellipsis in original. Okigbo, "Come Thunder," *Labyrinths*, 66.
34 Spender, *The Thirties and After*, 13.
35 See Gikandi's analysis of Picasso's abstraction of real Africans in "Picasso, Africa, and the Schemata of Difference."
36 Lazarus, " 'Unsystematic Fingers at the Conditions of the Times.' "
37 Douglass, "Reading the Wreckage."
38 Harish Trivedi, " 'Ganga Was Sunken.' "
39 Ibid., 56.
40 Yeats, *The Poems*, 295.
41 Said, *Orientalism*, 3.
42 Yeats, *Letters on Poetry from W. B. Yeats to Dorothy Wellesley*, 8–9.
43 Pound, *Lustra*, 53.
44 Pound, *Gaudier-Brzeska*, 89.
45 Among recent books on the impact of East Asian culture on modernism, see Qian, *The Modernist Response to Chinese Art*, *Orientalism and Modernism*, and his edited collection *Ezra Pound and China*; Huang, *Transpacific Displacement*; Xie, *Ezra Pound and the Appropriation of Chinese Poetry*; and Kern, *Orientalism, Modernism, and the American Poem*. See also Hayot's useful overview in "Critical Dreams."
46 On the poem and haiku, see Lin, "Pound's 'In A Station of the Metro' as a Yugen Haiku."
47 Perloff, *Twenty-first Century Modernism*, 1–14, 154–200.
48 Ramanujan, "Where Mirrors Are Windows," 8–9.

## Works Cited

Ali, Agha Shahid. "Ghazal." *The Country without a Post Office*. New York: Norton, 1997.

——. Introduction to *Ravishing DisUnities*. Edited by Agha Shahid Ali. Hanover, N.H.: Wesleyan University Press, 2000.

——. *T. S. Eliot as Editor*. Ann Arbor: University of Michigan Press, 1986.

Ashcroft, Bill, and John Salter. "Modernism's Empire: Australia and the Cultural Imperialism of Style." In *Modernism and Empire*, ed. Howard J. Booth and Nigel Rigby, 292–323. Manchester: Manchester University Press, 2000.

Bakhtin, M. M. *The Dialogic Imagination: Four Essays*. Edited by Michael Holquist. Translated by Caryl Emerson and Michael Holquist. Austin: University of Texas Press, 1981.

Bernstein, Charles. "Poetics of the Americas." *Modernism/Modernity* 3.3 (1996): 1–23.

Boehmer, Elleke. *Colonial and Postcolonial Literature*. New York: Oxford University Press, 1995.

——. *Empire, the National, and the Postcolonial, 1890–1920*. New York: Oxford University Press, 2002.

Brathwaite, Edward [Kamau]. "Calypso." *The Arrivants*. New York: Oxford University Press, 1973.

——. "Dies Irie." *X/Self*. New York: Oxford University Press, 1987.

——. *History of the Voice*. London: New Beacon, 1984. Reprint with slight alterations in *Roots*. Ann Arbor: University of Michigan Press, 1993.

——. "Irae." *Middle Passages*. Newcastle upon Tyne: Bloodaxe Books, 1992.

Chen, Xiaomei. *Occidentalism: A Theory of Counter-Discourse in Post-Mao China*. New York: Oxford University Press, 1995.

Chinweizu, Onwuchekwa Jemie, and Ihechukwu Madubuike. *Toward the Decolonization of African Literature* (1980). Reprint, Washington.: Howard University Press, 1983.

Clifford, James. *Routes*. Cambridge: Harvard University Press, 1997.

Dasenbrock, Reed Way. "Why the Post in Post-Colonial Is Not the Post in Post-Modern: Homer • Dante • Pound • Walcott." In *Ezra Pound and African American Modernism*, ed. Michael Coyle, 111–22. Orono, Maine: National Poetry Foundation, 2001.

Douglass, Paul. "Reading the Wreckage: De-Encrypting Eliot's Aesthetics of Empire." *Twentieth-Century Literature* 43.1 (1997): 1–26.

Egudu, Romanus. "Ezra Pound in African Poetry: Chistopher Okigbo." In *Critical Perspectives on Christopher Okigbo*, ed. Donatus Ibe Nwoga, 337–48. Washington: Three Continents Press, 1984.

Eliot, T. S. "*Ulysses*, Order and Myth." *Selected Prose*. Edited by Frank Kermode. New York: Farrar, Straus and Giroux, 1975.

——. *The Waste Land: A Norton Critical Edition*. Edited by Michael North. New York: Norton, 2001.

Gikandi, Simon. *Maps of Englishness: Writing Identity in the Culture of Colonialism*. New York: Columbia University Press, 1996.

——. "Picasso, Africa, and the Schemata of Difference." *Modernism/Modernity* 10 (2003): 455–80.

——. *Writing in Limbo: Modernism and Caribbean Literature*. Ithaca, N.Y.: Cornell University Press, 1992.

Glissant, Edouard. *Caribbean Discourse: Selected Essays*. Translated by J. Michael Dash. Charlottesville: University of Virginia Press, 1989.

Goodison, Lorna. "Country, Sligoville." *Turn Thanks*. Urbana: University of Illinois Press, 1999.

Hayot, Eric. "Critical Dreams: Orientalism, Modernism, and the Meaning of Pound's China." *Twentieth-Century Literature* 45 (1999): 511–33.

Huang, Yunte. *Transpacific Displacement*. Berkeley: University of California Press, 2002.

Jenkins, Lee M. *The Language of Caribbean Poetry: Boundaries of Expression*. Gainesville: University of Florida Press, 2004.

Kern, Robert. *Orientalism, Modernism, and the American Poem*. Cambridge: Cambridge University Press, 1996.

Lazarus, Neil. " 'Unsystematic Fingers at the Conditions of the Times': Afropop and the Paradoxes of Imperialism." In *Recasting the World: Writing after Colonialism*, ed. Jonathan White, 137–60. Baltimore: Johns Hopkins University Press, 1993.

Lévi-Strauss, Claude. *The Savage Mind*. Translation from the French. London: George Weidenfeld and Nicolson, 1972.

Lin, Jyan-Lung. "Pound's 'In A Station of the Metro' as a Yugen Haiku." *Paideuma* 21.1-2 (1992): 175–83.

North, Michael. *The Dialect of Modernism*. Oxford: Oxford University Press, 1994.

Ogundipe-Leslie, Molara. "The Poetry of Christopher Okigbo: Its Evolution and Significance" (1973). Reprint in *Critical Essays on Christopher Okigbo*, ed. Uzoma Esonwanne, 185–94. New York: G. K. Hall, 2000.

Okigbo, Christopher. "Come Thunder." *Labyrinths with "Path of Thunder."* New York: Africana Publishing Corporation, 1971.

——. "Lament of the Masks." In *W. B. Yeats: Centenary Essays on the Art of W. B. Yeats,* ed. D. E. S. Maxwell and S. B. Bushrui, xiii-xv. Ibadan: Ibadan University Press, 1965.

——. "Limits 3." *Labyrinths with "Path of Thunder."* New York: Africana Publishing Corporation, 1971.

Olson, Charles. "Projective Verse." *Collected Prose*. Edited by Donald Allen and Benjamin Friedlander. Berkeley: University of California Press, 1997.

Perloff, Marjorie. *Twenty-first Century Modernism*. Oxford: Blackwell, 2002.

Pollard, Charles W. *New World Modernisms: T. S. Eliot, Derek Walcott, and Kamau Brathwaite*. Charlottesville: University of Virginia Press, 2004.

Pound, Ezra. *Gaudier-Brzeska: A Memoir*. New York: New Directions, 1970.

——. *Lustra*. New York: Knopf, 1917.

Qian, Zhaoming, ed. *Ezra Pound and China*. Ann Arbor: University of Michigan Press, 2003.

——. *The Modernist Response to Chinese Art*. Charlottesville: University of Virginia Press, 2003.

——. *Orientalism and Modernism*. Durham, N.C.: Duke University Press, 1995.

Ramanujan, A. K. Afterword. *Poems of Love and War*. Translated by A. K. Ramanujan. New York: Columbia University Press, 1984.

——. *The Collected Poems of A. K. Ramanujan*. Delhi: Oxford University Press, 1995.

——. "Where Mirrors Are Windows: Towards an Anthology of Reflections" (1989). *The Collected Essays of A. K. Ramanujan*. Edited by Vinay Dharwadker. New Delhi: Oxford University Press, 1999.

Rushdie, Salman. "In Good Faith." *Imaginary Homelands*. New York: Granta-Penguin, 1991.

Said, Edward. *Orientalism*. New York: Vintage-Random House, 1978.

Spender, Stephen. *The Thirties and After*. New York: Random House, 1978.

Trivedi, Harish. " 'Ganga Was Sunken': T. S. Eliot's Use of India." In *The Fire and the Rose: New Essays on T. S. Eliot,* ed. Vinod Sena and Rajiva Verma, 44–62. Delhi: Oxford University Press, 1992.

Tuma, Keith. *Fishing by Obstinate Isles*. Evanston, Ill.: Northwestern University Press, 1998.

Walcott, Derek. *Omeros*. New York: Farrar, Straus and Giroux, 1990.

——. "Prelude." *Collected Poems, 1948–1984*. New York: Farrar, Straus and Giroux, 1986.

*W. B. Yeats: Centenary Essays on the Art of W. B. Yeats.* Edited by D. E. S. Maxwell and S. B. Bushrui. Ibadan: Ibadan University Press, 1965.

Whitelaw, Marjory. "Interview with Christopher Okigbo" (1965/1970). Reprinted in *Critical Essays on Christopher Okigbo*, ed. Uzoma Esonwanne, 52–60. New York: G. K. Hall, 2000.

Xie, Ming. *Ezra Pound and the Appropriation of Chinese Poetry*. New York: Garland, 1999.

Yeats, W. B. *Letters on Poetry from W. B. Yeats to Dorothy Wellesley*. New York: Oxford University Press, 1940.

——. *The Poems*. 2nd ed. Edited by Richard J. Finneran. Vol. 1 of *The Collected Works of W. B. Yeats*. New York: Macmillan, 1989.

# CONTRIBUTORS

NICHOLAS ALLEN, an associate professor of English at the University of North Carolina, Chapel Hill, is author of *George Russell (AE) and the New Ireland, 1905–30* (2003) and coeditor with Aaron Kelly of *The Cities of Belfast* (2003). He is also editor of the poet Gerald Dawe's collected essays, *The Proper Word: Ireland, Poetry, Politics* (2007), and is finishing a book on Irish postrevolutionary literature and art of the 1920s and 1930s.

RITA BARNARD is a professor of English and director of the Women's Studies Program and the Alice Paul Center for Research on Women, Gender, and Sexuality at the University of Pennsylvania. She is the author of *The Great Depression and the Culture of Abundance* (1995) and *Apartheid and Beyond: South African Writers and the Politics of Place* (2007), as well as numerous articles on twentieth-century literature and popular culture.

RICHARD BEGAM, a professor of English at the University of Wisconsin, Madison, is a former editor of *The Beckett Circle* (1996–99) and the author of *Samuel Beckett and the End of Modernity* (1996). He has published articles on modernism and postcolonialism and is currently working on a book entitled *Beckett's Philosophical Levity*.

NICHOLAS DALY is a professor in the School of English and Drama at University College Dublin, where he is Chair of Modern English and American Literature. He is author of *Modernism, Romance, and the Fin de Siècle* (1999) and *Literature, Technology and Modernity, 1860–2000* (2004), as well as articles on late Victorian and early modern literature.

MARIA DIBATTISTA, a professor of English and Comparative Literature at Princeton University, has written widely on modern narrative and film. Her books include *The Major Novels of Virginia Woolf: The Fables of Anon* (1980) and *First Love: The Affections of Modern Fiction* (1991). Her most recent book is *Fast Talking Dames* (2001), a study of women and classic American film comedy.

IAN DUNCAN, a professor and department chair of English at the University of California, Berkeley, is the author of *Modern Romance and Transformations of the Novel: The Gothic, Scott, Dickens* (1992). A second book, *Scott's Shadow: The Novel in Romantic Edinburgh*, is forthcoming in 2007.

JED ESTY is an associate professor in the English Department and in the Unit for Criticism and Interpretive Theory at the University of Illinois, Urbana-Champaign. He is the author of *A Shrinking Island: Modernism and National Culture in England* (2004) and coeditor of *Postcolonial Studies and Beyond* (2005). He is currently working on a book entitled *Tropics of Youth: The Bildungsroman and Colonial Modernity*.

ANDRZEJ GĄSIOREK is a reader in twentieth-century English literature at the University of Birmingham and coeditor of the electronic journal *Modernist Cultures*. He is the author of *Post-War British Fiction: Realism and After* (1995), *Wyndham Lewis and Modernism* (2004), and *J. G. Ballard* (2005), and is coeditor with Edward P. Comentale of *T. E. Hulme and the Question of Modernism* (2006).

DECLAN KIBERD is a professor of Anglo-Irish literature at University College Dublin, where he is chair of the Department of Anglo-Irish Literature. Among his many books are *Synge and the Irish Language* (1979), *Men and Feminism in Modern Literature* (1985), *Inventing Ireland* (1996), *Irish Classics* (2001), and with Edna Longley, *Multi-culturalism: The View from the Two Irelands* (2001).

BRIAN MAY, an associate professor of English at Northern Illinois University, is the author of *The Modernist as Pragmatist: E. M. Forster and the Fate of Liberalism* (1997) and the editor of a special issue of *Studies in the Novel* on postcolonial fiction. Recent essays in *ELH* and *Modern Fiction Studies* will be parts of a book that he is now completing, entitled *Extravagant Postcolonialism: Transcendent Vision, the Body, and Ethics in Postcolonial Fiction*.

MICHAEL VALDEZ MOSES is an associate professor of English at Duke University. He is the author of *The Novel and the Globalization of Culture* (1995) and the editor of a collection of critical essays, *The Writings of J. M. Coetzee* (1994). He serves as coeditor of the web-based journal *Modernist Cultures*. Presently he is completing a book entitled *Nation of the Dead: The Politics of Irish Writing, 1890 to the Present*.

JAHAN RAMAZANI, Edgar F. Shannon Professor of English and department chair at the University of Virginia, is the author of *The Hybrid Muse: Postcolonial Poetry in English* (2001), *Poetry of Mourning: The Modern Elegy from Hardy to Heaney*

(1994), and *Yeats and the Poetry of Death: Elegy, Self-Elegy and the Sublime* (1990). He is the coeditor of *The Norton Anthology of Modern and Contemporary Poetry* (2003) and *The Norton Anthology of English Literature* (2006).

VINCENT SHERRY is a professor of English at Washington University in St. Louis. His books include *The Great War and the Language of Modernism* (2003), *The Cambridge Companion to the Literature of the First World War* (ed., 2005), *James Joyce: "Ulysses"* (1995, 2004), *Ezra Pound, Wyndham Lewis, and Radical Modernism* (1993), and *The Uncommon Tongue: The Poetry and Criticism of Geoffrey Hill* (1987). He is currently writing *The Life of Ezra Pound* and working on a book on pan-European decadence and literary modernism in Britain and Ireland.

# INDEX

Abbey Theatre, 188, 219, 247
Achebe, Chinua, 4–5, 15 n. 16, 68 n. 2, 68 n. 12, 277, 303
Ackroyd, Peter, 116
Aeschylus, 118
Aesthetics, 1–12, 43–69, 70–72, 93–94, 139–44, 151, 155–56, 156 n. 1, 162, 167, 181 n. 37, 189–90, 204–6, 215; aestheticism of 1890s and, 10, 186, 191–203; of decolonization, 185–88; education and, 74–75, 82–86; experimentation and, 261. *See also* Representation; Wilde, Oscar
Africa, 2, 6, 23, 34–35, 43–57, 68 n. 2, 91, 179 n. 13, 179 n. 20, 181 n. 41, 289, 291, 295–96, 301, 308; Azania as Africa, 164–78. *See also* South Africa
Alasdair, Alasdair MacMhaighstir, 262
Ali, Agha Shahid, 297–98, 309 n. 27
*Allan Quatermain* (Haggard), 47, 50, 55
Alterity, 44, 71, 104, 295, 304, 307
America, 5, 28, 95–108, 111, 114–17, 220, 272, 298–99. *See also* North America; South America
*America and Cosmic Man* (Lewis), 105
Anachrony, 9, 53, 57, 64–65
Anderson, Benedict, 106
Anglo-American literary history, 116
Anglo-British cultural model, 247
Anglo-Irish, 10–11, 196, 202, 228, 244 n. 9, 244 n. 11; Anglo-Irish Ascendancy, 220; Anglo-Irish Treaty, 212, 233; gentry, 226–27; language and, 249; the Troubles and, 209, 227, 232–36
Anthropological turn, 194–95
"Apeneck Sweeney" (T. S. Eliot), 111, 119
Ashbery, John, 303
Auden, W. H., 5, 269, 272, 307
Austen, Jane, 73–74, 86, 88 n. 8, 240
Authenticity, 93, 117, 127, 167–68, 211, 289; inauthenticity and, 136, 262
Avant-garde, 193, 283; art of, 95; literary devices of, 9

Bakhtin, M. M., 74–75, 84, 87, 88 n. 11, 89 n. 17, 296, 299, 309 n. 23
Baraka, Amiri, 290
"Barbarity," 162–66, 170, 181 n. 39, 188; vs. civilization, 169
Barnacle, Nora, 276
Bathos, 257–60; bathetic mode, 137, 141–52; India and, 148
Baudelaire, Charles, 200
Beckett, Samuel, 56, 247, 278

Ben Jelloun, Tahar, 67
Bergson, Henri, 60, 104
Berlin Conference, 21, 72
Berman, Jessica, 100
Berman, Marshall, 46
Bhabha, Homi K., 1, 276
Big House, 226, 231
Bildungsroman, 9, 72–76, 78–86, 278; generic rules of, 71; modernist anti-bildungsroman, 73, 77, 87
*Black Mischief* (Waugh), 10, 162–181
Blavatsky, H. P., 213, 224 n. 12
Boer War, 2, 14 n. 13, 92, 112
Bolt, Christine, 92
Booth, Howard J., 7, 132 n. 5
Bowen, Elizabeth, 8, 11, 73, 226–45
*Bowen's Court* (Bowen), 227
Bradbury, Malcolm, 15 n. 17, 45, 157 n. 12, 166
Brathwaite, Edward [Kamau], 290–310
Britain, 3–4, 6–13, 79, 91–94, 103, 111–12, 117, 122, 197, 209–10, 249–50; imperialism and, 2, 5, 21, 29–32, 36, 119; Victorian, 27, 48
British empire. *See* Empire, British
Brontë, Charlotte, 86
Brown, Sterling, 307
Brown, Terence, 210–11
Buchanan, Robert, 126, 133 n. 29
Burke, Edmund, 75
Burns, Robert, 247, 252–63
Butler, Hubert, 226–32

Cabrera Infante, Guillermo, 67
"Caesarism," 220–22
"Calypso" (Brathwaite), 299
Capitalism, 3, 46, 74–75, 81–85, 97
Carlyle, Thomas, 223 n. 9, 256, 259, 262
Carpentier, Alejo, 67
Caudwell, Christopher, 269
Celtic Revival. *See* Ireland
Celtic Twilight. *See* Ireland
Cézanne, Paul, 163
Chakrabarty, Dipesh, 77, 88 n. 13
Chamberlain, Joseph, 92
Cheng, Vincent, 185, 190, 275
"Chicago Zen" (Ramanujan), 294–95
Christianity, 48, 298, 302–3; Catholicism and, 174, 201, 228; missions and, 291–92
Civilization, 50, 91–106, 169, 242; Roman, 112
Class, 27–30, 97, 249, 272; middle, 20, 73–74, 277, 280, 284
Clifford, James, 104, 108 n. 42, 293
Coetzee, J. M., 7, 55, 67
Coleridge, S. T., 75, 258, 271–72
Colonialism, 2–13, 70–72, 81–82, 91–92, 96, 137, 228; colonial imaginary and, 34–36, 44; colonized peoples, 71, 86, 111; cultural adaptation and, 55–56, 227; decolonization and, 91, 111, 175, 185–206, 248, 251, 292; internal, 250; violence and, 1, 94
"Come Thunder" (Okigbo), 301
Conrad, Joseph, 1, 5–13, 20–21, 46–47, 59–66, 67, 98, 124, 131, 143, 152, 154, 157 n. 7, 166, 170, 175, 227, 270–71; compared with Woolf, 71–86; delayed decoding and, 49–53; disorientation and, 43–45, 50–53; modernist style of, 52–57. *See also* Delayed decoding; Disorientation
Consciousness, 8, 93–105, 194–8, 209, 212; modern, 57, 228, 238–43. *See also* Stream-of-consciousness
"Cooking Egg, A" (T. S. Eliot), 120–21
Cosmopolitanism, 104, 185, 188; discrepant, 293
"Country, Sligoville" (Goodison), 288–89
Crawford, Robert, 263
Creeley, Robert, 290
Creole, 299, 308
Crews, Fredrick, 156

Cullingford, Elizabeth, 210–11
Culture, 1–13, 44, 70, 75, 86, 92, 103–4, 146, 169, 190–197, 213, 248–50, 281; cycles of, 220–22; hybridity and, 290; mass, 20, 37

Dante Alighieri, 254, 259–60, 270, 272
Danto, Arthur, 151
*Decline of the West, The* (Spengler), 11, 92, 210–6, 222
Delayed decoding, 9, 49–52, 63, 68 n. 10
De Man, Paul, 258
Desani, G. V., 7
Dickens, Charles, 20, 80, 86, 157 n. 17
"Dies Irae" (Brathwaite), 300
Disorientation, 43–45, 51, 53; of reader, 172; Western epistemology and, 44–45
Disraeli, Benjamin, 91
Dissociation of sensibility, 95, 100, 250, 256
Domesticity, 77, 89 n. 22, 251
Domestic novels, 23, 34–35, 85
Donoso, José, 67
Dos Passos, John, 66
Douglass, Paul, 302
*Drunk Man Looks at the Thistle, A* (MacDiarmid), 11, 246–65
Duffy, Enda, 185–86
Dunbar, William, 257–61

Eagleton, Terry, 1, 14 n. 1, 244 n. 11, 244 n. 12
East, the, 92–93, 97, 104–5, 302–7
Easter Rising, 127, 188
Education Act of 1870, 24, 36
Eliot, George [Mary Ann Evans], 73, 86
Eliot, T. S., 5–13, 46, 51, 115–16, 122–24, 132–34, 180 n. 30, 198–206, 269–74, 290–308; Decadence and, 125–30; empire and, 111, 117–21, 131; Roman civilization and, 112–14
Eliot, Vivien, 115
Ellmann, Richard, 12, 185, 273–76
Emecheta, Buchi, 7, 227
Empire, British, 1–6, 91, 92, 111, 122–23, 128–31, 132 n. 21, 249–50, 271, 291; crisis of, 271; economics and, 4, 92; "empire writes back," 111, 164–65; end of, 112, 133 n. 35; fictional and real, 22, 169; ideal and actual history of, 115–17, 137; imaginative attraction to, 114–15; myth and, 21, 34, 86, 96; peripheries of, 1, 13, 46, 58–67, 72, 88 n. 6, 177–78; pressures of, 11, 213; regimen of authority and, 4, 44, 112–14, 216; threats to hegemony, 75, 86, 112–15; wealth and, 21–23
England. *See* Britain
*England, My England* (Lawrence), 96
English departments, 273
Epistemological turn, 194
Ethnocentrism, 146
Europe, 44–45, 60–61, 93, 209, 248, 271–79; civilization of, 48, 50; European Union and, 274; humanism and, 270; idea of, 91, 274; metropole and, 66, 292; science and technology of, 2, 50, 250

*Fantasia of the Unconscious* (Lawrence), 95
Faulkner, William, 44, 54, 80
Fin de siècle, 19–39, 72
First World War, 2, 9, 11, 14 n. 3, 91–2, 96, 104, 112, 209–10, 248
Flaubert, Gustave, 73
Ford, Ford Madox, 154, 270
Forster, E. M., 1, 7–13, 46, 52, 67, 137–41, 146–60, 196, 227, 229, 240, 269; bathos and, 141–42; impressionism and, 143–46, 155
Foster, Roy, 211, 215, 218
Foucault, Michel, 4, 14 n. 12, 15 n. 14

Freedman, Carl, 254, 263
Freud, Sigmund, 270
Fuentes, Carlos, 67

Gaelic League. *See* Ireland
García Márquez, Gabriel, 67
Gaudier-Brzeska, Henri, 151
Gender, 20, 82, 84, 89 n. 21, 166, 288; feminization and masculinization, 34–35
Genette, Gérard, 53
"Gerontion" (T. S. Eliot), 122–23, 133 n. 35
"Ghazal" (Ali), 297–98
Gikandi, Simon, 1, 289, 308 n. 3
Ginsberg, Allen, 290
Glissant, Edouard, 289
Globalization, 2, 112, 116, 167, 178, 203, 248, 275, 292
Goethe, Johann Wolfgang von, 73–75, 83–86, 88 n. 8, 89 n. 17, 270
GoGwilt, Christopher, 92
Goldring, Douglas, 128–30
Goodison, Lorrna, 288–89, 296–99
Graham, Jorie, 303
Great Britain. *See* Britain
Great War. *See* First World War
Greene, Graham, 5, 227

Haggard, H. Rider, 8, 21–23, 31–99, 45–55
Hardy, Thomas, 86
Harlem Renaissance, 105
Hazlitt, William, 252
Heaney, Seamus, 262–63
*Heart of Darkness* (Conrad), 5, 8, 43–69, 82, 98, 131, 271
Hellenism, 10, 94, 187–88, 194, 202, 204 n. 7
Henley, W. E., 21, 24–32
Herbert, W. N., 255
Herder, Johann Gottfried von, 74
History, 2–13, 188–202, 209–22, 233–43, 247–59, 292; contemporary, 117, 200, 302; fantasy and, 123, 222; legendary, 122; literary, 20, 76, 86, 112, 117, 123, 126; pattern and, 211, 216
Holocaust, 274
Hospitality, 169, 227, 236
*Howards End* (Forster), 141, 147, 159 n. 58, 175–76
Hughes, Langston, 307
Hunt, Leigh, 252
Husserl, Edmund, 60
Hybridity, 53, 220, 228, 253, 288–308; and cultures, 4, 12; and literary strategies, 65, 288–308; the postcolonial and, 288–308
Hyde, Douglas, 10, 186, 194–98, 203; nationalism and, 10, 186

Imagism, 123
Imperialism, 5–15, 44–47, 73–76, 91–93, 167, 174, 229, 270, 276, 293; anti-imperialism, 252; contrasted with colonialism, 1–4; cultural, 128; ideology of, 52, 71, 73, 113, 131; Marxist theory and, 3, 14 n. 8; monologic, 307; systems of communication and, 2, 60
Impressionism, 157 n. 19, 158 n. 32; Conrad and, 46; Forster and, 136–56
"In a Station of the Metro" (Pound), 306
India, 2, 9, 91, 136–60, 274, 295, 303, 308
Individualism, 46, 60, 96–103, 215–19
Industrialization, 74–78, 87, 95, 101, 164
"Irae" (Brathwaite), 300
Ireland: culture of, 193–94, 213; Gaelic League, 197, 247, 280; Irish Celtic Revival, 188, 193–97, 219, 247, 262; Irish Civil War, 11; Irish Free State, 188, 220, 223 n. 8, 247; Irish Renaissance, 275, 280; and literary movements, 219; and nationalism, 185,

196, 227, 232, 273, 276; in political upheaval, 232; Treaty of 1922, 227, 233; the Troubles and, 11, 226–43

James, Henry, 20, 52, 116–17
James, William, 204 n. 9
Jameson, Fredric, 1, 46, 82–84, 176–78, 180 n. 24, 196, 230, 241, 244 n. 18; "imperialism" and, 3, 175, 196, 229; political unconscious and, 81, 175; "Third World" and, 205 n. 28
Joyce, James, 21, 46, 54, 56, 66–67, 72, 77, 85–86, 124, 162, 185, 194–97, 228–30, 238, 244 n. 18, 247–48, 263, 273, 275, 276, 277, 280–85; and aesthetics, 186; and cultural decolonization, 186, 203; and interior monologue, 278–79; and mythical method, 186, 194, 198–203, 277; and stream-of-consciousness, 186, 204 n. 8, 204 n. 9. *See also* Aesthetics; Mythical method; Stream-of-consciousness

Keats, John, 252, 271–72
Kenner, Hugh, 12, 206 n. 43, 273, 275
Khatibi, Parviz, 67
*King Solomon's Mines* (Haggard), 8, 21–22, 31–32, 35, 47
Kipling, Rudyard, 21, 52, 72, 76–78, 86, 117, 132 n. 21, 175, 270–71
Köhler, Wolfgang, 59

"Lament of the Masks" (Okigbo), 295–96
Lang, Andrew, 19–34
"Lapis Lazuli" (Yeats), 304
Larisch, Marie, 200
*Last September, The* (Bowen), 11, 226–43
Lawrence, D. H., 7, 10, 54, 91–98, 106–8, 269; and the "African," 99–100; New Mexico and, 100–105
Lees, George Hyde. *See* Yeats, George
Lenin, V. I., 3, 14 n. 9; Marxist-Leninism, 247
Lessing, Gotthold Ephraim, 74, 194
Lewis, Wyndham, 8, 10, 91–106, 130, 151, 157 n. 7
Literary marketplace, 34, 47. *See also* Mass market
Lloyd, David, 185, 197
Lloyd's Bank, 115–17, 126
*Longest Journey, The* (Forster), 147, 156–57 n. 12
Lowell, Robert, 307
Lowry, Malcolm, 54, 56

MacDiarmid, Hugh, 8, 11–12, 246–63
MacIntyre, Duncan Bàn, 262
MacLean, Sorley, 262
Macpherson, James, 250, 256, 262
Mao, Douglas, 149–50
Marcus, Jane, 71
Marcus, Steven, 163, 178
Mass culture, 20
Massis, Henri, 92–93, 104
Mass market, 8, 19–27; audience for, 36; elite and popular, 20
Materialism, 8, 93–96, 101; Aristotelian, 187
Maxwell, Stephen, 248
McClintock, Anne, 34
McGee, Patrick, 71, 87 n. 5
Mediated narration, 57, 62
Metropole, 66–67, 231, 289, 292, 304, 308
Mexico, 101–2
Middle class, 20, 73–74, 277, 280, 284
Milton, John, 2, 271
Modernism: apocalypse and, 299, 301; bricolage and, 288–308; canon formation and, 163, 188, 247; collage and, 11, 210, 222, 303; "high," 37, 51, 54, 66–67, 163, 248, 255, 273; international, 11, 276; modernist

Modernism (*continued*)
heteroglossia and, 298; modernist nationalism, 246–65; protomodernism, 20; relation to postcolonialism, 11; vernacular, 6, 203
"Modernism and Imperialism" (Jameson), 1, 175–76, 196, 205 n. 28, 244 n. 18
Modernity, 57, 73–76, 87, 162, 168, 178, 179 n. 21, 200, 210, 238, 290, 300–301; Africa as antidote to European, 35; ambivalent, 308; youth as master trope of, 73
Moretti, Franco, 46, 73–74, 84, 88 n. 8
*Mornings in Mexico* (Lawrence), 95, 100–104
Moses, Michael Valdez, 198
"Mr. Eliot's Sunday Morning Service" (T. S. Eliot), 126
Myers, William, 174, 179 n. 17, 181 n. 37
Mythical method, 11, 186, 199, 204 n. 8, 204 n. 9, 255, 273, 297
Mythical syncretism, 294–95, 298

Naipaul, V. S., 7, 67
Nairn, Tom, 248, 255–56
Narrative: experimentation with, 9; language and, 74–75; Marxist theory of, 86; master, 219; metanarrative of modernity, 85; modernist, 44, 49–56, 59, 243, 276; nation and, 3, 88 n. 8, 188, 231–32, 270, 274–75; of Western superiority, 70
Nationalism, 10, 74, 93, 96–98, 185–203, 226–32, 246–65, 273–76
National Socialism, 98
New Mexico, 10, 93–95, 100–101, 104–5
Ngugi, wa Thiong'o, 7, 67
Nietzsche, Friedrich, 60, 305
*No Longer at East* (Achebe), 4, 15 n. 16
Nolan, Emer, 185, 204 n. 4, 276
North, Michael, 299
North America, 279

O'Casey, Sean, 219
O'Connor, Frank, 277
O'Duffy, Eoin, 220–21
*Odyssey*, 187, 192, 230, 238, 277
Okigbo, Christopher, 291–308, 309 n. 22
Olson, Charles, 291
Orientalism, 9, 303, 307; disorientalism and, 43–69
Orwell, George [Eric Arthur Blair], 227, 269–70

*Paleface: The Philosophy of the "Melting-Pot"* (Lewis), 97–98, 104–5
Paris, 200, 228, 273, 280, 306; *Ulysses* and, 196, 284
Parody: in Joyce, 198–202; in Waugh, 166, 177
Parry, Benita, 1, 138, 156
*Passage to India, A* (Forster), 3, 9, 13, 44, 136–60, 166, 176, 240, 269
Pater, Walter, 123, 125, 130, 191; style and, 187
Patriarchy, 71, 84, 87 n. 5
p'Bitek, Okot, 291
Perspectivism, 9, 53, 57, 59, 292
Phoenix Park murders, 30
Picasso, Pablo, 162
*Plumed Serpent, The* (Lawrence), 95, 100–102
Politics, 1–12, 50–52, 70–85, 91–102, 123, 146, 151–56, 175, 185–86, 210–23, 226–28, 256, 269
Popular literature, 19–39. *See also* Mass market
*Portrait of the Artist as a Young Man, A* (Joyce), 73, 187–190, 273, 275
Postcolonialism, 12, 67, 136, 269–86, 289, 293
Postcolonization, 290

Postmodernism, 66, 146, 158 n. 32, 289
Pound, Ezra, 8, 12, 21, 130, 274, 291–93, 295–305; modernist poetic style and, 123–25, 302, 306–8; Orientalism and, 306–7; "super-position" and, 294, 306
"Prelude" (Walcott), 292
Primitive, 10, 30–31, 54, 103–5, 111, 119, 132 n. 1
Primitivism, 10, 91–108, 146
Proust, Marcel, 72, 233–34, 245 n. 25; Proustian novel and, 11, 235–36; retrospective intimation and, 11, 237–38, 242–43
Public, 20–24, 29. *See also* Readership

Race, 92–93, 105, 166, 174, 197, 219
Racism, 68 n. 2, 292
*Rainbow, The* (Lawrence), 54, 95–101
Rainey, Lawrence, 19
Ramanujan, A. K., 291–98, 308
Readership, 23–25, 164; children and, 24–25; after Education Act of 1870, 23–24
Redfield, Marc, 86, 255
Representation, 62, 122, 137, 140, 162, 167, 176
Rhys, Jean, 7, 54, 56, 67, 73
Rigby, Nigel, 7
Roa Bastos, Augusto, 67
Romance, 23, 27, 31, 34–36, 65, 148; colonial, 83; elementalist, 149, 152–54; Victorian imperial, 8–9, 21, 47, 73, 77, 85
Romanticism, 146, 158 n. 34, 248–63
Roy, Arundhati, 7, 227
Rushdie, Salman, 7, 67, 227, 295
Ruskin, John, 127–30, 133 n. 30
Russell, George [Æ], 187, 280
Russian Revolution (1917), 11

Said, Edward, 1, 44, 48, 70, 85, 93, 136, 155–56, 156 n. 1, 305
Sandburg, Carl, 151
Schiller, Friedrich von, 74, 83, 86
Schreiner, Olive, 73, 76
Scotland, 6, 10, 246–63
Scots language, 247–53, 256–59, 261–63; "Synthetic Scots," 11, 246, 254, 260
Scott, Sir Walter, 23, 86, 114
Scottish Renaissance, 246
Second World War, 5, 12, 91, 106; literary culture after, 273, 290
Seeley, John Robert, 92
Sex, 78, 83–84, 98–99; homosexuality and, 270, 281–83
Shakespeare, 2, 129, 190, 192, 201, 202, 270
Shaw, George Bernard, 193, 195, 280, 284
Shelley, Percy Bysshe, 148, 307
South Africa, 22, 31–32, 55
South America, 22, 71–79
Soyinka, Wole, 291–92, 295, 297
Space, 2, 13, 79, 92, 123, 205 n. 28; colonial, 22, 31, 37, 229–30; poetic discourse/counterdiscourse and, 289, 305; political, 210
Spender, Stephen, 269, 272, 301
Spengler, Oswald, 11, 92, 104, 209–24
Stein, Gertrude, 80
*Stephen Hero* (Joyce), 190
Stevenson, Robert Lewis, 8, 121, 23, 29, 31, 34, 35–36; as children's writer, 24–27, 30; mass market and, 22, 37
*St Mawr* (Lawrence), 95
*Strange Case of Dr Jekyll and Mr Hyde, The* (Stevenson), 30–31
Stream-of-consciousness, 11, 46, 186, 204 n. 8, 204 n. 9
*Studies in Classic American Literature* (Lawrence), 101
Style, 45–46, 185, 230, 275, 285; city and, 45; colonial context and, 71, 81; comparison of Conrad and Woolf, 81. *See also* Conrad, Joseph

Subjectivity, 84, 87, 98, 195–96, 204 n. 8, 205 n. 28
Suleri, Sara, 1, 76, 136–37
"Sweeney Among the Nightingales" (T. S. Eliot), 118–21
Swift, Jonathan, 221, 275, 278, 284
Swinburne, Algernon Charles, 9, 123–25, 130
Synge, John Millington, 191, 194, 202, 219, 280

"Third World," 229, 231, 248, 301; modernism, 205 n. 8, 289; poets, 292, 301
Time (temporality), 71–74, 83–87; historical, 75–76, 123, 258; imperialism and, 76, 112, 130; narrative and, 73, 236
*Time and Western Man* (Lewis), 97, 104
Tinsley, Molly B., 147, 155
Transhemispheric currents, in Euro-modernist poems, 301–6
Translocalism, 308; postcolonial and modernist, 294–95
*Treasure Island* (Stevenson), 8, 21–38
Trojans: Trojan horse and, 10, 185–203; Trojan War and, 118

*Ulysses* (Joyce), 10, 12, 44, 54, 66, 230, 244 n. 18, 247, 273–83, 284; and decolonization, 186; as Trojan horse, 185–203
"*Ulysses*, Order and Myth" (T. S. Eliot), 198
United States. *See* America

Vargas Llosa, Mario, 67
Versailles Peace Conference, 209, 248
Victorianism, 5–9, 19–39, 47–48, 75–84, 92, 112, 146, 292; and romance, 5, 256, 291
Virgil [Publius Vergilius Maro], 112–17, 259, 271
*Vision, A* (Yeats), 11, 209–24, 272–74
Vorticism, 94
*Voyage Out, The* (Woolf), 9, 71–89

Walcott, Derek, 7, 291–99
Walpole, Horace, 201
*Waste Land, The* (Eliot), 131, 180 n. 30, 199–200, 206 n. 39, 247, 269–71, 290–91, 298–306
Watt, Ian, 53, 57; delayed decoding and, 49, 68 n. 10
Waugh, Evelyn, 8, 13, 166–67, 168–73; "barbarism" and, 164–65, 169, 181 n. 39; compared with Ousmane, 163–65, 178 n. 13; representation and, 162, 167, 174, 176–78, 181 n. 37. *See also* Representation
West, 10–12, 45, 85, 91–108, 209–24, 300–307
Wilde, Oscar, 12, 36, 72–73, 130, 157 n. 19, 190, 199–203, 204 n. 8, 273, 280–81, 284; aestheticism and, 10, 186, 192–98; and the English, 191–93, 198; impressionism and, 142–43
Williams, Patrick, 14 n. 7
Williams, Raymond, 70, 87 n. 5, 100
*Women in Love* (Lawrence), 95–102, 269
Woolf, Virginia, 7–9, 46, 54–56, 66, 74–87; and temporality, 71–73, 87; views on aesthetics and colonialism, 71, 82
World English, 263
Wyndham, George, 113–14

Yeats, George [Bertha Georgina Hyde-Lees], 210–11
Yeats, William Butler, 5, 7–14, 20, 151, 187, 197, 199, 212–19, 247, 269, 273–84, 288–89, 295; compared with Okigbo, 295–96; Orientalism and, 304–6; politics and, 209–11, 215, 220–23, 274

RICHARD BEGAM, a professor of English at the University of Wisconsin, Madison, is a former editor of *The Beckett Circle* (1996–99) and the author of *Samuel Beckett and the End of Modernity* (1996). He has published articles on modernism and postcolonialism and is currently working on a book entitled *Beckett's Philosophical Levity.*

MICHAEL VALDEZ MOSES is an associate professor of English at Duke University. He is the author of *The Novel and the Globalization of Culture* (1995) and the editor of a collection of critical essays, *The Writings of J. M. Coetzee* (1994). He serves as coeditor of the web-based journal *Modernist Cultures.* Presently he is completing a book entitled *Nation of the Dead: The Politics of Irish Writing, 1890 to the Present.*

*Library of Congress Cataloging-in-Publication Data*

Begam, Richard
Modernism and colonialism : British and Irish literature, 1899–1939
/ edited by Richard Begam and Michael Valdez Moses.
p. cm.
Includes bibliographical references and index.

ISBN-13: 978-0-8223-4019-5 (cloth : acid-free paper)
ISBN-10: 978-0-8223-4038-6 (pbk. : acid-free paper)

1. Modernism (Literature)—Great Britain.
2. English literature—20th century—History and criticism.
3. English literature—Irish authors—History and criticism.
4. Politics and literature—Great Britain—History—20th century.
5. Imperialism in literature. I. Moses, Michael Valdez. II. Title.

PR478.M6B45 2007
820.9′112—dc22 2007014125